P9-DXM-291

DATE DUE

MY 7 '95			
MY 5 '95			
DE 22 '95			
DE 9 '97			
JE 7 '01			

DEMCO 38-296

16 45

Born in Larkana, Pakistan, Dilip Hiro received his higher education in India, Britain and America, where he obtained his Master's degree. He has been living in London since 1964, and is a full-time writer and journalist. His articles on the Middle East and allied subjects have appeared in many leading British and North American publications, including the *Sunday Times, Guardian, Washington Post, Wall Street Journal, Toronto Star* and *Atlantic Community Quarterly.* He has published several books including *Inside India Today* (1976), *Inside the Middle East* (1982), *Iran Under the Ayatollahs* (1985) and *Holy Wars: The Rise of Islamic Fundamentalism* (1988). A member of the Middle East Studies Association of North America, he is a frequent commentator on Islamic affairs on British and American radio and television.

By the same author

Dilip Hiro

THE LONGEST WAR

The Iran-Iraq
Military Conflict

ROUTLEDGE
NEW YORK

Riverside Community College
Library
4800 Magnolia Avenue
Riverside, California 92506

OCT   '92

Published in 1991 by
Routledge, an imprint of
Routledge, Chapman and Hall, Inc.
Copyright © 1991 by Routledge Chapman & Hall, Inc.

Printed in the United States of America

All rights reserved. No part of this book may be reprinted or reproduced or utilized in any form or by any electronic, mechanical or other means, now known or hereafter invented, including photocopying and recording, or in any information storage or retrieval system, without permission in writing from the publishers.

Library of Congress Cataloging-in-Publication
Hiro, Dilip.
    The longest war : the Iran-Iraq military conflict / Dilip hiro.
        p.   cm.
    Reprint. Originally published: London : Grafton, 1989.
    Includes bibliographical references.
    ISBN 0-415-90406-4.   ISBN 0-415-90407-2 (pbk.)
    1. Iran-Iraq War.   1980-1988.   I. Title.
DS318.85. H57   1991
955.05′4—dc20   90-45641

CONTENTS

ILLUSTRATIONS

ABBREVIATIONS

ABSP	Arab Baath Socialist Party	Nato	North Atlantic Treaty Organization
ADIZ	Air Defence Interception Zone	NLA	National Liberation Army
Awacs	Airborne Warning and Control Systems	OPEC	Organization of Oil Exporting Countries
BBC	British Broadcasting Corporation	PUK	Patriotic Union of Kurdistan
b/d	barrels/day	RCC	Revolutionary Command Council
CIA	Central Intelligence Agency	RDF	Rapid Deployment Force
EASSP	European Association for the Study of Safety Problems	SAIRI	Supreme Assembly of Islamic Revolution in Iraq
GCC	Gulf Co-operation Council	Sam	Surface-to-air missile
GDP	Gross Domestic Product	SHORAD	Short Range Air Defence
GNP	Gross National Product	SNPE	Société Nationale des Poudres et Explosifs
ICO	Islamic Conference Organization	Tow	Tube-launched Optically-tracked Wire-guided
ID	Iraqi Dinar	UAE	United Arab Emirates
IR	Iranian Rial	UN/UNO	United Nations Organization
IRP	Islamic Republican Party	UNIIMOG	United Nations Iran–Iraq Military Observer Group
KDP	Kurdish Democratic Party		
MERIP	Middle East Research and Information Project	US/USA	United States of America
		USS	United States Ship
NAM	Non-Aligned Movement	USSR	Union of Soviet Socialist Republics

GLOSSARY OF ARABIC AND FARSI WORDS

adha: sacrifice
al/el/ol/ul: the
Alawi: follower or descendant of Imam Ali
ashura: (lit.) tenth; (fig.) tenth of Muharram
Ayatollah: sign or token of Allah

baath: renaissance
bait: place or home
basij: mobilization
bint: daughter

daawa: call
din: faith

-e: of
eid: festival
Eid al Adha: the Festival of Sacrifice
Eid al Fitr: the Festival of 'Breaking the Fast'

fajr: dawn
faqih: religious jurist
fatah: victory
fitr: breaking the fast

hadith: action or speech of the Prophet Muhammad or a (Shia) Imam
hajj: pilgrimage (to Mecca)
haram: religiously forbidden
harram: holy

haur: marshes
hojatalislam: proof of Islam
hukumat: government

ibn: son
imam: (lit.) one who leads prayers in a mosque; (fig.) religious leader
islam: state or act of submission (to the will of Allah)
ittihad: unity
ittilaat: information

jihad: (lit.) struggle in the name of Allah; (fig.) holy war or crusade
jumhouri: republic

kayhan: world
khalq: people
kharaji: outsider or seceder
khums: one-fifth (of gains)

mahdi: one who is guided by Allah
majlis: assembly
majnoon: mad
medina/medinat: town or city
mobin: clear
mubarak: blessed
muhammad: praiseworthy or blessed
mujahedin (sing. mujahid): those who conduct jihad
mullah: cleric or preacher

muqaddas: holy
Muslim: one who accepts Islam
mustazafin (sing. mustazaf): the
    needy or the oppressed

nasr: victory

oghab: eagle

quds: holy
quran/koran: recitation or
    discourse

resalat: mission
rud: river

sayyid: (lit.) lord or prince; (fig.)
    title applied to a male
    descendant of Imam Hussein
shah: king
shaikh: (lit.) old man; (fig.) a title
    of respect accorded to a wise
    man

Sharia: sacred law of Islam
shatt: river
shehadat: martyrdom
shia: partisan or follower
shiraa: sail
sultan: ruler
sunna: tradition or beaten path
sunni: one who follows sunna

thawra: revolution
tudeh: masses

ulama (sing. alim): body of
    religious-legal scholars

wa: and or by
waqf: religious endowment

-ye: of

zafar: victory
zakat: alms or charity

TURKEY

Tabriz

Mahabad
Zanjan

Mosul ● Arbil

Kirkuk ● ● Suleimaniya ● Sanandaj

● Hamadan

SYRIA

Tikrit ● Bakhtaran

Samarra ● Ar

● Ilam ● Khorramabad

● Rutba ● Baghdad
Mehran

IRAQ Karbala ● ● Hilleh
Kut ● Dezful

Kufa ● Amara ● Ahvaz

Najaf ●

Qadasiya ● Khorramshahr

Basra ● Abadan ● Banda
Khom

Fao

KUWAIT Kha

Kuwait ●

Neutral Zone

SAUDI ARABIA

BAHRA

Tigris
Euphrates

	Iranian territory occupied by Iraq; November 1980
—·—·—	International Boundary
●	National Capital
●	City or Town

0   50   100   150   200
└────┴────┴────┴────┘ Miles

● Riyadh

THE LONGEST WAR

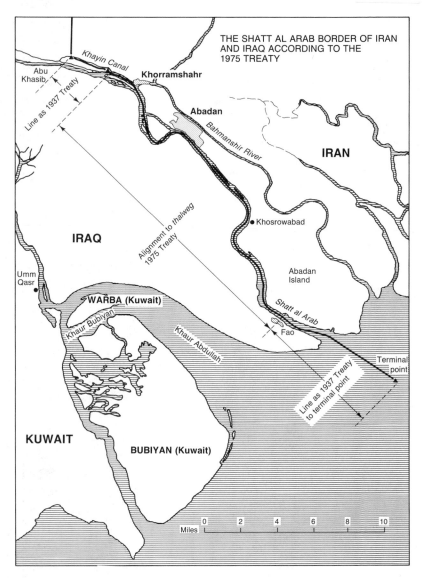

THE SHATT AL ARAB BORDER OF IRAN
AND IRAQ ACCORDING TO THE
1975 TREATY

Khayin Canal

Abu
Khasib

Line as 1937 Treaty

Khorramshahr

Abadan

Bahmanshir River

IRAN

IRAQ

Alignment to *thalweg*
1975 Treaty

Khosrowabad

Umm
Qasr

WARBA (Kuwait)

Abadan
Island

Khaur Bubiyan

Khaur Abdullah

Shatt al Arab

Fao

Terminal
point

Line as 1937 Treaty
to terminal point

KUWAIT

BUBIYAN (Kuwait)

0   2   4   6   8   10
Miles

THE LONGEST WAR

THE LONGEST WAR

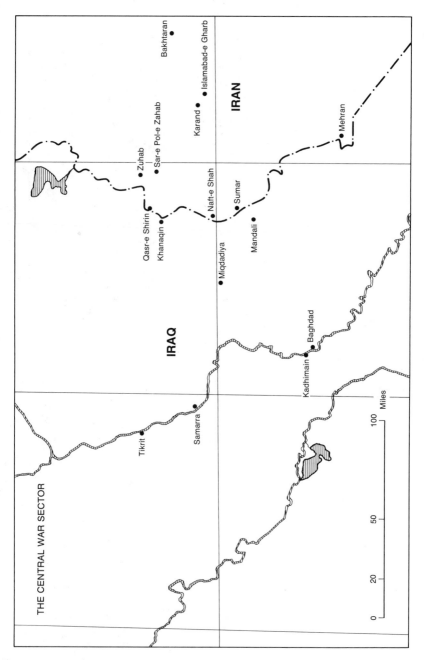

THE CENTRAL WAR SECTOR

IRAQ

IRAN

Bakhtaran

Islamabad-e Gharb

Karand

Sar-e Pol-e Zahab

Zuhab

Qasr-e Shirin

Khanaqin

Naft-e Shah

Sumar

Mandali

Mehran

Miqdadiya

Baghdad

Kadhimain

Tikrit

Samarra

Miles

0   20   50   100

THE LONGEST WAR

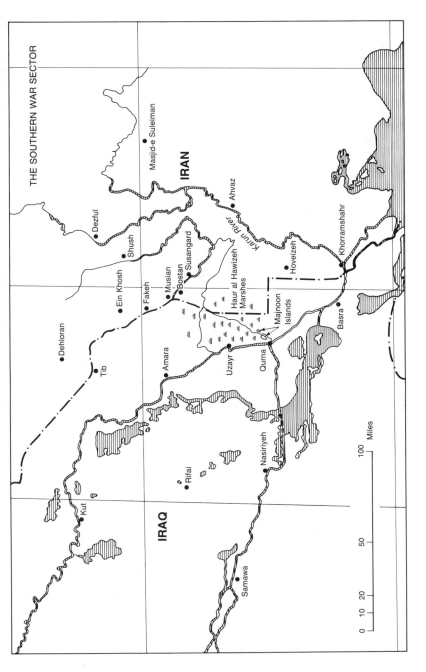

THE SOUTHERN WAR SECTOR

IRAN

IRAQ

Masjid-e Suleiman

Dezful

Shush

Ein Khosh

Fakeh

Musian

Bostan

Susangard

Ahvaz

Karun River

Haur al Hawizeh
Marshes

Hoveizeh

Khorramshahr

Majnoon
Islands

Basra

Dehloran

Tib

Amara

Uzayr

Qurna

Kut

Rifai

Nasiriyeh

Samawa

0   10 20   50   100   Miles

THE LONGEST WAR

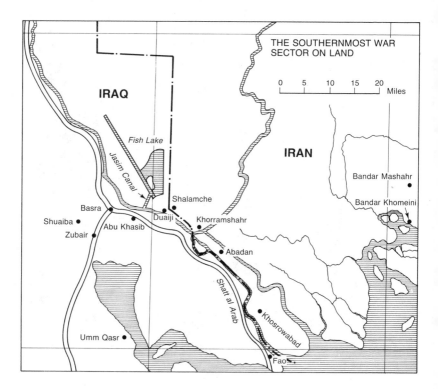

THE LONGEST WAR

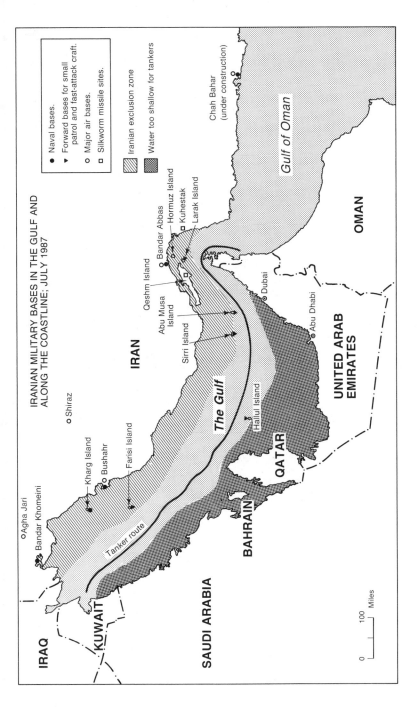

IRANIAN MILITARY BASES IN THE GULF AND
ALONG THE COASTLINE; JULY 1987

- Naval bases.
▼ Forward bases for small
  patrol and fast-attack craft.
○ Major air bases.
□ Silkworm missile sites.

Iranian exclusion zone
Water too shallow for tankers

IRAQ
KUWAIT
SAUDI ARABIA
BAHRAIN
QATAR
UNITED ARAB EMIRATES
OMAN
IRAN

Agha Jari
Bandar Khomeini
Kharg Island
Bushahr
Farisi Island
Shiraz
Hallul Island
Tanker route
The Gulf
Sirri Island
Abu Musa Island
Qeshm Island
Bandar Abbas
Hormuz Island
Kuhestak
Larak Island
Dubai
Abu Dhabi
Chah Bahar
(under construction)
Gulf of Oman

0   100
Miles

THE LONGEST WAR MAP

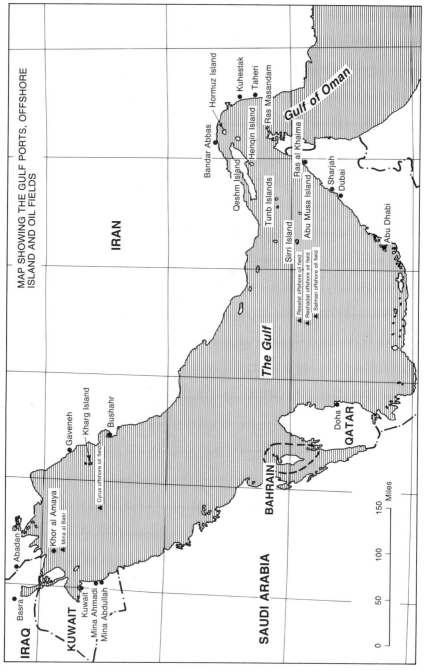

MAP SHOWING THE GULF PORTS, OFFSHORE ISLAND AND OIL FIELDS

IRAN

Bandar Abbas
Hormuz Island
Qeshm Island
Kuhestak
Taheri
Henqin Island
Ras Masandam
Gulf of Oman
Ras al Khaima
Sharjah
Abu Musa Island
Dubai
Tunb Islands
Abu Dhabi
Sirri Island
Resalat offshore oil field
Reshadat offshore oil field
Salman offshore oil field

The Gulf

Gaveneh
Kharg Island
Bushahr
Cyrus offshore oil field

Abadan
Khor al Amaya
Mina al Bakr

IRAQ
Basra

KUWAIT
Kuwait
Mina Ahmadi
Mina Abdullah

SAUDI ARABIA

BAHRAIN

Doha
QATAR

Miles
0   50   100   150

THE LONGEST WAR - MAP 6

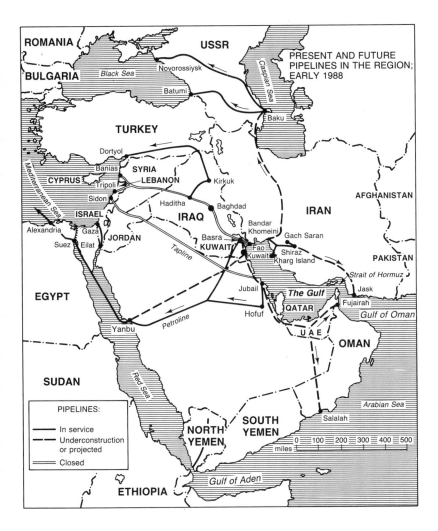

THE LONGEST WAF

THE LONGEST WAR - MAP

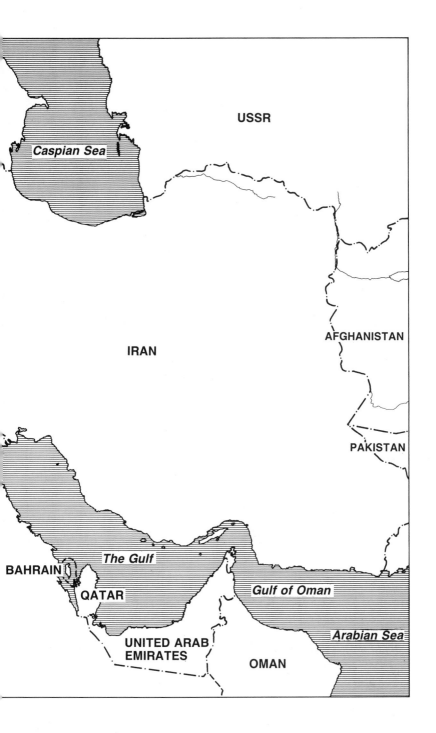

PREFACE

Several features of the Iran–Iraq War make it unique among the conflicts of modern times. It is the longest conventional warfare of the twentieth century. Unlike the Arab–Israeli or India–Pakistan hostilities, it was not a brief but intense encounter between the combatants. Instead, it developed a pattern of its own: constrained, episodic action interspersed with bouts of feverish fighting.

In so far as neither America nor the Soviet Union had any leverage over Iran, it was a purely Third World phenomenon. Unlike most of the post-Second World War conflicts, this one did not lead to a sharp division between the two superpowers.

The Gulf conflict was not about territory – as was the case, say, with Argentina and Britain over the Falkland Islands in 1982 – or hostile ideologies like capitalism and socialism, as in the 1950–53 war between North Korea and South Korea. It was a violent manifestation of the struggle between the secular Arab nationalism of Iraq and the universalist, religious ideology of Iran's revolutionary Islamic regime.

Competition and conflict between Iran and Iraq have been endemic since the mid-seventeenth century when Iraq became the easternmost province of the Ottoman empire and Iran was the heartland of the Safavid empire. That is why I begin this book with a chapter tracing the roots of conflict to earlier centuries.

I divide the war, which lasted from September 1980 to August 1988, into four parts, and each part into two chapters: one describing the progress of the fighting and its impact on the domestic scene of the combatant nations, and the other dealing with the roles played by outside forces, principally the neighbouring countries, Europe and the superpowers.

Chapter 2 deals with the period until mid-1982 when the battle-fronts were inside Iran, while the next chapter gives a survey of the involvement of the main foreign players in the war.

From then on the front lines were almost always in Iraq. Chapter 4 takes the reader up to Iran's successful Majnoon Islands offensive in early 1984, followed by a chapter describing the parts played by the Gulf monarchies, the Europeans and the superpowers in the continuing conflict.

The next chapter begins with the Tanker War initiated by Iraq in the spring of 1984 and traces the progress of hostilities up to the end of 1985. Then follows a survey of the war-related activities of the outside powers.

Iran's Fao and Basra offensives, the major events of the last part of the war, form the core of Chapter 8. The succeeding chapter gives, *inter alia*, a summary of the Irangate affair in the United States, and shows how the conflict was internationalized by Kuwait's success in securing superpower protection for its oil tankers.

The shooting down of an Iranian airbus by the US navy on 3 July 1988 marks the beginning of the end of the Gulf War. Chapter 10 takes the narrative to the ceasefire on 20 August 1988 and beyond, offering a brief résumé of the subsequent talks between Iran and Iraq.

In the final chapter I give an analytical summary of the causes of the outbreak of the Gulf War and its long duration as well as the impact it has had on the belligerent nations and the outside powers which tried to influence its outcome.

A word about place names, and the spellings of Arabic and Farsi words. I have used the term 'the Gulf' for the gulf that divides Iran from the Arabian Peninsula, but I have listed the two other names in general use – the Arabian Gulf and the Persian Gulf – in the index. There is no standard way of transliterating Arabic and Farsi names. In each case I have chosen one of the most widely used spellings in the English-speaking world, and stuck to it – except when the spelling of a book author is different from mine. There I have simply reproduced the published spelling. A particular difficulty arises when different spellings of a proper name, or an object, begin with a different letter. Common examples are Koran and Quran, and Ghom and Qom. I have solved this problem by using one spelling in the text but including both in the index. In general I have tried to be simple and consistent.

Some of the place names in Iran have been changed since the revolution. I have given both versions at the first mention and then stayed with the current name.

Since many of the Arabic words which appear in the text are also part of the Farsi vocabulary, I have prepared a combined glossary of Arabic and Farsi words.

Dinar is the Iraqi unit of currency, and Rial is the Iranian unit. The official exchange rate varies between 0.31 and 0.28 Iraqi Dinar to one US dollar. Though in Iran the official exchange rate has fluctuated between 70 to 85 Rials to a US dollar I have used the rate of 80 Rials to one US dollar.

The following Arabic and Farsi words signify religious or secular titles: ayatollah, hojatalislam, imam, sayyid, shah, shaikh and sultan.

INTRODUCTION

The 1980–88 Iran–Iraq conflict is the longest conventional warfare of this century. Neither the First World War nor the Second lasted eight years. The other major conflicts of the century – in the South and North Vietnams of the 1960s and 1970s, and between China and Japan in the Manchuria of the 1930s – do not qualify as conventional wars between sovereign states.

America intervened in what was essentially an incipient civil war in South Vietnam in the mid-1960s. The strife between China and Japan in the province of Manchuria never reached a point where one state declared war against the other. In 1931 Japan converted the Chinese province of Manchuria into the State of Manchukuo under a puppet ruler: Henry Pu Yi, the long deposed emperor of China. It was not until 1937 that the Chinese government tried to retrieve Manchuria/Manchukuo militarily, an armed conflict which was to merge with the Second World War.

With more than a million casualties the Gulf War is also one of the bloodiest. The cost of conducting it, and the direct and indirect damage caused by it, is put at an astronomical figure of $1,190 billion.

Its repercussions extended far beyond the region. Unable to resist the gains, financial or political, accruing from clandestine weapons trade with Iran, scores of Western companies and several governments sold arms to Tehran. The result was a series of scandals, the best known of which was the Irangate affair in America. The startling revelations in late 1986 that the United States had been selling arms to Iran – officially branded as a terrorist state – in exchange for the release of American hostages in Lebanon immobilized the US administration for the best part of a year. President Ronald Reagan never quite recovered from the drop in his approval rating from 67 per cent to 46 per cent.

Among the European countries to be hit by scandals stemming from illegal weapons sales to Tehran were France, Italy, Sweden, Belgium and Austria. In France commissions from such dealings were allegedly paid by the state-owned arms manufacturing companies to the functionaries of the governing Socialist Party. In Sweden there were persistent rumours of a connection between illicit arms sales to Tehran, consummated or thwarted, and the still-unsolved mystery of the assassination of the prime minister, Olaf Palme, in early 1986. Then there were large-scale clandestine supplies of explosives to Iran by a cartel of 14 European companies based in Austria, Belgium, Britain, Finland, France, Holland, Italy, Norway, Spain, Sweden, Switzerland and West Germany.

These were but outer ripples emanating from the centre of a bitter war which has left a profound mark on the Gulf region – a most strategic territory containing 54 per cent of the world's known oil reserves.

The roots of conflict between Iran and Iraq are deep and varied. They date back to the rivalries between the Ottoman and Persian empires of earlier times, when Iraq was the easternmost province of the Ottomans. What brought the two states to open warfare was the 1979 Islamic revolution in Iran and its consequences. The military and economic chaos that followed the political upheaval in Iran tempted the Iraqi leader, Saddam Hussein, to settle old scores with his bigger and more populous neighbour. More specifically, he wanted to regain the half of the Shatt al Arab (lit. The Arab River), forming the common border in the south, that he had surrendered to Tehran in a treaty signed in 1975.

It transpired later that the reports of Iran's military weakness were highly exaggerated. The source of these accounts were monarchist generals and politicians who had found a congenial refuge in Baghdad and who dreamt of resuming their past roles of authority and power in Tehran.

The net effect of Saddam Hussein's invasion of Iran was to provide the regime of Ayatollah Ruhollah Khomeini with a rallying cause to mobilize its citizens in the name of defending both Islam and the nation. This was a powerful call. By successfully resisting and then expelling the Iraqi invaders the Iranian government consolidated the Islamic revolution.

Saddam Hussein reckoned that Tehran would now cease fighting and settle the border and other disputes through negotiations. He was mistaken. In the war that had been imposed upon them Iranian leaders sensed a powerful vehicle for the export of their revolution. And what better target could they have than Iraq, where at least 55 per cent of the nationals belong to Shiaism, the Islamic sect predominant in Iran? But by invading Iraq in mid-1982 the Khomeini government committed the same kind of mistake as the Saddam Hussein regime had done in September 1980. This time it was the Iraqi president who exhorted his citizens to defend the homeland and fight the 'mad mullah' intent on expanding his domain under the banner of Islam.

Iraq's president had a daunting task, given that his nation is divided along sectarian lines – Shia and Sunni – as well as ethnic – Arab and Kurd. The technique he employed, successfully, was an amalgam of persuasion and coercion. It worked not only at home, but also abroad with his foreign allies, principally the oil-rich monarchies of Saudi Arabia and Kuwait. They had a solid reason to dread the revolutionary message emanating from Tehran. According to Khomeini, there is no place for hereditary power in Islam. That is, monarchy is unIslamic.

Not surprisingly, short of declaring war against Iran, both Saudi Arabia and Kuwait aided Iraq materially and logistically. When Iran retaliated by targeting its oil tankers, Kuwait turned to the superpowers for the safety of its vessels, and got a positive response, particularly from the United States. The Pentagon boosted its naval presence in the Gulf region from six warships to 32. Thus in the summer of 1987 Kuwait succeeded in internationalizing the conflict, something Iraq had attempted to do, in vain, three years earlier, when it initiated the Tanker War by repeatedly hitting Iran's oil carriers and thereby invited Iranian attacks on non-Iraqi ships (since Iraq had no merchant ships plying in the Gulf).

The other military technique Iraq used was to bomb Iranian cities in order to demoralize the population. Given the parlous state of Iran's air force and air defence systems, the government was unable to defend urban centres. Yet, to Baghdad's surprise and frustration, Iranian morale was not sapped. Indeed, Tehran kept up periodic major land campaigns, which the Iraqis had learnt to block with overflowing armouries and their ever-active air force. Yet the Iranians managed to seize and retain enough Iraqi soil in each big offensive to maintain morale and hope on the front lines and behind.

Thus the war dragged on for six years after Iran had dislodged the Iraqis from its territory.

In the end Tehran gave up the gun for an olive branch in the face of unbearable pressures from Iraq and its regional and international allies. Washington's concerted, world-wide campaign after the Irangate fiasco to deny arms and ammunition to Tehran began to bite. US warships engaged the Iranian navy in a series of damaging confrontations. The USSR and France armed Iraq to the teeth, an enterprise funded as much by rising Iraqi oil exports as by Saudi and Kuwaiti financial aid.

Then there was Baghdad's enhanced military power, combined with its newly adopted tactic of using chemical weapons regularly and extensively in its offensives against Iran to recover its territories. Along with this went Iraq's success in raising its standing army to one million and supporting it with an armed militia of 600,000. Thus a country of 16 million put one-tenth of its population under arms. At this rate the US would have 24.5 million men in its military and the National Guard; and Britain 5.5 million in its armed forces and the Territorial Army.

The comparative figures for Iran were unimpressive. Despite the three to one advantage that it had in population, its clerical leaders could only shore up their aggregate fighting force to the level of Iraq's: 1.6 million. It was the same in the application of economic resources. At its highest Iran spent no more than 12 per cent of its Gross Domestic Product on the war – against Iraq's 57 per cent. In short, while the Iranian clergy were long on rhetoric they proved woefully short on results.

However, a general point could be made that Iraq fought the war on borrowed money and manpower. It spent some $95 billion on the war in 95 months; and its foreign loans and grants amounted to $85–90 billion. To keep its civilian economy ticking over it engaged 1.5–2 million foreign workers, who on average provided 40 per cent of the civilian workforce. Not only did Iran fight the war completely on its own, spending about $85 billion, but it paid off its modest pre-revolution foreign loans in the course of the conflict. Despite the long war and an acute need for manpower at the fronts, Iran had an unemployment rate of at least 15 per cent.

In short, while Iranian leaders projected an image of dogmatic revolutionaries urging their followers to take the path of martyrdom, in practice they were pragmatic, even cautious. Small wonder that the official figure of nearly 200,000 Iranian troops and civilians killed in the conflict was lower than even the most conservative estimate by the Pentagon: 262,000.

Iran's Islamic leaders did not want the war. But once it was thrust on them they saw its potential for welding the nation together under the revolutionary Islamic banner: warfare was to be a means of consolidating the revolution. As long as it served that purpose they waged it. Given the religious network of clerics in daily touch with the populace, the leadership had its hand on the pulse of the nation all along. When it realized that ordinary people had tired of the war it concluded that continuing the armed conflict would only undermine the revolution and destabilize the present system. The speed with which the Iranian government turned round on the question of a ceasefire was remarkable. But by doing so it reaffirmed its ultimate loyalty to the Islamic revolution: how to consolidate it and advance it in Iran.

As for Iraq, its president convinced himself and his fellow citizens that they had won the Gulf War. His first step after the ceasefire was to punish the rebellious Kurds in the north for having actively co-operated with Iran during the conflict. He used chemical weapons extensively, this time against his own nationals: an unprecedented act. With a million men in the regular army not engaged in active warfare, he had plenty to spare to curb Kurdish insurgency and attack his rival in the Arab world, President Hafiz Assad of Syria.

Having survived an armed adventure against Iran – indeed having emerged stronger militarily and politically as a result of it – Saddam Hussein might undertake another. What is likely to restrain him are the financial penalties. As the leader of a cripplingly indebted country, he does not have the political and military freedom he enjoyed in the summer of 1980 when Baghdad held $35 billion in foreign currencies.

So while a peace treaty between Iran and Iraq is not imminent, the chance of conventional war breaking out again between the two unreconciled neighbours is slim.

1 ROOTS OF CONFLICT

The Iran–Iraq War was the result both of long-term and immediate causes. A study of the conflict shows that the points of contention between the two neighbours have not altered for centuries and that some of the events of the past seem uncannily contemporary.

Competition and rivalry between Iran and Iraq go back to the days of the Ottoman Turkish empire (1517–1918) and the Persian empire under the Safavids (1501–1722). Iraq was then the easternmost province of the Ottomans and Iran the nucleus of the Safavid realm. Disputes between the competing empires revolved around boundaries and interference in each other's internal affairs, conducted through ethnic and sectarian minorities across the common border.

Though the nature of the disputes remained unaltered, the context in which they occurred changed. Until the first quarter of the nineteenth century the presence of migratory tribes in the frontier areas militated against fixed boundaries. Then tensions continued under the tutelage of European imperial powers. Finally, from the 1920s onwards the nominally independent states of Iraq and Iran sustained historical animosities in changed circumstances, at first still under the direct influence of Britain, and later (after 1958) as truly independent countries pursuing their respective national interests.

After the Safavid chief, Shah Ismail (1501–24), had consolidated his newly won territories he adopted Twelver Shiaism[1] as the official religion so as to appeal to the heterodox sentiments of his subjects and differentiate himself from the competing Sunni Ottoman Turks eager to incorporate Iran into their empire. Under Shah Ismail, Shia theology and jurisprudence were systematized. The resulting religio-ideological unity helped him to lay a strong foundation for the Safavid empire. On the other hand, the Ottomans feared that the Safavids might incite their own Shia subjects in Central Asia to rebel. The result was that some 40,000 Shias in the Ottoman empire were massacred as spies of the Safavids.[2]

Because the Safavids considered themselves the guardians of Shiaism they wanted free access to Shia holy shrines in Najaf and Karbala in southern Iraq. The Iraqi cities of Basra, Kufa, Najaf, Karbala and Samarra

figure prominently in the early history of Islam, when divisions in the
ranks of Muslims led to the creation of two major sects: minority Shias –
derivative of Shiat Ali, 'Followers of Ali', the cousin and son-in-law
of the Prophet Muhammad – and majority Sunni, people of Sunna,
'Tradition'. Of the twelve Imams of Twelver Shias, six are buried in Iraq
and the last one went into occultation in the Iraqi town of Samarra.

The Safavids occupied Iraq for 15 years, from 1623 to 1638. Following
its recapture by the Ottomans the two sides signed the Treaty of Zuhab
in 1639. It recognized Iraq as part of the Ottoman empire and dealt with
frontier demarcation, as well as with the thorny problems of the Kurdish
tribes settled in the northern Zagros Mountain region and the annual
pilgrimage of Persian Shias to the holy shrines in Iraq.

Though the treaty held for over a century the problem of the frontier
areas persisted. In the north the Kurdish tribes continued to ignore the
international boundaries and in the south, Arabic-speaking tribes, keen
to maintain their autonomy from the Ottomans, offered (nominal)
allegiance to Persia.

In fact the emergence of Muhammara in 1812 as an autonomous
principality ruled by the leader of the Muhaisin tribe sharpened tensions
between the adjoining empires. War broke out between them in 1821. By
now Britain and Tsarist Russia were the leading European imperial
powers in the region. They came to regulate Ottoman–Persian relations.
In 1821 Britain mediated between the belligerent neighbours, resulting
in the Treaty of Erzerum in 1823. Among other things each of the
signatories promised not to grant political asylum to dissident groups
from the other empire.

But the two sides continued to interfere in each other's affairs. Persia
encouraged the Kurds in Iraq to rebel. Tensions rose between 1834 and
1840 when the Ottomans attacked the port of Muhammara (later
renamed Khorramshahr) and persecuted the Persian Shias living in Iraq.
Britain and Russia again intervened to resolve the conflict. A joint
commission appointed in 1843 produced results two years later. Persia
ceded Suleimaniya in Iraqi Kurdistan and received Muhammara/
Khorramshahr in return. And for giving up some territory in the Zuhab–
Qasr-e Shirin area Persia got the Island of Khizr (later renamed Abadan)
and the land between the Bahmanshir river and the Shatt al Arab, a
400–1300-yard-wide-waterway – called Arvand Rud by the Persians –
which originates at the confluence of the Euphrates and Tigris rivers. In
short, the Second Treaty of Erzerum of 1847 moved the fluvial borders

between the two countries from the western bank of the Bahmanshir river to the eastern bank of the Shatt al Arab for about the last third of its length of 120 miles.

The Delimiting Commission appointed in 1848 produced a detailed map in 1869, and functioned for seven more years. But the signatories to the Second Erzerum Treaty did not stop interfering in each other's domestic affairs. Muhammara continued to function as an autonomous district, while the free movement of the Arab tribes across the Shatt al Arab preserved the Arab character of the waterway's eastern bank. However, tensions were kept under control by the supervising powers of Britain and Russia.

A new factor was added to the complex equation when, in 1908, the British discovered oil in commercial quantities near Masjid-e Suleiman in Arabistan/Khuzistan. The Shaikh of Muhammara persisted in his drive for independence while faction fighting among the Kurds showed no sign of abating. This was the background to the signing of the Protocol of Tehran in 1911: it outlined a basis for negotiations to settle all outstanding problems and set up a Joint Delimitation Commission. In November 1913 the representatives of the Ottoman empire, Persia, Britain and Russia met in Constantinople (later renamed Istanbul) to delineate the boundary from Mount Ararat to the Gulf and redefine navigational rights in the Shatt al Arab. Britain was keen to develop an oil industry in Iran and needed extensive port facilities along the waterway. Not surprisingly, the new protocol awarded to Iran five small and one largish islands in the Shatt al Arab between Muhammara and the sea. The 1913 Constantinople Protocol was confirmed in 1914 and followed by the appointment of a Delimitation Commission on which Britain and Russia had powers of arbitration. By the time the First World War broke out a definitive map of the frontier had been produced and 227 boundary pillars installed.

The First World War, the Bolshevik revolution and the dissolution of the Ottoman empire caused profound changes in the region. Iraq emerged as a quasi-independent state under British mandate in 1921. With this began the third phase of Iran–Iraq relations, where two (nominally) independent nation-states faced each other.

Britain passed on the Basra Port Authority it had created to the Iraqi government. Iran refused to recognize the exclusive Iraqi control of the Shatt al Arab and used its own pilots to steer ships along it, arguing that the 1913 Constantinople Protocol had recognized the thalweg – the median line of the deepest channel – as the international boundary. In the mid-1920s trouble erupted in the Kurdish part of Iraq and in the Khanaqin–Qasr-e Shirin frontier area. It was only in April 1929 that Tehran formally accorded diplomatic recognition to Iraq. By now Iran was ruled by Reza Pahlavi Shah, who had seized the throne in 1926 after proving his military prowess by crushing the semi-autonomous Shaikh Khazal of Muhammara and renaming the province Khuzistan.

In 1931 the two countries exchanged envoys; and the following year Iraq, having acquired full independence, became a member of the League of Nations. The nature of the inter-state problems, however, remained the same. This was well encapsulated by Tawfik al Suwaidi, the first Iraqi representative in Iran, in his memoirs. 'One of the most complicated issues exhausting both sides, Iraq and Iran, was the Kurdish border problem which included the return of criminals and related issues,' he wrote. 'The Iranian government believed that the Arabs of Khuzistan were encouraged by the Iraqi government to rebel. At the same time the Iraqi government believed that harsh oppression was exercised by Iran against the Arabs of Khuzistan. This policy resulted in a number of uprisings which forced the Arabs of Arabistan/Khuzistan to seek refuge in Iraq . . . The third issue which required debate between the two governments was the position of Iraq in regard to the Shatt al Arab and its right to complete sovereignty over the whole river.'[3]

Iraq took the dispute to the League of Nations in November 1934, but in the spring of 1936 both states agreed to withdraw the case from the League and resume direct negotiations. While these were in progress internal developments in Iraq weakened its position. A military coup in October 1936 ushered in a government which was feeble and confused. Under continued pressure from Iran, bolstered by the British oil interests and government, Iraq conceded the thalweg principle for 4 miles opposite Abadan, which housed a vast oil refinery owned by the Anglo-Persian Oil Company. The result was the Iran–Iraq Frontier Treaty signed on 4 July 1937. It stated that the Shatt al Arab was open for navigation to all the countries of the world. It confirmed the land boundaries as set out in the 1913–14 accords, and amended only the fluvial frontiers. Later Iraq was to state that it had signed the treaty under duress – an argument it was to repeat regarding the March 1975 Algiers Accord with Iran.

Even though the 1937 Treaty was between two sovereign states the domineering presence of Britain was all too obvious. British interests exercised influence in both Baghdad and Tehran. A British-dominated oil company had struck oil in northern Iraq in 1927, and the Anglo-Persian Oil Company was a giant in Iran's industrial and commercial life.

The Second World War destroyed whatever illusion the two states had of their sovereignty. In 1941 London intervened militarily to overthrow the nationalist government of Rashid Ali Gailani in Baghdad. During the same year Britain and the Soviet Union deposed Reza Pahlavi Shah and occupied Iran. Both Iran and Iraq were used as staging areas by the Allies to supply weapons and goods to the beleaguered Soviet Union. This led to the building of a bridge across the Shatt al Arab and improved rail and road systems between the two neighbours.

Following the signing of the Treaty of Good Neighbourly Relations in June 1949 mutual ties were raised to the ambassadorial level. Relations improved further with the establishment of a military alliance between Turkey, Iraq, Iran, Pakistan and Britain in February 1951, officially called the Middle East Treaty Organization and popularly known as the Baghdad Pact. Among other things this alliance was a device for Britain in conjunction with America, which had emerged as the leader of the West following the Second World War, to maintain influence over Iran and Iraq. Little wonder that in January 1957 Iran and Iraq endorsed the doctrine of the American president Dwight Eisenhower which promised support to any Middle East government against 'overt armed aggression from any nation controlled by international communism'.

A generation of fairly peaceful co-existence between the two countries ended in July 1958, when the pro-Western Iraqi monarchy was overthrown by nationalist, republican military officers. The event heralded the final expulsion of Western imperialism from Iraq; and Baghdad and Tehran entered a period when, as truly independent states, they were free to regulate their relations in the light of their sovereign rights, territorial integrity and national interests.

While republican Iraq adopted a non-aligned policy by withdrawing from the Western-sponsored Baghdad Pact in March 1959, monarchical Iran, under Muhammad Reza Pahlavi Shah, moved closer to the US. In March 1959 it signed a Military Co-operation Agreement with Washington, providing for American defence of Iran in case of external aggression. Thus fortified, the Shah in November 1959 revived the old Iranian demand that the thalweg formula be applied to all of the Shatt al Arab. The Iraqi leader, Premier Abdul Karim Qasim, rejected the demand, explaining that Iraq had made the concession on the thalweg in 1937 to provide an anchorage area for Abadan because of unsettled conditions at home. Tension mounted. Iran threatened to use its own river pilots and cease paying tolls to Baghdad.

Baghdad continued to be the weak party, partly because it lacked the military strength of Iran and partly because its internal situation was unstable. During the decade 1958–68 Iraq experienced three coups and five different governments. Only in July 1968, with the success of a coup dominated by the Arab Baath Socialist Party, did the situation stabilize.

Meanwhile, to the earlier list of problems a new one was added: exploration for oil in the offshore continental shelf. This subject cropped up in the spring of 1963. There was already the contentious issue of Iran and Iraq tapping a common oilfield in the central sector of Khaneh and Naft-e Shah.

So when an Iranian delegation went to Baghdad in February 1969 to confer with the new Baathist administration it discussed three issues: the offshore continental shelf; joint exploration of the oilfield near Khaneh; and demarcation of unsettled boundaries. On the last point the Iranians declared that Iraq had failed to meet its obligations under the 1937 Treaty and repeated the demand that the fluvial frontier be redrawn along the thalweg of the Shatt al Arab. Baghdad refused. In March there was a revival of Kurdish rebellion in Iraq which diverted the attention of the central authority in Baghdad and emboldened the Shah. On 19 April Tehran unilaterally abrogated the 1937 Treaty, and went on to pilot its own ships in the Shatt al Arab. Iranian gunboats steamed up the waterway along the middle channel. Iraq complained to the United Nations, but nothing came of it. As before, Iraq expelled resident Iranians in large numbers and began helping dissident Iranian groups against the Shah. It revived the issue of Khuzistan/Arabistan which, in Baghdad's view, was Iraqi territory that had been surrendered to Iran during 'the foreign mandate [of the Ottomans]'.[4] It announced the formation of the Popular Front for the Liberation of Arabistan. A war of words ensued between the two capitals, with Iraq setting up three radio stations to transmit anti-Shah propaganda.

The Shah went beyond hostile words. On 21 January 1970 Baghdad stated that he had tried to engineer a coup led by Major-General Abdul Ghani al Rawi, and that the attempt had been foiled. Forty-four plotters, three-quarters of them military men, were executed.

Earlier, in 1966, the Shah had agreed to act as a conduit for arms supplies from Israel and the US to the Kurdish insurgents in Iraq. The Kurdish problem was endemic to Iraq when it was part of the Ottoman empire and after. As descendants of the Indo-European tribes who settled in south-eastern Turkey, north-eastern Iraq and north-western Persia, Kurds trace their distinct history as mountain people to the seventh century BC, appearing as Medes in the Bible. Racially, they are different from Turks and Semite Arabs, and their language, a member of the Indo-European family, is akin to Farsi (Persian). After the dissolution of the Ottoman empire the Kurds in Mosul province mounted periodic rebellions, first against Britain, the mandate power, and then against the central Arab authority in Baghdad. The importance of the Kurdish area rose sharply in 1927 when a British dominated company struck oil near Kirkuk, the largest find in the world so far. A Kurdish insurgency for independence led by Shaikh Ahmad Barzani in 1931–2 was crushed in 1935 by a joint Iraqi-Turkish campaign, a strategy to be re-employed half a century later. During the Second World War Mustafa Barzani, a brother of Ahmad, led another rebellion which failed. He escaped to Iran where, under the banner of the Kurdish Democratic Party, he founded the Kurdish Republic of Mahabad in 1946. When the Republic was crushed by the Shah, Barzani fled to the Soviet Union.

Following the 1958 coup Barzani returned to Iraq, and backed the new regime under Qasim. In exchange Qasim legalized the Kurdish Democratic Party and promulgated a constitution which stated: 'Arabs and Kurds are associates in this nation.' This was a formal recognition of Kurds – who formed 16–25 per cent of the national population – as a distinct ethnic minority. However, when Barzani advanced a plan for autonomy Qasim rejected it; and in September 1961 he mounted an all-out campaign against Kurdish insurgents. Even though Qasim was ousted from power in February 1963 the Kurdish rebellion continued. It was not until June 1966 that a 12-point agreement was signed between Barzani's KDP and the Baghdad government, which had been obliged to commit three of its five army divisions to fighting Kurdish guerrillas.[5] The pact included the official recognition of the Kurdish language and proportional representation for Kurds in the civil administration. But in the absence of mutual trust the agreement failed to resolve the problem.

Soon after seizing power in 1968 the Baathists began implementing part of the 12-point agreement. But the KDP considered the move inadequate, and inaugurated an armed rebellion in March 1969 with an attack on the Kirkuk oil refinery. The government struck back. The fighting went on for a year, costing Baghdad about 30 per cent of its annual budget.[6] The high cost of the conflict and the discovery of a military plot against it in January 1970 led the Baathist regime to conclude a 15-point pact with Barzani's KDP in March, to be implemented during the next four years. The new accord promised a fair degree of autonomy to the region where Kurds were in the majority (as recorded by a census to be conducted) and the appointment of a Kurd as the republic's vice-president. An interim constitution, promulgated in July 1970, recognized Kurds as one of the two nationalities of Iraq, and the Kurdish language as one of the two official languages in the Kurdish region. But the ruling Baathist Revolutionary Command Council rejected the KDP's nominee for vice-president.

Once again the pact failed to hold. Since the central government earned three-fifths of its oil revenue from Kurdistan it was unwilling to loosen its authority over the region. It failed to hold the promised census in Kurdish areas and continued the previous regime's policy of Arabizing the oil-rich Kirkuk district through such means as deporting some 40,000 Fali (Shia) Kurds to Iran. On the other hand, contrary to his promise, Barzani enlarged his guerrilla force, and maintained contacts with Iran, Israel and the US.

About this time another crucial element was added to the historic rivalry between Iran and Iraq: leadership of the Gulf region. The issue came to the fore as Britain, the imperialist power in the Gulf, began implementing its plan to withdraw from the region by December 1971. Both the US and Britain had chosen Iran to be the new guarantor of the security and safety of the Gulf and a bulwark against revolutionary changes in the area. To assume this role the Shah decided to add three strategically placed islands – the Lesser and Greater Tunbs (belonging to the Ras al Khaima principality) and Abu Musa (belonging to the Sharjah principality) – to a group of islands it already possessed: Qeshm, Larak and Hormuz. Together these six islands form a crescent which covers the entrance to the Hormuz Straits, through which a substantial portion of Gulf oil was shipped to the West and Japan. It was significant that on 30 November 1971, a day before the termination of the British treaty with the principality of Ras al Khaima, Iran occupied the uninhabited Lesser Tunb Island and captured Greater Tunb Island after some fighting. Britain aided the Shah to secure part possession of Abu Musa with a promise by Tehran of an annual grant to Sharjah's ruler. The Shah declared that he would not tolerate revolution on the Arab side of the

Gulf. Iraq's radical Baathist rulers were incensed. As fervent Arab nationalists they condemned the usurpation of Arab territory by the Shah, and saw in his move a ploy by Western imperialism to weaken the Arab side by first enfeebling Iraq. As revolutionaries they decided to confront the arch-reactionary of the region: the Shah of Iran.

Baghdad broke off relations with Tehran and London. It turned more and more towards Moscow, and formalized its close ties with the Soviet Union with a 15-year Treaty of Friendship and Co-operation in April 1972. The signatories pledged to contact each other in case of 'danger to the peace of either party or . . . danger to peace', and to refrain from joining an alliance (with another country or group of countries) aimed against the other. They also resolved to 'continue to develop co-operation in the strengthening of their defence capacity'.[7] At home the Baathist government expelled several thousands of Iranian theological students, pilgrims and merchants despite their long residence in Iraq. It increased its aid to the Popular Front for the Liberation of Arabistan.

Iraq's treaty with Moscow led America to back Tehran even more strongly. President Richard Nixon announced in May 1972 that the Shah could buy any non-nuclear American weapons he wanted, and that Washington would co-operate with Iran in instigating Kurdish insurgency in Iraq.

Iran regarded itself as the gendarmerie of the region and its monarchical Arab regimes, whereas Iraq perceived itself as the standard-bearer of militant, republican Arab nationalism in the Gulf. The conflict between the pro-West, conservative Iran, determined to maintain the status quo, and the pro-Soviet, radical Iraq, committed to revolution, was sharp and irreconcilable. At the same time the competition was unequal. Iraq was militarily and strategically much weaker than Iran. Since its coastline of a mere 40 miles was short and shallow, its seaports could not maintain extensive and reliable communications with other ports in the region: an Iraqi claim to be a Gulf power was hard to substantiate. On the other side, Iran's coastline not only ran the length of the Gulf but also extended into the Arabian Sea. Politically, too, Iraq was isolated in the region. Because of the support that the Baathists provided to republican forces against what they called 'Arab reaction', they were much feared and hated by the Gulf's Arab monarchs.

The outbreak of the Arab–Israeli war in early October 1973 demolished the Iraqi thesis that the Shah was a greater enemy than Israel and the West. Indeed during the hostilities Iraq despatched troops to the

Syrian–Israeli front, and re-established diplomatic links with Iran. However, there was no improvement in Baghdad–Tehran relations. Flushed with funds in hard currencies thanks to the quadrupling of oil prices, the Shah vastly increased his armed forces and military arsenals. He tried actively to destabilize the Iraqi government of Baathist leaders whom he described as 'a group of crazy, bloodthirsty savages'.[8] His best bet lay in bolstering up Barzani's Kurdish Democratic Party. Its agreement with Baghdad had collapsed, and in July 1973 it had refused to join the Baathist-led Progressive National Front government.

In March 1974 the Baghdad government enforced the Kurdish autonomy law, stemming from the March 1970 accord, as planned, and set the scene for the convening of a (nominated) legislative council in Arbil, the Kurdish capital. Protesting against the exclusion of such oil-rich areas as Kirkuk, Sinjar and Khanaqin from the Kurdish region, the KDP demanded that the enforcement of the autonomy law be postponed until a fresh census revealed the exact distribution of Kurds in the northeastern region. Baghdad ignored the demand; and the KDP resumed its armed struggle against the central government. At its peak the fighting involved 45,000 Kurdish guerrillas who pinned down four-fifths of Iraq's 100,000-plus troops and nearly half its 1390 tanks.[9] Barzani claimed to have liberated 25,000 square miles with a population of 1.5 million Kurds adjacent to the Iranian border. This was achieved with the direct assistance of the Shah who, besides supplying US and Israeli arms to the Kurds, used his forces to cover the insurgents with artillery fire and anti-aircraft missiles. In January 1975 the Shah posted two regiments of his uniformed army into the 'liberated' Kurdish areas of Iraq. Elsewhere, border skirmishes erupted between the armed forces of Iran and Iraq. (In contrast, Iraq's effort to support secessionist elements among Iran's Arab and Kurdish minorities was puny, costing Baghdad less than $50 million in 1973 and 1974.[10]) By early 1975 tension between Baghdad and Tehran had reached such a pitch that it threatened to lead to full-scale war between them. Both sides realized the danger, keenly aware that warfare would lead, *inter alia*, to immediate destruction of their crucial oil installations, something neither could afford. They therefore encouraged mediation, first by Turkey and then by Algeria.

The other major reason which led the Shah to ease the pressure on Baghdad was his realization that the activities of the Iraqi Kurds were creating secessionist aspirations among Iranian Kurds. As for Iraq, it had suffered great losses in men and materials. The year-long conflict resulted in some 60,000 military and civilian casualties.[11] Moreover, the conflict brought home the depressing message to Baghdad that it was internationally isolated. Neither the Soviet Union nor any of the members of the 21-strong Arab League came to its military rescue. The Iraqi president was to reveal later that, in the absence of resupplies from the Soviet Union, Iraq was left with only three bombs for its air force.[12]

This was the background to the conclusion of an accord on 6 March 1975 in Algiers by the Shah of Iran and Saddam Hussein, the vice-president of Iraq, during a summit conference of the Organization of Petroleum Exporting Countries. The signatories agreed to delimit their river boundaries 'according to the thalweg line' and 'to end all infiltrations of a subversive nature'.[13] A Treaty concerning the Frontier and Neighbourly Relations between Iran and Iraq was signed in Baghdad on 13 June and ratified by both parties on 17 September. A joint commission was appointed to demarcate the new border in the wake of Iran's conceding territory around the villages of Zain al Qaws and Saif Saad in the Qasr-e Shirin area to compensate Iraq for its concession on the Shatt al Arab.

The Algiers Accord signified victory for Iran. It incorporated the Iranian demand, first made over 60 years earlier, that the thalweg principle be applied to the frontier along the Shatt al Arab. And, just as in 1937 the weakness of its government had led Iraq to yield to Iranian pressure to accept this formula for Abadan port, so too now. Harassed and exhausted by the Iranian-backed Kurdish insurgency, the Baghdad regime agreed to extend the thalweg formula to the rest of the fluvial border. It was a bitter pill for Iraq to swallow which, as was to be revealed later, left its leaders acutely divided, with military officers among them opposing the accord.

Domestic consequences for the signatories of the Algiers Accord, however, turned out differently. Iraq benefited far more than Iran. Released from the debilitating pressure to counter Kurdish rebellion, the Iraqi government focused on an accelerated programme of socio-economic development. It applied itself to tackling the long-simmering problem of the Shias, partly by increasing expenditure on economic projects in the south where Shias were concentrated. The funds for these ambitious plans came from exporting oil, the price of which had risen fourfold during 1973–4. By then Baghdad had nationalized all foreign holdings of the oil companies operating in Iraq, and was in full control of its most precious resource. Moreover, the Baathists had consolidated their hold over state and society, and provided firm ideological underpinning to the regime.

This was in marked contrast to the situation in Iran. The Shah headed a strong, highly centralized state which lacked an ideological foundation. According to the 1906–7 Constitution, Twelver Shiaism was the state religion, and only a Twelver Shia could become king. Another article enjoined the monarch to promote the sect. But, in practice, Iran under Muhammad Reza Pahlavi Shah was a secular state run by a highly Westernized ruling elite, uninterested in religion, politics or ideology. The Shah lacked a well-oiled party machine, inspired by a comprehensive, self-contained social philosophy to underwrite the legitimacy of his regime.

The situation was parallel to that which had prevailed in Iraq under the monarchy, from 1922 to 1958, when all political activity was banned. During the early 1950s the Arab Baath Socialist Party in Iraq was in its infancy, and clandestine. It came into being as the Arab Baath Party in the Syrian capital, Damascus, in April 1947 with a pan-Arab congress. Its founders were three teachers: Michel Aflaq, a Greek Orthodox Christian; Zaki Arsuzi, an Alawi (i.e., follower of Imam Ali) Muslim; and Salah al Din Bitar, a Sunni Muslim. The party's basic principles were described as: the unity and freedom of the Arab Nation within its homeland; and a belief in the 'special mission of the Arab Nation', the mission being to end colonialism and promote humanitarianism. To accomplish it the party had to be 'nationalist, populist, socialist and revolutionary'. While the party rejected the concept of class conflict, it favoured land reform; public ownership of natural resources, transport and large-scale industry and financial institutions; trade unions of workers and peasants; co-option of workers into management; and acceptance of 'non-exploitative private ownership and inheritance'.[14] It stood for a representative and constitutional form of government, and for freedom of speech and association within the bounds of Arab nationalism. Its programme was summed up by the slogan: 'The eternal mission of the Arab Nation: Unity, Freedom, Socialism'.

According to the Baath Party, Arabs form one nation which is currently divided into various regions(countries). Therefore the party has at the top the National Command which encompasses the whole Arab world and which serves as the central executive authority. Under it are certain Regional Commands pertaining to those Arab states where the party is strong enough to justify establishing one. Below a Regional Command are branches, composed of sections, made up of divisions, each one consisting of a few three-member cells.

In 1952 the union of the Arab Baath Party with Akram Hourani's Arab Socialist Party in Syria led to the composite name Arab Baath Socialist Party (ABSP). The new entity's strength in Syria rose to 500 members. The party became active in Iraq in 1952, and two years later it claimed membership of 208. It held its first (clandestine) regional congress in late 1955, when it decided to co-operate with other nationalist groups. Against the background of the repressive, pro-Western monarchical regime's joining the Baghdad Pact, and refusing to condemn the November 1956 Anglo-French-Israeli aggression against Egypt, the strength of the Baath Party rose steadily. However, it played only an insignificant role in the military coup which destroyed the monarchy in 1958.

The Baathists fell out with the republican leader, Abdul Karim Qasim, and attempted unsuccessfully to assassinate him because he refused to further Arab unity by agreeing to unify Iraq with the United Arab Republic – consisting of Egypt and Syria – led by Gamal Abdul Nasser. Despite suppression by Qasim, the party increased in size. By the time the Baathists, joined by non-Baathist sympathizers, overthrew Qasim in February 1963, the party had 850 active members and 15,000 sympathizers, and its own militia, called the National Guard.

Once in power the Baathists fell out among themselves on the questions of union with Nasser's Egypt and the degree of socialism to be achieved, thus allowing the prestigious but non-Baathist Abdul Salam Arif to usurp power as president in November 1963. His death in an accident in April 1966 led to the installation of his brother, Abdul Rahman, as president. He was overthrown on 17 July 1968 by an alliance of Baathist leaders and non-Baathist military officers. Within a fortnight the Baathists had rid themselves of their non-Baathist allies and assumed total power.

The Arab Baath Socialist Party of 1968 was quite distinct from the one which had captured state authority five years earlier. It was more down-to-earth than before, having learnt to concentrate on such practical issues of policy as land reform. It was better organized and bigger, with 5000 active members; and yet more conspiratorial and more paranoid about co-operating with non-Baathist elements. It had passed through a particularly volatile period, not only in Iraq but also at the level of the National Congress and the National Command. The young, radical delegates at the Ninth National Congress in Damascus in February 1966 eliminated the old leadership, including General Secretary Aflaq, causing the party to split. The Iraqi contingent sided with Aflaq, and under its aegis a separate Ninth National Congress was held in Beirut in February 1968. From then on the two National Commands of the ABSP functioned as bitter rivals – a fact reflected in acute rivalry between Damascus and Baghdad, culminating in Syria siding with Iran in the Gulf War.

The ruling five-member Baathist Revolutionary Command Council in Baghdad resolved to avoid the fatal pitfall of division within its ranks, quickly consolidate its grip over state apparatus, and ensure that there was no military coup against the regime. It combined the immediate purging of military officers of dubious loyalty with the rehabilitation of 117 Baathist officers dismissed after the fall of the 1963 Baathist-dominated regime. It appointed party activists as director-generals of government departments.

It then set out to institutionalize the interweaving of the party with the state machinery and with secular society at large. It decided to transform the military into an organ of the Baath by placing party members with freshly acquired military training in crucial positions and directing them not to execute any significant order without clearance from Baath headquarters. The same strategy was used for domestic intelligence services. Concurrently the military hierarchy ordered that the ranks and officers be imbued with Baathist ideology. In addition, the party set up its own bureaus in parallel with such major institutions as the military, police and intelligence. The interim constitution of July 1970 formalized party supremacy by stating that the Revolutionary Command Council, the highest state body, had the right to select new members of the Council from 'among the regional [i.e., national] leadership of the Arab Baath Socialist Party'.

Initially all five members of the RCC held military rank; but its chairman and the republic's president, Ahmad Hassan Bakr, a former major-general, and his closest adviser Saddam Hussein (who was not a RCC member), were intent on reducing the importance of military officers and imposing civilian control over the armed forces. This was achieved in stages. In November 1969 RCC membership was expanded to fifteen, all but one of the ten fresh members, including Saddam Hussein, being civilians. The 1970 constitution specified a two-thirds majority on the RCC for selecting new members, thus institutionalizing civilian control. The RCC kept a watchful eye on the air force and directed the deployment of loyal army units.

The Arab Baath Socialist Party set up cells in government departments, professional syndicates, educational institutions, publicly- and privately-owned businesses, trade unions, agricultural co-operatives and women's associations. These cells were all the more effective because the Baathist cadres were required to keep their party affiliation secret. The party units met regularly to evaluate the performance of the government departments in the light of Baathist principles and guidelines, and report to their headquarters. A similar procedure was followed in the armed services. By the time the ABSP held its Eighth Regional Congress in January 1974 to clarify, *inter alia*, the party-state relationship, Baath membership had risen to 20,000. A strict procedure for becoming a full/working member started with the position of a sympathizer and graduated to supporter, candidate and trainee over a total minimum period of seven years. A working member was required to attend weekly party meetings and monthly symposiums, participate in the activities of the Popular Army, give above average performance at work, and dress and behave unostentatiously.

As the Baathist regime's oil income shot up from $75 million in 1972 to $8000 million in 1975,[15] it enlarged its popular base by awarding hefty wage and salary increments, expanding educational, health and public welfare services, and implementing ambitious economic projects. Simultaneously, the party tightened its grip over the military, police and intelligence. By 1978, according to one estimate, a fifth of all state employees were working for various security services.[16] A well-planned internal security system held Baathist members responsible for the safeguarding of their street or neighbourhood.

While the Kurdish crisis receded with the signing of the 1975 Algiers Accord, disaffection among Shias came to the fore. The roots of the problem went back to the period when Iraq was part of the Sunni Ottoman empire. The Ottomans excluded Shias from public office. While they allowed Sunni ulama (religious-legal scholars) to control substantial waqfs (religious endowments), and derive income from them, they denied these rights to Shia ulama. They did not permit Shias to exercise jurisprudence except in internal matters in their own centres. On the other hand the Ottoman rulers let Najaf and Karbala – the holy cities containing respectively the shrines of Imam Ali and his son Imam Hussein, the most revered figures of Shias apart from the

Prophet Muhammad – function as semi-independent enclaves. The ulama in Najaf and Karbala had the prerogative to issue fatwas, religious verdicts, which were binding on Shias. They also acted as intermediaries between Shia tribal chiefs and the government.

A religious verdict issued in June 1922 by the chief Shia cleric of Karbala called on the faithful to defend Islam against the infidel British who exercised ultimate power in Iraq. This led to the arrest of many Shia clergy and the expulsion of their leaders to Iran. It seemed the Ottomans' replacement by Faisal I, a Sunni Arab king functioning under British hegemony, would make no difference to the fate of Shias, who made up at least 55 per cent of the population of the newly formed state of Iraq. Indeed, using co-option and threats, the new monarch ruptured the traditional alliance between Shia tribal leaders and the ulama. The situation of Shia clergy was summed up by Faisal I in 1933 in a secret memorandum thus: 'The Shia ulama have no connection with the government and are at present estranged from it, particularly in as much as they see the Sunni ulama in possession of funds and properties of which they are deprived'.[17] Apparently, King Faisal I continued the Ottoman practice of depriving Shia ulama of the privilege of managing the religious endowments of their deceased followers.

Shia clerics remained dependent on the contributions of their flock, mainly in the form of *zakat* (tithe for the poor) and *khums* (one-fifth of profits as due to the descendant Imams of the Prophet Muhammad). Shias were mostly nomadic tribal people who had later settled as peasants or shepherds in the predominantly rural south. While they enthusiastically celebrated Ashura – the commemoration of Imam Hussein's death on a battlefield near Karbala in 680 – they were not particularly strict about daily prayers and fasting during the holy month of Ramadan. The 1947 census revealed that religion was poorly organized among the rural Shias of southern Iraq, with only one religious institution for 37,000 people.

By then Shia peasant tribesmen had begun migrating in large numbers to Basra and Baghdad, where they congregated in a shanty town later to be called Medinat al Thawra (Town of the Revolution). From the 1940s onwards the Iraqi Communist Party began to organize the Shia underclass in Basra and Baghdad. Later the Communists won supporters among the sons of the ulama in Karbala and Najaf, the leading centre of Shia theological learning, which had fallen on bad times in the 1950s, with the student body down by two-thirds from the 1918 total of 6000.

On the eve of the 1958 coup the Shia religious establishment was in a poor state, with its social and economic power at its nadir.

The socio-economic reform effected by Qasim's republican regime had an impact on the ulama. The more reactionary among them declared nationalization and land redistribution to be *haram*, religiously forbidden. For the first time an attempt was made to establish religion as a political movement with the formation of the Islamic Party of Iraq, which declared itself inimical to 'all atheistic ideas and concepts which only recognize materialism'. It was allowed to function openly until 1961, when all political parties were outlawed.

Since one of Qasim's parents was Shia, he was neutral between Sunnis and Shias, in contrast to his successor Abdul Salam Arif, a rabid Sunni. During Arif's rule discrimination against Shias increased. This led to the formation in 1964 of an anti-government Shia group called Fatimiya; but before it could do anything substantial it was infiltrated by intelligence agents and neutralized. What is more, the government set up a special section – the Second Branch – in its Directorate of Public Security to counter the Shia underground. In the coming years the Second Branch was to expand dramatically and become an extremely important arm of the internal security apparatus.

Though the Fatimiya group was eliminated the conditions which had spawned it persisted. There was a feeling abroad among Shia ulama that many of their co-religionists, both urban and rural, were drifting away from the faith, its practices and rituals, and that their own standing in the community was declining. With the secular Baathists seizing power in mid-1968, the government imposed strict censorship of religious publications, shut down various Islamic institutions, including a theological college in Najaf, began harassing Shia ulama and, for the first time in Iraqi history, allowed the sale of alcohol in the Shia holy places. These official steps goaded Shia clergy to rally their followers to protest, a development which in turn brought government repression.

It was against this backdrop that in 1969 Al Daawa al Islamiya (The Islamic Call) was formed, clandestinely, with the blessing of Ayatollah Muhsin Hakim, the most senior Shia cleric, based in Najaf. As the Baathist regime, dominated by Sunni leadership, tried to interfere with some of the characteristically Shia rituals, impose certain political slogans on them, and weaken the authority of the religious hierarchy, Al Daawa gained ground. It began to win increasing support among junior, younger ulama in the holy cities of Najaf, Karbala and Kadhimain, a suburb of Baghdad. Since these cities drew Shias in their hundreds of thousands during several religious ceremonies, Al Daawa activists, both clerics and laymen, had ample opportunities to disseminate their message disguised as pious sermons. 'The fall of [Imam] Hussein as a martyr in the struggle to regain authority from the Sunni caliph in 680 is a symbolic event which reminds the Shia community each year that it is still under Sunni rule though the members of the Shia community form the majority of the population in the country,' notes Majid Khadduri, an American specialist on Iraq.[18] Al Daawa members were aided in their endeavour by the economic downturn caused by the drought that struck the Najaf–Karbala region and other Shia-dominated areas in the south during 1973 and 1974.

In early December 1974 Shia religious processions turned into indignant political demonstrations against the Baathist regime. This was the first time in the history of independent Iraq that Shias had, as a religious body, violently confronted the state. The Baathist government reacted sharply. It tried 25 Shia leaders clandestinely and executed five of them.[19] It also tried to placate the Shias by increasing development funds to the south, something it could afford with the sudden jump in oil revenue. But such decisions take time to show results.

In any case Shia grievances went beyond redistribution of national wealth. They felt, rightly, that they were grossly under-represented in the upper echelons of the police, military, intelligence, civil service and Baath Party hierarchy. The eight-member Revolutionary Command Council had no Shia on it; and the 13-member Regional Command had only three. All this was true but somewhat irrelevant to Al Daawa leaders. They attacked the rule of a party whose National Command was headed by a Christian, Michel Aflaq, who (then residing in Baghdad) was also its chief ideologue. They deplored the Baathists' neglect of Islam and Islamic institutions, and their alliance with the Communists at home and the atheistic state of the Soviet Union abroad. Thus unexpressed tension between Shia masses and the regime built up steadily over the next few years.

It erupted violently at the height of a Shia ceremony in early February 1977 when the government sealed off Karbala, claiming that an agent of Syria (with whom it had hostile relations) had been caught trying to smuggle explosives into Imam Hussein's shrine. The police intercepted a procession of pilgrims on its way from Najaf to Karbala. This triggered off riots, with the crowds chanting 'Saddam, remove your hand / The

Iraqi people don't want you', and taking over a police station at Haidariya. The police opened fire to restore order, causing several deaths. The news caused riots in Najaf. These persisted for several days; and troops had to be called in to crush the uprising. Several dozen people were killed and some 2000 Shias, including Hojatalislam Muhammad Baqir Hakim, son of Muhsin, were arrested.[20]

This was the most widespread, persistent and bloody challenge by an important section of the population to the nine-year-old Baathist rule. It caused acute anxiety and fractious debate within the party leadership which had only just recovered from the divisive effect of the March 1975 Algiers Accord and launched its ambitious 1976–80 Development Plan. Some leaders, headed by President Bakr, wanted to conciliate Shia dissidents and accommodate party ideology to the rising wave of Islamic revival, while others led by Vice-President Saddam Hussein advocated using an iron fist against the Shia protestors and strict adherence to the Baathist commitment to secularism and separation of religion and politics. Saddam Hussein won. This became apparent when two of the three ministers, who were also Regional Command members, were stripped of their party and government positions after the special tribunal – to which they had been appointed – to try the Shia dissidents was judged to have been 'lenient' towards the accused.[21] As it was, the tribunal had ordered the execution of eight Shia dignitaries, five clergy and three laymen.

Saddam Hussein grasped the gravity of the situation if only because Shias formed 70 per cent of the Arab population, which was about 80 per cent of the total, the rest being Kurds. Unlike the Kurdish insurgents, who were confined to a certain mountainous region, Shia activists were part of the mainstream both socially and geographically.

The vice-president followed a two-track policy: merciless repression of Al Daawa went hand in hand with determined moves to placate the Shia masses through economic and political concessions. Further sums were allocated to the development of the Shia-dominated south. Attempts were made to attract Shias to the general rolls of the Baath Party, a ploy which kept the top leadership firmly in Sunni hands. For instance, the expansion of the Regional Command from 13 to 21 members at the Extraordinary Session of the Eighth Regional Congress on 10 January 1977 increased the Shia strength only from three to four. It was not until September that a constitutional amendment placing all Regional Command members on the RCC invested meaningful power in the hands of a small group of Shias in the Regional Command. At the same time the latest constitutional change completed the process of monopolization of power by the Baath. With most of the RCC/Regional Command members being cabinet ministers, the Baath Party was now in charge of forming policies as well as legislating and executing them. Within the party Saddam Hussein, though nominally number two, enjoyed supreme authority.

His moves to tackle the Shia problem had not come a day too soon. For in Iran a revolutionary movement led by Ayatollah Ruhollah Khomeini, a towering Shia personality, against the autocratic, secular regime of the Shah was about to gather momentum. As it happened, Khomeini had been living as an exile in Najaf, only several blocks away from Imam Ali's shrine, since October 1965, having clashed with the Shah in 1963–4. It was common for Shia clergy the world over to seek refuge in the shrine city of Najaf. Given the animosity then existing between Iran and Iraq, there had been no objection from President Abdul Salam Arif to granting political asylum to Khomeini. Later the Baathist President Bakr solicited the ayatollah's backing in Iraq's quarrel with the Shah: Khomeini refused to oblige. Indeed, being unhappy at the way the Baathist regime had been treating Shia clerics in Najaf and Karbala, he had expressed a wish to leave for Lebanon, only to have it rejected by the authorities. At the same time he kept scrupulously away from the Iraqi Shia underground. His one and only interest lay in overthrowing the Pahlavi dynasty. As the anti-Shah movement gathered momentum in 1978 and reached a critical stage in October, with widespread strikes crippling the economy, the Iranian monarch became anxious. He pressed the Iraqi government to honour the Algiers Accord regarding suppressing subversive activities directed against the fellow-signatory. Baghdad complied with alacrity. The expulsion of Khomeini was resented by Iraqi Shias, especially when it was soon followed by Saddam Hussein's escorting the Shah's wife, Farah Diba, around the Shia holy places. Khomeini flew to France where he discovered that he had greater freedom of action than in Najaf. He returned to Iran in triumph a fortnight after the Shah had left the country in mid-January 1979.

The victory of the revolutionary forces, led by Khomeini, over an apparently invincible Shah gave a fillip to Iraqi Shias. An indication of this came when Ayatollah Muhammad Baqir Sadr of Najaf stated in his congratulatory message to Khomeini that 'Other tyrants have yet to see their day of reckoning.'[22] It was obvious that by 'other tyrants' Sadr meant the Baathist rulers, particularly Saddam Hussein. So while Saddam Hussein had taken steps to conciliate disaffected Shias their expectations and aspirations underwent a qualitative change as a result of Iran's Islamic revolution. Now neither the Baathist regime nor Iraqi Shias could define their relationship without reference to the Iranian revolution.

AFTER THE IRANIAN REVOLUTION

For Iraqi Baathists the Iranian upheaval could not have come at a worse time. The signing of a peace accord by Egypt's President Muhammad Anwar Sadat with Israel in September 1978 at Camp David, a mountain resort in Maryland, USA, made Baghdad revise the ultra-radical, isolationist position on the Arab–Israeli dispute it had taken since the October 1973 war. Alarmed at the loss of Egypt as Israel's enemy on the western front, the Iraqi regime invited Syria's President Hafiz Assad to Baghdad, and offered to unite Iraq with Syria so as to create a strong eastern front against Israel. Through this move, and the holding of the Arab summit in Baghdad against the Camp David Accords, the Iraqi regime ended its isolation and improved its standing in the Arab world. The Iranian drama caused a miscarriage of the Iraqi–Syrian unity plans. While Assad openly praised the Iranian revolution and recognized the new regime immediately, Baghdad maintained a studied silence.

The overthrow against all odds of the powerful Shah, commander-in-chief of 415,000 troops, in the midst of a booming economy made Iranian revolutionaries feel that their example would inspire the oppressed masses elsewhere to rise up against their unjust, repressive rulers. They divided the world into oppressors and oppressed, and declared it to be their Islamic duty to support the national liberation movements of the 'deprived peoples' of the world.[23] They were particularly keen to aid the oppressed Muslim masses in the Gulf region to depose their rulers whom they considered either 'corrupt' (as in the Arab Gulf monarchies) or 'atheistic' or 'non-Muslim' (as in Iraq). Referring to the national liberation movements in the region and elsewhere, Ibrahim Yazdi, Iran's foreign minister, stated in July 1979: 'These movements stemmed from internal and natural conditions. They only wanted to benefit from Iran's experience [of national liberation] and gain strength from Iran's support.'[24] Certainly, in Tehran's view, the Iraqi Al Daawa was one such movement. That such a policy specifically violated Iran's 1975 treaty with Iraq, which specified non-interference in each other's domestic affairs, did not seem to enter Tehran's revolutionary thinking.

For Tehran three factors made Iraq the prime target for the engineering of Islamic revolution: the secular nature of the Baathist regime; the oppression of the Shia majority; and the existence of six Shia holy shrines in Iraq. The Baathists, having consolidated their hold on state and society over the past decade, were determined to meet the challenge from Iran head on. It was ironic that a pro-Western, conservative, secular Iranian regime had been transformed into a revolutionary proselytizer threatening the status quo which the erstwhile radical, pro-Soviet Iraqi regime was keen to preserve in the region.

It soon became obvious that unless one or other state changed tack they would clash on a large scale. The escalation, which culminated in the outbreak of war in September 1980, came in three stages: (a) the formal assumption of supreme authority by Saddam Hussein in July 1979; (b) the unsuccessful attempt to assassinate Iraq's deputy premier, Tariq Aziz, followed by the execution of Ayatollah Sadr in April 1980; and (c) the thwarting of an attempted military coup in Iran on 9/10 July 1980.

Ayatollah Sadr's much publicized congratulatory telegram to Khomeini made him a marked man. He was put under surveillance. Along with Ayatollah Abol Qasim Khoei he was a leading Shia cleric, an outstanding jurist and thinker, and the author of authoritative works on the Islamic state and economics. He also inspired strong devotion among the Shia masses. In early June 1979 he was put under house arrest, first in Najaf and then in Baghdad, ostensibly to prevent him from leading a delegation of Shia dignitaries to Iran to congratulate Khomeini, his friend of long standing, on the success of the Islamic revolution. The news triggered demonstrations in southern cities and Baghdad's Shia township of Al Thawra. The authorities used army units, who fired to disperse the demonstrators. Scores were killed and about 3000 arrested. Tehran Radio's Arabic service referred to Sadr as 'the Khomeini of Iraq' and called on the faithful to replace 'the gangsters and tyrants of Baghdad' with 'divine justice'.[25]

On 10 June Saddam Hussein reportedly submitted a list of men to be executed to President Bakr for his signature. It included not only the Shia leaders of the demonstrations but also a number of senior military officers alleged to have been in secret touch with them. Bakr objected to the inclusion of armed forces officers, and found himself put under house arrest.[26] He resigned on 'health grounds' some weeks later. On 16 July 1979, on the eve of the eleventh anniversary of the Baathist coup, Saddam Hussein became chairman of the Revolutionary Command Council, president of the republic and general secretary of the Regional Command of the Baath Party.

This was quite an achievement for a man born 42 years earlier, on 28 April 1937, in a landless family of the Albu Nasir tribe's Began clan (of Sunni persuasion) in Auja, a village near Tikrit, a town 100 miles north of Baghdad. Saddam's father had died before his birth, and he was raised by his maternal uncle, Khairallah Talfa, who had lost his military post for backing the nationalist Rashid Ali Gailani during the Second World War. In 1955, when he was 18, Saddam went to Baghdad for further schooling, and became involved in opposition activities. At 20 he joined the Baath Party. After the 1958 coup he engaged in fights between the Baathists and the followers of Premier Qasim. He was part of the team that tried, unsuccessfully, to assassinate Qasim in October 1959, and was injured in the leg. He escaped to Syria and then to Egypt where he studied law at Cairo University.

Soon after the Baathists seized power in early 1963, Saddam Hussein returned to Iraq and married Sajida Talfa, the schoolteacher daughter of his maternal uncle. During the regime of Abdul Salam Arif he was involved in a failed attempt to mount a Baathist coup and imprisoned, but escaped in July 1966. He was elected assistant general secretary of the Iraqi Baath Party. For the next two years he worked hard to reorganize the party and supervised its rejuvenated militia. He was only 31 when the Baath captured power in 1968. Though not a member of the ruling RCC, he was quite influential thanks to his close relationship with the 54-year-old RCC chairman, Ahmad Hassan Bakr, a cousin of Khairallah Talfa. In late 1969 he secured a place on the RCC. Thereafter the Bakr-Hussein duo came to dominate the party as a result mainly of their cunning decimation of their RCC colleagues. Saddam Hussein had many opportunities to use his considerable conspiratorial abilities, developed during his formative years as an underground Baathist activist often on the run. He also busied himself with restructuring and strengthening the party as well as resolving the Kurdish problem. As a youthful, energetic figure, Saddam Hussein appealed to those Baathists who believed in strong ideology and commitment to socio-economic progress. By the mid-1970s he had outstripped Bakr in leadership, cunning, ruthlessness, organizational ability and charisma. It was he who signed the Algiers Accord with Iran in 1975. He still needed Bakr, a former military officer with an avuncular personality whose moderation and piety went down well with the older, conservative segments of society. But as the Shia problem escalated into a series of crises it strained the long sustained alliance, since Bakr advocated compromise and Saddam Hussein confrontation.

Having reached the peak Saddam Hussein wasted no time in consolidating his position and removing any possible challenge to his supremacy. In late July 1979 he discovered a major 'anti-state conspiracy' involving 68 top Baathist civilian and military leaders. Following a summary trial by a specially appointed tribunal of half a dozen of Saddam Hussein's closest allies on the RCC, 21 of them were executed in August. The list included five of the 22 RCC members, including Muhyi Abdul Hussein Mashhadi, one of the alleged masterminds of the plot. He had been bold enough to suggest that the successor to President Bakr ought to be elected through a free vote of RCC members. One of the four Shias on the RCC, he had earlier questioned the severity with which the government had dealt with the Shia demonstrations in June. Having decimated all doubters at the highest level, Saddam Hussein carried out a widespread purge of dissident elements in trade unions, the Popular Army, student unions, and local and provincial governments.

He combined these moves with such popular actions as raising the salaries of the military, police, intelligence, civil service and judiciary. This strategy of ruthless suppression of opposition at higher or more fundamental levels, sweetened with open-handed generosity towards large constituencies, was a replica of the strategy Saddam Hussein had been following concerning the Shia problem.

In 1979 he allocated $80 million for Shia and Sunni shrines, mosques and the welfare of pilgrims.[27] He was munificent towards those clerics who publicly backed the regime. He was successful in winning the endorsement of such eminent Shia ulama of Najaf as Shaikh Ali Kashif Ghita and Shaikh Ali Saghir. At the same time he continued his merciless persecution of Al Daawa and the recently formed Mujahedin Movement.

In the ideological sphere Saddam Hussein shifted his focus somewhat within the overall Baathist view of Islam as originally articulated by Michel Aflaq, the party's principal ideologue. Describing Islam as civilization, Aflaq defined it as the embodiment of Arabism, Arab nationalism, which had existed long before the arrival of the Islamic faith. If cultural and civilizational aspects of Islam, and not its religious and legal aspects, were emphasized, then Islamic and Arab identities merged imperceptibly, he argued. This concept had particular appeal for the intellectuals and power-wielders in a heterogeneous society like Iraq because it provided a bridge between Kurd and Arab, Sunni and Shia, Christian and Muslim. By opting for the model of a secular state, Aflaq stated, the Baath had chosen 'to avoid religion being weighed down by the burden of politics, to avoid its implication in political ambiguities'.[28] Another reason for adopting this policy was that the state's secular character underlined the freedom it offered to citizens in pursuing their moral-spiritual life.

Saddam Hussein reiterated for party members the guidelines on this thorny issue, which he had formulated in the wake of the February 1977 Shia disturbances, in a speech given in August and published the following year. 'Our party is not neutral between belief and unbelief; it is on the side of belief always,' he stated. He referred to 'certain oppositional forces' trying 'under the cover of religious observances' to provoke the government into interfering in matters of faith in 'an undisciplined manner' so as to isolate the Baath from the masses. They had reckoned that 'We would make a tactical mistake whose consequences they would generalize with negative effects on our strategy.' It was therefore essential for the government and party to avoid the 'politicizing of religion' and to allow every sect to observe its rites according to its wishes.[29]

The concept of division between religion and politics was anathema to Khomeini, who considered it antithetical to Islam. He tackled this and other issues in a series of lectures delivered in January–February 1970 in Najaf, and published the following year as *Hukumat-e Islami* (Islamic Government). In this work Khomeini urges the subordination of political power to Islamic precepts, criteria and objectives; prescribes it as a duty of all Muslims to achieve 'the triumphant political revolution of Islam' to end injustice and corruption; exhorts the ulama to participate in the legislative, executive and judicial organs of the Islamic state; and offers a programme of action to establish such a state.

Khomeini describes the movement to reduce Islam to a mere system of ritual and worship as a deviation from the true faith: a development much encouraged by the imperialist West to weaken Muslims and their countries. Since Islam is above all a divine law – in the form of a compendium of the Quran, the Word of God, and the Hadiths, the Sayings and Doings of the Prophet Muhammad – it needs to be applied as a form of state. Only a government can properly collect the Islamic taxes of *khums* and *zakat*, and spend them honestly on the needy – as well as enforce Islamic injunctions about the duties of the believer and punishment of the transgressor of the divine law, Sharia. An Islamic administration requires an Islamic ruler. All Muslims agree that an Islamic ruler must be a religious jurist, one who is well-versed in 'the Islamic creed, laws, rules and ethics', and is absolutely just in its application – a Just Faqih (Religious Jurisprudent). He is to be assisted by jurists at various levels of legislative, executive and judicial bodies. The function of a popularly elected parliament is to resolve the conflicts likely to arise in the implementation of Islamic doctrines. The overall supervision and guidance of parliament and judiciary is to rest with the Just Faqih, who must also ensure that the executive does not exceed its powers. This, in summary, was Khomeini's outline of the rule of the Sharia as interpreted and applied by the Just Faqih. (Later the constitution of the Islamic Republic of Iran was to incorporate these principles.) Since the position of the Just Faqih is not hereditary the system is not monarchical. Nor is it dictatorial, since the Just Faqih does not govern according to his own free will. Given that the people are to be allowed the right to choose the Just Faqih (directly or indirectly), the system is republican but within an Islamic context. How is such a system to be installed? 'The great reformist movements in history did not possess power at their inception,' Khomeini states. 'The cadres of the [reformist] movement would draw the attention of the people to oppression and awaken them to the dangers of submitting to the rule of the tyrants, then the people became the active force which sweeps aside all the obstacles in its way.'[30]

If a convincing proof was needed of the ability of Khomeini's line of action to overthrow an unjust, oppressive ruler by a popular movement, inspired mainly by pious, courageous ulama, the success of the 1978–9 anti-Shah movement in Iran provided it. On 11 February 1979, the day the revolutionary forces finally triumphed, Khomeini declared: 'We will export our revolution to the four corners of the world because our revolution is Islamic; and the struggle will continue until the cry of "There's no god but Allah, and Muhammad is the messenger of Allah" prevails throughout the world.'[31] Sayyid Ruhollah Musavi Khomeini, now 77 years old, had waited and actively agitated for 15 years for this day.

He was born to Sayyid Mustafa Musavi, the chief cleric of Khomein, a town 220 miles south-west of Tehran. His father was murdered when Ruhollah was a year old. At 19, after he had finished his Persian schooling and religious instruction, he joined a seminary run by Ayatollah Abdul Karim Hairi-Yazdi in Arak; and when Hairi-Yazdi moved to Qom, a leading Shia centre, Khomeini went with him. In 1925 he completed his studies in the Sharia, ethics and spiritual philosophy. He married Khadija Saqai at 25; and two years later published his thesis on ethics and spiritual philosophy in Arabic, a language he had learnt as a child. Over the years he established himself as a teacher who inter-related ethical-spiritual problems with contemporary social issues. After Hairi-Yazdi's death in 1936 Khomeini followed the leadership of Ayatollah Muhammad Hussein Borujerdi. In 1941 he published a book which attacked secularism and Reza Pahlavi Shah's dictatorial rule. Four years later he graduated to the rank of hojatalislam (proof of Islam), one below that of ayatollah (sign of Allah).[32] This meant that he could now collect his own circle of disciples who would accept his interpretations of the Sharia. Following the death of Borujerdi in 1961 his admirers pressed him to publish his interpretations of the Sharia under the title *Clarifications of the Points of the Sharia*. It immediately secured him the rank of ayatollah. In a series of sermons delivered at Qom's most prestigious seminary in early 1963 Khomeini attacked the Shah's 'white revolution' as phoney. Later that year, on the eve of the anniversary of Imam Hussein's death in early June, he vehemently attacked the Shah and his secular, dictatorial, pro-Western policies. This speech transformed him into a national hero among the religious masses who despised the royal autocracy but dared not express their feelings. He was in and out of jail until November 1964 when he was deported to Turkey. A year later he arrived in Najaf, and kept up a steady campaign against the Shah.

His efforts received a boost when, following the Algiers Accord, Iran and Iraq eased border crossings, and the Baghdad government allowed 130,000 Iranian pilgrims a year to visit the Shia holy places in Iraq.[33] With this, it became comparatively easy for Khomeini to maintain regular contact with his acolytes, and guide them in their anti-Shah struggle through smuggled tape recordings. It had become amply clear by then that Khomeini was a pious, principled man of strong convictions, extremely patient and shrewd, fearless and uncompromising. He led a spartan life and was incorruptible. All these qualities gave him a charisma which no other Iranian leader, religious or secular, had so far enjoyed. He was rooted completely in Islam; and this enabled him to appeal directly and effectively to the religious masses in Iran, 90 per cent of whom were Shia and another 8 per cent Sunni.

Once Khomeini had achieved power at the head of a revolutionary movement he expounded a universalist view of Islam and revolution. Out of this soon flowed a series of appeals from Tehran that in Muslim lands Arab or state nationalism be eradicated, or subjugated, in order to achieve the higher unity of Islam. 'The Ummayad rule [661–750] was based on Arabism, the principle of promoting Arabs over all other peoples, which was an aim fundamentally opposed to Islam and its desire to abolish nationality and unite all mankind in a single community, under the aegis of a state indifferent to the matter of race and colour,' stated Khomeini in an interview with a Tehran newspaper. 'It was the aim of the Ummayads to distort Islam completely by reviving the Arabism of the pre-Islamic age of ignorance, and the same aim is still pursued by the leaders of certain Arab countries who declare openly their desire to revive the Arabism of the Ummayads.'[34] No doubt, among 'the leaders of certain Arab countries' promoting Arabism was Saddam Hussein who, along with his 'infidel Baath Party', was one of the three enemies listed by Khomeini in an interview he gave during his brief exile in France in late 1978.[35]

It was to such ideological offensives mounted from Tehran that Saddam Hussein felt obliged to respond. He tried to turn the argument around. 'In order for the Islamic Revolution [or] any [other] revolution to be Islamic, it must be a friend of the Arab revolution,' he stated in October 1979. 'As an Arab revolutionary I understand the matter as such . . . A true Islamic revolution would absorb the Arab ideology . . . and remove any contradiction between it and this [Arab] ideology.'[36]

At the same time Saddam Hussein resorted to projecting himself as a pious Muslim by praying at numerous holy shrines, Sunni and Shia. He undertook an extensive tour of the Shia region and announced programmes for its socio-economic betterment. He declared Imam Ali's birthday a national holiday. He began identifying with the historical figures of early Islam and employing Islamic symbols. In a significant gesture, during a speech in Najaf near Imam Ali's shrine, he pledged to 'fight injustice with the swords of the Imams' and called for 'a revival of heavenly values'.[37] In a move made in December 1979 he held out the possibility of sharing power with Shias – as members of the popularly elected National Assembly, a body mentioned in the 1970 constitution but never convened.

In March 1980 came the execution of 97 civilian and military men, half of them members of Al Daawa. Membership was now punishable by death; and its activists had resorted to attacking police stations, Baath Party offices and Popular Army recruiting centres. State repression of Shia militants had already impelled Ayatollah Sadr to issue a religious verdict that the Baathist regime was unIslamic and that dealings with it were *haram*, religiously forbidden.

To avenge the execution of their cadres Al Daawa activists tried on 1 April 1980, the first anniversary of the founding of the Islamic Republic of Iran, to assassinate Tariq Aziz, the (Christian) deputy premier of Iraq. They failed. But the attempt raised tensions between Baghdad and Tehran, and made Saddam Hussein more ruthless in his drive against the Shia underground. He ordered the bombing of Qasr-e Shirin, an Iranian border town, and the expulsion of thousands of Iranian residents and Iraqi nationals of Iranian descent. He called on Iran to vacate the three Arab islands of Abu Musa, Lesser Tunb and Greater Tunb, which had been occupied by the Shah. More importantly, he decreed the execution of Ayatollah Sadr and his sister Bint al Huda. These sentences were carried out in the utmost secrecy on 8 April 1980. It took about a week for the news to leak and reach Tehran. It shocked and incensed Khomeini, who delivered his most bitter attack yet on the Baathists. 'The war that the Iraqi Baath wants to ignite is a war against Islam,' he declared. 'As the Iranian army joined the people [in their struggle against the Shah], oh Iraqi army, join your people . . . The people and army of Iraq must turn their backs on the Baath regime and overthrow it . . . because this regime is attacking Iran, attacking Islam and the Quran . . . Iran today is the land of God's messenger; and its revolution, government and laws are Islamic.'[38]

Iran initiated a programme of giving guerrilla training to Iraqi Shias and then sending them back to Iraq. It had already begun assisting Iraq's Kurdish Democratic Party, now led by Mustafa Barzani's sons, Idris and Masud, who had crossed into Iran in July 1979. Baghdad expelled 16,000 Iraqis of Iranian origin, and increased its aid to the secessionist elements among Iranian Kurds and Khuzistani Arabs. In a way it was a re-enactment of past events during heightened tension between the two neighbours. Yet this time there was a major difference: Baghdad had become an important centre of activity by major political and military figures of the Pahlavi era. Most prominent among them were Shahpour Bakhtiar, the last premier under the Shah, and General Gholam Ali Oveissi, joint chief of staff under the deposed monarch. Each of them was given a radio station in Iraq. Besides conducting anti-Khomeini propaganda, these stations broadcast specific advice to the partisans of Bakhtiar and Oveissi among the armed forces and Iranian tribals. This occurred in an environment where since early 1980 minor border skirmishes between Iran and Iraq were happening at the rate of ten a month.

The Bakhtiar–Oveissi camp wanted to set up an anti-Khomeini base inside Iran with a view to initiating a civil war. After the failure on 24–25 April 1980 of Washington's armed rescue operation to retrieve its 53 diplomats held hostage in Tehran since November – a mission the pro-American Iranians had planned to use to overthrow the Islamic regime – the pro-Shah camp tried to mount a military coup on 24–25 May. It was thwarted by Khomeini loyalists. On 9–10 July a further attempt by pro-Shah military officers, orchestrated and funded by Bakhtiar, to topple the Tehran regime failed.[39] On 27 July the Shah, the continuing inspiration of monarchist generals and politicians, died of cancer in Cairo.

These events marked the start of the final phase of the pre-war confrontation between Tehran and Baghdad. Until then Saddam Hussein had counted on the success of the endeavours of the US and/or anti-Khomeini Iranian forces to overthrow clerical rule in Tehran, or at least to destabilize it. Now there was no alternative to his performing the task himself.

Baghdad was buoyed up by accounts of rapid military, political and economic decline in Iran. Persistent reports of conflict between the Iranian president Abol Hassan Bani-Sadr and religious leaders, low morale among military officers who had seen thousands of their erstwhile colleagues purged, and rapid deterioration in the effectiveness of Iranian weaponry went hand in hand with accounts of shortages of consumer goods, growing unemployment, and rising disaffection among the professional classes as well as ethnic minorities. Diplomatically, Iran was isolated. It had broken ties with America, which until recently had been its most important arms supplier. By refusing to release the American hostages it had invited an economic embargo by

Western nations. Its relations with Moscow had soured in the wake of the Soviet military intervention in Afghanistan, a Muslim country. Its virulent attacks on the Gulf monarchs as unjust, corrupt rulers had left it friendless in the region.

Iraq had several internal and external reasons for invading Iran. Saddam Hussein feared that any recurrence of widespread Shia riots would encourage Kurdish secessionists to revive their armed struggle and plunge Iraq into a debilitating civil war. In his view the only certain way to abort such a possibility was by destroying the source, moral and material, of Shia inspiration: the Khomeini regime. Soon after assuming supreme power in July 1979 Saddam Hussein aired the strategy of a campaign against Tehran as a way of solving the Shia crisis at home. He told a Baathist gathering that Khuzistan could be Iraq's best line of defence against an internal Shia uprising.[40]

As the months rolled on the question he increasingly faced was not whether or not to invade, but when. He seems to have decided to act before the US presidential poll in early November. It was likely that a new American president would settle the hostage crisis and re-establish normal relations with Tehran, thus inadvertently robbing him of the opportunity to attack Iran during its most vulnerable period.

The personalities of Saddam Hussein and Ruhollah Khomeini impinged strongly on the course of events. Both were strong-willed, intransigent men, who could not be intimidated. They believed absolutely in themselves and their doctrines. But their experiences were poles apart, and they ran different types of regimes. Khomeini had every reason to be confident of his inspirational charisma, but the social system he led was in a formative stage. In contrast, Saddam Hussein was in charge of well-oiled state and party machines which were awash with money and confidence. Additionally, the Iraqi leader had the active co-operation of the recently deposed Iranian military and political leaders, who possessed vital information and commanded the loyalties of hundreds of Iranians in key positions in the Islamic republic. For once Baghdad felt that in its long tussle with Tehran the military and diplomatic balance was in its favour. So, it concluded, the time was right to strike Iran. The current confusion and division among Iranian leaders was bound to end, with the Islamic regime establishing itself and reconstructing Iran's superior military and economic might. The Baathist regime had never really accepted the thalweg principle for the Shatt al Arab, enshrined in the Algiers Accord, as final. Here was a golden opportunity for it to retrieve its honour.

Iraq's economy was doing wonderfully well, with the oil income expected to reach a record $30,000 million in 1980. Its prestige in the Arab world was at its highest, with relations with the Gulf monarchies at their most cordial. By August 1980 Saddam Hussein had visited the rulers of Saudi Arabia and Kuwait, and discussed his military plans with them. With Egypt suspended from the Arab League, owing to its peace accord with Israel, Baghdad was actively pursuing the ambition of replacing Cairo as leader of the Arab world. If the Iraqi army could cross the Iranian border and liberate the Arabs of Arabistan/Khuzistan – who were reportedly engaged in an armed struggle against the racist, Persian clerical regime in Tehran – and restore an Arab territory to the Arab Nation,[41] then it would entitle Iraq to a leading role in the Arab councils. In case this claim was not approved by all Arab countries, the triumphant Iraq – having vastly expanded its coastline along the Gulf and deprived Iran of its largest source of oil in Khuzistan – would undoubtedly be accepted as the foremost power in the region. So in the course of settling old scores with Iran the Baathist regime expected to realize the dream of breaking out of the narrow straits of the Gulf coastline and having a larger economic stake in the region known to possess more than half of global oil reserves. Thus opportunities for Iraq were immense; the risks, if any, minimal.

The anti-Khomeini Iranian leaders, particularly Bakhtiar and Oveissi, were an integral part of the Iraqi design. If nothing else, they provided Saddam Hussein with a guise to project himself as a liberator not only of Khuzistani Arabs but of all Iranians suffering under the chaotic rule of fanatical mullahs. Together, Saddam Hussein and his Iranian collabor-ators visualized the Iraqi forces, greeted as liberators by the Arabs of Khuzistan, capturing the oil-rich province in a week, and then linking up with the Iranian Kurdish insurgents already fighting Tehran's forces. These liberated areas were then to be declared the 'Free Republic of Iran' under Bakhtiar, operating from the temporary capital of Ahvaz. This was seen as a catalyst to set off widespread uprisings against the Khomeini regime by discontented civilians as well as the armed forces.[42]

Once Saddam Hussein had finalized his plans and secured the Saudi and Kuwaiti rulers' active backing in August, events moved fast. On 2 September 1980 clashes erupted between Iraqi and Iranian troops near

Qasr-e Shirin. Two days later Iran shelled the Iraqi towns of Khanaqin and Mandali from the disputed area of Zain al Qaws village. According to Baghdad, the Iranian air force bombed Khanaqin and Mandali and oil installations.

On 6 September Iraq threatened to seize 115–145 square miles in the Zain al Qaws area – reportedly awarded to it according to an unpublished clause of the Algiers Accord – if Iran did not cede the territory within a week.[43] Tehran responded with more artillery fire at Iraqi border towns in the area. Baghdad claimed to have taken Zain al Qaws on 7 September followed by Saif Saad three days later and five border posts on 12–13 September, thus forcibly settling its dispute with Tehran on land boundary differences. The absence of any meaningful Iranian resistance to the Iraqi advances seems to have convinced Saddam Hussein that time was ripe for regaining full sovereignty over the Shatt al Arab.

In a televised speech to the recently elected National Assembly on 17 September, after accusing the Iranian leaders of violating the Algiers Accord by 'intervening in Iraq's domestic affairs by backing and financing ... the leaders of the mutiny [by Kurdish guerrillas] ... and by refusing to return the Iraqi territory', Saddam Hussein added that 'We consider the Accord as abrogated from our side, also.' He then tore up Iraq's copies of the Algiers Accord and the subsequent Treaty concerning Frontier and Neighbourly Relations.[44] With this, according to the Iraqi president, his country regained full sovereignty over the Shatt al Arab. He therefore insisted that henceforth the Iranian ships using the waterway must engage Iraqi pilots and fly the Iraqi flag. Tehran refused. Heavy fighting broke out along the Shatt al Arab. To meet the situation Iran called up its reserves on 20 September. Two days later Iraq invaded Iran.

The complex motivation behind Baghdad's action was summed up by Shahram Chubin, a specialist on Gulf security, thus: 'Motivated by fear, opportunism and overconfidence, a mixture of defensive and offensive calculations, Iraq's decision to resort to force was a compound of a preventive war, ambition and punishment for a regional rival.'[45]

2 EMBATTLED IRAN

Iraq's war plans were both offensive and defensive. It wanted to block possible Iranian advance in the north to its oilfields in the Mesopotamian plain, and in the central region towards Baghdad, thus guarding two of its three strategic targets, the remaining one being the southern port city of Basra. In the south Iraqi intentions were to seize not merely all of the Shatt al Arab but also Khorramshahr and Abadan on its eastern bank – as well as Ahvaz, the capital of Khuzistan, and the strategic city of Dezful. Baghdad's operational strategy was a duplicate of Israel's during the June 1967 Arab–Israeli War: knock out the enemy's aircraft on the ground in a surprise pre-emptive strike; and then pour armour into its territory on a large scale.

ACTIVE CONTINUOUS WARFARE

On the night of 22 September 1980 two waves of Iraqi jets raided ten Iranian air bases – including half a dozen with combat planes parked in sheltered areas – and two early warning stations. They intended to hit enemy aircraft or runways, thus further damaging the capacity of the already attenuated Iranian air force. By and large they failed. Their bombs either missed the targets or misfired, partly because the crews did not possess the degree of expertise needed and partly because their Soviet warplanes, fitted with mediocre avionics, lacked accurate targeting equipment.

Later that night several Iraqi divisions invaded Iran at eight different points to achieve half a dozen major goals. In the north an Iraqi infantry division advanced near Panjwin into Iranian Kurdistan to thwart any possible march by the Iranian infantry division posted near Sanandaj, a provincial capital, towards Suleimaniya to reach the Kirkuk oilfields.

In the central-north region an Iraqi division seized the garrison town of Qasr-e Shirin, guarded by one armoured brigade, and captured the strategic heights along the main Baghdad–Tehran road. By so doing the Iraqis threatened the provincial capital of Bakhtaran (called Karmanshah before the revolution), protected by a depleted armoured division, and blocked any potential move by Iran towards Baghdad barely 75 miles from the international border. In the central-south region an Iraqi infantry division captured Mehran and reached the foothills of the Zagros Mountains (620 miles long and 120 miles wide), thus capturing the road network connecting northern Iran – west of the Zagros – with Dezful, a strategic road junction as well as the site of a pumping station linking the Khuzistan oilfields with Tehran, the vast airbase of Vahidyeh and a hydro-electric dam.

Further south, three armoured and one mechanized Iraqi divisions penetrated Khuzistan, the oil-rich province with a population of 3.5 million (of whom only 35–40 per cent were ethnic Arabs) and an area of 9800 square miles. One of these divisions made a two-pronged attack, its left column seizing the disputed border territory near Musian and moving on to Dezful, and its right column heading for Ahvaz. Another division marched straight ahead towards Ahvaz. The remaining forces focused on the Shatt al Arab and the port cities of Khorramshahr and Abadan. The only way Iraq could secure the Shatt al Arab was by capturing Khorramshahr and Abadan Island, thus totally insulating the waterway in the south and east.

Other than border militia units Tehran had only one depleted armoured division at Ahvaz. Little wonder that, though lacking air cover, the Iraqi forces moved fast into Khuzistan, an integral part of the Tigris–Euphrates plain. On 25 September Baghdad claimed that its troops had laid seige to Dezful, Ahvaz and Khorramshahr.

Iran made the most of its navy, far better equipped than its enemy's, and four times larger in personnel than Iraq's 4250. On 24 September Iranian gunboats fired on Basra and attacked two oil terminals near Fao. They imposed a naval blockade of the Shatt al Arab, trapping many ships and incapacitating Basra port. The Iranian navy operated with virtual impunity because Iraq's airmen had no training in hitting naval targets. In any case, most of Tehran's naval craft were deployed beyond the range of the Iraqi planes.

Moreover, having realized that Iran's air force was functioning quite efficiently, and that all Iraqi air bases were within the striking range of its warplanes, the Baghdad government despatched most of its 332 combat aircraft – two-thirds of these being of offensive nature – to Jordan, Kuwait, Saudi Arabia, North Yemen and Oman.[1] In contrast, the Iranian air force, with twice as many personnel as its rival's 38,000, was very active, sometimes carrying out 150 sorties a day. On paper Tehran had 450 combat aircraft including 350 offensive planes, half of these being US-made ground attack F-4s and F-5s equipped with sophisticated avionics; but due to lack of spare parts only about half of these machines were airworthy. On the other hand the American-trained Iranian pilots were daring and innovative, and important Iraqi oil and other economic targets were within 100–200 miles of the border. The Iranians soon discovered that low-flying formations of two to four Phantom F-4s could easily dodge Iraqi air defences and fighter aircraft. When the Iraqis hit the Abadan refinery – the world's largest – with artillery on 25 September, Tehran unleashed 140 warplanes on Iraq's poorly defended oil facilities in Basra and Zubair in the south and Mosul and Kirkuk in the north, with devastating effect.[2] On 26 September both sides suspended their oil shipments.

By then the southern front was the scene of fierce warfare involving aerial bombing and strafing, gunboat barrages, artillery duels and tank salvoes, not to mention the small arms exchanges. The net result was a slowing down of Iraq's march towards its prime targets of Dezful, Ahvaz and Abadan. By 30 September, the ninth day of the war, the Iranians had succeeded in stopping the Iraqis at the peripheries of these cities.

Declaring that Iraq's territorial objectives had been achieved, Saddam Hussein announced his government's readiness to cease fire on 28 September – the day the United Nations Security Council called for cessation of hostilities and mediation – if Iran accepted Iraq's complete rights over the Shatt al Arab and 'other usurped Iraqi territories', promised to 'abandon its evil attempts to interfere in the domestic affairs of the region's countries' and ended its occupation of three islands in the Arab Gulf.[3] The claim that Iraq had attained its territorial aims ran counter to the fact that the Iranian naval blockade had made the Shatt al Arab unnavigable. The reason behind Hussein's peaceful overture was that he very much wanted to minimize Iraqi war casualties by avoiding hostilities in Iranian cities. In this he was to be disappointed.

For the next few days the Iraqis attempted to overrun Dezful, Ahvaz and Khorramshahr. They employed the tactics used earlier against the poorly equipped and trained Kurdish insurgents: sealing off the target, taking up entrenched positions, and then softening up the enemy with artillery salvoes and strafing, often using tanks as artillery pieces. This strategy failed to take into account the wide difference between the situations in Iraqi Kurdistan and Iran, where there was no dearth of men and materials and where a large city defied total encirclement.

As it was, Iraq's aggression resulted in a surge of patriotism in Iran, induced partly by the wanton damage caused by the Iraqi artillery attacks on civilian targets in Khorramshahr and Abadan. Patriotism engulfed the military, the newly formed Islamic Revolutionary Guards Corps and civilians – including Khuzistani Arabs and most of the Kurdish autonomists. The vehicles that were used to evacuate women, children and old men from the threatened cities of Ahvaz, Khorramshahr and Abadan returned with volunteers from all over the country. Instead of being welcomed as liberators by Khuzistani Arabs – the majority community in Khorramshahr and Abadan – as the Iraqi forces had been made to believe, they found themselves facing spirited resistance.

The war unified Iranian leaders hitherto divided on the issue of the sharing of power by President Bani-Sadr and Premier Muhammad Ali Rajai, the nominee of the radical clerics. Listening to Bani-Sadr's pleas the revolutionary authorities virtually halted the purges and executions that had been in train in the armed forces following the failed military coup in July 1980, thereby improving morale in the armed services. Speedy arrival of urgently needed weapons and ammunition from Syria, Libya and North Korea helped too. On 13 October Khomeini appointed Bani-Sadr chairman of the seven-member Supreme Defence Council, consisting of leading political and military figures, charged with conducting the war. (The parallel Iraqi body, the ten-member National Defence Council, headed by Saddam Hussein, not only included the state's six highest civilian and military officials but also the ministers of the interior and information as well as the director-general of public security.)

Two days earlier the Iraqis had crossed the Karun river 10 miles north-east of Khorramshahr, severed the strategic Ahvaz–Abadan road and advanced towards Abadan, cutting it off in the north and east. (But with the Shatt al Arab to the west and the Persian Gulf to the south, Abadan was still open to the outside world.) With Dezful and its air base firmly in its hands, the Iranian government was able to reinforce and resupply its combatants in the 'besieged' cities of Khuzistan, thus reducing the 5:1 superiority in manpower that Iraq initially enjoyed. The revolutionary guards, steeped in Islamic ideology and fiercely loyal to Khomeini, were in the forefront of resistance, relying heavily on small arms and Molotov cocktails, and extracting a heavy price from the Iraqis in lost lives and limbs. The Iranians had taken increasingly to using helicopter gunships in combat and achieved good results. Also their intimate knowledge of the terrain and superior intelligence gave them an edge over the occupying forces.

Baghdad had hoped to end the conflict with victory by Eid al Adha (The Festival of the Sacrifice), an Islamic festival due on 20 October. Instead, on the eve of the Eid, Saddam Hussein explained in a long televised speech that victory had eluded Iraq because of 'geographical injustice' and Iran's superiority in arms and military training. 'Their aircraft can . . . reach any spot in Iraq with full loads because their range is greater than that of many of our aircraft, and because Iraq has a smaller area than Iran,' he continued. 'Their artillery pieces have a greater range, fire heavier shells and are more numerous than ours. Their tanks are among the most sophisticated Western tanks. Their navy is greater in number and can operate at a greater range than our naval forces.'[4] In fact, Iran's 1000-plus artillery pieces were only slightly greater in number than Iraq's 800, while Iraq possessed nearly 3000 Soviet tanks versus Iran's 2000 British and American tanks (on paper). Moreover, many of the Iranian machines were unusable due to the long distances they had traversed from the Soviet and Afghan borders to the Iraqi frontier.[5]

Another important aspect of Saddam Hussein's speech was that he declared the current conflict as jihad, holy war, against Persian infidels. He called on his soldiers to cut off their enemies' heads. 'Strike powerfully, because you are truly Allah's sword on earth,' he said. 'The necks you are striking are those of aggressor Magians, collaborators with the lunatic Khomeini.' He tried to reinforce his pan-Arab line with Islamic history, describing the war as the 'Second Qadasiya' – referring to the battle of Qadasiya in 637 when Arab Muslims defeated the Persian army of Zoroastrian Sassanians – and the present foes as the descendants of Khosrow, the last Sassanian ruler, and Rustam, the Persian commander at Qadasiya.[6] He introduced a programme of inducting pro-regime Sunni and Shia clergy into the war effort by despatching them to the fronts and the occupied Iranian territory. There they reaffirmed their support for the Iraqi regime and denounced Khomeini for implementing a heretical interpretation of Islam which conferred positions of state power on clerics.

During the following three weeks – 21 October to 10 November – Iraq made visible gains against a spate of reports from Tehran that Bani-Sadr was not receiving wholehearted support and co-operation from clerical leaders and some senior cabinet ministers.

On 24 October Iraqi forces entered the outskirts of Khorramshahr after crossing the Shatt al Arab by a pontoon bridge. Their familiar tactic of subduing a target with artillery fire failed in the face of heavy resistance by the enemy lodged into thousands of homes and shops. The only way to defeat the Iranians was by engaging in hand-to-hand combat, something which the Iraqi commander-in-chief, Saddam Hussein – shrewdly aware of the adverse political consequences of high casualties – wanted to avoid. All was not well in Tehran either, where Khomeini publicly appealed to clerics, lacking in military theory and practice, to refrain from interfering in the conduct of the war.[7] On 10 November Baghdad claimed it had captured Khorramshahr. But the price was high – 1500 Iraqis dead and another 4000 wounded – partly because the special forces sent to Khorramshahr arrived without street maps of the city.

The first bout of bitter fighting exposed the ideological weakness of the largely conscripted Iraqi army with its Shia majority. There were several instances of Shia troops directing their weapons against their colleagues. A clear hint of this came in a radio broadcast in early November 1980 citing Saddam Hussein's statement about 'cowards' in the army. 'Is he [the attacked soldier] not your brother with you at the [anti-aircraft] guns?' the Iraqi president asked the military turncoats rhetorically. 'So why do you kill him when he fires at [enemy] planes?'[8] Such incidents strengthened Saddam Hussein's resolve to avoid high casualties which might cause disaffection at home as well as mass desertions by Shia troops. Therefore he opted for the siege of Abadan – rather than its capture involving house-to-house combat – an objective within his reach after his troops had constructed pontoon bridges across the Karun river. (However, access to Abadan from the sea remained open to the Iranians, who continued to provide civilian and military supplies to the fighters inside the largely abandoned city.)

By now Iraq occupied Iranian soil along about half of the 735-mile international border varying in depth from 6 miles in the north to 25 miles in the south. In all, Iraq had taken about 10,000 square miles of Iranian territory.[9] The Iraqi media were full of tales of heroic victories and pictures of jubilant troops which they described as forming a glorious chapter in modern Arab and Islamic history. They routinely called Saddam Hussein 'the second great conqueror of the Persian enemy' and the conflict 'Saddam's Qadasiya', thus establishing an indissoluble link between him and the war. He now appeared regularly in military uniform. As Field Marshal of Iraq he was shown frequently on television conferring with military officers at the front or at headquarters. But this in no way detracted from his other assiduously cultivated image: an accessible, generous father-figure ready to shower gifts on the populace. He resorted to convening regular sessions of the National Assembly, first elected in June 1980, to underline popular backing for the war with Khomeini's Iran.

It was a supremely confident Saddam Hussein who raised the stakes at a press conference on 10 November. He reiterated the official line that it was Iran which had started the war on 4 September 1980 by using its air force to bomb Iraqi border towns and oil installations. But once hostilities had erupted and Iraqi lives had been lost, these sacrifices entailed 'additional rights' for Iraq. The extent of these rights would be 'revealed' by 'future battles'. In other words, the extent of Baghdad's territorial claims on Iran would depend solely on the ability of its forces to capture and hold Iranian land. He disavowed any Iraqi ambitions to cause the break-up of Iran through the secessionist activities of its ethnic minorities. 'However,' he added, 'if the Arabistanis [i.e., Khuzistanis], the Baluchis or the Azerbaijanis want their stand and decision to be different, then this will be another matter.' To his earlier demands Saddam Hussein added another – freedom of navigation in the Hormuz Straits and the Arab/Persian Gulf's navigation route – thus restressing the pan-Arab nature of the conflict.[10] Earlier Iraq's deputy premier, Taha Yassin Ramadan, had stated that his country would continue 'to clean up the region and take the cities of Arabistan [Khuzistan]' and that 'Arabistan oil will remain Iraqi' so long as Tehran refused to negotiate.[11]

Saddam Hussein's demands were totally unacceptable to Tehran. 'There is absolutely no question of peace or compromise, and we shall never have any discussion with them [Baathists],' Khomeini had declared on 30 September in response to the Iraqi president's offer of a ceasefire. 'We cannot compromise with [Saddam Hussein], a perpetrator of corruption. We will fight to the end . . . because we have to implement our religious duties.' Khomeini constructed a connection between the duty to counter Saddam Hussein's aggression and participation in the revolutionary struggle against the Shah. 'We are religiously bound to protect and preserve Islam . . . This was the same logic we pursued in our fighting against the corrupt Pahlavi regime . . . Islamic teachings were going to be eradicated and Islamic principles erased, therefore we were bound by our religion to resist as much as we could.'[12] Khomeini's views were echoed by Bani-Sadr, who maintained that there would be no ceasefire or talks as long as Iraq occupied Iranian soil.

The onset of the rainy season on the Tigris–Euphrates plain (encompassing Khuzistan) in November imposed a stalemate on the war in Khuzistan – criss-crossed by 640 major and minor water barriers – with Iraq following a policy of limiting its casualties by merely consolidating its gains after its failure to capture Susangard during its 14–17 November offensive. The only substantial event during this period was Iran's combined naval, air and commando strikes on the night of 29–30 November against Fao and the five-year-old offshore oil terminal of Mina al Bakr with 2.5 million barrels per day capacity. This slashed Iraqi oil exports from 3.24 million b/d on the eve of the war to 550,000 b/d through the Turkish pipeline during the last quarter of 1980.[13]

For all practical purposes a continuous, full-scale war between Iran and Iraq lasted about two months: from 22 September to 29 November 1980. After that the conflict was sustained with constrained, episodic action interspersed with bouts of feverish fighting.

Despite the several advantages Iraq enjoyed initially it failed to win, and had to reconcile itself to a protracted war. The Iraqi National Defence Council had many months and vast sums available to make war preparations. The military command and control system in Iraq was impeccable, with Saddam Hussein as the commander-in-chief and the Revolutionary Command Council containing top military leaders. The officers and ranks had long experience of fighting Kurdish insurgents and these war veterans were still active in the armed forces. They were equipped with arms from a single source – the Soviet Union – and were well-versed in using and maintaining them. The military geography of Khuzistan, adjoining the Iraqi border, favoured the invader furnished with tanks and armoured vehicles. It was easy to drive up to Dezful beyond which the Zagros Mountains made vehicular traffic problematical. Finally, the Iraqis were stronger than the Iranians in both men and materials.

On paper the military manpower of the combatants was almost equal: 240,000. But Iraq's army at 200,000 was larger than its rival's at (nominally) 150,000. The Iraqi high command committed seven of its 12 well-equipped, full-strength divisions to confront, immediately, two depleted Iranian divisions. Additionally, Iran fought under other disadvantages. The period before the outbreak of the war had been full of turmoil, with the armed services hierarchy undergoing a purge in the

wake of a failed military coup in July 1980. The rift between President
Bani-Sadr, the acting commander-in-chief (Khomeini being the constitutional commander-in-chief), and the cabinet headed by Rajai, whose
clerical backers had the effective control of the Revolutionary Guards
Corps, militated against an efficient command and control system. It
was not until three weeks into the war that Khomeini appointed
Bani-Sadr chairman of the Supreme Defence Council charged with
conducting the war. But the policy of assigning the Revolutionary
Guards Corps to defend towns and villages – an activity widely covered
in the media – while using the army to mount local counterattacks in
the countryside was not conducive to easing tension between the two
forces.

Yet after the initial setbacks the Iranians did well in blocking the Iraqi
advance. Their achievement stemmed primarily from the flaws in the
leadership and training of Baghdad's armed forces as well as the overall
failure of Saddam Hussein, the supreme leader, to co-ordinate specific
military strategy and general security policies with wider political
objectives. Iraq's military, reared on the Soviet doctrine of massive,
static defence, was ill-trained to mount combined arms offensives.
Various factors impeded the efficient working of the Iraqi air force. All
its effective squadrons were controlled personally by Saddam Hussein,
who was afraid of the force mounting a coup against his civilian regime.
This meant limited combat training for airmen. Nor was the force
proficient in providing air cover to ground troops. Its personnel failed to
use their anti-aircraft guns properly; and the Soviet surface-to-air missiles performed poorly (as indeed did Iran's American and British missiles). The force lacked a command and control system to implement an
integrated air defence. So poor was the military planning that the Iraqis
had failed to provide adequate air defences for their vital oil facilities, on
the cosy assumption that after Iraq's pre-emptive attacks on the Iranian
air bases, the few enemy aircraft capable of taking off would be unable to
use the damaged runways.

Generally speaking the military planners, particularly Saddam
Hussein, failed to make a correct assessment of the capabilities of their
troops. Baghdad's armed forces were capable of quickly achieving a
limited objective such as securing both banks of the Shatt al Arab or
severing Dezful from the rest of Iran; but not both. More specifically,
Saddam Hussein failed to choose between capturing Khorramshahr
–Abadan or Ahvaz–Dezful. By pursuing both objectives simultaneously

he lost valuable time as well as the advantage of surprise. Khorramshahr and Abadan were not crucial if the intention was to deprive Iran of precious Khuzistani oil, for which the capture of the pipeline junction east of Dezful and Ahvaz was essential. The reason why Saddam Hussein focused on the port cities was that the majority of their residents were Arabic-speaking, and Iraqi intelligence was confident they would switch sides. The main flaw here was that Iraq's intelligence officials were inclined to provide their president with the kind of information he wished to have. Failure to capture Dezful and its vital Vahidyeh air base, and thus cut off Iranian supply lines, was in due course to lead to Iraq's expulsion from Khuzistan.

This happened primarily because Iran's reserves totalled 400,000 whereas Iraq's were 230,000 in the form of the Popular Army. Baghdad's aggression helped the Islamic regime to regain most of the soldiers who had deserted during the long anti-Shah movement as well as to secure fresh recruits. At the same time the size of the Revolutionary Guards Corps, which stood at 30,000 at its first anniversary in mid-June 1980,[14] rose sharply. Also the military arsenal that the Khomeini government had inherited from the Shah was so vast that, notwithstanding the revolutionary turmoil, it was able to supply its troops adequately with arms and ammunition which were superior to those used by the Iraqis. Thus at the end of three months of warfare Tehran had reduced the Iraqi superiority in men and armour in the southern sector from 5:1 to 5:2.

SPORADIC WAR

In late December 1980 Iraq made an unsuccessful foray into Iranian Kurdistan to link up with Iran's Kurdish insurgents, a move which built up irresistible pressure on Bani-Sadr from clerical leaders to mount a counter-offensive. On 5 January 1981 Tehran launched a badly prepared, but highly publicized, counterattack in the Dezful-Susangard area with three under-strength armoured regiments backed by insufficient infantry. The Iraqis let the attacking force advance all the way to Hoveizeh near the border. Then the well-entrenched Iraqi armour and infantry pounced upon the Iranians. For a loss of 50 tanks of their own they wrecked 40 Iranian tanks and seized 100 more.[15] Though the Iraqis, for once, made effective use of their air force to support ground actions, they failed to build on this success. However, they had by now constructed an asphalt road linking Basra with the front lines near Ahvaz to keep their forces well supplied during the wet winter. The two armies had by and large settled into a routine of periodic artillery exchanges. In the north Iran made an unsuccessful attempt in early February to expel the Iraqis from its territory, and lost another 50 tanks.

Neither side was able to achieve a decisive military breakthrough, raising outside hopes that the situation was conducive to negotiations under the auspices of the United Nations, the Non-Aligned Movement or the Islamic Conference Organization based in Jiddah, Saudi Arabia. On 1 March 1981 Khomeini met the nine-member ICO delegation visiting Tehran. He urged them to 'sit in judgement on Iraq' and fight whosoever had 'launched the aggression'.[16] After consulting Baghdad, the ICO team offered a peace plan on 5 March. It specified a ceasefire in a week's time, to be followed by an Iraqi withdrawal from Iran. The Iranian Supreme Defence Council rejected the ICO plan unanimously. Two days later Baghdad said that it would not withdraw from 'a single inch of Iranian territory before Tehran recognizes Iraqi rights.'[17]

Khomeini had shrewdly allowed the ICO delegation a chance to define the terms of truce and thus test Iraqi morale. When Baghdad showed itself eager for peace, Khomeini was encouraged to fight on until victory – and Saddam Hussein's downfall. Realizing the trap that he had fallen into, the Iraqi president tried to reverse the process. His forces made a determined attempt on 19–20 March to capture Susangard, an enclave left untouched by the previous Iraqi moves. They failed. This was a turning point in the six-month-old war. It confirmed that Iraq had exhausted its capacity to make further gains. It was a measure of Iraq's frustration that on 12 and 22 March it hit Dezful and Ahvaz with Frog-7 surface-to-surface missiles (with a range of 75 miles), ostensibly to scatter Iranian troops gathered for a counter-offensive.

In return, on 4 April 1981, Iran's Phantom F-4s hit Iraq's bomber air base at Walid near the Syrian border – a distance of 506 miles from their base at Rezaiyeh – and destroyed up to 46 planes. They apparently managed this by flying at a low level to dodge radar detection, although Baghdad claimed to have tracked on its radar the Iranian warplanes flying towards Syria and then reappearing over Iraq 67 minutes later. Damascus denied any collusion with Tehran in terms of either providing the Iranian Phantoms with air cover or allowing them to refuel.[18]

There was a marked escalation in the war aims of both sides. Iraq's deputy premier Tariq Aziz declared in mid-April 1981, 'Now we don't care if Iran is dismembered.'[19] On the Iranian side the parliament's speaker, Hojatalislam Ali Akbar Hashemi Rafsanjani, asserted: 'Removal of Saddam Hussein's regime is our strategic goal on which we will not compromise.' A measure of domestic tranquillity prevailed in Iran from mid-March to late May 1981 when a three-man conciliation committee studied complaints and problems concerning 'the war and other disputed issues': a development which also improved military morale.

Since spring is the time of floods in the Tigris-Euphrates plain, caused by the melting of snow in the Caucasus Mountains, both sides were inhibited from mounting major military operations. The stalemate revealed disagreement between Iraq's political and military leaders. In a wider sense this stemmed from the incompatibility of the highly centralized, regimented nature of the Baathist regime, rooted in the conspiratorial, clandestine history of the ruling party, with the independent creativity of professional military strategists. (In contrast, the Iranian Revolutionary Guards Corps and its commanders, free from over-centralized control and unaffected by traditional military staff college training, manifested much innovation and ingenuity in the midst of a battle.)

Once the war had started it became difficult for Saddam Hussein to control the field commanders to the extent he was used to. Initially, many of the professionally trained lieutenants of Saddam Hussein – the supreme commander who lacked formal military training – felt that he did not advance quickly enough into Iran. Later they grumbled about the orders to retreat. None of them had prepared for a protracted war.

As the conflict dragged on, and Khomeini repeatedly appealed to Iraqi military personnel to rebel against the 'infidel' Baathist regime, the loyalty of many Shia soldiers and officers came under strain. The result was the emergence of an anti-Saddam Hussein network led by senior Shia officers, the existence of which was reportedly discovered by Baghdad's military intelligence in June 1981. The dissident officers were alleged to have been behind five unsuccessful attempts to assassinate the Iraqi president during the previous six months.[20] The unveiling of an opposition network in the military made Saddam Hussein intensify his attempts to bolster army morale. As it was, the government had decided earlier to pay each dead soldier's family two months' remuneration, and to link pension rises to increases in military salaries. Now Saddam Hussein resorted to doling out plots of land and television sets to the martyrs' families during his extensive tours of the country. He was generous with military promotions and decorations. Furthermore, he deployed units of the ideologically reliable Popular Army – which had originated as the militia of the Baath Party – at the front. As the ideologically committed armed force dedicated to upholding the current regime, the Iraqi Popular Army had much in common with Iran's Islamic Revolutionary Guards Corps. One of their tasks was to keep a watchful eye on professional military officers. At the same time Saddam Hussein visited the fronts regularly, thereby manifesting personal involvement in the struggle as well as improving the morale of the fighters and re-establishing himself as the focus of loyalty for the officers.

On the war front, of the three front-line Iranian cities – Abadan, Ahvaz and Dezful – Abadan had come to acquire top priority in Baghdad. Only by seizing Abadan Island could Iraq regain access to the Gulf and end its dependence on its neighbours for vital military and civilian imports. By mid-1981 the Iraqi high command had deployed 60,000 troops and 1000 tanks to capture the city being defended by 10,000 Iranians belonging to a naval battalion, a mechanized brigade and an armoured battalion of 50 tanks.[21] The defenders were supplied by river from Bandar Mashahr and by road from Khosrowabad.

In June 1981 the long, festering political crisis in Iran reached its denouement. Following President Bani-Sadr's impeachment for incompetence by parliament on 20 June, Khomeini removed him from office. Immediately the Iranian joint chief of staff declared his loyalty to Khomeini. Rajai, the next elected president, was a favourite of the clerical leadership. Radical fundamentalists now controlled all three organs of the state: legislative, executive and judicial. This environment was conducive to co-operation between the military – under the overall command of President Rajai – and the Islamic Revolutionary Guards Corps and its auxiliary volunteer force, named Basij-e Mustazafin (Mobilization of the Oppressed), established in early 1980. The result was improved performance by the Iranians on the battlefield.

Another factor which helped create cohesion in Iran's fighting forces was Islamic education and indoctrination imparted by the political-ideological departments in the military and the Revolutionary Guards Corps. These were manned by clerics who drew heavily on the early history of Islam, when battles between believers and non-believers were common, to motivate the forces to fight in defence of Islam. They constantly stressed the Islamic nature of the struggle, and explained

Ayatollah Khomeini's statements issued at the outbreak of the war. Khomeini had characterized Saddam Hussein as 'an infidel' who was 'corrupt, a perpetrator of corruption and a man who resembles the Shah'. Addressing the Iranian people he had said: 'You are fighting to protect Islam and he [Saddam Hussein] is fighting to destroy Islam. At the moment Islam is completely confronted by blasphemy, and you should protect and support Islam . . . There is no question of peace or compromise, and we shall never have any discussion with them [the attackers of Islam].'[22] According to Khomeini, by invading the Islamic Republic of Iran, where a true 'government of God' was installed in 1979, Saddam Hussein had attacked not just Iran as a geographical entity but also Islam itself; and this had earned him the epithet of 'infidel'.

In Iraq Saddam Hussein was now more entrenched and the state-controlled media more fulsome in their praise of him than ever. He was variously described as 'the greatest Arab hero since the fall of Baghdad to the Mongols in 1257', 'the saviour of the nation from darkness, backwardness and disunity' and 'the symbol of Arab revival'.[23] His birthday, 28 April, was now a national holiday. On the eve of the thirteenth anniversary of the Baathist coup in July, 400,000 posters of Saddam Hussein were distributed in Iraq. A film on the historic battle of Qadasiya was released showing the Arabs to be the victors because of their faith in Islam. Saddam Hussein decreed that the war dead be called 'martyrs' because they had fallen fighting for Islam against 'the Persian infidels'.[24]

His enemies, Iran's military and political leaders, inspired and guided by Khomeini, were diligently implementing a complex plan to break the siege of Abadan. They mounted a series of small attacks in adjoining areas in July–August to compel Iraq to station some of its forces away from the city. In late September two Iranian infantry divisions poured into Abadan by crossing the Bahmanshir river at night (thus making it difficult for the Iraqis to manoeuvre their tanks) and penetrating the Iraqis' weak points while fighting them at their strong positions. Taken by surprise, the Iraqis, lacking innovation or initiative, stuck to their posts while awaiting orders. They were soon encircled by the Iranians. Their losses included 600–1500 lives, injuries up to twice as many, the capture of about 2500, and the destruction of hundreds of armoured vehicles. By 29 September, when the Iranians succeeded in expelling the Iraqis to the western bank of the Karun river, their human losses stood at about 3000 dead.[25]

At the end of the first year of the war the approximate death toll was 38,000 Iranians and 22,000 Iraqis.[26] Twice as many combatants were wounded. Given that Iran was three times more populous than Iraq, the Tehran government could afford a higher loss of life. Psychologically, too, the Iranian nation, having been in the grip of revolutionary and religious ardour since 1978, was ready for a high toll on the battlefields. Finally, Iranians viewed death in the current war as martyrdom in the path of God, a lofty ideal, described thus in the Quran, the Word of Allah revealed to humanity by the Prophet Muhammad: 'Count not those who are slain in God's way as dead, but rather living with their Lord, by Him provided, rejoicing in the bounty that God has given them.'[27] This was apparent from the wills of the combatants, and from the official offerings of 'blessings' to the families who had lost their sons or husbands in the warfare. At the same time the Martyrs Foundation – funded by the government, religious trusts and income from exiled Iranians' properties – looked after their welfare, assuring the widow or parents a monthly income of $280 plus a child allowance of $56 a month, and giving the survivors in the family preference in the allocation of such scarce goods and services as cars, motorcycles, refrigerators, housing and university places. In the case of military personnel an outright grant of $24,000 was also made.[28] So the government combined material incentives with an appeal to the Islamic zeal of the potential combatants.

No such innovation was displayed by either of the warring parties in the wider political arena. Saddam Hussein could not conceive an unconditional pull-back; anything less than a new concord on the contentious Shatt al Arab would have lost him the respect of senior military officers increasingly critical of his conduct of the war. Khomeini was rigidly against negotiating with Iraq while it occupied Iranian land. Had he done so it would have highlighted his failure to preserve Iran's sovereignty and territorial integrity, which had been unimpaired during the rule of the Shah he had overthrown.

The regaining of Abadan improved the morale of the Iranians who, though unable to mount large assaults owing to the impending wet winter in Khuzistan, adopted a decidedly offensive posture to retake their land. They did so despite economic problems made worse by the Iraqi strike on Iran's main oil terminal at Kharg Island in late October 1981. This attack reduced Tehran's oil exports from 500,000 to 300,000 b/d – about one-tenth of its exports of 3.2 million b/d achieved within a few months of the February 1979 revolution. Since oil exports provided 95 per cent of Tehran's foreign currency earnings the steep drop in oil shipments caused a crisis by driving down the foreign reserves to $500 million, just enough for a fortnight's imports.[29] This was the case despite the fact that in April the government had banned the import of such consumer durables as cars, videos, colour televisions, freezers and dishwashers. To control inflation by ensuring adequate supplies of basic necessities at subsidized prices, the authorities had introduced rationing of rice, sugar, cooking oil and petrol within six weeks of the war. At the same time Khomeini deplored 'consumerism' and advocated lowering consumption as part of the Islamization of society: a value system quite different from the one prevalent in Baathist Iraq. In the field of labour, unlike Iraq, Iran had an oversupply, with an unemployment rate of 15 per cent, which had resulted from the turmoil of the 1978–9 revolutionary movement and the subsequent economic downturn. The outbreak of the war, which resulted in the doubling of the conscription period from one to two years, helped alleviate joblessness, particularly among new entrants to the labour market. Now the aggression by Iraq, combined with the charisma of Khomeini, not only led young Iranians to volunteer on a large scale for the armed forces but also to fight with unprecedented fervour.

IRANIANS REGAIN LOST TERRITORY

From mid-November 1981 to the end of May 1982 the Iranians implemented an offensive strategy in three phases: mid-November 1981 to February 1982; March to April 1982; and May 1982.

During the wet, cold season of November–February they launched a series of minor attacks on the static Iraqi lines and succeeded, generally, in demoralizing the enemy and, particularly, in regaining the territory around Abadan and north of Susangard. They followed the same tactic in the central sector of Qasr-e Shirin.

The next phase witnessed the Iranian Supreme Defence Council amassing forces in the Dezful–Shush area to the tune of seven divisions, including two armoured divisions and two infantry divisions of revolutionary guards and Basij militia. They were poised to confront three Iraqi divisions and eight independent brigades.

On the night of 19 March the Iranians co-ordinated the landing of their commando units behind enemy lines with a two-pronged armoured attack, taking the Iraqis by surprise: they had ruled out a major offensive by Tehran on the eve of the Iranian New Year (the spring equinox), an occasion of long, joyful holiday. Having caught their foes unawares, the Iranian commanders kept up the pressure by unleashing large contingents of fighters for a whole week. Waves of about 1000 combatants, each armed with a shoulder-held rocket launcher, advanced at intervals of 200–500 yards, straining the ammunition supplies of the Iraqis and eventually overpowering them. They were followed by regular troops. Finally, Iran's armour surrounded the entrenched Iraqi armoured forces. Thanks to the Iranians' familiarity with the terrain they performed well in manoeuvring their machines. In contrast the Iraqi responses were slow and laboured, with many of the drivers getting stuck in mud. About 320 Iraqi tanks and armoured vehicles were wrecked; and another 350 tanks fell into the hands of the Iranians. According to Tehran, 10,000 Iraqis were killed, 15,000 injured, and 15,450 captured.[30] Iranian losses were put at 4000 dead, twice as many wounded and 6000 imprisoned. Iran claimed to have regained 940 square miles and moved to within 5–10 miles of the Iraqi border by pushing the enemy forces 25 miles westwards.

The success of the Iranian tactics led Colonel Bahruz Suleiman, deputy commander of the 21st Division, to declare: 'We are going to write our own [military] manuals, with absolutely new tactics that the Americans, British and French can study at their staff colleges.'[31] In contrast Saddam Hussein, now thrown on the defensive, tried to put a gloss on the setbacks suffered by his forces. 'I hope you will not be bitter about the land you are leaving voluntarily, as dictated by the requirements of defensive positions in the rear,' he told the Fourth Army Corps. 'We never told you to keep this land as part of Iraqi land.'[32]

An important feature of this battle – codenamed Fatah al Mobin, The Clear Victory – was the extensive use the belligerent camps made of their air power. The Iraqi air force was active – having made up some of its losses of 110–175 aircraft partly with French F-1s – operating as many as 150 sorties daily. Their impact was dulled by the extensive use that the Iranians made of their Soviet-made Sam-7 surface-to-air missiles and the curtain fire from their anti-aircraft guns. The loss of up to 175 planes had reduced the Iranian air force to 250-odd combat jets, only about half of which were airworthy. Since no aircraft manufacturing country was prepared to sell warplanes to Tehran, it had to conserve its limited stock.

The Iranians resorted to using attack helicopters to provide air cover to ground troops using heat-seeking missiles to target enemy tanks.

On 8 April 1982 Iraq suffered another major setback. Protesting against Saddam Hussein's aid to the dissident Muslim Brotherhood in Syria, President Hafiz Assad closed the Syrian border with Iraq. Two days later he shut off the pipeline carrying Iraqi crude oil to the Syrian and Lebanese ports of Banias and Tripoli. This cut the Iraqi exports from 1.4 million b/d in August 1981 to 600,000 b/d by the Turkish pipeline, and caused an economic crisis.

When the war started Iraq's average total petroleum output was running at about 3 million b/d, with exports of 2.8 million b/d expected to fetch nearly $30 billion in 1980. Its foreign reserves then amounted to an impressive $35 billion. The fighting resulted in severe damage to oil and other economic targets in Mosul, Kirkuk, Basra and Zubair, as well as to the oil terminals of Mina al Bakr and Khor al Amaya, and led to a steep decline in oil shipments. Saddam Hussein persuaded Saudi Arabia and Kuwait to save Iraq from defaulting on its oil contracts by supplying its customers. With its ports of Basra and Umm Qasr rendered inoperable by Iran, Iraq had to develop major land routes through Saudi Arabia, Kuwait, Jordan and Turkey. It managed this – but at a price, financial and diplomatic. It pledged to resolve its long-festering border demarcation problems satisfactorily with Jordan, Turkey and Saudi Arabia. In addition it gave financial aid to Jordan. By offering tempting transit fees it succeeded in persuading Syria to reopen the pipeline connecting Iraqi oilfields with Syrian and Lebanese ports. With this, and the use of the pipeline through Turkey, Iraq built up its oil exports to 1.4 million b/d by the first anniversary of the war – that is, half of the 1980 average.

Saddam Hussein was intent on proving to the Iraqis that the war would not interfere with the government's development plans and that their living standards would keep on rising steeply – by as much as 20 per cent annually – as they had for the past several years. Following the outbreak of hostilities, the government filled the markets with the kind of imported consumer goods which had been in short supply before: a sharp contrast to what had happened in Iran. The 1981 budget showed a 29 per cent increase in development projects over the previous year.[33] By the first anniversary of the war in September 1981 the Iraqi government had got most of the foreign construction companies to resume work, interrupted by the flight of their skilled personnel due to the war, by threatening to penalize them if they did not. Such projects as the highway between the capital and Zakho (on the Turkish border) and the Baghdad underground railway continued unabated. There was no slow-down in the implementation of the plans to renovate and expand Baghdad at a total cost of $7 billion for the Non-Aligned Movement summit in September 1982. If there was any slackening in socio-economic development it was due to the paucity of civil servants and vital machinery and spares requisitioned by the military.

Vigorously following the 'guns and butter' policy, Saddam Hussein kept up the expansion of the military machine. In early 1981 he announced that Iraq had signed contracts worth billions of dollars for weapons and ammunition in 'black' and 'white' markets. (In contrast, Iran's defence expenditure of $4.2 billion in 1981 was a fraction of the $12.1 billion it undertook in 1978 under the Shah, chiefly because the Khomeini regime eschewed the policy of buying large quantities of advanced aircraft and tanks which Saddam Hussein was now feverishly acquiring.) The total annual cost of the war to Baghdad was estimated at $12 billion. Its development budget amounted to $22.5 billion. Its imports actually rose by $5 billion over the previous year's $14 billion, producing a trade deficit of $9.6 billion.[34] Iraq managed to keep up this rate of expenditure by drawing heavily on its own reserves and securing grants and loans from the Gulf states. At the end of 1981 its foreign reserves were down by $15 billion. Its income from oil exports of about 900,000 b/d for the year was $10.4 billion, far below the previous year's $26.14 billion.[35] Following the closure of the Syrian pipeline in April 1982, Saddam Hussein decreed an austerity plan. It involved cancelling many foreign and domestic contracts, postponing public welfare pro-jects, curtailing the Five Year Development Plan, and slashing imports. However there was no retrenchment in the current development proj-ects, which were running at 12 per cent above the previous year's level.

By mid-1981 the manpower demands of the war had escalated to the extent that according to Tahir Tawfik, a Baathist leader, 40 per cent of the total Iraqi manpower was engaged in the war effort.[36] This caused a decline in production and led to the government ordering all employees to work overtime. The popular organizations of workers, students, women and peasants affiliated to the Baath Party held rallies to bolster support for the war and higher production. They also mounted cam-paigns to collect funds for the families of war victims. The common theme was that the war burden must be shouldered equally by com-batants and non-combatants.

The formal burial of the 'guns and butter' policy was coupled with a marked softening of the war aims. On 12 April 1982 Saddam Hussein stated that Iraq would withdraw from Iran if it had assurances that this would end the conflict. No such statement was forthcoming from Tehran, which was buoyed up by reports of, *inter alia*, rising Kurdish insurgency in Iraq. The outbreak of the war had compelled Baghdad to reduce its troops in the north. This led to an expansion in the border area under the control of the opposition Kurdish Democratic Party led by Masud and Idris Barzani. Following the March 1982 Iraqi setbacks, Baghdad's cancellation of cultural concessions made to Kurds in the early 1970s, so as to forge 'Iraqi unity', triggered protest demonstrations in major Kurdish cities and increased skirmishes between Kurdish insurgents and the security forces.

Iran prepared to implement the final phase of its plans to expel the Iraqis. On the night of 29–30 April it launched an offensive codenamed Bait al Muqaddas – The Sacred House (meaning Jerusalem) – south of the regained Dezful–Shush region along three axes, deploying 70,000 troops and 200 tanks and using the tactics they had by now perfected. They mounted infantry assaults at night which were backed by armour. Then came repeated thrusts by tanks and armoured vehicles combined with operations by attack helicopters. The Iraqis made better use than before of their tanks and their newly acquired Mirage warplanes. The weak element among them were the units of the Popular Army who, lacking both training and morale, were too ready to surrender. The net result was the Iraqi loss of 300 square miles to the Iranians. On 3 and 4 May the Iraqis counterattacked and retook some ground. Iran responded by invading the border town of Fakeh to interdict Iraqi supplies and divert enemy forces. The tactic succeeded. On 9 May the Iranians severed two Iraqi divisions, and regained 116 square miles north of Khorramshahr, reaching Shalamche on the Shatt al Arab, about 13 miles south-east of Basra. Three days later they captured Shalamche and brought their new territorial gains to 366 square miles. Operation Bait al Muqaddas cost each side about 15,000 lives.[37]

These victories brought Iran to the second phase of Operation Bait al Muqqadas, and close to Khorramshahr whose loss had left a scar on national honour. By mid-May 1982 the Iranians had captured all the roads leading to the city, which was surrounded by marshes, leaving the Iraqis only one means of access: across the Shatt al Arab. Khorramshahr's defence was in the hands of 35,000 Iraqi troops stationed behind three fortified barriers of earthworks and minefields. On 21 May 70,000 Iranians converged on the perimeter of the city. Two days later, fearing an Iranian onslaught, the Iraqi president invoked the Arab League's 1950 Joint Arab Defence Agreement to secure military aid from fellow League members.[38] But nothing came of it. On the night of 22–23 May Tehran launched a series of attacks. Iraqi defences collapsed. Within a day and a half the Iranians broke through the enemy minefields and trenches, and began pouring into the city. Iraq's regular troops withdrew in an orderly fashion while sustaining heavy casualties whereas the Popular Army personnel surrendered en masse, thus increasing the number of Iraqi prisoners of war by 12,000 to 15,000.

The news of the recovery of Khorramshahr was greeted with widespread jubilation in the streets of Iran: the Iranians had reversed their biggest and most humiliating loss in the war. All told, Operation Bait al Muqqadas secured Iran 2077 square miles.

Iraq's military was battered. Between March and June 1982 its strength fell from 210,000 to 150,000, with two of its four armoured divisions down to brigade size, and the ranks of its generals depleted by death or imprisonment. Its airworthy combat planes were down from 335 to about 100.[39] The long-suspected friction between political and military leaders came out into the open. Tariq Aziz told _Le Monde_ (The World): 'There were mistakes by some commanders, negligence by others, and especially incompetence and lack of composure in the [Khorramshahr] sector.'[40]

Baghdad's reverses had resulted from a combination of logistical, military and political factors. Its forces performed well only as long as they were near their own border. Once deep into Iran their communications and supply lines became overstretched, and the high command had difficulty in redeploying forces quickly. The Iraqis faced problems in finding suitable posts for their artillery: weaponry which was integral to Baghdad's tried and tested tactics against the Iraqi Kurds. The deployment of Popular Army units complicated the situation. Many regular army officers considered these inexperienced reservists more of a cumbersome liability than an asset, more inclined to surrender than fight. Unlike Iran's revolutionary guards they showed no innovation, daring or fierce dedication to a cause. In their eagerness to conquer or besiege Iranian territory, the Iraqi military planners, headed by Saddam Hussein, neglected to carve out defensive positions. Above all, they attacked Iran without any clear-cut idea of minimum and maximum war aims, or how to end the armed conflict through military and/or diplomatic effort. Now they found themselves deprived of any area of manoeuvre and at the mercy of Tehran.

Rafsanjani, in his capacity as the spokesman of the Iranian Supreme Defence Council, stated that there would be no ceasefire until and unless Saddam Hussein had been punished as a 'war criminal' and the Iraqi people had 'a legitimate government', and Iran had been paid war reparations of $150 billion.[41]

The Iranian victories set off a chain of riots on 30 May in Karbala, Basra, Hilleh and Nasiriyeh – southern Iraqi places with predominantly Shia populations – as well as the Shia quarters of Baghdad. This was not surprising. Even in such a regimented institution as the army Shias had expressed their dissidence through the age-old techniques of dereliction of duty, absenteeism and desertion, particularly when the fighting took place on the soil of the Islamic Republic of Iran. By and large they had shown themselves to be less receptive to ideological indoctrination, administered by civil and military authorities, than their Sunni colleagues. The existence of these problems could only be implied by such official actions as the April 1981 decree offering exemption from punishment for 'deserters, absentees and transgressors' if they rejoined their units within a month.[42]

Al Daawa militants took advantage of the daily blackouts, necessitated by the war, and intensified their campaign of sabotage and assassinations, encouraged by the infiltration of arms and trained Iraqi refugees-turned-guerrillas from Iran. Among the many acts of sabotage and clashes with Iraqi security forces that were claimed by Al Daawa, the blowing up of an ammunition depot and fuel storage tanks near Baghdad airport on 28 May 1981 was confirmed.[43]

Saddam Hussein tried to tackle the problem by intensifying the repression of Al Daawa, drafting sympathetic ulama more firmly into the war effort, increasing the state's involvement in religious affairs and energetically projecting himself as a pious Muslim. The government increased its surveillance of dissident clerics, Shia and Sunni, laying particular stress on the Shia region, especially the holy cities, with Popular Army units performing security tasks in the countryside. The verdict of Shaikh Ali Kashif Ghita, the imam of Najaf, and other Shia clerics that the war with Iran was a jihad and that Khomeini was a heretic proved a valuable tool for the regime to legitimize the conflict. However, government success was only partial. For, despite the media claims that Ayatollah Abol Qasim Khoei, the most senior Shia cleric in Iraq, had prayed for Saddam Hussein's health and co-operated with the monarchist Iranian leaders, Bakhtiar and Oveissi, against the Khomeini regime, Khoei maintained a sullen silence on the issue of war.[44] The authorities curtailed sharply the size of his seminary in Najaf and imprisoned many of his students.

On the positive side, in late 1981 Saddam Hussein reorganized and expanded the ministry of waqfs (religious endowments) and religious affairs, and incorporated it into the presidential office. It enlarged its Committees for Religious Indoctrination, made up of politically reliable clerics and Baath members, which *inter alia* monitored the preachers' sermons. It also decided to distribute 5 million copies of the Quran abroad.[45] Its increased budget allowed it to continue vigorously the policy of renovation and construction of mosques, especially in Shia areas. The example of Saddam Hussein praying in different mosques under the glare of television lights was emulated by other Baathist figures. In March 1982 the Iraqi leader made it a point to offer prayers on Imam Ali's birthday at his shrine in Najaf. 'They [our enemies] imagined that Najaf could become part of Iran,' Saddam Hussein said. 'But Najaf is an Iraqi and Arab town. Its soil is Arab and its symbol is our grandfather Imam Ali ibn Abi Talib, who is definitely not the grandfather of Khomeini.'[46]

All these measures helped to alleviate the problem of Shia reluctance to identify wholeheartedly with the war, but did not solve it. Indeed, with Iraq's military suffering reverses in the spring of 1982, it became more serious. This could be inferred from the reported decision of Saddam Hussein in early May to order the shooting of any soldier fleeing from battle. This proved counterproductive in so far as it encouraged thousands of Iraqi combatants in Khorramshahr to surrender to Iran.

Keenly aware of the crisis facing Baghdad, Iranian leaders insisted that they would talk to their counterparts only if Saddam Hussein was replaced as president. This led to a flurry of diplomatic activity, with President Assad of Syria and King Fahd of Saudi Arabia playing a leading role. Assad reportedly favoured Ahmad Hassan Bakr as the successor to Saddam Hussein while Fahd proposed Shafiq Daraji, the Iraqi ambassador to Riyadh.[47] They also agreed on the formation of the Gulf Reconstruction Fund, to be financed by the six-member Gulf Co-operation Council, as a means of paying reparations to Iran. On 2 June 1982 GCC foreign ministers meeting in Riyadh offered a peace plan: a ceasefire, withdrawal of the warring parties to the 1975 borders, and negotiations to resolve the outstanding issues. But these concerted efforts were blown off course by the Israeli invasion of Lebanon on the night of 5–6 June.

Israel's attack was triggered off by an attempt to assassinate Shlomo Argov, the Israeli ambassador to Britain, on the night of 3 June. The London operation was masterminded by Nawal Rosan, an Iraqi 'carpet dealer', who was later found to be a colonel in Iraqi intelligence.[48] Subsequent Iraqi behaviour lends credence to the theory that the Iraqi authorities ordered the killing of the Israeli envoy in order to provoke an Israeli invasion of south Lebanon – then a base for Palestine Liberation Organization operations against Israel – and create conditions suitable for an immediate ceasefire in the Gulf War to enable the combatants to fight their common foe: Israel.

The Islamic Conference Organization secretariat immediately appealed to Iran and Iraq to stop fighting and direct their weapons against Israel. Iraq responded quickly. On 9 June Baghdad witnessed an extraordinary gathering of the Regional and National Commands of the Arab Baath Socialist Party and the Revolutionary Command Council – as well as the Iraqi armed forces general command – to consider the ICO call. Following this the ruling RCC issued a statement that Iraq was ready for a ceasefire and a withdrawal to the international border, and would accept the verdict by a fact-finding commission of Muslim states to determine the 'aggression' that caused the war.

It was significant that Saddam Hussein did not attend this meeting; and, contrary to protocol, he did not sign its decision. Observers, domestic and foreign, concluded that this was the end of the road for Saddam Hussein, who had been gripped by a deep crisis since the spring, which among other things had emboldened a group of cabinet ministers to call for his replacement by Bakr.[49] The other rumoured scenario visualized the Iraqi president being replaced by the triumvirate of Taha Yassin Ramadan, first deputy premier, commander of the Popular Army and head of the party's military bureau; Tariq Aziz, deputy premier and the leading ideologue of the party; and Sadoun Hamadi, foreign minister, who was Shia.

But it transpired later that, following the Iraqi defeat in the Dezful–Shush area in March, the Iraqi president had held long, intensive consultations with senior field officers. They seemed to have concluded that despite the strategic and tactical mistakes of the armed forces high command headed by Saddam Hussein, which had led to the present sorry state, the military and political leaders needed one another to survive the worsening crisis, and that an Iraqi retreat to the international frontier – which increasingly looked inevitable – would be accompanied by a reshuffle of the party hierarchy.

Khomeini was among those who were quietly confident of Saddam Hussein's imminent downfall. He spurned Baghdad's peace offer, arguing that Iraq was using the same tactic as Israel: first occupying the neighbouring country's cities and land, and then seeking a ceasefire. To Iraq's offer of safe conduct through its territory for the Iranian volunteers ready to aid the beleaguered Lebanon, Khomeini rejoined that before Iran could help in the liberation of Lebanon and Palestine, 'we must deliver Iraq from this accursed [Baath] Party'.[50] His call for the uprooting of the Baath had the opposite effect: it made the party hierarchy rally round the Iraqi president.

Saddam Hussein showed an extraordinary capacity for survival. He announced on 20 June that the unilateral Iraqi withdrawal, begun that day, would be completed by the end of the month. He presented the Iraqi move as 'tactical', designed to enable the high command to reorganize the forces to give better protection to the fatherland. Based within its own borders Iraq's military would give battle more valiantly. In any case Iraq had never planned to keep Iranian territory, he added. Its primary aim all along had been to wreck Iran's military machine, a strategy which entailed withdrawals from 'here and there in order to reduce our sacrifices'. However, the Iraqi pull-back was not to apply to the Iranian border areas which Baghdad had claimed and occupied on the eve of the war.

On 24 June 1982 Saddam Hussein presided over the Ninth Regional Baath Party Congress, held secretly and attended by 250 delegates who had been 'elected' earlier: an exercise which showed that age had not diminished the Iraqi leader's expertise in clandestine operations. At the end of the four-day session parts of the adopted resolutions were published in the media. Saddam Hussein's opening speech set the tone for the dramatic reshuffle he had in mind. He blamed 'enemies of the Baath' for infiltrating the party with the objective of 'killing it from inside' – alluding to the success they had had in influencing students and workers (a reference to the less than satisfactory performance of the party in the early 1982 elections of labour and students unions' officials)

– and advocating 'old and outdated social and religious customs and concepts'. This situation had arisen from the party's dramatic expansion and the weak, incompetent behaviour of 'certain Baath officials'. They needed to be replaced by those capable of 'great courage in adversity' and of accepting 'supervision by higher leadership'.[51]

Towards the end of the congress Saddam Hussein and his few close aides reshuffled the party and state hierarchy. He ended the practice of Regional Command members automatically functioning as members of the ruling RCC. He nearly halved the size of the RCC, from 17 to nine, restricting it only to his close allies: Izzat Ibrahim (Duri), assistant general secretary of the Regional (Iraqi) Baath Party; Ramadan; Aziz; Adnan Khairallah (Talfa), defence minister (and a cousin of Saddam Hussein); Sadoun Shakir (Tikriti), interior minister (also a cousin, and close friend of the president since the latter's underground days); Hassan Ali Amiri, trade minister; Naim Haddad, speaker of the National Assembly; and a new appointee, Taha Muhyi al Din Maruf, the Kurdish vice-president of the republic since 1974. Of these Haddad and Amiri were Shia. Saddam Hussein loaded the reorganized Regional Command with nominees who were personally loyal to him. The new 15-member Regional Command included eight men from the RCC (excluding Maruf) and seven fresh appointees. Four of the new appointees were long-standing party functionaries, being secretaries of the regional bureaus, and owed their rise to Saddam Hussein. In sectarian terms four of the new nominees (including Sadoun Hamadi, foreign minister) were Shia. This meant that six or seven of the Regional Command members were now Shia. In that sense the new Regional Command had about the same proportion of Shias as the National Assembly: 40 per cent.[52] The Iraqi leader also reshuffled provincial governors as well as lower state and party bureaucrats. Through these decisions he rewarded those who had been loyal to him, injected new life into the state and party machines and, most importantly, succeeded in shifting the responsibility for military reverses from his shoulders to those of the sacked or demoted leaders.

He achieved these objectives at the cost of an increasing risk to his life. Soon after the party congress, on 11 July, he became the target of an assassination attempt by a group of soldiers belonging to Al Daawa in Dujayal, a town of mixed Sunni–Shia population, 40 miles north of the capital, used by him as a rest place. The assassins ambushed his motorcade with machine-guns and rocket-propelled grenades, killing ten of his bodyguards. His car was hit, but he was unhurt. The government reprisal that followed resulted in 150 casualties and the destruction of parts of the town.[53]

A remarkable feature of the Ninth Congress's political resolution was its stance on Islam – a subject which had not even been mentioned in the deliberations of the previous congress. 'The party considers Islam a great revolution in the history of mankind and that the Arab Nation has the historical credit for spreading the revolution,' stated the newly adopted resolution. 'The modern Arab must be inspired by the spirit of Islamic mission.' The party reiterated its calls for the creation of a state 'based on patriotic links within the framework of one country and based on Pan-Arab links within the parameters of the Great Arab Homeland'. But in a significant departure from the past, the resolution declared: 'Such a state should be inspired by Islam as a mission and a revolution.' Furthermore, the party regarded 'Islam as the basis of Arab nationalism' and advocated 'strengthening of ties between the Arab Nation and other Islamic nations on the basis of spiritual links'.[54] However, this view was at loggerheads with that of Khomeini: for him the concept of nationalism *per se* was anathema.

As it was, the Baath Party was still vehemently opposed to those whom its resolution accused of exploiting 'political-religious trends' for tactical and opportunistic reasons, an oblique reference to Al Daawa. Citing Saddam Hussein's work, *The Arab Heritage and Contemporary Life*, the resolution stated: 'What is requested is that we be against the state's politicization of religion. We have to oppose dragging revolution into the issue of religion. We have to go back to the origins of our faith and be proud of religion yet without its politicization.'[55] In that sense the Baath Party's secular creed remained intact.

Baghdad kept up its propaganda against Khomeini – who was always given derogatory labels and grossly caricatured in the Iraqi media – and Iran, which was routinely presented as the aggressor. The Israeli invasion of Lebanon and Khomeini's refusal of Baghdad's ceasefire offer were presented as further evidence of an Iranian–Zionist conspiracy. 'They [Iranian leaders] aimed at inciting sedition in Iraq in order to destroy it by dividing it into weak states belonging to Iran, Zionism and the [Arab] Nation's enemies,' Saddam Hussein said. 'They wanted to destroy Iraq's independence and unity.'[56] Along with such statements went claims that Iraq's superior position on the battlefield had altered only after the arrival of 'foreign expertise in an organized manner inside the Iranian lines', with the Iraqi president specifically mentioning 'Israeli expertise'.[57]

The Iraqi reverses had a many-sided impact on the country. Firstly, they made the leadership take an increasingly pragmatic view of Baathist socialism. Secondly, they helped forge genuine unity between political and military leaders, with the armed forces as an institution treated progressively on a par with the Baath Party, and not as its subordinate. Thirdly, the significance of the secret services, already high, rose as the government redoubled its effort to quell dissent and disaffection. Finally, the military defeats resulted in an intensification of official efforts to foster the personality cult of Saddam Hussein, who drew a strong security curtain around himself in the face of repeated assassination attempts.

The pressures of war overstretched the public sector, the favoured sphere of the economy in the Baathist state. Therefore the government let the private sector grow not merely in agriculture, where the existing co-operatives were found to be unpopular with peasants, but also in commerce and industry.

Adversity brought senior politicians and military officers together. They were aware that each side had its share of blame for the present crisis. By and large they were Sunni and secular. They had a common interest in blocking the ascendance of Shias in the Iraqi state and society as a consequence of Iran's victory in the fields of war and ideology. Armed forces officers knew the value of a cohesive civilian government, led by a strong personality like Saddam Hussein, willing to overlook their defeats and guard them against demoralizing public censure. In return civilian leaders wanted reliable military officers who would keep out of politics. This was the compact that Saddam Hussein seems to have struck with senior military commanders in March 1982. From then on he was meticulous in ensuring that the military high command was in total agreement with the RCC's decision to sue for peace, and was seen as such by the public.

Iraqi intelligence – already noted for its efficiency and ruthlessness – was bolstered further as the government feared adverse responses from the already alienated groups, now emboldened by a general disenchantment among the people due to the poor performance of the military.

As the crisis deepened Saddam Hussein stopped his random forays into the country to ply the local communities with schools or mosques and the families of the dead soldiers with land or television sets. None the less he constantly stayed in the public eye through extensive television coverage of his activities. Besides, he was to be seen in pictures and posters displayed in all public buildings and shops. Stage-managed events to show popular love and admiration for the 'struggler-leader' included a steady stream of poems, articles and songs in his praise in the media. On the other hand, the growing despondency and fear among ordinary Iraqis increased tensions, thus necessitating further tightening of the security net around the president – a job assigned to his stepbrother, Barzan Tikriti, the intelligence chief. He turned the presidential palace, hitherto accessible to the general public, into something more like a fortress, ringed by tanks and paratroopers, and put the presidential bodyguard through fresh training by former British commandos and other experts. But that did not deter assassins from attacking Saddam Hussein twice in July 1982.

Saddam Hussein stood at the apexes of the three power centres of Iraq: the party, the military and the secret services. He was the general secretary of the Baath Party and the commander-in-chief of the military. The deputy commander-in-chief and defence minister was none other than his cousin and brother-in-law Adnan Khairallah (Talfa). While one of his stepbrothers, Barzan Tikriti, was the head of the secret services, the other, Sabri Ibrahim, was the deputy chief of police.

According to the Iraqi media, Saddam Hussein was the only saviour the nation possessed. The political resolution of the Baath Party's Ninth Congress referred to the efforts of 'Zionist and colonialist circles, the old and new regimes in Tehran as well as all other powers hostile to Iraq and the Arab Nation's progress' to 'defame and endanger the life of the historic leader Saddam Hussein who is now shouldering the duties of the indispensable leader'. It went on to describe him as 'a symbol of freedom, independence, pride, integrity and a hope for a better, brighter future for Iraq and the Arab Nation'.[58] Equally, on the other side, the Tehran regime described Saddam Hussein as a war criminal and insisted on his overthrow as the primary condition for agreeing to a ceasefire. It considered him not merely an infidel who delighted in persecuting pious believers, laymen and clerics, but also an evil person, cruel, vain and treacherous. The manner in which Saddam Hussein swiftly and clandestinely turned the tables against his strong opponents within the party and state hierarchy reinforced hatred against him in Tehran.

Not surprisingly, when the Iraqi government announced on 29 June 1982 that its troops had voluntarily vacated all Iranian territory, Tehran called it a lie. Later events showed Iran to be right. The Iraqis had withdrawn from some, but not all, Iranian areas.

For the next several days the Iranian Supreme Defence Council weighed the pros and cons of attacking Iraq. In the end the hardliners won.

Part of the reason for the hawks' success was the optimistic mood prevalent in Tehran. This stemmed from the improved political and economic environment in the republic. Its government had succeeded in suppressing the armed struggle launched by the Mujahedin-e Khalq, People's Mujahedin, in the wake of the June 1981 dismissal of President Bani-Sadr, which claimed the lives of scores of religious and political leaders including President Rajai and Premier Muhammad Javed Bahonar. With the nation engaged in bloody battles with the Iraqis, it was comparatively easy for the Khomeini regime to label Mujahedin activists as traitors in league with the enemy. This lost the Mujahedin whatever popular sympathy they had and further encouraged Iran's security forces to crush them.

Also, from the spring of 1982 oil sales had improved sharply. In the aftermath of the revolution, determined to loosen its economic links with the West, the Iranian oil ministry signed a series of barter deals with socialist and Third World countries. Soon Tehran discovered that what it got in return for its oil were overpriced, low quality goods it did not really need. In the wake of the Gulf War Iran needed to import vital military goods to be paid for in foreign currencies, so its salvation lay in selling petroleum for hard currencies to the West and Japan. But when the Iranians realized this in the autumn of 1981 they found the oil market depressed by oversupply, and Western and Japanese companies reluctant to do business with them. So the National Iranian Oil Company let it be known through intermediaries that its crude was available for less than the official OPEC price of $30 a barrel. By early 1982 fresh orders for Iranian oil began arriving in Tehran. The other way to conserve precious foreign exchange was by controlling civilian imports. The government devised a plan for nationalizing foreign trade in October 1981 whereby the functions of a middleman were taken over by the ministry of commerce. Nationalization of foreign trade and sale of oil for cash to the West and Japan gave the government much leeway in managing the economy, and contributed strongly to an economic upturn. These measures also helped it to pursue the war with greater vigour than before, and win the battles it did from March to June 1982.

All in all, therefore, the situation in mid-1982 was radically different from that prevailing at the outset of the war 21 months earlier. Then a strong, united Iraq, heady with bulging foreign reserves and arms arsenals, commanding the largest military force ever, its economy roaring ahead fuelled by ever increasing oil output selling at $37 a barrel, started the war with the expectation of ending it within a few weeks with total control of the Shatt al Arab and a stranglehold over the oil-rich Iranian province of Khuzistan, and an anti-Khomeini government installed in Ahvaz: achievements guaranteed to establish Saddam Hussein as the leader of the Arab world and the protector of the Gulf monarchies. By now the war had turned into a struggle for survival for both Iraq and its supreme leader. Through some swift, deft moves the wily Saddam Hussein had managed to keep his position. But he as well as his nation looked to the immediate future with trepidation as Tehran prepared to invade Iraq. For a country which seemed embroiled in acute political, economic and military crises in September 1980, Iran had surprised all, friend and foe alike, by its performance in the war. It had proved more resilient and cohesive than its most ardent well-wishers had hoped.

Historically, popular revolutions have always proved to be strong in defence because they quickly give a stake in the new system to the previously disenfranchized masses. When attacked, the freshly empowered working and lower middle classes fight fiercely to preserve their recently acquired gains. Revolutionary Iran fell neatly into this pattern of behaviour.

3 OUTSIDE POWERS

The diplomatic standing of Tehran and the timing of the US presidential election were important factors for President Hussein in deciding the date for the invasion of Iran. Having antagonized Washington by taking American diplomats hostage, the Khomeini regime had soured its relations with Moscow by virulently condemning the Soviet military intervention in Afghanistan. Iran's estrangement from both super-powers – particularly the US, its leading source of military supplies – augured well for Iraq's war plans. By the same token the Iraqi leader feared the prospect of a resolution of the American hostage crisis as the US presidential campaign reached its peak in October 1980.

When the war erupted both superpowers expressed their neutrality. Washington lacked formal diplomatic ties with Iraq but had one of the largest missions in Baghdad in the 'interests section' of the embassy of Belgium, which had been looking after American interests since June 1967. In any case this did not preclude direct contacts between the two governments at the United Nations headquarters in New York or third countries' capitals. According to the Iranian president, Bani-Sadr, in early August 1980 his government had purchased secret documents containing a detailed account of the conversations in France between several deposed Iranian generals and politicians, Iraqi representatives and American and Israeli military experts. If so, the administration of President James Carter had an inkling of the Iraqi plans.[1] By supplying secret information, which exaggerated Iran's military weakness, to Saudi Arabia for onward transmission to Baghdad, Washington encour-aged Iraq to attack Iran – seeing in the move the making of a solution to the hostage crisis on the eve of the presidential poll. Given that US intelligence had predicted Iran running out of spare parts for its predomi-nantly American arsenal in three weeks, presidential aides visualized Tehran growing desperate to secure them from the Pentagon – a situ-ation tailor-made for a swap: American spares for hostages. Out of this arose the rumours of a 'mid-October surprise' by the Carter camp which alarmed the rival Ronald Reagan camp. Contrary to President Carter's expectations, however, Iran did not turn to him immediately for spares and ammunition. It approached Vietnam, which had huge stocks of left-over American spare parts and weapons. Vietnam helped Iran.

However, unpublicized talks between Washington and Tehran continued. As the *Washington Post* of 17 October 1980 reported, a spares-for-hostages deal was an element in the hostage settlement. Carter was keen to win the contest on the coat-tails of the American hostages freed before 4 November, election day. Polls showed that a pre-election hostage release would earn the incumbent five to ten per cent of the vote, thus ensuring him a second term. To placate Tehran, President Carter stated on 18 October that the Iraqi forces had gone beyond 'the ultimate goal' expressed by President Hussein, and that the US would like to see any 'invading forces withdrawn'. Two days later the American Secretary of State said that the Iraqi 'invasion' of Iran was threatening the Gulf's stability and that territory must not be seized by force. On 23 October the US ambassador to the United Nations said that the 'national integrity of Iran' was threatened by the Iraqi 'invasion'.[2] These statements were enough to make Iraq's foreign minister express doubts about Washington's neutrality in the conflict.

On 28 October Carter, feeling desperate, promised that if the hostages were released the US would airlift the $300–500 millions-worth of arms and spares that Iran had already paid for. But nothing came of this mainly because – as has become known since then – Reagan's campaign office secretly struck a deal with the emissaries of Iran in meetings held in Washington in early October and in Paris on 19–20 October. In return for the Iranian promise not to release the hostages before election day, the Republican candidate's emissaries promised that, if elected, Reagan would supply Iran with US-made weapons and spares.[3] Reagan won. After taking office in January 1981 he publicly pledged to honour the terms agreed by Carter (just before relinquishing office) to resolve the hostage crisis, and lifted US economic sanctions against Iran.

Moscow was genuinely troubled by the outbreak of war on its own periphery. It was angry and disappointed with Baghdad on two counts. Iraq had violated the spirit of the 1972 Friendship and Co-operation Treaty which implied that Soviet weapons were to be employed only for defence. Secondly, it had not even shown the courtesy of informing Moscow of its impending action. The Kremlin's immediate appeal to both sides to show restraint and common sense was followed by an authorized article by the Tass news agency on 28 September 1980. This contained a reminder to Iran and Iraq that their war was 'undermining the national liberation movement in the Middle East in its struggle against imperialism and Zionism'. In order to help end the hostilities, the Kremlin stopped supplying arms, or even spare parts, to Baghdad. This was confirmed when Iraqi sources stated later that Soviet ships carrying 140 tanks to Basra had turned round at the Hormuz Straits and returned home on Moscow's orders.[4] Since 85 per cent of Iraqi weapons were Soviet-made, this policy hurt Iraq.

The Soviet authorities immediately assured Iran that they would remain neutral in the conflict; and this allowed Tehran to move troops and equipment from the north to the south. They believed that Iraq had been encouraged by America and its Arab allies to resort to force. 'Certain people in the West do not conceal their hopes that the present Iranian-Iraqi conflict will reduce the ability of the Republic of Iran to resist the imperialist pressure which is being exerted on it [to resolve the American hostage crisis],' wrote *Izvestia* (News) on 23 September 1980. 'They also hope that the involvement of Iraq in military operations against Iran will enable the West to achieve changes in Iraqi policy in the West's favour.'

A week later the Soviet leader Leonid Brezhnev warned that the war might provide Washington with an excuse to move into Iran militarily and control Gulf oil under the pretext of freeing American hostages. In order to help Iran preserve its anti-imperialist stance in the face of the combined pressures of war and Western economic boycott of Iran – equipped almost exclusively with American, British and French arms – Moscow offered to sell weapons to Tehran. According to Iran's premier, Muhammad Ali Rajai, the Soviet ambassador in Tehran made the offer on 4 October 1980, and he rejected it.[5] The Iranian decision stemmed from its displeasure with Moscow's military intervention in Afghanistan, a neighbouring Muslim country, and its commitment to a 'Neither East nor West' foreign policy. But the snub from Tehran did not stop the Kremlin from giving permission to Syria and Libya to airlift arms and ammunition to Iran.

An article in *Krasnaya Zvezda* (Red Star), the Soviet army daily, on 26 October 1980 indicated where Soviet sympathies lay. 'The declared aims of the [Iraqi] military actions are being changed,' said the article. 'At first Iraq claimed the comparatively small area of 508 sq km . . . But now the Iraqi press is publishing maps in which the whole province of Khuzistan, called Arabistan in the Iraqi capital, is marked as Iraqi territory.' In the Soviet view Iraq had compounded its culpability by combining its expansionist intent with co-operation with the US.

This analysis was remarkably similar to the one prevalent in Tehran. There the regime believed that, given the Iraqi weakness in strategic terms – possessing only one quarter of Iran's area and about one-third of its population – Baghdad could only have invaded the Islamic Republic at the behest of the US and its regional agents. It therefore redoubled its attacks on America, vowing to fight until total expulsion of its influence in the region.

As for the Soviet Union, it refrained from officially condemning the Iraqi action partly to preserve the spirit of the Friendship Treaty with Iraq which was still in force. This drove the Iranian ambassador in Moscow, Muhammad Mokri, to press the Soviets to condemn the Iraqi aggression and confirm that they had stopped supplying arms to Baghdad. In early November 1980 Mokri informed the Tehran-based *Kayhan* (World) that 'This has now happened.'[6]

Three months later Baghdad publicly complained that the USSR had stopped implementing 'its pre-war contracts with Iraq' since the outbreak of the war.[7] However, the Soviet embargo applied only to direct supplies. Iraq succeeded in purchasing Soviet-made weapons and ammunition from Somalia, North Yemen and Egypt – which had in the past received Soviet arms – as well as Poland, and having them shipped through Saudi Arabia. 'If we had failed [to procure Soviet weapons altogether] we might have become irritated, very hostile, very hysterical against the Soviet Union which would have been a mistake,' said Tariq Aziz in mid-April 1981. 'Now we can behave serenely with the Soviet Union without being hostile to it.'[8] Since Iraq could not expect to replace Soviet arms supplies with shipments from the West it was careful not to antagonize Moscow further.

But the situation changed in early June 1981 when an Israeli air raid destroyed the Iraqi nuclear reactor near Baghdad. This softened the Soviet stance towards Iraq, particularly as it had become obvious that Saddam Hussein's dream of becoming the region's supreme leader had been dashed, and that sooner or later he would be forced to defend his country's territorial integrity.

This became evident when Iraq's deputy premier, Ramadan, met the Soviet chief of staff, Nikolai Ogarkov, during his visit to Moscow in mid-June; and the final communiqué referred to both sides as ready to 'broaden trade and economic relations and supplies in other areas on a stable and mutually profitable basis'.[9] 'Supplies in other areas' was a coded phrase for military shipments. It seems that the Kremlin decided in principle to resume arms supplies to Iraq if and when it needed them for defending itself, provided it paid in hard currency.

Lack of diplomatic ties with Baghdad did not inhibit Washington's options. The US policy, defined by President Carter in the wake of the Soviet military intervention in Afghanistan in December 1979, was to keep open the Gulf, declared vital to America's national security; and for this purpose Carter had set up the special joint task force of infantry, marine, navy and air force personnel, to be called the Rapid Deployment Force. His other (unstated) objective was to protect Saudi Arabia, the largest and most important oil-rich Gulf kingdom. Within a fortnight of the outbreak of war his administration despatched four Airborne Warning and Control Systems (Awacs) to Saudi Arabia, and declared that it would respond 'positively' to requests for assistance from 'non-belligerent friends' in the region. The US built up its naval presence in the region to 37 ships. The Reagan administration confirmed the Carter doctrine.

Responding to Saudi advice the new American president sent a special emissary to Baghdad in April 1981. Three months later Saddam Hussein announced that he intended to treat the head of the US interests section in the Belgian embassy in Baghdad as a *de facto* ambassador.

THE GULF AND THE ARAB WORLD

Saudi Arabia seemed to have figured prominently in the Iraqi war plans. On 5 August 1980 Saddam Hussein visited Riyadh where he had meetings with the Saudi king, premier and foreign minister on 'the current situation in the Middle East and the Gulf region'.[10] By then the Gulf rulers, including the Saudi monarch, had tired of trying to establish rapprochement with Iran's revolutionary regime, which combined its attacks on monarchy as an unIslamic institution[11] with denunciation of the Gulf rulers as corrupt men, who depleted the valuable oil resources of their countries to satisfy the ever-growing demands of America, the Great Satan, and who denied their subjects any role in policymaking. They felt that something had to be done to meet the Iranian menace. For its part Iraq promised its Gulf allies that it would strike militarily only after it had exhausted all peaceful avenues and that it would 'limit military action while offering negotiations'.[12] One of the factors to determine the timing of the Iraqi invasion was Saudi anxiety about Iranian subversion during the hajj pilgrimage due in October. According to Tehran, on 12 September Saudi Arabia and Kuwait signed secret agreements to raise their oil outputs by one million and 800,000 barrels per day respectively, and contribute the sales revenue to Iraq's war effort.[13]

While fulfilling the terms of their clandestine pacts both Gulf states refrained from openly joining Iraq in the war. Indeed, for various reasons, the Saudi government took a deliberately ambiguous stand in public so as not to antagonize Iran. About a year earlier it had experienced rioting by its Shia nationals, a disliked minority, living almost exclusively in the oil-rich eastern region. Also it was aware that its oil installations, concentrated in a small area in the Gulf, were vulnerable. Still another restraining factor was the fact that half of its petroleum production came from offshore wells which were hard to defend. Besides, it felt ideologically inhibited. It gave equal importance to its Arab responsibilities and its Islamic obligations – the latter consideration weighing in favour of Iran which was, in the final analysis, an Islamic state.

When the Saudi ruler, King Khalid ibn Abdul Aziz, telephoned Saddam Hussein on 25 September 1980, according to the Saudi Press Agency, he expressed 'his interest and good fraternal feelings' towards Iraq. In contrast, the Iraqi News Agency reported that King Khalid had 'affirmed the support of the Kingdom of Saudi Arabia in its pan-Arab battle' and had referred to Iran as 'the enemy of the Arab Nation'.

On the one hand there were persistent reports of Riyadh allowing Iraqi warplanes to use Saudi airspace and even its air bases. On the other, in a television interview in New York, the Saudi foreign minister, Prince Saud al Faisal, described the war as 'a conflict between two brother Muslim countries that had to be brought speedily to termination' and not a conflict in which 'we want to support one side against the other'.[14] However, expressing such sentiments did not stop Saudi Arabia later from letting its ports in the Red Sea and the Gulf be used for civilian and military imports for Iraq – or from financially aiding Baghdad. By the end of 1981 it had loaned Iraq $10 billion.[15]

Existing in the shadow of the powerful states of Saudi Arabia, Iraq and Iran, Kuwait felt most threatened. A country of a mere 7300 square miles, with a population of 1.6 million, it lacked military muscle to protect its vulnerable oil facilities or stand up to either of the belligerents. Being a monarchy with a quarter of its nationals belonging to the Shia sect, it was particularly susceptible to threats from Iran, which warned that it would take 'appropriate action' against any regional state that transformed its discreet backing for Baghdad into active cooperation. Indeed, to show that it meant business, Iran launched air raids on Kuwaiti border posts on 12 and 16 November 1980 in retaliation for alleged Kuwaiti involvement in the Iraqi military effort. Under the circumstances the Kuwaiti regime continued its policy of permitting the media to take up a pro-Iraqi stance while banning its officials from endorsing this stand.

As the tide began to turn against Iraq on the battlefield, Kuwait increased its financial and logistical aid to its northern neighbour, with 500 to 1000 heavy trucks a day carting goods to Iraq. To its interest-free loan of $2 billion to Iraq in the autumn of 1980, it added two further sums of $2 billion each in April and December 1981.[16] Iran disapproved of Kuwait's actions. On 1 October 1981 the Kuwaiti oil refinery at Umm Aayash was hit in an air raid. Though Tehran denied responsibility the Saudi-based Awacs reportedly tracked the attacking planes from their Iranian base. The moral was clear: Kuwait must pay a price, periodically, if it persisted in its policy of allowing Iraq to use its ports, airfields and highways.

Bahrain, Qatar and the United Arab Emirates maintained strict official silence on the Iranian-Iraqi hostilities. In the UAE's case neutrality was the result of differences among the seven constituent principalities: three were pro-Iranian, two pro-Iraqi, two non-partisan. The pro-Iraqi emirates of Abu Dhabi and Ras al Khaima loaned Baghdad $1–3 billion by the end of 1981, with Qatar providing another $1 billion.[17] Receipts of such largesse from the Gulf states enabled Iraq actually to increase its civilian imports in 1981 by $5 billion.

Because of its location Oman had a particular interest in keeping the Gulf open to international shipping through the Hormuz Straits. Tehran was quick to declare that it would keep the waterway open for navigation. This made interference by the West, keen to maintain the flow of oil through the Straits, unnecessary. It also led to a decision in major Western capitals to try to localize the conflict. When British intelligence in Oman discovered that Iraq had assembled helicopters and troops in Oman to invade and occupy Abu Musa and the Greater and Lesser Tunb Islands, the British and American governments pressured the Omani ruler, Sultan Qaboos ibn Said, to scuttle the Iraqi plan.[18] Later Saudi Arabia persuaded Iraq to abandon the idea of retaking the islands in the Gulf.

Britain and France actively advised Saudi leaders to create a supra-national body of the Gulf states, which could call upon the West for military assistance in the event of internal or external threat to one or more of its members. Previous attempts to form a regional organization had failed owing to the rivalry between Iran, Iraq and Saudi Arabia. Now, with Iran and Iraq engaged in a bloody conflict, Saudi Arabia got its chance to spawn the formation of the Gulf Co-operation Council in February 1981 with its headquarters in Riyadh. Its objectives were to co-ordinate internal security, arms procurement and national econ-omies of the member states, and to settle border disputes. These were incorporated into the charter of the Council which was officially established on 25 May.

Debates within the GCC on external security were conducted within the parameters set by Kuwait on one hand and Oman on the other. Kuwait advocated the formation of a joint military command which would be self-reliant, whereas Oman proposed a joint Arab Gulf force for the purpose of defending the Hormuz Straits under the umbrella of a multinational naval force of America, Britain and West Germany. The issue was unresolved.

However, consensus grew around the idea of co-ordinating the de-fence plans of the members, and letting Oman, Bahrain and Saudi Arabia strengthen their individual military and intelligence links with the US. In February 1982 the US defence secretary obtained Riyadh's agreement to form a joint Saudi–American Military Committee, something the Saudis had refused to do in the past. The Iranian threat brought about the change. This was the background against which the Pentagon issued a secret directive in March which widened the scope of American mili-tary involvement in the Gulf. It stated: 'Whatever the circumstances, we should be prepared to introduce American forces into the region should it appear [that our] security of access to the Persian Gulf oil is threatened.'[19] Clearly this was meant to include the 'circumstances' created by Iranian activities in the Gulf, and was Washington's re-sponse to Tehran's professed aim of destroying its influence in the region.

Overall, GCC members tried to use the absence of Iraq from their midst to underline their neutrality in the war. But Iran was not convinced. It saw the establishment of the GCC as a step directed against it and the Islamic revolution.

As for Iraq, its president was affronted by the exclusion of his country from the GCC. He was also offended by Kuwait's refusal to lease its offshore islands of Bubiyan and Warba to let Iraq have wider access to the Gulf. He described the Iraqi effort as a means to stop an international Zionist conspiracy linked with Iranian expansionism aimed at the Arab world in general and the Gulf in particular. 'Had it not been for Iraq and its army the Iranians would have seized the entire Gulf, moved into the [Arabian] Peninsula and even occupied Iraq itself,' Saddam Hussein said.[20] He classified Arab states as pro-Iraqi, neutral and traitor. In the first category came Jordan and, to a lesser extent, North Yemen and Morocco. Saddam Hussein did not name the neutral countries, whose behaviour, according to him, verged on the irresponsible. Despite the generous material and logistical aid he received from Saudi Arabia and Kuwait, he described their contributions as 'much less than what duty dictates'.[21] The Iraqi leader was so incensed with the 'traitor' and 'opportunist' states of Syria and Libya that he severed diplomatic ties with them in October 1980. To a lesser extent he was unhappy with Algeria and South Yemen for maintaining cordial relations with Tehran.

The division in the Arab League on the Gulf War helped Egypt, which had been suspended from the League in March 1979 following its unilateral peace treaty with Israel. The Egyptian president, Muhammad Anwar Sadat, who condemned both sides, saw in the Arab split an opportunity to consolidate the Egyptian–Israeli treaty. Ignoring the League's boycott resolution against Egypt, Saddam Hussein approached Cairo for Soviet-made arms and ammunition, and received them. Sadat was only too willing to oblige, seeing the new development as the first sign of a diminution of hostility towards Egypt in the Arab world.

For various reasons King Hussein ibn Talal of Jordan proved to be the most vociferous supporter of Iraq. Before the war his country had been a recipient of generous aid from Baghdad, and he had been aligning himself closely with Iraq, which had been trying to occupy the centre stage in the Arab world. He felt particularly stung by Khomeini's attacks on monarchy. Since his kingdom lacked a Shia minority and was far away from Iran, he felt secure enough to pursue a strong anti-Khomeini line. He expressed solidarity with Iraq in its battle for Arab rights, and moved 40,000 troops to the Iraqi frontier. He allowed Aqaba port, expanded with Iraqi funds, to be used for civilian and military imports for Iraq. According to Tehran, he let the Iraqis use Mafraq air base. Not surprisingly, Iran cut off its links with Jordan in January 1981.

In contrast to King Hussein's flamboyant backing for Baghdad, President Hafiz Assad of Syria offered Iran prudent, yet highly effective, support. His regime had been hostile to Iraq ever since he seized power in November 1970 with a brief period of friendship during 1978–9. His hostility towards Saddam Hussein endeared him to Tehran. Another factor which favoured him was that he belonged to the Alawi sect, a derivative of Shiaism. Assad was the first Arab leader to recognize the Khomeini regime, whose militant anti-imperialism and anti-Zionism appealed to him. As for Tehran, it perceived Syria, the leader of the radical Front of Steadfastness and Confrontation (with Israel), as militantly anti-Zionist.[22]

Following the outbreak of the Gulf War, Damascus Radio condemned Saddam Hussein for starting the wrong war against the wrong enemy at the wrong time. It would exhaust Arab resources, divide Arab ranks and divert their energies from 'the holy battle in Palestine'.[23] The Syrian chief of staff, Hikmat Shihabi, accused Iraq of 'serving imperialism by fighting marginal battles which weaken the Arab Nation's steadfastness'. Soon, with the Kremlin's consent, Syria discreetly airlifted Soviet-made arms and ammunition to hard-pressed Iran by staging flights over Greece, Bulgaria and the USSR.[24] It also provided Tehran with intelligence on Iraq. Syrian warplanes repeatedly violated Iraq's airspace in order to divert the Iraqi air force. In April 1981 Syria apparently co-operated with Iran in the latter's destruction of many Iraqi planes at Walid air base near the Syrian border.

Six months later Iran concluded an arms deal with Syria, a prelude to long-term economic links between the two states. In March 1982 they signed a ten-year trade pact. Over the next five years Iran agreed to sell 100,000 b/d of oil to Syria for cash, and exchange another 14,000 b/d of crude for Syrian phosphates and manufactured goods. Having thus secured its oil needs, Syria closed the Iraqi pipelines passing through its territory on 10 April 1982. Damascus severed all ties with Baghdad, and declared: 'Syria will stand beside the Iraqi people in their struggle to topple the Saddam Hussein regime until they succeed.'[25] Syria thus adopted the same objective as Iran: the overthrow of the Hussein regime.

The other Arab country which airlifted Soviet-made weapons to Iran in October 1980 was Libya. Its leader, Muammar al Qadhafi, was an admirer of the Islamic revolution in Iran and saw the hand of the US in the Iraqi invasion. In a cable to other members of the Arab League he stated, 'Islamic duty dictates that we ally ourselves with the Muslims in Iran in this crusade instead of fighting them on behalf of America.'[26]

With such prominent Arab League members as Syria and Libya openly siding with Iran, it was hard for Saddam Hussein to gain credibility for his view that Iraq was fighting Iran on behalf of the whole Arab world. Matters came to a head in May 1982 when, fearing a massive Iranian offensive to retake Khorramshahr, Saddam Hussein invoked the Arab League's collective security pact to secure military aid from its members, including Egypt. Assad warned that if Egypt fought on the Iraqi side then Syria would line up with Iran, thus dissuading Egypt's new president, Hosni Mubarak, a cautious man, from joining the fray.

Both warring parties shared their borders with Turkey, a member of the North Atlantic Treaty Organization, which provided them with their only overland access to Europe. Therefore Turkey's stance on the war mattered a great deal. It declared itself neutral in the conflict. None the less two important elements gave it a pro-Baghdad tilt. Its Kurdish minority had been up in arms for the past many years in an area contiguous with the Iraqi Kurdish region, and it had been co-operating actively with Baghdad in counter-insurgency. Secondly, as a secular society since 1924, Turkey had much in common with Baathist Iraq, and shared Baghdad's fear of Islamic fundamentalism within its borders.

THE EUROPEAN POWERS

Neutrality in the war was also expressed by the major European powers. Since Britain had been Iran's second largest arms supplier its neutral stance hurt Iran more than Iraq. London even refused to release the weapons and spares – including tanks and tank engines – already paid for by Tehran. In July 1981 there were reports of a London arms dealer having shipped British tank engines to Iran in defiance of the official ban[27] – one of the earliest instances of illicit military supplies from the West to Iran which were later to become endemic. In contrast, Britain's relations with Iraq improved considerably. Following the Iraqi foreign minister's visit to London in March 1981 – the first since 1958 – Iraq concluded a technical and economic agreement with Britain. Later, in

February 1982, Baghdad signed a contract with London for repairs to 50 Chieftain tanks captured from the Iranians on the battlefield.

France applied its declared policies of neutrality and suspension of arms shipments to the combatants one-sidedly. While it refused to deliver even the three missile patrol boats for which Tehran had already paid, it airlifted weapons and spares to Iraq in November 1980. The French foreign minister stated that there was no reason to deny arms to a country like Iraq 'which could always get them somewhere else'.[28] Nothing established the closeness of Iraqi–French ties better than the fact that he received the Iraqi deputy premier, Tariq Aziz, in Paris four times between September 1980 and March 1981. The change-over in the French presidency in May 1981 from the conservative Valéry Giscard d'Estaing to the socialist François Mitterrand made no difference to Iraqi–French relations. Sixty French construction companies had development and other contracts in Iraq, including the building of a nuclear reactor, and France was a prime customer for Iraqi oil. The first batch of the 60 Mirage jet fighters that Iraq had contracted to buy before the war was delivered to Baghdad in January 1981. A year later Iraq placed military orders worth $660 million with France.[29]

Elsewhere, to get round the arms embargo applied to both warring parties, Iraq used its oil customers to act as intermediaries to buy arms and spares. In the first 18 months of the war it spent at least $2000 million on missiles from Brazil, light tanks from Austria, Roland surface-to-surface missiles from France, and jet aircraft and infantry fighting vehicles from Spain.[30]

THE SUPERPOWERS

Being equipped with mainly American weapons, the Iranian government had to continue procuring US-made arms and spare parts. Through the office of Sadiq Tabtabai, a former deputy premier, in West Germany, it set up a network in Western Europe, Dubai, Singapore and Hong Kong to obtain the necessary weapons and spares. Customs checks in such places as Amsterdam, Singapore and Hong Kong were so lax that it was easy to redirect consignments arriving from the US or Canada straight on to Iran without any inspection. Even during the period of American economic boycott of Iran (from April 1980 to January 1981) there was no ban on the export of food, medicines and agricultural machinery from the US to Iran. One American company regularly sent goods marked 'tractor engines' from Boston to Tehran for two years until a customs inspector with a military background, noticing that the machines were equipped with superchargers, discovered that they were replacement engines for US-manufactured M-60 tanks.[31]

With the Iranians in the market for buying US-made weapons and spares, those countries possessing the same military hardware had a chance to play a role. Vietnam was one such country, Israel another. Israel had all along followed a strategic policy of befriending the periphery of the Arab world, a stance that had led it in the past to assist among others the Marxist regime in Ethiopia. Iran was another example. Whether under the Shah or Ayatollah Khomeini, it was seen as a non-Arab state and therefore worth cultivating. Once Iran was locked in a bloody war with Iraq – seen as a staunch enemy still technically at war with Israel[32] – the Jewish state attempted to keep the hostilities going by supplying much-needed spares to Iran through private arms dealers. During 1981 and 1982 Israel supplied from its own stocks arms and spares worth $50–70 million, and procured a further $50–100 millions-worth of spare parts and ammunition from Western European sources, for the middlemen acting for Iran.[33]

As for Iran, its premier, Mir Hussein Musavi, expressed his preference for buying arms and spares in the open market to avoid 'dependence on the East or the West'.[34] Therefore Tehran combined its efforts to refurbish its stocks of Western-made weapons and ammunition with purchases from non-Western sources. It built up its stores of Soviet-manufactured arms and ammunition from its Arab allies – Syria and Libya – as well as North Korea, East Germany and Cuba, which were eager to buy Iranian oil. Indeed, in February 1982 the Iranian foreign minister confirmed that his country had made small purchases of arms and ammunition from the USSR.[35] This happened at the time of the signing of an economic protocol between the neighbours whereby the Soviets contracted to expand the existing steel plants in Iran and construct a new hydro-electric dam. The two-way trade in 1981–2 exceeded $1 billion, a record.

But Moscow did not want to befriend Tehran at the expense of its close links with Baghdad. As it was, its trade with Iraq in mid-1982 was running at only one-third the rate for Baghdad–Washington trade at $1 billion a year.[36] Earlier that year the Reagan administration had decided to clear the sale of 'civilian' transport aircraft to Baghdad. This worried

Moscow, since it held out the possibility of a major alternative source of Western weapons for Iraq apart from France.

By June 1982 the situation on the battlefield had altered dramatically, with the possibility of Iran invading Iraq looming large on the horizon. The Kremlin urged restraint on Tehran. At the same time it showed itself amenable to resuming arms deliveries to Baghdad should Iran attack Iraq, and said as much to Tariq Aziz during his visit to Moscow. The reasons for this change were threefold: Article 8 of the 1972 Friendship Treaty specified that the signatories were to 'continue to develop co-operation in the strengthening of their defence capacity'; Iraq had repeatedly expressed its willingness to settle the conflict through talks; and Iran continued to paint the USSR with the same brush as the US, treating them both as equally threatening.[37] Moreover, Moscow felt that it would be easier to deal with a chastened Baghdad than with a triumphant Tehran with all the consequences of destabilization that an Iranian victory would cause in the region.

Moscow was consistent in its policy towards the Gulf War. It viewed the warring states as anti-imperialist, deplored the conflict between them, and wanted to see it end. Concurrently it wanted to meet its obligations towards Iraq under the 1972 Friendship Treaty but not at the expense of abandoning cordial relations with Iran. Washington pursued the opposite line. Having encouraged the war – if only as a device to secure the release of its hostages in Iran and weaken the hostile Khomeini regime – it ensured that it would remain localized and leave navigation in the Gulf undisturbed. Once this was achieved it was content to let the belligerents slug it out. US officials knew that as long as the hostilities went on Iran would be in continued urgent need of American arms and spares, thus providing them with opportunities to influence Iran's policies.

But Ayatollah Khomeini was impervious to pressures from either superpower, determined to show Iranians and others that his republic, deriving its inspiration and strength from Islam, was truly independent and self-reliant. In contrast, Saddam Hussein's Iraq became more and more dependent on outside forces. It relied increasingly on the Gulf monarchies for financial subventions, put (by Tariq Aziz) at $18–20 billion by the end of 1981, to conduct the war.[38] Diplomatically too it came to rely increasingly on the superpowers. In his radio broadcast on 20 June 1982 Saddam Hussein said, 'It is strange that the superpowers ... made no tangible effort to stop the war ... raging in one of the most dangerous and vital regions of the world.' It was in the same speech that he announced the unilateral withdrawal of Iraqi troops from Iranian territory, thus inadvertently conceding the moral wrong he had committed by attacking Iran in the first place.

4 EMBATTLED IRAQ

Having recaptured the lost Iranian territory in four major offensives from September 1981 to May 1982, Iran's Supreme Defence Council debated the merits and demerits of taking the war into Iraq.

The doves argued that attacking Iraq would destroy much of the popular sympathy Iran had aroused in Muslim countries as a victim of Baghdad's aggression, and undermine the Islamic Republic's moral standing. They were backed by professional military officers on the Council. In order to seize Iraqi land, they reasoned, Iran needed more heavy weaponry, warplanes and logistical support than it possessed. The hawks argued that these limitations could be overcome by deploying large numbers of fighters imbued with revolutionary Islamic zeal and by appealing to Iraqi Shias to rebel against the infidel regime of Saddam Hussein. They buttressed their case with two practical considerations: to silence the Iraqi artillery which had been pounding Iranian civilian areas since the beginning of the conflict, and to capture Iraqi oilfields near the border for use as bargaining counters for securing war reparations from Baghdad.

The argument to move into Iraq to knock out the Iraqi artillery was much too emotion-laden to be set aside easily. More importantly, there was a feeling among political leaders that the national unity forged in the face of the war would start to crumble once a ceasefire was agreed. Finally, the economy was in a good shape, with oil revenue rising sharply. Little wonder that the hawkish view prevailed.

On 9 July 1982 Rafsanjani listed the Iranian conditions for a ceasefire: retaining the 1975 Iran–Iraq Treaty; repatriation of over 100,000 Iraqi citizens expelled by the Baghdad government; placing of war guilt on Iraq; payment of $100 billion to Tehran for war damages; and punishment of Saddam Hussein as a war criminal.

The prospect of Iran attacking Iraq disturbed both superpowers. They had been neutral in the conflict and wanted it ended, a sentiment that was shared by others in the international community. Reflecting this, the UN Security Council passed a resolution on 12 July 1982 calling for a ceasefire and a withdrawal of the warring forces to the international border.

Tehran rejected the resolution. The next day, the beginning of the holy month of Ramadan, it launched an offensive named Ramadan al Mubarak, the Blessed Ramadan, on the southern front. With it the nature of the conflict changed.

Iran was no longer fighting to expel the Iraqi aggressor: now it was the invader. This marked the fourth phase of the Gulf War, the earlier phases being the Iraqi advance into Iran (until late March 1981), the stalemate (until mid-March 1982), and the Iraqi retreat from Iran (until the end of June 1982).

The Iranians made a resolute effort to capture Basra, the second largest Iraqi city with about a million people and a Shia majority. The Iraqi defences consisted of earthworks and trenches, followed by minefields, barbed wire fences and well-placed machine-gun and artillery positions. But by deploying five divisions the Iranian commanders were able to break through Iraqi defence lines, and penetrate up to ten miles into Iraq about ten miles north of Basra. Iraq staged an immediate counter-offensive with four divisions. Thus some 130,000 troops were locked into the largest infantry fighting since the Second World War. Faced with spirited Iraqi resistance and swampy conditions, Tehran's forces – weakened by large losses in men and armour, and handicapped by long supply lines – became bogged down. At the end of a week of fighting the Iraqis managed to drive the Iranians back, although not to the border proper.

Determined to succeed, the Iranian commanders mounted another major offensive on 22 July. This time their troops advanced five miles into Iraq. Once again their air cover, armour and logistical backing proved inadequate to withstand the subsequent Iraqi counterattack. But this did not deter Tehran from launching one more major assault on 28 July. It too was thwarted by the Iraqis.

The two weeks of intense fighting ended in stalemate. Having at one point occupied 120 square miles of Iraqi territory, Iran had to give up all but 32 square miles – a strip ten miles long and 'a few miles wide. However, Basra was now within range of the Iranian artillery. Tehran also gained diplomatically.

Intense fighting on Iraqi soil led the preparatory committee of the Non-Aligned Movement to move the venue of the seventh summit conference from Baghdad to Delhi.[1] If the conference had been held in Baghdad in September 1982 as scheduled, and chaired by Saddam Hussein, he would have become the leader of the 97-member Non-

Aligned Movement for the next three years, boosting Iraq's diplomatic standing in the Third World at the expense of Iran.

However, for these modest gains Iran paid a heavy price in casualties. Independent observers put the number of Iranians killed, wounded or captured during the three weeks of hostilities at 1000 a day. In contrast, Iraqi losses were put by official Iranian sources at 7000 killed or injured, and 1400 taken captive.[2]

For various reasons Iraq performed well. It was adequately prepared because Iran had (out of overconfidence) virtually broadcast in advance the date of its major offensive. On the battlefield Iran's revolutionary guards proved more vulnerable to enemy ambushes than professional soldiers. Owing to poor leadership and insufficient experience the guards failed to time precisely their infantry attacks. Because of lack of spares Tehran's one and only armoured division failed to perform optimally. (Overall, the Iranians had only about 900 tanks to Iraq's 3000.) The same was true of Iran's air force, particularly of its ground attack F-4 contingent, given the F-4's unusually high maintenance requirements. Even those combat planes which could fly often had erratic avionics and air-to-air missiles; and this made them unsuitable for aerial dogfights. With Tehran now possessing only about 120 airworthy jet fighters (to Baghdad's 300), and 900 heavy artillery pieces (to Baghdad's 1800), Iran had lost its earlier superiority over Iraq in air power and artillery.[3] This imbalance began to manifest itself in Iran's poor performance on the battlefield. The Iraqis were well entrenched, and knew the terrain and the people intimately. Since they were now fighting a defensive war on their home ground their morale was high.

The Shia fifth column, which Saddam Hussein dreaded and Ayatollah Khomeini desired, failed to materialize. Like the Iraqi leaders' predictions about the Iranian Arabs of Khuzistan in the summer of 1980, officials in Tehran had visualized popular uprisings against the Baghdad government by Shias when Iran's 'Islamic combatants' marched towards Basra. To encourage such an outcome, Hojatalislam Baqir Hakim – the much revered Iraqi Shia leader living in exile in Tehran – had crossed the international border with the Iranian forces, and exhorted co-religionists to rise up against Saddam Hussein. But neither this nor Khomeini's calls for rebellion against the Iraqi president had worked. Facing a foreign invader Iraqi Shias behaved in the same way as Iranian Arabs and Kurds had done in September 1980: they rallied round their government. They shared the fears of Iraqi Sunnis that an Iranian occupation of their homeland would be a national dishonour and cause a violent disruption of their lives.

But to mobilize Iraqis proved to be an uphill task for Saddam Hussein. His decision to withdraw troops unilaterally from Iran had brought many Iraqi urban centres into the Iranian artillery range. This aroused criticism in certain sections of the military and civilian establishment. He found it necessary to justify his decision publicly. 'The feelings of the soldier while defending his land are different from his feelings when defending his rights and lands 80 km inside enemy territories,' he explained.[4]

There was the practical problem of manpower shortage on the front. The successive Iranian onslaughts reduced the Iraqi army by a third from its peak of 210,000 in March 1982. In order to maintain popular morale and the war effort, the government decided in late June to stop announcing battlefield casualties. Another problem that needed to be tackled was the unacceptable level of desertions. The government came up with a multi-track policy to solve these interlinked issues. It attempted to reduce desertions by promulgating a decree in early June which stated: 'Those who committed the crimes of desertion or absence [of more than five days] or failure to rejoin their units shall be punished by execution.'[5] It tried to increase its military strength by withdrawing exemptions given to certain groups – college graduates and those who had been discharged from the armed forces – and calling up all volunteers and conscripts. It vigorously pursued the policy of opening up the Popular Army – conceived and spawned as the Baath Party militia as a counterforce to the military – to non-Baathists. To buttress the Popular Army, voluntary special task brigades were established. Of the 400,000 men in the Popular Army in early 1982, more than 55,000 were deployed at the front line on a rota basis.

Successful blunting of the Iranian offensives of July 1982 provided a breathing space for Saddam Hussein to re-form and reinforce the Iraqi war machine. He expanded the air force and the armoured corps, and channelled the most competent Baathist officers into their command structure. At the same time he began treating Baathist and non-Baathist officers on a par when it came to promotion. It was along these lines that during the summer of 1982 the Iraqi president implemented a major reshuffle of the armed forces command. By obtaining advanced weaponry from France he bolstered military morale.

What further raised fighting spirit, and curtailed desertions, was the fact that once combat shifted away from the soil of the Islamic Republic of Iran, Iraqi Shia troops lost the physical and psychological grounds for defection. To consolidate this situation Saddam Hussein initiated an intensive programme of 're-education' for the ranks and officers.

He combined these moves with frequent visits to the front line to stress his leadership role and supervise the field commanders at close quarters. He initiated an active policy of reward and punishment for military officers with the overall objective of bringing them under his direct control. Before he had assumed the presidency in mid-1979 the military establishment had been beholden to President Bakr who was a career army officer. Lacking formal training in warfare, Saddam Hussein had been suspicious of professional military men. In the wake of battlefield setbacks he was quick to punish those officers who had performed poorly due to an inadequate grasp of military theory and fieldcraft, lack of proper training, low morale in the ranks, or failure to learn from past mistakes. Conversely, he was generous to those who offered stiff resistance to Iranian incursions into Iraq by taking up forward positions, or inspiring their subordinates with patriotic words or brave actions. By pursuing these policies Saddam Hussein succeeded in securing the loyalty of a large majority of military leaders, as well as denying any chance to upper-level commanders to settle with Tehran directly by agreeing to his removal from the presidential palace.

Saddam Hussein dealt summarily with dissidents in the Baath Party. In the wake of Baghdad's military defeats in the spring and summer of 1982 some Baathist leaders called for the reinstatement of Bakr as president. This angered Hussein because Bakr's return would have signalled the ascendancy of the orthodox wing of the party over the pragmatic faction which he headed. Following the Ninth Regional Congress of the Baath Party in late June 1982, and the failed assassination attempt on him in mid-July, the portraits of Bakr – which had continued to be displayed in public places along with Saddam Hussein's – were removed. Riyad Ibrahim Hussein, health minister and a vocal proponent of Bakr, was dismissed from his job in June 1982 and executed in mid-October, some days after the (natural) death of Bakr – puportedly for importing a medicine which proved fatal to the injured.[6]

Having failed to capture Basra, Iran resorted to shelling it. In reply Saddam Hussein opted for an offensive posture in the Gulf proper. On 12 August 1982 he declared the northern end of the Gulf – demarcated by a line 30 nautical miles east of Kuwait City and running down the middle of the waterway – a 'maritime exclusion zone'. The Iranian ports and offshore installations as well as vessels in this zone thus became legitimate targets for the Iraqis. As Baghdad had no operating oil facilities in the region it did not risk reciprocal attacks by Tehran. It therefore felt free to raid Iranian ships, Bandar Khomeini port and the Kharg oil terminal. Its actions caused a temporary drop in Iranian oil exports from 2 million to 800,000 b/d.[7]

It was against this background that Saddam Hussein attended the summit conference of the Arab League on 11 September 1982 in Fez, Morocco. He strengthened Baghdad's diplomatic position by subscribing to the Saudi King Fahd's peace plan adopted by the conferees: a ceasefire during the imminent hajj pilgrimage season, complete evacuation of Iranian territory by Iraq, and compensation of $70 billion to Iran through the Islamic Reconstruction Fund to be financed by the Gulf states. In contrast, Tehran summarily rejected the terms of the Arab summit. It considered itself strong enough to evict the Iraqis from its soil in the central and northern sectors.

On 1 October 1982 Iran mounted an offensive – named Muslim ibn Aqil after Imam Hussein's younger brother – on the central front near the Sumar Hills overlooking Mandali, 65 miles north-east of the Iraqi capital. This time Iran's target was Baghdad. It deployed 50,000 to 70,000 troops. On 5 October the UN Security Council called for an end to the hostilities and mutual withdrawals from the occupied territories. Iraq accepted the ceasefire proviso of the resolution; Iran rejected it outright. Once again Tehran tried to compensate for its deficiency in armour and combat planes needed to penetrate Iraqi defence lines by resorting to human wave assaults. The result was bloody, with the Iranians all the worse for it. Their commanders attempted to overstretch the Iraqis by activating the southern front near Basra, but Baghdad had enough troops in place in the area to blunt the Iranian thrust.

Undeterred, Tehran mounted a second major offensive on Mandali on 10 October. This time its forces entered the town; but, lacking adequate air, armour and logistical backing, they failed to retain it. The net gain made by them was 60 square miles of Iranian territory.

Iraq tried to get even with Iran. Later in the month it fired Scud-B surface-to-surface missiles at Dezful, killing 21 people. Its aircraft raided Kharg Island and Iranian tankers. Consisting mostly of sheltered and buried facilities, and equipped with dense anti-aircraft and surface-to-surface missiles, Kharg was a hard target to damage. Thanks to the limitations of the range and ammunition of Iraq's Mirage and MiG warplanes, and the lack of skill and daring of its pilots, Baghdad failed to hurt Kharg's oil installations seriously. Often the Iraqi pilots would drop their ammunition offshore rather than risk infiltrating Kharg's formidable air defences.[8]

Disregarding the rainy season, Tehran launched another offensive codenamed Muharram al Harram, the Holy Muharram, on the night of 31 October–1 November along two fronts: in the oil-bearing areas of Naft-e Shah in the central sector and Tib, to the south, in the Musian area. Khomeini personally backed the drive. In a speech on 31 October he said: 'War can be as holy as prayer when it is fought for the sake of defending Islam.'[9]

Tehran deployed four army divisions as well as several divisions of revolutionary guards and Basij militia. To offset the Iraqi advantage in air power and artillery, the Iranian infantry, backed by tanks about 800 yards to the rear, attacked the Iraqi positions in large numbers. Despite the virtual absence of Iranian jet fighters, which gave an almost free rein to Iraq's large warplane and helicopter force, the Iranians achieved a tactical breakthrough. They strained the enemy to the extent that the Iraqi high command was compelled to fall back on its last reserves: an army corps stationed south of the capital and two under-strength brigades in the northern oilfields. The Iraqi forces resorted to using the military supplies, including advanced T-72 tanks, as soon as they arrived from the Soviet Union, which had resumed its shipments to Baghdad in the wake of the Iranian invasion. They suffered a substantial loss of warplanes and helicopters owing to the extensive use of anti-aircraft guns and Sam-7s by their antagonists.

In the central sector the Iranians captured the Bayat oilfield and seriously threatened Mandali. Further south they broke the enemy lines and penetrated 6 miles into Iraq, seizing 50 oilwells on the way to Tib. With this reverse the situation became critical in Baghdad.

In Iraqi ruling circles pressure mounted on Saddam Hussein to accede to Tehran's prime demand and give up power in order to prevent a massive invasion by Iran, and bring the war to an end. But he was in no mood to step down. On 9 November he bravely proposed referendums in Iran and Iraq to determine who was more popular in his own country: Khomeini or Saddam Hussein. The next day he declared that Iran was trying to overthrow the Baghdad regime not because 'a certain person [i.e. himself] was in the regime' but because it wanted to 'control all of Iraq'.[10] On 13 November an informal referendum materialized in Baghdad when reportedly some four million people participated in huge demonstrations. Carrying pictures of Saddam Hussein, the marchers shouted, 'Yes, yes, Saddam / This is the referendum.' In response the Iraqi leader said, 'I am staying even if [the war] lasts for another 10 years. I consider this condition [by Iran] as silly and it should be trampled under my foot.'[11] These events had an uplifting impact on the Iraqi forces at the front. They succeeded in retaking Tib. Yet, overall, they lost 330 square miles to Tehran, including 120 square miles of Iranian land, as a result of Iran's latest offensives.

In October 1982, after two years of war, independent observers put the number of dead Iraqi soldiers at 40,000. The figure for Tehran's regular troops, according to an Iranian source, was about 50,000. This excluded the number of revolutionary guards and Basij militia killed.[12]

Having frustrated the Iranian attempt to advance to Baghdad, and succeeded in mounting an impressive show of popular support for himself in the capital, Saddam Hussein tried to consolidate his position further. In January 1983 he published the authorized version of the proceedings of the Ninth Regional Congress of the Baath Party held seven months earlier.

The report was remarkable in more ways than one. It differed substantially both in the subjects covered and in content from the preliminary texts published at the end of the congress. While making no mention whatsoever of either Bakr or Aflaq it portrayed Saddam Hussein as the leading figure of the party since the 1968 coup. It thus put the stamp of approval on the pragmatic line advocated by him and put to rest the orthodox line as represented by Bakr.

It scuttled the objective of Arab unity, one of the primary elements of Baathism. 'The question of linking unity to the removal of boundaries is no longer acceptable to the present Arab mentality,' Saddam Hussein declared. 'It could have been acceptable 10 or 20 years ago . . . The Arab reality is that the Arabs are now 22 states, and we have to behave accordingly.'[13] Stress on pan-Arabism gave way to Iraqi nationalism, which became all the more significant in view of the war. The exigencies of the hostilities with Iran were used to impress on the public sector the need not to hinder private enterprise, which in turn was exhorted to fill the deficiency left by the public sector due to the war. Thus socialism, another leading element of Baathism, was downgraded.

Once the report and Saddam Hussein's guidelines on party activities were out, he encouraged members to hold meetings and adopt both documents. It was announced that the members, apprentices and supporters of the Baath totalled a million, and that they were all required to join the Popular Army.

The Iraqi president used the occasion to call on party and state to provide an opening to the masses. He took the initiative by making himself available to the public on the telephone at certain well-publicized times, holding weekly meetings and travelling all over the country. The media too were instructed to provide channels for complaints about bureaucratic lethargy, high prices or the failings of the welfare system. All this was part of Saddam Hussein's plan to divert popular criticism away from himself and the war on to the ubiquitous bureaucracy, and give his administration an aura of democracy.

There was much need for such an approach. The war, which had been expected to yield victory to Iraq in three weeks, was now in its third year with no end in sight.

THE WAR IN 1983

One of the salient features of the Gulf War was that while Iran had by and large limited its air raids to military and economic targets, Iraq had not been so discriminating. In late December 1982, for instance, Baghdad claimed to have mounted 74 air raids on targets in Khuzistan in a single day. Then fighting flared up on the southern front, and on 18 January 1983 Iraq reported 66 bombing missions in the region. It renewed attacks on 26 January and continued them for five days. By then Iraq had lost 117 warplanes,[14] but because it had been taking delivery of military aircraft from France, and had been receiving Chinese-made MiG-19s and MiG-21s from Egypt, it had maintained its total of combat aircraft around the pre-war strength of 332.

In contrast, Iran had failed to procure warplanes owing to the strict ban maintained by the aircraft manufacturing states. Losses in the war, and the lack of spares for its American-made fighter planes, had reduced Iran's airworthy military aircraft to about a quarter of its pre-war size of 440-plus. Iran was therefore compelled to use its warplanes mainly for defensive purposes: protection of airfields, oilfields and installations, refineries and important cities.

Because of lack of adequate air cover for its ground forces, Tehran's offensives resulted in heavy casualties. This was particularly true of the offensive of 7 February 1983 in the Fakeh region of Khuzistan, code-named Wa al Fajr, By the Dawn. Its aim was to capture the strategic Basra–Baghdad highway near Amara, the capital of Misan province. Tehran deployed six divisions, or about 100,000 troops, which crossed the border at Fakeh and penetrated many miles into Iraq. But the Iraqi forces, led by Major-General Hisham Sabah Fakhri, commander of the Fourth Army Corps stationed in the Basra region, stopped the Iranian drive. They made extensive use of warplanes and helicopter gunships and succeeded in pushing back the enemy troops, inflicting heavy losses on them. Rafsanjani, who had described the offensive as 'the final move towards ending the war', rationalized the setback thus: 'It is in Iranian interests to spare enemy soldiers who are to serve the future Islamic Republic of Iraq.'[15] The final Iranian gain was modest: the recovery of 100 square miles of its own territory. Major-General Fakhri's achievement had a tonic effect on the Iraqi armed forces. It helped them to recover their much shaken confidence. Indeed, in late March 1983 Iraq launched an offensive near Miqdadiya in the central sector, something it had not done for two years. But Iran had no difficulty in repulsing it.

On 10 April 1983 Iran staged its second offensive in the region, codenamed Wa al Fajr-One, west of Ein Khosh, again with a view to seizing the Basra–Baghdad highway. Iraq countered the Iranian move with a massive force aided by warplanes and attack helicopters, inflicting heavy losses. After a week's fighting Rafsanjani conceded that Iran's progress had been slow. 'I don't consider the time ripe to tell the nation what had taken place,' he said. 'Our forces crossed the enemy lines and then returned to positions more easily defensible.'[16] Tehran's new front line included the freshly recovered Iranian territory of 60 square miles, but this still left Iraq in possession of 330 square miles of Iranian land in scattered pockets along the international border.

Iran's repeated failures stemmed from a variety of factors. There was a continued paucity of sophisticated weaponry. Then there was a profound and debilitating difference between the thinking of the military planners and their revolutionary guards counterparts. Professional army officers believed in meticulous planning of the offensives: sufficient training of the forces, robust logistic build-up and limited tactical objectives. In contrast, the revolutionary guards commanders and clerical leaders stressed the virtues of deploying volunteers imbued with revolutionary fervour, exercising surprise, innovation and human wave tactics.

On the whole the revolutionary guards' view prevailed. The problem was that their commanders had not yet mastered the professional army technique of maintaining sufficient resupplies of men and weapons. Enthusiastic advance units forged ahead without a proper plan for succeeding waves to replace them as they reached the point of collapse out of sheer physical and mental exhaustion. In their zeal, the Islamic combatants left the overrun enemy positions undermanned. Consequently, once the counterattacking Iraqis had broken the Iranian front line, they had little difficulty in retaking most of their lost positions. In a sense, the revolutionary guards behaved like a large-scale guerrilla force, adept at harassing and exhausting enemy troops rather than overrunning and securing their territory.

On top of this the Iranians had to cope with an unusual and unprecedented factor: the deployment of US intelligence satellites over the battle regions. The information from these sources was made available to Iraq through Saudi Arabia. Not only did this enable Baghdad to make adequate preparations to meet any impending Iranian threat, but it also inhibited Iranian commanders from following the normal tactics of troop concentration before an offensive, thus severely impairing the efficiency of their forces.

Despite its failure to capture Basra, storm Baghdad, or cut off the Basra–Baghdad road, the Iranian Supreme Defence Council showed no sign of giving up the struggle. Its mood in June 1983 was summed up in the words: 'Now that we have come thus far we must persevere, resist and make sacrifices to rid the region of this [Baathist] cancer or [at least] weaken it to teach others a lesson.'[17] But the Council was now prepared to consider modifying its strategy of staging grand offensives at specific points. It saw merit in building up pressure against Iraq all along the border with a view to overstretching its resources, and so inducing the collapse of the Baathist regime. Also, by waging a staggered war of attrition it expected to reduce Iranian losses in men and materials, and incur these over a long period. A corollary of the new thinking was to do something dramatic to upset Baghdad's strategic and logistic concepts, and thus unbalance its war machine.

With this strategy in view, and the more specific objective of retaking the lost Iranian territory, Iran mounted an offensive, codenamed Wa al Fajr-Two, on 22 July 1983 along the route from Piranshahr in Iran to

Rawandoz in Iraq. The rebellious Iraqi Kurds, belonging to the Kurdish Democratic Party, and armed Iraqi Shias, Al Mujahedin, fought along-side Tehran's troops. The KDP's intimate knowledge of the local people, language and terrain was a great asset to the joint forces. They marched nine miles into Iraq, and captured Mount Karman and the garrison town of Hajj Umran.

Baghdad launched a counteroffensive, but failed to dislodge the enemy. In such mountainous terrain the Iraqis could not use tanks. Their air raids, even when mounted from helicopter gunships, were ineffective since the opposing infantry had ample cover. Finally, the Iranian side found the high ridges an ideal setting for ambushing the counterattacking Iraqi troops. Altogether Tehran secured 150 square miles, half of them in Iraq. By so doing it also cut off Iraqi supplies to the Iranian Kurdish insurgents.

Iranian officials allowed the Tehran-based Supreme Assembly of Islamic Revolution in Iraq to open offices in Hajj Umran. Formed in November 1982 with the primary assistance of Al Daawa, the Mujahe-din Movement and the Islamic Action Organization, the SAIRI, was led by Hojatalislam Baqir Hakim, a 39-year-old cleric with a long history of resistance to the Iraqi Baath regime. Arrested in 1972 and 1977 during the Shia riots, he was sentenced to life imprisonment. When he was released in an amnesty in 1980 he escaped to Iran. The SAIRI set up the armed force called Al Mujahedin, consisting of volunteers from among Iraqi exiles and prisoners of war, and despatched them to the front. By letting it establish its presence on Iraqi soil, Tehran wished to give succour to Iraqi opposition which was then in disarray.

On 30 July 1983 Iran staged the Wal al Fajr-Three offensive west of Mehran in the central sector. Its forces advanced six miles into Iraq. Fierce fighting ensued, with the counterattacking Iraqis mounting 150 air sorties daily. Yet Iran managed to retain 60 square miles of territory, half of it inside Iraq.

The relentless attacks by Iran had a demoralizing effect on the Iraqi president. To forestall any moves towards his overthrow he redoubled his efforts to bolster the personality cult. His forty-sixth birthday on 28 April 1983 was made an occasion for exhibitions, demonstrations and public celebrations, a joyous feast designed to deflect popular attention away from the grimness of the war which had by then claimed 200,000 casualties in a country of about 14 million nationals.[18] Some of the adulation, no doubt, was genuine. After all Saddam Hussein had shown extraordinary resolve in adverse circumstances, daring, tenacity and robust leadership. Through these populist manoeuvres he demonstrated to the military and party leaders that above and beyond the backing they offered him he had a firm base in the Iraqi public at large.

But none of this made an iota of difference to the Islamic leadership in Tehran or to his staunch domestic adversaries in the armed forces and elsewhere. The discovery in early 1983 of an assassination plot against him by certain military officers showed the persistence of murderous opposition to him in the defence services.

Interestingly enough, in May his stepbrother Barzan Tikriti published a highly publicized book, *Assassination Attempts on the Life of President Saddam Hussein*, listing seven attempts on the Iraqi president's life, excluding the one at Dujayal. By so doing Saddam Hussein stressed the efficiency of Iraqi intelligence and warned those currently plotting against him. The significance of the secret services, already high, had risen sharply with the outbreak of the war. Secondly, since these 'plots' were more in the nature of intra-party scheming rather than serious murder attempts, the book gave Saddam Hussein a chance to get even with his past and present adversaries. Finally, the book helped to direct popular anger at the plotters, and aroused sympathy for the president.

It prepared the people to understand why their 'struggler leader' had to limit his public appearances, skipping even the annual celebration of the Baathist coup on 17 July. During the summer and autumn of 1983 – a period of acute economic, political and military crisis – Saddam Hussein curtailed his visits to the battlefronts, often limiting himself to the inspection of air bases, since they were an integral part of the air force, a crucial wing of the armed forces.

Militarily, the only area where the initiative lay with Saddam Hussein was in the Gulf. Here Iraq's naval exclusion zone in the Upper Gulf remained in force. In the first half of December 1982 the Iraqis claimed to have sunk six Iranian merchant and naval vessels in the Bandar–Khomeini–Kharg region, most probably by using French-made heat-seeking Exocet air-to-ship missiles fired from helicopter gunships. The following month Iraq hit the Nowruz oil rig in the northern Gulf, causing an oil slick. In February and March 1983, when Iran staged land offensives, Iraq mounted naval and air strikes against Bandar Khomeini, damaging Iranian installations. Both sides lost war vessels.

As the third anniversary of the war approached, Iraq and France tried to dissuade Tehran from mounting yet another offensive in the north.

They did so by exaggerating the threat to the Kharg oil terminal by the five Super-Etendard planes and Exocet missiles about to be delivered to Baghdad. Khomeini responded with a counter-threat. 'It should be announced to the world and emphasized that if they [the major powers] continue to help Saddam [Hussein], their hands will be cut off from oil resources,' he said in a speech on 19 September. 'If they help Saddam to attack our economic resources, they will not see any more oil.'[19]

Iran moved its elite troops to Larak, Henqin and Sirri Islands in the Hormuz Straits, and increased its artillery and anti-aircraft guns on Qeshm and Greater Tunb Islands. On average 50 departing ships sailed through Hormuz daily, including 20 tankers carrying eight million b/d, amounting to one-fifth of the non-Communist world's consumption. Two-thirds of Japanese oil imports and a quarter of West European imports passed through Hormuz. Not surprisingly, France rushed emergency military supplies worth $500 million – including Exocet missiles, fragmentation bombs and anti-tank missiles – to Iraq. Bahrain put its security forces on alert. Qatar closed its borders to all foreigners. Oman moved its troops to Ras Masandam facing the Hormuz Straits.

The Khomeini regime, which issued a warning to the world about oil supplies, was more secure in power than ever before. In February 1982 the Iranian security forces dealt the Mujahedin-e Khalq a near-fatal blow when in a raid they killed the party's central committee members. Two months later the government uncovered a plot involving 70 military officers and a former foreign minister, Sadiq Qutbzadeh. The officers were tried secretly by a military court, but Qutbzadeh was put on television where he confessed his crime. He was executed on 15 September. This marked a dramatic end to the co-option by the Islamic regime of lay Iranian intellectuals who, during their residence in the West, had been active in the Islamic anti-Shah movement abroad. With this the civilian and military establishments in Iran became more ideologically homogeneous.

Iran accelerated the Islamization programme which it had initiated earlier. In late May 1982 the cabinet approved comprehensive plans to bring the current penal and legal codes, civil law, trade law and registration of documents and land in line with Islamic law. In August the government declared all secular laws null and void.

Islamization in the military and the Revolutionary Guards Corps was intensified. The political-ideological department, manned by clerics, was complemented by personnel from the Islamic guidance ministry and voluntary Islamic Associations. The function of the former was to inform and educate the ranks and officers about the Islamic nature of the current policies and decisions of the government. The Islamic Associations, existing in all units of combat forces, consisted of pious Muslims concerned with raising their religious consciousness, safeguarding the security and well-being of their unit, and keeping a watchful eye on possible dissidents and 'hypocrites' – i.e., people who while professing to be good Muslims followed a secular ideology.

Ideological cohesion aided the Iranian leadership to improve working relationships between the Revolutionary Guards Corps and the military. The organization of the guards in the form of battalions helped, too. These were either allowed to function independently or integrated into army brigades.

The Revolutionary Guards Corps, estimated as 150,000 strong in 1982, was equally active on the domestic front, and acted as the regime's prime agency to stamp out the armed opposition spearheaded by the Mujahedin-e Khalq. Since the Mujahedin were active in the Farsi-speaking heartland of Iran they had caused the most severe turmoil since the revolution. The Islamic regime surmounted the challenge – which lasted from July 1981 to September 1982 – by using unrestrained force and propaganda. With war against Iraq raging along the border, the government convincingly labelled those creating disorder at home as unpatriotic agents of Baghdad. Its efforts received a boost when the Mujahedin leader, Masud Rajavi, publicly met the Iraqi deputy premier, Tariq Aziz, in Paris on 9 January 1983.

In a wider, more positive context the Khomeini regime transformed patriotic feelings into a sustained drive for self-sufficiency, and was particularly successful in bringing Iranian oil output to the full quota of 2.4 million b/d fixed by OPEC. By painting the war in Islamic colours, Iranian leaders were able to galvanize the nation as well as raise Islamic consciousness in the country. They had thus turned the tide on the battlefront, and put Iraq on the defensive. In turn this increased the Islamic regime's popularity at home. On the other hand numerous instances of indiscriminate violence used by the Tehran government against its opponents tarnished its image in the region. The Iraqi regime was quick to exploit this, and did so effectively, implanting in the minds of its citizens the image of mad mullahs violently persecuting their own people.

Once the Iranian administration had successfully met the armed challenge of the Mujahedin, it felt confident enough to relax its iron fist. In December 1982 Khomeini issued an eight-point decree, entitled 'Islamization of Judiciary', designed to protect 'the dignity and honour of individuals'. It outlawed arbitrary searches and arrests, and stressed that citizens were to be judged only by their present deeds without any reference to their past actions. One of the main reasons behind the decree was to reassure the middle and upper classes at home, and encourage affluent and professional Iranian expatriates to return, in order to reduce the shortage of skilled personnel and help rebuild the economy.

Among the political groups which were allowed to function was the Tudeh (i.e., Masses) Party, which believed in Marxism–Leninism and the socialist system as existing in the Soviet Union. It supported the revolution at home and accepted Khomeini as the national leader. So long as hostilities were being conducted on Iranian soil, Tudeh backed the war effort. However, in July 1982, when government officials were weighing the pros and cons of marching into Iraq, the Tudeh Party journal warned that an Iranian invasion of Iraq would be detrimental to the future of the Islamic Republic. The government's attitude towards Tudeh hardened.

Relations between the regime and Tudeh soured as Moscow resumed arms supplies to Baghdad in the late summer of 1982. Among the weapons received by Baghdad were Frog-7 surface-to-surface missiles with a range of 75 miles. In April 1983 Iraq fired a few of these missiles on Dezful, apparently intending to hit the nearby Vahidyeh air base. Instead they struck civilian areas and killed 67 people. This led the government in Tehran to dissolve the Tudeh Party on 4 May. During the next month the authorities arrested 1500 party members, including many serving in the armed forces. Trials and convictions of those suspected of spying for Moscow were conducted later, and ten of those found guilty, all of them military personnel, executed.

This left the Freedom Movement led by Mahdi Bazargan as the only recognized opposition group in Iran. At one stage it had a dozen deputies in the Majlis (lit., assembly), the parliament. In a parliamentary speech in August 1983 Bazargan, who opposed the Iranian invasion of Iraq, criticized the government for labelling those who disagreed with it heretics, a habit which, he said, vitiated the atmosphere and encouraged violence.[20] When the party tried to organize a seminar in late October as part of its campaign to secure an official guarantee that the Majlis elections due next spring would be free, it was denied permission. A parliamentary debate on the ban proved unruly and ended in disorder.

The silencing of anti-war opposition was conducive to bolstering the Khomeini regime's military effort which manifested itself as the Wa al Fajr-Four offensive in the northern sector on 20 October 1983. After expelling the units of Iraq's First Army Corps (stationed in the north) from the area between the Iranian towns of Baneh and Marivan, Iran's forces marched 25 miles into Iraq, capturing 250 square miles north and east of Panjwin. To dislodge the Iranians Saddam Hussein despatched the elite Presidential Guard units from Baghdad to this sector, a gesture intended to show that the security of the presidential palace came second to safeguarding the territorial integrity of Iraq. But they failed. So too did the use of mustard gas bombs by Iraq against the Iranians.[21] Tehran's success further raised the spirits of Kurdish guerrillas intent on securing genuine regional autonomy. Kurdish desertions from the Iraqi military had become a vexing problem for Baghdad – reaching, according to official sources, 48,000 by early 1983 – all the more so because the deserters joined the ranks of Kurdish insurgents.[22]

To avenge the loss of its territory the Baghdad government, in late October, mined Bandar Khomeini and fired missiles at six Iranian cities. It was the first time the Iraqis used Soviet-made Scud-B surface-to-surface missiles with a range of 185 miles. Far from demoralizing the Iranians, such attacks seemed to steel their resolve to continue the war and 'punish' Saddam Hussein.[23]

On 10 December 1983 Kuwait experienced five bomb explosions set off by a group of resident Iraqi and Lebanese nationals believed to be members of Al Daawa. Six people were killed and 80 wounded. In retaliation Iraq fired Scud-B missiles at five Iranian towns, killing 21 people and injuring 222.[24] Iran responded with artillery barrages on six Iraqi towns.

Having made minor gains in the northern sector, Tehran seemed to have turned its attention once again to the southern and central-southern fronts defended by Iraq's Third and Fourth Army Corps. By early 1984 it had acted to thwart the Iraqi plan to drown attacking Iranians by diverting the waters of the Tigris. It constructed a 36-mile-long canal from Karun river to drain the overflowing waters of the Tigris. It also trained and equipped its forces to cross water barriers.

THE MAJNOON OFFENSIVE

Repeating the past year's pattern, the Iranians prepared to stage a multi-pronged offensive around the anniversary of the Islamic revolution in February. They did this in three stages, starting with a probing operation. But the target was always the same: to seize the Basra–Baghdad highway in order to cut off Shia-dominated southern Iraq from the Sunni-dominated north, and weaken the Baghdad government by depriving it of an oil-rich region. On 16 February the Iranian forces advanced west of Dehloran to cross the Iraqi lines and capture the Basra–Baghdad highway between Amara and Kut. But Iraq's Fourth Army Corps, which had been expecting an attack and was well-prepared, stopped the Iranian march.

The second phase of Iran's offensive started on 22 February under the codename of Khaibar – the Jewish oasis north of Medina which was conquered by the Prophet Muhammad before his victorious return to his birthplace, Mecca. The Iranian forces, consisting mainly of several divisions of the revolutionary guards, collected at Hoveizeh, situated 18 miles from the border which ran through marshes. The marshy terrain – called Haur al Hawizeh – extended westwards beyond the Tigris, towards the lower reaches of the Euphrates before the beginning of the Shatt al Arab at the confluence of the two rivers. Baghdad's military planners regarded the Haur al Hawizeh as a natural defence barrier unlikely to be crossed by enemy forces. But the Iranians surprised them by staging a helicopter and water-borne attack, utilizing small craft and rubber boats to penetrate the marshes, with a view to capturing Qurna at the Tigris–Euphrates confluence, and the Basra–Baghdad highway that passed through the town.

On 25 February, in the course of their advance to Qurna, the Iranians assaulted the Northern and Western Islands of Majnoon (lit., mad), situated relatively deep in the marshes. These were artificial islands created out of mud and sand dunes by the Iraqi authorities as part of an oil extraction project involving an estimated seven billion barrels of crude, about a sixth of the total Iraqi reserves. However, with the onset of the war, Baghdad had sealed off the 50-odd oil wells on the islands. Swampy conditions helped the attackers to offset the defenders' advantage in tanks as they negotiated the marshes in boats and on foot along the narrow strips of dry land in the area. The Iranian tactics were sufficiently innovative to be compared by an Iraqi commander to those of the North Vietnamese in fighting the Americans in South Vietnam. The informal, decentralized functioning of the revolutionary guards proved an important asset to Tehran, just as the highly centralized, hierarchical set-up of the Iraqi military proved a weighty liability to Baghdad. On 27 February the Iranians captured the Majnoon Islands.

Steady progress brought the Iranians on 29 February to the outskirts of Qurna and within rifle-shot of the strategic Iraqi highway. But since they were now in open country without proper air cover, and since they had to halt to execute their plans to cross the Tigris to reach the Basra–Baghdad road, they became easy targets of Iraq's well-entrenched forward positions.

By then the Iraqi high command had got over its initial surprise and reorganized the East of Tigris Command responsible for the defence of the area. It pressed the Popular Army into action. They and the professional soldiers performed with bravery born out of despair, and repulsed the Iranian attack with massive artillery shelling combined with attacks from warplanes and helicopters with conventional and chemical bombs and rockets.

But Tehran would not give up. Having established a bridgehead over the marshes, on 1 March, it pressed into action two revolutionary guards divisions well equipped with armour and heavy earth-moving machinery. But lack of adequate air cover and detailed command instructions exposed them to the kind of losses suffered earlier by their comrades.

Having beaten back the Iranian assault on Qurna, the Iraqis tried to evict the enemy from the Majnoon Islands, but encountered severe problems. The Iranians controlled the floating roads and platforms that criss-crossed the reed-filled marshes. They proved adept in using helicopters, motorcycles and boats to move about and fight. In contrast the Iraqis could not use the narrow causeways to counterattack or press home their superiority in artillery and tanks. Still, they managed to recover the southern part of the larger Western Island nearer to Qurna, depriving the Iranians of an immediate opportunity to use the Western Majnoon Island as a springboard to capture the Iraqi lifeline: the Basra–Baghdad highway.

At their peak these three-week-long offensives and counteroffensives involved a total of 500,000 combatants, 300,000 of them Iranian. An estimated 27,000 died: 20,000 Iranians and 7000 Iraqis.[25]

Iran kept up its attempts to reach the highway for the rest of March deploying its regular armoured division. But it performed no better than had the revolutionary guards earlier.

In the end Iraq came through this series of massive attacks with relatively little loss of land. But during the course of it – facing the probability of Iraq's two most important cities being cut off, with consequent collapse of public and military morale – the Iraqi high command grew panicky. This manifested itself in its use of mustard gas (and possibly nerve agents) on a much larger scale than before: on 25 and 26 February, and again on 2, 3, 7 and 9 March. Because mustard gas acts slowly – producing blisters first on the skin and then inside the lungs – it proved efficacious against the foot-slogging Iranian infantry. Iraq had been producing this chemical at Samawa, 145 miles south of Baghdad, and nerve agents at Rutba near the Jordanian border. So far, Iran claimed, Iraqi chemical bombs had killed 1200 Iranians and injured 5000.[26] Iraq was a signatory to the 1925 Geneva protocol which outlaws chemical weapons. It reportedly used chemicals normally employed in manufacturing pesticides to produce poison gases and nerve agents.

What initially favoured Tehran was its choice of the marshy terrain and the surprise it caused in Baghdad. But it could not score solid achievements for the same reasons as before: its insufficiently trained revolutionary guards marched against the enemy without adequate combined arms backing and proper resupply facilities. They could succeed only so long as they fought in the reed-filled marshes. On the dry plain approaching the Tigris and heavily fortified Iraqi positions, it was another matter altogether. Hurling human waves at these targets without a proper air umbrella proved suicidal for the Iranians. The imbalance in the air power of the belligerents was obvious from the fact that while Iraq staged over 100 sorties daily, Iran could rarely muster 10. Elsewhere, lacking precise battle management techniques, the revolutionary guards persisted in their habit of congregating indecisively once they had achieved their objective, providing ideal targets to the well-entrenched Iraqis backed by amply stocked artillery emplacements in the rear.

As a result of the February–March 1984 offensives the number of casualties on both sides rose. It was estimated that since the start of the war over 170,000 Iranian combatants (i.e., military personnel, revolutionary guards and Basij militiamen) had died and twice as many had been injured – versus some 80,000 Iraqi troops dead and 150,000 wounded.[27]

Iran was not particularly disheartened by the rising toll. It was intent on consolidating its position on the Majnoon Islands and staging another offensive to take Qurna. Indeed by mid-April it had assembled a force of over 300,000 for launching major assaults. To forestall the Iranians, the Iraqis flooded the marshes along their southern and western perimeter – an exercise in which they were helped by the rising waters of the Tigris due to the melting of snow in the Caucasus Mountains, a process which continued throughout summer.

For religious and demographic reasons Iran was in a better position to accept high casualties. Each year 422,000 males, amounting to about one per cent of the total Iranian population, reach the conscription age of 18. The figure for Iraq is 161,000. In addition there was the Basij militia force, operating from 9000 mosques and thousands of workplaces and educational institutions, open to those under 18 and over 45, and all women. By the spring of 1983 the Basij authorities, functioning as part of the Islamic Revolutionary Guards Corps, claimed to have trained 2.4 million Iranians in the use of arms, and sent 450,000 to the front on a rota basis.[28]

Underlying all this was the deep religiosity of the Iranian Shias with strong overtones of 'martyr complex'. They considered it their religious duty to fight evil and oppression which, in this case, they associated with Saddam Hussein. This struggle, to them, was part of another: to liberate Jerusalem from its Zionist occupiers and oppressors. They saw the march either to the holy cities of Najaf and Karbala in southern Iraq, or Kadhimain[29] near Baghdad, as part of the advance to Jerusalem, the third holiest city of Islam, which in Arabic is called Al Quds (The Holy) or Bait al Muqqadas (The Holy Place). Since Syria was an ally of Iran and a staunch anti-Zionist state, all that stood between the Islamic Republic and Jerusalem was the infidel regime of Saddam Hussein. To die in removing this hurdle was to ensure passage to heaven in the afterlife.

The concept of afterlife is deeply embedded among Muslims. Earthly life is useful only in so far as it helps the believer to show his commitment to Islam and his yearning to close the distance between himself and Allah, the Creator. On Iranian radio and television the audiences were frequently reminded of the Prophet Muhammad's saying to the believers: 'Wish death and welcome afterlife.' A striking example of the popularity of the martyr complex among Iranians was the disproportion between the war captives on each side. In early 1984 Iraq held only 7300 Iranian prisoners of war, whereas Iran held more than 50,000 Iraqis.[30]

Interestingly, as hostilities dragged on, the Iraqi regime resorted to lauding 'martyrs', with the military adopting as one of its mottos Saddam Hussein's statement: 'The martyrs are more noble than all of us.'[31] In order to upstage Iran in the religious arena the Iraqi president sponsored the Popular Islamic Conference in Baghdad in April 1983. It was attended by 280 clergy and pious laymen from 50 countries, and presided over by Shaikh Ali Kashif Ghita, a leading Shia cleric of Najaf, noted for his religious verdict branding Khomeini as a heretic. Since Iraq was a newcomer to this activity it drafted Maruf Dawalbi, an Islamist aide to King Fahd ibn Abdul Aziz, to implement the project. He drew on the Saudi network of Islamic affiliations to attract participants. Addressing the gathering, Saddam Hussein said: 'When we sensed that Muslims wanted us to withdraw from Iranian territory . . . we responded to Muslim opinion, to world public opinion and to Iranian public opinion, and withdrew to the borders.'[32] Having backed Iraq's stand on the war the conference tried to mediate between the belligerents – a venture doomed to failure.

Earlier, official invitations to the Shia ulama of Najaf were by and large spurned. Among those who refused to attend were the families of Ayatollah Khoei and the late Ayatollah Hakim. This resulted in the arrest of 90 members of the Hakim household. Six of them, including three brothers of Hojatalislam Baqir Hakim, were executed on 20 May 1983. The government increased the surveillance of Najaf, regarded as the prime centre of Shia dissidence, to the extent that almost every hotel, coffee-house and restaurant was reportedly monitored by secret service agents.[33] At the time of the Popular Islamic Conference the minister of waqfs and religious affairs stated that 58 per cent of the 3183 religious sites were under total government supervision, and the rest partial; and that all the 2294 religious caretakers had become civil servants.[34] The state also took charge of all religious ceremonies of Islam, thus ensuring that its adversaries would not turn these occasions into anti-government demonstrations and riots as had happened in the 1970s.

On the whole the task of the regime to isolate and suppress Shia opposition became easier once the Iranians marched into Iraq. It was convincingly able to label the backers of Khomeini as traitors to Iraq. Given the patriotic feeling that existed among most Shias, their history of passivity and dread of the government's repressive apparatus, and the success of the Iraqi media in creating a repulsive portrait of the

Khomeinist system in Iran, Iraqi Shias by and large upheld nationalism rather than their sectarian loyalty. This meant a sharp drop in the backing for Al Daawa, the Mujahedin Movement and the Islamic Action Organization. None the less, these bodies continued their terrorist acts – the Islamic Action Organization claiming in November 1983 to have carried out sabotage which destroyed the security directorate and military directorate buildings in Baghdad.

Among the factors that encouraged the leaders of militant Shia organizations was the high level of military casualties suffered by the Iraqis. By the third anniversary of the Gulf War in September 1983 most extended families in the country had suffered a war casualty. The authorities actively discouraged public mourning or funerals so as to preserve failing morale. Indeed, they tried to raise the spirits of the citizenry. They did so by reassuring the people of their tenacity and military muscle while encouraging the troops to fight hard and exhorting the public to enrol in the Popular Army. They intensified their campaign to present Iranians and their supreme leader grotesquely, portraying Khomeini variously as an insect, a donkey and a decrepit old man. Iraqi television combined its violently anti-Persian rhetoric with the screening of the dead and mutilated bodies of Iranians for hours on end to drive home the point that the enemy was being resolutely crushed.

Iraqi commanders made it a point to denigrate and dehumanize the foe. 'Great Sir, we gladly inform you of the annihilation of thousands of harmful magian insects that carried out an abortive offensive late last night,' stated Major-General Mahir Abdul Rashid, commander of the Basra-based Third Army Corps, in his cable to Saddam Hussein on 28 February 1984. 'We . . . will turn what is left of these harmful insects into food for birds of the wilderness and the fishes of the marshes.'[35] In contrast, Iran focused on denigrating only Saddam Hussein. It refrained from any ethnic caricaturing and never presented the conflict in Persian–Arab terms. Indeed the government continued its policies of teaching Arabic on television and Arabizing the Farsi language.

Use of vituperative language against Iran was also meant to demonstrate at large the confidence that Iraq's military had in defending the homeland. The recourse to chemical bombs, too, was to be seen in this light. In the wake of the October 1983 Iranian successes in Iraqi Kurdistan, officials in Baghdad began talking ominously of a 'new and secret weapon'. Following the Iranian allegations of the use of chemical arms by Baghdad, the Iraqis coupled their routine denials (issued in order to maintain abroad the image of a rational, moderate party facing a fanatical foe) with ambivalent statements. For instance, in mid-March 1984, Major-General Abdul Rashid said, 'If you gave me a pesticide to throw at these swarms of insects . . . then I'd use it.'[36] The general idea was to reassure Iraqis that even in the worst possible case their military had the means of repulsing the enemy.

The defence forces and their commanders were given higher status in society and the state apparatus than before. Efforts were made to inculcate among Iraqis such martial values as 'high morale, steadfastness, love for the homeland to the point of martyrdom, leadership qualities, honour and valour'. Saddam Hussein decreed in September 1983 that soldierly culture and thought should be spread among government and Baath Party officials. Conversely, stiff punishment awaited those who failed on the battlefield, however high their rank – a job performed by the specially appointed 'Punishment Corps' operating in the rear lines.[37] The creation of a martial ambience was thought necessary for the success of the official drive to maintain the professional military force above 500,000. In November 1983 the authorities drafted for reserve service all those aged 36, and urged the 14- to 17-year-olds to enrol for arms training.

These measures, combined with efforts to boost the Popular Army, had an adverse effect on the economy. So too did the decline in oil prices during 1983, reducing Iraq's foreign income from the commodity by a third, against the previous year's level, to about $7 billion. According to the Bank of International Settlements, at the end of 1982 Iraq's foreign exchange reserves did not exceed $1.2 billion.[38] Since the latter half of 1982 Iraq had been unable to pay cash to foreign firms for their services or goods. During 1982 the per capita (domestic) income fell by 12 per cent on top of a decline of 26 per cent in the previous year; and the trend was downward.[39] Little wonder that during the summer and autumn of 1983 Baghdad found itself in the midst of an acute economic crisis.

To meet it the government took various steps. It reversed the upward trend in development expenditure by cutting it by a third in 1983. It reduced the size of the civil service and decreased its salaries by one-fifth. It slashed civilian imports to $250 million a month from the peak of $975 million a month in 1980.[40] But, given the pressure of war, there was no decline in imported military goods which cost the country three times as much as civilian imports. The only way Iraq could cope was by raising fresh loans and grants from friendly nations, rescheduling current debts, and seeking moratoriums on contract payments.

It took to appealing to its population for contributions to the war chest. One such exhortation in June 1983 to the people to donate their cash, gold, jewellery and family heirlooms yielded $500 million and 8800 pounds of gold and jewellery. Lists of donors were broadcast on television to encourage the recalcitrant. To increase state revenue tax collection procedures were made stringent. In November 1982 the remittances ceiling for foreign workers – who in 1982 sent home $4 billion – was lowered by about a third, which saved foreign currencies but worsened the labour shortage. It resulted in the departure of a third of the 1.5 million Egyptians, who had so far accounted for two-thirds of the workforce in agriculture and construction. Iraqi women were increasingly drawn into the labour market, and now constituted a quarter of the total workforce.

In 1983 the interlinked problem of hoarding, profiteering and black market became worse. It stemmed from severe shortages of basic necessities, particularly food, in part caused by the transfer of the food trade from the public sector to merchants in order to strengthen the private sector. Inflation reached a peak of 50 per cent in late 1982 before declining to 25 per cent in early 1984.

Iran faced similar problems. Once the threat of arbitrary arrest was dispelled by Khomeini's December 1982 judicial decree, traders began overcharging. The subsequent public complaints disturbed the leadership. In late January 1983 Khomeini addressed Tehran's mercantile leaders. Reminding them of the Islamic war that the country was waging against the infidel Iraqi regime, he said that he expected every Muslim to make sacrifices for the holy struggle, not enrich himself from it. This reproof caused some fall in prices.

The government combined such appeals with a campaign against 'economic terrorists': a term applied to all those counter-revolutionaries who, having failed to overturn the revolutionary order by military or political measures, had taken to economic means. In July 1983 trials for economic offenders were referred to the stringent revolutionary courts which prescribed stiff sentences for those found guilty. The prosecutor-general of economic crimes established patrols of 'assistants of God' to catch economic offenders – described by him as being no better than Saddam Hussein for 'sucking the blood of the families of war victims'.[41] At the same time the authorities argued that the main reason for high prices was faulty distribution, not actual shortages. To rectify the situation they encouraged consumer co-operatives in workplaces and mosques. Already the government had nationalized foreign trade, handing over the functions of private middle-men to the commerce ministry. In contrast to Iraq, war conditions encouraged the growth of public and co-operative sectors in Iranian commerce and trade.

In tackling economic difficulties the Iranian government remained conscious of its political priorities. For instance, it did not tinker with subsidies on basic necessities or the Islamic system of social security. These cost the public exchequer $4 billion, or about 10 per cent of the national budget. Subsidies amounted to $1.9 billion, the one on flour and wheat alone costing $500 million.[42] The government was keen to make a success of the rationing system, particularly for the poor. Whenever it received urgently needed imports of food, it first distri-buted them in the working-class areas of cities and towns. At the same time it allowed the black market to function freely to allow the middle and upper classes to obtain whatever they could not get through the rationing system.

It managed to keep inflation around 20 per cent by sustaining the efficiency of the rationing system through imports, and curbing public expenditure through such means as cutting civil servants' salaries and banning recruitment. Due mainly to an abrupt rise in oil output from early 1982 onwards, the Gross National Product had risen modestly by 2.2 per cent in 1981–2, reversing the trend of the past three years when the GNP had declined by an annual average of 10.5 per cent.[43]

Stress on self-sufficiency, accentuated by the war, began to show results in agriculture. In 1982–3 its output (by value) was about one-fifth higher than in 1978–9, the last year of the Shah's rule. But industry presented a sorry state. It continued to suffer from poor management and paucity of skilled personnel as well as shortages of industrial raw materials and spare parts stemming from a drive to save foreign curren-cies required for more pressing military needs. In 1982–3 its output (by value) was about seven-eighths of the figure of five years before.[44]

On the other hand strict import controls and improved oil output – running above 2.3 million b/d in 1982 and 1983 – helped Iran to turn its trade deficit of $3.2 billion in 1980–81 into a surplus of $6.3 billion two years later. By mid-1983 Tehran had reduced its foreign debts to $1.1 billion from $15 billion before the revolution.[45] So not only had Iran refrained from raising external loans – something that Iraq had done on a prodigal scale – but it had almost completely wiped out its outstanding debts. For a country which had undergone a revolution, and was in the throes of a war, this was a remarkable achievement.

Part of the reason lay in the way Iran controlled its defence budget. Without impairing the efficiency of the war machine, the government tried to economize. It used captured weapons to equip the newly formed units of the military or the Revolutionary Guards Corps. It paid a paltry stipend of $1 a day to conscripts. It encouraged the public to contribute cash and goods to the war chest. At $7 billion, the military budget was just above 15 per cent of the total in 1983–4. But when war-related expenses – the running of the Basij and a large section of the Revolutionary Guards Corps, the compensations and pensions to the war disabled and the families of the fallen, the financing of the Martyrs Foundation, and the war reconstruction fund – were added to military expenditure, the total amounted to 30 per cent of the $45 billion budget.[46]

The direct military cost of the warfare to Iran was only about 60 per cent of Iraq's, primarily because, whether out of choice or necessity, Tehran's expenditure on heavy and advanced weaponry and ammunition was a fraction of what Baghdad spent. In other words, while Iran was waging a 'labour intensive' struggle Iraq was fighting a 'capital intensive' war.

This was not the only disparity that the Gulf War created. In Iraq it led to pro-private sector policies whereas in Iran it gave rise to contrary tendencies. It made the Baathist regime less secular than before, with the state not only sponsoring international Islamic gatherings but also putting the Islamic sites at home under its supervision and turning their caretakers into state employees. In a sense this development was a moral victory for Tehran. Under the pressure of the Iranian offensives Saddam Hussein came to promote professionalism in the military, downgrading Baathist credentials for officers. The reverse was the case in Iran. Here, with the continuation of the war, the importance and size of the ideologically-inspired Islamic Revolutionary Guards Corps increased – as did its direct involvement in the planning and execution of combat.

In Iran the war strengthened revolutionary fervour, and made society and government more ideological, not less. In Iraq, the opposite happened. When the hostilities started the country was a civil society where the Baathist party and ideology ruled supreme: a little over three years of warfare turned it into a military society where the civilian ruling party came to play second fiddle. Political leaders, particularly Saddam Hussein, realized increasingly that not only Iraq's territorial integrity but also the very survival of their regime depended entirely on the performance of the military. They realized, too, that the defence forces were a more effective institution to rally the nation than the Baath. Little wonder that Saddam Hussein paid less and less attention to party activities. His speeches made scanty references to the Baathist ideals of pan-Arabism, socialism and secularism, instead stressing military qualities of valour, patriotism, discipline and martyrdom.

Iraq's movement away from its radical, revolutionary moorings was well received by its newly acquired allies in the region and elsewhere. They increased their financial and diplomatic backing of Baghdad.

5 IMPACT OF THE WAR ABROAD

The Iranian invasion of Iraq had a mixed impact on the Gulf monarchies. Freshly impressed by Tehran's power, the Lower Gulf states became genuinely neutral. In contrast, Saudi Arabia and Kuwait drew nearer to Iraq. Here again there was a difference. Kuwait's backing for Iraq stemmed from two factors: its anxiety about the internal subversion likely to be caused by its substantial Shia minority, and genuine fear of its strong northern neighbour, Iraq, which persisted in its demand to lease Kuwait's Bubiyan Island. Rioting by Kuwaiti Shias during the Ashura ceremony in October 1982, which the authorities blamed on Tehran, highlighted Kuwaiti anxiety about Iran. To counter the Iraqi pressure, the Kuwaiti government consolidated its hold over Bubiyan by building a bridge between the mainland and the offshore island in early 1983.

In the absence of any such competing claims straining relations between Saudi Arabia and Iraq, Riyadh's links with Baghdad were very tight. Iraq was swift in backing King Fahd's peace plan at the September 1982 Arab summit in Fez. When the Iranians staged their offensive at Mandali on 1 October1982 with a view to capturing Baghdad, the Saudi monarch telephoned Saddam Hussein to reassure him of his backing. Riyadh Radio warned that Iran would face war with 'the whole Arab world' if it refused mediation and broke through the Iraqi defence lines.[1] The failure of the Iranian attack was welcomed as much in Baghdad as in Riyadh. In March 1983 Crown Prince Abdullah ibn Abdul Aziz declared: 'Iran cannot enter Baghdad because that would mean an all-out war with Iran [by us].'[2]

The events of 1983 established clearly that among the Gulf states Saudi Arabia was the most important regional supporter of Iraq. During that year there were a dozen exchange visits involving top officials of these countries, including Saddam Hussein's arrival in Riyadh on 15 January. In his talks with King Fahd he reportedly secured the monarch's permission for an oil pipeline through Saudi territory. Equally importantly, Saudi Arabia convinced France, a major arms supplier to the rich oil kingdom, to deliver five highly advanced Super-Etendard warplanes to Iraq. The deal was facilitated by Saudi Arabia's agreement to pay for the jet fighters in oil – out of the 200,000 b/d that it contracted to ship to Iraq's customers. This arrangement came into being due to Riyadh's reluctance to provide cash to Baghdad because of falling oil prices and its much reduced OPEC quota – down from 9.5 million b/d in 1979 to 4.5 million b/d in early 1983. During that year Saudi Arabia ran a deficit of $15.5 billion in its current trade account, a contrast to its surplus of $7.6 billion in 1982.

Riyadh helped Baghdad in another way. It provided 10 per cent down payment to the foreign companies signing contracts with Iraq, and guaranteed the balance. Kuwait did the same. Lacking the generous oil income of the immediate past, it opted for supplying 130,000 b/d of oil to Baghdad's customers.

Following the December 1983 bomb explosions at the US and French embassies in Kuwait, the international airport and the compound of an American residential complex accommodating US missile experts, relations between Kuwait and Tehran deteriorated sharply. Though none of those arrested for these acts was Iranian, the government deported hundreds of Iranian residents. Iraqi retaliation, in the form of strikes against five Iranian towns, won much appreciation in Kuwait and further strengthened mutual ties. The same happened during the Iranian offensives of February–March 1984. In the wake of the Iraqi loss of the Majnoon Islands to Iran, Kuwait announced a 'public mobilization plan'.

In a general sense Tehran's gain of the Majnoon Islands made Gulf Co-operation Council members realize that time was running against Iraq. GCC foreign ministers meeting in mid-March 1984 tried to mediate in the war. As before, their effort proved futile. Later, at a meeting of the Arab League foreign ministers – boycotted by Syria and Libya among others – GCC members backed a call by the League to all states to cease selling arms and spares to Iran.

Tehran remained hostile towards the GCC, particularly its military activities. When GCC members announced a joint military exercise under the aegis of the GCC Rapid Deployment Force to be conducted in the UAE desert in early October 1983, Iran reacted sharply. 'Who will the RDF of the GCC confront?' asked Tehran Radio's Arabic service on 26 September. 'Just as the formation of the GCC [in May 1981] was intended to confront the Islamic tide, it is equally true that these exercises have the same purpose.'

Khomeini's regime pursued a two-tier policy towards the Gulf states.

It reiterated its pledges of non-aggression and non-interference in their internal affairs while urging them to dissolve their links with Baghdad and Washington. In February 1983, for instance, Rafsanjani declared that if the Gulf states refrained from intervening in the war, Iran would honour their territorial integrity and defend their security.[3] Four months later Khomeini stressed that Iran had no territorial ambitions on the Arab side of the Gulf, and added: 'Islamic Iran is ready to help the countries of the region to regain their liberation and salvation from the arrogant forces [the superpowers].'[4]

The Gulf country most amenable to Iran's gestures was the United Arab Emirates. In November 1982, when Tehran sent its first ambassador to the UAE since the revolution, the UAE's foreign ministry described relations with Iran as 'friendly'. The UAE maintained genuine neutrality in the Gulf War because of the rising fears for its own security, and the urge to preserve its own federal unity as well as its commercial interests. If there was an individual emirate or principality offering cash to Iraq, it was most probably Abu Dhabi, whose ruler was the president of the UAE. However, in early 1983, his financial aid to Baghdad was reportedly running at no higher than $500 million a year. The UAE kept up its trade with Iran. Dubai, where most of the UAE's 20,000 Iranian merchants were based, did thriving business with Iran.

Tehran was pleased to see a diminution in the Gulf monarchies' cash subventions to Iraq. Having concluded that by late 1982 Baghdad had derived the maximum aid it could from the Gulf states, Saddam Hussein felt the need for a fresh powerful alliance in the Arab world. Egypt was the obvious choice. The Iraqi leader, who only four years earlier had played a leading role in the expulsion of Egypt from the Arab League, now stated: 'Iraq is looking forward to Egypt's resumption of its influential role in the pan-Arab movement at large.'[5] Exchanges of visits by the countries' foreign ministers and military delegations ensued. Baghdad raised its weapons procurement from Cairo to the extent that by early 1984 it had bought $2.7 billion worth of arms and ammunition during the period 1981–3.[6] In addition to the 15,000 Egyptian 'volunteers' already in Iraq's armed forces by mid-1983, Cairo supplied military instructors to train Iraqi soldiers.

Rapprochement between Baghdad and Cairo suited both parties. It provided a welcome opportunity to Egypt to worm its way back into the pan-Arab fold, a task made easier by the assassination in October 1981 of

President Sadat who had signed the much-criticized Camp David Accords. Given that Libya and Syria were siding with Iran, it seemed natural that the respective adversaries of each – Egypt in the case of Qadhafi's Libya, and Iraq for Assad's Syria – would draw together. Moreover, President Mubarak and President Hussein were equally opposed to Khomeini's version of Islamic fundamentalism.

Links between Iran, Libya and Syria were fortified in January 1983 with a conference of their foreign ministers in Damascus. In a joint communiqué issued by the Syrian and Libyan ministers they condemned Iraq for its invasion of Iran and pledged to stand by Iran against 'hostile forces'.

The Syrian government derived political and diplomatic advantages from its alliance with Iran. With Iraq locked in a bloody conflict with Iran, it had a quiet eastern front for itself. Saddam Hussein was unable to instigate destabilizing activities against the Assad regime. This allowed the Syrian president to concentrate on resolving the Lebanese crisis caused by the Israeli invasion and occupation of June 1982. However, these factors did not stop Tehran from showing its appreciation of the Syrian stand on the Gulf War. When drawing up trade terms for the financial year 1983–4 Iran agreed to sell Damascus not only five million tonnes of oil for cash and barter but also offered it a grant of one million tonnes – worth $200 million – to assist the Syrian struggle against Israel.

Such a gesture flew in the face of the Iraqi thesis that there was a strategic alliance between Iran and Israel against Iraq in particular and the Arab world in general. But then Baghdad had something substantial to back up its assessment: the reports of Israeli sale of arms to Iran, which appeared in the American press in March and May 1982.

Based on information that has since become available, the following picture of the Israeli military supplies to Tehran can be constructed. According to the memoirs of Zbigniew Brzezinski, the National Security Adviser to President Carter, the US administration in 1980 (when Washington's embargo against Iran was in force) learned, 'much to its dismay, that the Israelis had been secretly supplying American spare parts to the Iranians'. This happened in late June 1980 and involved one planeload of non-lethal materials. When Carter objected there were no more shipments. But following the outbreak of the Gulf War, Israel again offered military goods to Iran through intermediaries. This overture was accepted and shipments made through such countries as

Portugal, Italy and Cyprus. According to Bani-Sadr, by using intermediaries and third countries, Israel shipped $50–100 millions-worth of
arms and spares to Iran between May 1980 and June 1981. These
shipments probably included $40 millions-worth of weapons and spare
parts that were believed to have been agreed between Iranian envoys and
Reagan campaign officials in Paris on 20 October 1980.[7]

In the spring of 1981 Iranian officials and British middlemen working
for an Israeli firm concluded a $27 million contract in London, involving
12 planeloads of military supplies, including spares for US-made tanks
and warplanes. An Argentine CL-4 turboprop cargo plane was used to
ferry the equipment between Tel Aviv and Tehran via Nicosia, Cyprus.
It made four such trips. On its fifth flight on 18 July 1981 it strayed into
Soviet airspace; and, following interception by Soviet warplanes, it
crashed near the Soviet–Turkish border. Tehran denied that it had
bought any war materials (directly) from Israel. In November Tel Aviv
reportedly sold Tow (Tube-launched Optically-tracked Wire-guided)
anti-tank missiles of US origin to Faroukh Azizi, an Iranian arms dealer,
in Athens.[8]

By supplying arms to Iran, either independently or in collusion with
others, Israel intended to further its national interests by keeping its
long-term enemy, Iraq, embroiled in a bloody conflict. Since Baghdad
was allied with Moscow through a friendship treaty, Israel regarded an
Iraqi victory as heralding further gains for the Soviet Union in the
region: something the staunchly anti-Soviet Israel felt compelled to
thwart by all means. Also, by judiciously supplying scarce and valuable arms, ammunition and spares, it meant to exercise some power,
however indirectly, in the military and political circles of Iran.

Israel entered the Iraqi planners' estimation as well. By destroying a
nuclear reactor near Baghdad in June 1981 it had set a precedent, which
the Saddam Hussein regime could not afford to overlook. The publication of information in early March 1984 about a chemical complex near
Rutba manufacturing poison gases made Iraq fearful of a secret Israeli
strike against the factory. It mounted a propaganda campaign on the
issue warning Tel Aviv against any such action, and despatched its
deputy foreign minister, Ismat Katani, to Washington to dissuade the
US from co-operating with Israel in such a venture. The fact that the
chemical plant was left untouched illustrates the success that Iraq
had, and was a measure of the goodwill it had by then generated in
Washington.

THE SUPERPOWERS

The first overt sign of change in Iraqi–American relations came in January 1983 when Saddam Hussein published the text of his talks with US Congressman Stephen Solarz during the latter's visit to Baghdad five months earlier. In it the Baathist leader declared that Iraq had never been part of the Soviet strategy in the region, and that it was in the interests of Washington to be 'present in the region when any other big or super-power is present'.[9] This was an obvious reference to the Soviet Union, and constituted an open invitation to the US at the cost of Moscow. It was a reversal of the previous Iraqi policy of keeping both superpowers out of the Gulf.

Washington reciprocated. US Secretary of State George Shultz met Tariq Aziz in Paris in October 1982 and again in May 1983. The next month, despite the continued inclusion of Iraq in the State Department's list of 'nations that support international terrorism' – along with Libya, South Yemen, Syria and Cuba – the Reagan administration authorized the sale to Iraq of 60 helicopters for 'agricultural use'. These were capable of being converted to military machines. More import-antly, it provided credit of $460 million for the sale of 147,000 tonnes of American rice to Baghdad. Such a gesture by the US had wide and favourable international repercussions for Baghdad, then in the midst of a severe economic crisis. It reassured many European and Arab govern-ments and banks of the future of the Saddam Hussein regime, and raised its badly bruised credit-worthiness.

As 1983 progressed American policymakers concluded that an Iraqi triumph was out of the question, and that there were two possible outcomes to the present conflict: Iranian victory or continued stale-mate. In the case of an Iranian triumph they visualized a collapse of the pro-Western monarchies in the Gulf. Though the subsequent Islamic republics in Iraq and elsewhere were not expected to side with Moscow, the overthrow of a group of pro-Western rulers in a region that contained more than half of the world's known oil reserves was perceived as an unprecedented catastrophe. In short, an Iraqi defeat was seen as a major blow to US interests. This was the overall conclusion of a study by the US National Security Council in the autumn of 1983.[10] Washington therefore formulated plans to shore up Iraq morally and materially.

In November 1983 the US National Security Adviser issued a secret directive to this effect, outlining the diplomatic and military steps

America should take to aid Baghdad. The Pentagon prepared contingency plans to assist Iraq militarily if it was approached to 'stabilize the border' by Iraq or one of its Arab allies. In that case the US would use A-10 warplanes to attack the Iranian tanks inside Iraq, fragmentation bombs to disperse Iranian troop concentrations, and 'air defence weapons' to enable Iraq to retain control of its airspace.[11]

As for its public policy, in late November Washington removed Iraq from its list of 'nations that support international terrorism' thus, theoretically, opening up the possibility of arms sales to it.[12] In mid-December a special envoy, Donald Rumsfeld, was sent to Baghdad with a letter for Saddam Hussein from President Ronald Reagan. Then a delegation, headed by a deputy assistant secretary of state and a deputy assistant secretary of defence, visited the six Gulf capitals. It informed the rulers that Washington would regard Iraq's defeat as 'contrary to US interests'.[13] Besides making public its pro-Baghdad tilt to reassure Iraq as well as the Gulf states, such a statement by the United States was meant to dissuade Iran from launching its much anticipated offensive against Iraq.

On 23 January 1984 America added Iran to the list of the nations that support international terrorism, thus subjecting it to rigid export controls. This action was mainly due to the 23 October 1983 truck-bombing of the barracks of the US marines stationed at Beirut airport by Lebanese Shia militants, which resulted in the death of 259 servicemen: an attack in which Washington claimed to see the hand of Tehran. Now the US – which had instituted its Operation Staunch in the spring of 1983 to discourage its allies from selling arms to Iran – began to pressure Britain, Israel, Italy, South Korea, Turkey and West Germany among others not to supply weapons to Iran or allow their territory to be used for the purpose.

This was a major shift in the US policy of 'balance' in the Iran–Iraq War. In the early stages of the conflict Washington had turned a blind eye to the shipments of weapons and spares originating in the US to Iran by private companies either directly or through third parties. Simultaneously it passed on satellite and high-altitude reconnaissance pictures of Iranian troop movements to Riyadh, knowing that the latter was transferring these to Baghdad. The same applied to the information collected by four American-manned Awacs, leased by the US to Saudi Arabia, for round-the-clock surveillance of the Gulf, a fact confirmed by Saddam Hussein.[14]

When Iraq managed to blunt the Iranian offensives in July 1982, Washington was relieved. The subsequent stalemate suited the US: two unlikeable regimes were battering each other, and in the process dividing the Arab world and diverting Arab attention from the Palestinian problem. The military sales were made either by American companies such as Ramco International, a New Jersey-based aviation parts company, or arms dealers based in the US, or third countries such as South Korea and Israel. On its part the Tehran government encouraged exiled Iranian businessmen to establish front companies in the US and elsewhere to procure American arms and spares. The Office of Munition Control of the State Department was deliberately lax about enforcing the ban on exports of weapons and spares to Iran. 'We don't give a damn as long as the Iran–Iraq carnage does not affect our allies or alter the balance of power,' said a State Department official in July 1983. 'Why save Iranians from themselves with the US customs resources needed to protect Americans from the drug traffic [in America]?'[15]

In September 1983 the interests of Washington's allies in the region came under a shadow when Tehran threatened to close the Hormuz Straits if its Kharg oil terminal were destroyed. President Reagan reiterated the earlier position that the US would intervene to keep Hormuz open to shipping. He increased the American naval presence in the area to 30 warships. The British and French governments followed suit. The Soviets had 26 war vessels in the Arabian Sea.

Moscow had been disappointed in Tehran's rejection of the UN Security Council's July 1982 resolution calling for a ceasefire and withdrawal to the international border. It compared unfavourably the Iranian response with the earlier Iraqi decision to withdraw unilaterally from the occupied Iranian territories. On 21 July the *Literaturnaya Gazeta* (Literary Gazette) commented that the Iranian invasion benefited the US and Israel by distracting Arab states from Lebanon (then being invaded by Israel) and by giving a pretext to the US for increased military activity in the Gulf region. To Tehran such statements echoed sentiments expressed earlier by Baghdad.

Once Iraq was attacked, Moscow reassessed its position in the war in the context of its Friendship and Co-operation Treaty with Baghdad, which provided for defence co-operation and liaison between the signatories when the peace of either was endangered. The Kremlin decided to honour its pre-war contracts with Iraq, including those for advanced warplanes and tanks, but did so secretly. However, in late September

1982 Saddam Hussein revealed the Soviet decision in order to deter Iran from staging its offensive against Iraq.

Ignoring the ploy, Iran launched its attacks in October 1982. It made some gains; but these were unequal to the effort it put into the offensives. The Iraqis performed better than in the past. Tehran attributed this to their newly received Soviet weapons – crucial to Iraq, given that Soviet military supplies formed nearly seven-eighths of the Iraqi arsenals.[16] It felt bitter towards Moscow. In mid-December 1982 the Iraqis fired two freshly acquired Soviet-made Frog-7 surface-to-surface missiles on Dezful, killing 62 people. Iran also experienced more severe artillery shelling of its border towns. On 19 January 1983 a Tehran Radio commentary attacked Moscow's stand on the war. 'The Soviet Union took sides seeing Saddam [Hussein] suffer one defeat after another, gradually making public its pro-Saddam attitude,' it said. A week later Iran expelled the Tass correspondent, Oleg Zuinko, by refusing to renew his visa.

With this the Kremlin lost any hope of furthering its ties with Iran. It came to perceive the possible fall of the Baathist regime as an unmitigated strategic loss offering nothing in compensation. In addition it was apprehensive of the overspill of Islamic fundamentalism into the Muslim-majority southern Soviet republics that it visualized following in the wake of an Iranian victory – not to mention its destabilizing impact on the shaky Marxist regime in Afghanistan, embroiled in a debilitating conflict with Islamic guerrillas.

The Soviet Union now signed fresh military contracts worth $2 billion with Baghdad, which included MiG-23 and MiG-25 warplanes, T-72 tanks and Sam-8 and Sam-9 missiles. The number of Soviet military advisers increased. The media in the USSR provided wider coverage of events in Iraq. Baghdad reciprocated in kind, with Saddam Hussein receiving the Soviet ambassador in May 1983, something he had not done for many months.

In contrast, during that month the Khomeini government combined its dissolution of the Tudeh Party with the expulsion of 18 Soviet diplomats, including four military attachés and four first secretaries, for maintaining contacts with 'mercenary [Iranian] agents'. Referring to the incident, Rafsanjani said: 'The expulsion of the Soviet spies proved that getting rid of one superpower does not mean falling into the arms of another.'[17] Moscow retaliated by expelling three Iranian diplomats.

It blamed Tehran for the continuation of the Gulf conflict. On 8 June

1983 *Krasnaya Zvezda* accused America of secretly supplying weapons and spares to Iran to keep the war going, thus extending destabilization in the region and giving itself an excuse to increase its military presence in the Gulf and the Arabian Sea. The actual American build-up came three months later.

It was against the October 1983 Iranian offensive in Iraqi Kurdistan, and the UN Security Council's call for a ceasefire (rejected by Iran), that Tariq Aziz arrived in Moscow in mid-November. He held a series of meetings with his counterpart, Andrei Gromyko. The joint statement expressed 'the shared desire of the two countries . . . to develop bilateral relations on the basis of the Soviet–Iraqi Treaty of Friendship and Co-operation'. What the communiqué did not state was that the Soviet Union had agreed to sell fresh quantities of weapons to Baghdad.[18]

In mid-January 1984 the USSR Supreme Soviet sent a message to the Iranian parliament urging co-operation of their countries 'in the struggle against world imperialism and US acts of aggression'. Rafsanjani received the Soviet ambassador bearing the Supreme Soviet's message with attentive courtesy. He pointed out that Saddam Hussein had attacked Iran as 'an agent of America' and that he was now being aided by 'Jordan, Sudan, Egypt, Morocco and reaction in the region'. He advised the Soviet Union to notice 'Iranian aid and presence, together with the Lebanese people, being active in Lebanon against the Western occupiers and Israel, and actively engaged in the anti-imperialist struggle'.[19] However, none of this changed the basic position of either party.

Over the years Iran had developed close military ties with North Korea which had excellent relations with both the Soviet Union and the People's Republic of China. Sometimes the two Communist giants used their small neighbour as a conduit to supply military materials to Tehran. In 1983 estimates of the arms and ammunition sold by North Korea to Iran varied between $500 million and $3000 million, with Tehran selling much-needed oil to its ally in the Far East.[20]

THE EUROPEANS

On the other side, France became crucially important for the military and financial survival of the Iraqi regime, a relationship highlighted by the number of exchange visits between top officials of the two states.

Between January and June 1983 the French defence minister was in
Baghdad twice, and Tariq Aziz in Paris three times. By then France had
given up any pretence of neutrality. The French foreign minister declared in December 1982 that his government would not let Iraq lose the
war. Such an outcome, he argued, would threaten Western interests in
the Middle East. His statement was endorsed by President Mitterrand.
This stance stemmed from political, military, strategic and economic
considerations.

France had made substantial economic, financial and military invest-
ment in Iraq. By early 1983 about 1000 French companies were active in
the Baathist republic, and between 6000 and 7000 French specialists
were based there. As much as 40 per cent of total French military exports
were destined for Iraq.[21] Military co-operation between the two states
had developed to such an extent that the French government decided to
lease to Baghdad the five Super-Etendard warplanes originally meant for
use by the French air force. This step met criticism at home as well as
from France's allies abroad: Britain, America and West Germany. To
help pacify the controversy inside France, Baghdad pledged that it would
engage French companies and experts in the future to modernize its
military. France's Western allies argued that the supply of the Super-
Etendards to Iraq, and the consequent destruction of the Kharg oil
terminal, would escalate the conflict by pushing Iran to retaliate by
blocking the Hormuz Straits, thus severely disrupting oil shipments to
the West and Japan. France replied that since an Iraqi defeat would
destabilize other Arab regimes – thereby hurting Western interests in a
vitally strategic region – it was justified in despatching the advanced
warplanes to Iraq. Leaving aside the issue of the general strategic
well-being of the West, for France there was the more immediate
lucrative prospect of selling scores of expensive Exocet missiles to be
used by the Super-Etendards.

The fact that France had already staked large amounts of money and
expertise in Iraq became a powerful motive to back the Saddam Hussein
regime to the hilt. It encouraged its Western allies to pursue an active
policy of stemming the flow of arms or ammunition to Tehran and
provide credits to Baghdad. It helped Iraq to cope with its debts to French
companies which, at the end of three years of the Gulf War, amounted to
$5–$8 billion. It persuaded the civilian companies, which were owed
about $2 billion by Iraq, to reschedule part of the loans and accept the
rest in oil to be supplied by Saudi Arabia.[22]

Paris felt that by actively siding with Iraq it was bolstering its own standing in the Arab world, since most Middle Eastern states were backing Baghdad. It played a crucial role in bringing about rapprochement between Cairo and Baghdad.

In 1983, the year of an acute crisis in Baghdad, France emerged as a vitally important military-cum-financial prop for Iraq's long-term war effort. By the same token, relations between Paris and Tehran turned frosty. While France was over-eager to sell arms to Iraq it refused to deliver to Iran the weapons for which it had received cash before the revolution.

Tehran worked hard to persuade France to reverse its decision to provide Super-Etendard planes and Exocet missiles to Iraq. Rafsanjani said on 23 September 1983 that the sale of these weapons would turn France into 'Iran's enemy' and that it would endanger French interests throughout the world. When Paris ignored these warnings and delivered the warplanes to Iraq in early October, Tehran ended the special status accorded to French banks nearly a century before. It also placed French products on its blacklist, something it had done earlier with American products. Though the much reduced French embassy in Tehran was not closed down, France was now put in the same category as the US.

Later that month French troops posted in Beirut as part of a Western multi-national force became a target of truck bombing by Lebanese Shia militants, losing 59 servicemen in the attack. There was no conclusive proof that the action had been sponsored by Tehran: none the less, Iranian officials expressed sympathetic understanding of it, seeing in it a well-justified means for oppressed Muslims of Lebanon to take revenge on their foreign oppressors.

Even within France itself the Khomeini regime had gained militant supporters from among the 2.5 million Muslims living in the republic. By late 1983, according to a French counter-intelligence report, the Iranian embassy had set up an extensive network of individuals or cultural associations whose religious activities provided cover for their subversive activities. This state of affairs was highlighted by the expulsion from France of eight Iranians, three diplomats and five students, in December 1983.

What went unnoticed for some years was the clandestine network of a cartel of West European companies, including a French government-owned firm, that supplied huge quantities of explosives to Iran.

The cartel came into existence under the aegis of the European

Association for the Study of Safety Problems (EASSP). This organization was founded in 1975 by seven leading privately- and publicly-owned chemical companies based in Belgium, Britain, France, Holland, Italy, Sweden and West Germany. It was recognized by the French government in 1977 and had its headquarters in Paris, with Guy Chavallier of the state-owned Société Nationale des Poudres et Explosifs (SNPE) acting as secretary-general. Later it acquired five associate members from Britain, Finland, Norway and Switzerland. The constituents of the EASSP met about once a month in a private hotel in a different country. It was customary at these meetings for the members and associates to discuss their plant capacities and the state of their order books.

With the outbreak of the Gulf War these meetings would start by discussing safety and then move on to appraising the state of the arms and ammunition market. Mats Lundberg, commercial director of the Swedish weapons manufacturing company Bofors-Nobelkrut, emerged as the co-ordinator of the informally constituted cartel to take advantage of the Iran–Iraq conflict. In early May 1982, acting on behalf of this body, he approached an official of Iran's Defence Industries Organization. The result was an Iranian order for several tonnes of nitrocellulose and one million gun cartridges. On 1 July came the second Iranian purchase order for 100 tonnes of nitrocellulose for 7.62 calibre guns and 200 tonnes of explosives for guns and rockets.

The problem was that Swedish law banned export of arms or ammunition to a state either at war or forming part of a 'zone of conflict', a term which included all of the Middle East. But the law could be circumvented by falsifying the country of destination. That is, a third country could be used as the point of transit to Iran. To be on the safe side the purchaser too was falsified: from the Defence Industries Organization to the state-owned (civilian) Parchin Chemical Industries. Having secured the order Bofors-Nobelkrut shared it with two other members of the cartel.

As Iran began planning more offensives against Iraq in 1983 the need for explosives rocketed. An Iranian order for 650 tonnes of nitrocellulose was so large that Bofors-Nobelkrut decided to share it with SNPE of France, a company which had so far been selling military materials only to Iraq. For shipping it to Bandar Abbas in Iran, these firms considered intermediate stops in Italy and East Germany. Italy was particularly suitable as one of the few members of the North Atlantic Treaty Organization not to have imposed an arms embargo against Iran, and the fact that a Nato country could export war materials to another member of the alliance on the basis of a mere import certificate also made Italy a very convenient candidate. Little wonder that in January 1984 Tirrena Industriale, situated near the Italian port of Talamone, known for the arms trade, placed an order for 150 tonnes of Pentyl NSP 46 and 130 tonnes of another explosive with Bofors-Nobelkrut. This was nothing more than a repeat of the order that Bofors-Nobelkrut had received earlier from Iran's Defence Industries Organization. During the past year Tirrena Industriale had acted as a conduit for the supply to Iran of a staggering total of 5300 tonnes of explosives for 105mm and 155mm shells provided by the constituents of the EASSP cartel – now made up of 14 members and associates based in Austria, Belgium, Britain, Finland, France, Holland, Italy, Norway, Spain, Sweden, Switzerland and West Germany.

Besides the explosives sold by this cartel there were large exports of 105mm and 155mm shells by Luchaire, a company owned by SNPE, to Iran through third countries. One such transaction, consummated on 25 January 1984, was nominally destined for the Ecuadorian capital of Quito.[23]

The moral of this tale is that the basic law of demand and supply overrides the public policies of governments, particularly in capitalist countries. Here was the French administration committed to unequivocally backing Iraq, with one of the state-owned companies clandestinely supplying large quantities of ammunition to Iraq's enemy Iran. The reason for the company's behaviour was that it needed these export orders to stay solvent.

The position of such small, traditionally neutral countries as Sweden was quite tricky. In order to preserve its neutrality Sweden had established a strong military industry, but to sustain it the government had either to subsidize it heavily or let it export. Having chosen the foreign sales option, the government tried to salve its conscience by outlawing shipments to countries in a zone of conflict, the ones most in need of arms and ammunition. The managements of arms manufacturing companies found themselves in a dilemma. For instance, Bofors-Nobelkrut had its first (ever) sale of RBS-70 laser-guided missiles to Bahrain in October 1978 blocked by the government. It was then that a company official discovered that the missiles could be legally exported to, say, Singapore, which was outside any 'zone of conflict'. It was thus that Far Eastern states like Singapore and Thailand, such European destinations as Austria and Yugoslavia, and South American states like Brazil and Ecuador became popular with arms and ammunition exporters in Sweden and elsewhere.

As it was, Sweden had an above-average diplomatic interest in the Gulf conflict. Olaf Palme, a Swedish politician who later became prime minister, was chosen as the mediator by the UN secretary-general soon after the outbreak of the war. In that capacity he developed good relations with top leaders in Baghdad and Tehran. Of these two capitals, Tehran was believed to be more friendly with Palme. Since the revolution it had developed warm relations with such neutral European states as Austria, Switzerland, Yugoslavia and Sweden. Ideologically, Iran – committed to countering the 'arrogance' of major powers – was well-disposed to small states, whether in the Western or Eastern bloc or in the Third World. More specifically, the trading companies based in the small, neutral states of Europe had stepped in to provide Iran with the Western goods that had been banned by the US and European Economic Community countries. As a result, by the early 1980s Iran became Austria's second largest trading partner – after America. Likewise, in 1984 Sweden exported civilian goods worth $500 million to Iran. These included 40 speedboats – designed as pleasure cruisers by a Swedish shipbuilder – which were delivered to the Iranian coastguard.[24] Later these were to be converted to military vessels.

Palme's mediation effort was one of several that had been in train since the start of the war. The Islamic Conference Organization had been active as a mediator. So too had been the Non-Aligned Movement. As for individual states, Algeria and Turkey were in the forefront. Having successfully mediated between Iran and Iraq in 1975, and between Tehran and Washington in 1980 on the hostage crisis, Algeria was hopeful of success. But nothing came of its efforts. Nor did Turkey, on excellent terms with both belligerents, make any progress. Khomeini insisted on the ousting of Saddam Hussein from power, and showed no sign of compromise on that point.

6 TOTAL WARFARE: TANKERS AND CITIES

Having realized that Iraq had lost the initiative on the land fronts, its leaders decided to change the nature of the conflict by putting their superior air power to maximum use, giving rise first to the Tanker War and then to the War of the Cities.

TANKERS IN THE FIRING LINE

Once Iraq and Iran had reached a UN-mediated agreement on 18 February 1984 not to attack population centres, Baghdad concentrated its combat aircraft on Iran's port facilities and vessels in the Gulf. Between 25 February and 1 March it claimed to have struck seven Iranian naval targets. On 27 February Iraq announced that the Kharg oil terminal was under siege. Though it in fact lacked the air and naval power to besiege Kharg, this declaration, followed by repeated hits on the vessels trading with Iran, made shipping companies reluctant to use the terminal. On 27 March Baghdad announced that it had used the Super-Etendard–Exocet combination for the first time in its attacks on two small tankers south-west of Kharg.

This new phase of the armed conflict began in earnest on 18 April 1984, when the Iraqis struck a small Panamanian tanker near Kharg. Eight days later they hit a Saudi-owned vessel carrying Iranian oil to France, thereby signalling their resolve to target all ships, irrespective of their ownership, serving Iranian ports. On 7 May came another attack on a tanker.

As there were no vessels transporting Iraqi oil, Iran could only retaliate by targeting ships trading with Iraq's allies: Kuwait and Saudi Arabia, although without acknowledging its actions then or later. The first victim was a Kuwaiti tanker hit on 13 May near Bahrain. Within five weeks of the opening attack of 18 April, 11 ships were hit by both sides, 10 of them petroleum tankers. Surprisingly, oil prices in the usually sensitive spot market showed no movement; but insurance rates for ships trading with Kharg rose steeply, from 0.25 to 7.5 per cent of the cargo value. This translated into an increased cost of $1 to $1.50 a barrel of oil. Iran quickly offered its buyers compensatory price discounts of up to $2 a barrel on the official rate of $30. Yet Iranian exports fell as its customers diversified their supplies.

On 1 June 1984, responding to the Gulf Co-operation Council members' complaint, the UN Security Council condemned, by 13 votes to nil, attacks on the ships trading with Kuwait and Saudi Arabia. It called on all states to respect free navigation in the Gulf. This led the UN secretary-general to take steps to de-escalate the conflict which had once again been extended by the combatants to population centres.

On 3 June the Iraqis sank a Turkish-registered tanker off Kharg. Two days later Saudi warplanes, assisted by the US-operated Awacs, downed an Iranian jet fighter over Gulf waters. Tehran protested, saying that its aircraft had been in international airspace. Riyadh stated that the plane had been in Saudi airspace, but added that it did not wish to escalate the conflict. It reiterated its non-belligerent intentions through Damascus. Equally, on 8 June, President Ali Khamanei of Iran said, 'We do not want to fight Saudi Arabia, Bahrain and others . . . but this is on condition that they do not get mixed up in this war.'[1] Yet the Iranians had no intention of discontinuing their attacks on vessels trading with Saudi Arabia or Kuwait – to make the point that if the Gulf were not safe for their ships it would not be safe for others either. On 10 June Tehran's planes hit a Kuwaiti supertanker in the Lower Gulf, about 100 miles off the Qatari coast, the first such incident in this region.

By then the air raids on civilian populations had escalated to the extent of causing 900 casualties in a week. The UN secretary-general accelerated his peacemaking efforts. As a result, on 11 June 1984 both sides accepted another UN-initiated halt to attacks on each other's urban centres. They also agreed to have UN observers in their capitals to monitor breaches. On 15 June Iran proposed extending the limited truce to include Gulf shipping as well. Iraq insisted that any such agreement must allow it to repair or replace its own oil export facilities in the Gulf. To this Iran made no response. Its own exports from Kharg had by then returned to near normal at 1.6 million b/d, and insurance rates for Kharg-bound ships had fallen back to 5 per cent of the cargo value. There was such a glut of oil tankers in the international market that the owners gained a lot more in compensation for the loss of a vessel on the high seas than from scrapping it. Also there were plenty of 'cowboy sailors' ready to earn $5000 for a single trip to Kharg. Prominent among the companies which kept up traffic to and from the Iranian ports in the

Upper Gulf were those registered in Norway, Sweden, Denmark and Greece.

After lengthy consultations GCC members rejected the idea of restricting the movement of ships trading with them to their territorial waters, and opted for providing them with air cover in the international waters of the Gulf. The arrival in Saudi Arabia from the US of 400 Stinger anti-aircraft missiles and a super-Awacs plane, capable of monitoring air and sea traffic, bolstered Saudi defences. Eight American warships began escorting Saudi and Kuwaiti tankers in the Gulf. On 20 June Washington announced that Saudi Arabia had set up an Air Defence Interception Zone (ADIZ), known as the Fahd Line, which went beyond the Saudi territorial limits.[2] This would allow Saudi warplanes, guided by US Awacs and refuelled by US air tankers, to engage other aircraft threatening shipping in the region.

On 24 June Baghdad's claim that its planes had hit Kharg was confirmed by Tehran. Iran conceded that the Iraqi raid had damaged oil loading facilities on the western side of the island. Kharg, an island measuring 40 by 20 miles, is situated 140 miles south of the Iraqi coast. It is connected to the on-shore oil facilities at Gavaneh, with most of its well-dispersed major pipelines and other equipment either buried or sheltered, and the oil flowing to the loading points through underwater pipes mainly by gravity. On the eastern side of the island is a large T-shaped jetty with 14 berths suitable for small to medium tankers, on the western side is a J-shaped jetty with 20 berths, including three for supertankers, a total of 34 berths capable of handling 6.5 million b/d. In this massive complex the only vulnerable targets are the tanker loading points. They are difficult to hit from the air because they are comparatively small and they are well protected by Hawk and other surface-to-air missiles and low altitude anti-aircraft guns. To safeguard against gunshots or missiles the Iraqi pilots often flew at high altitudes; this militated against accurate results. But since 85 per cent of the Iranian oil exports were shipped from Kharg, and since these foreign earnings paid for essential military imports, Kharg was the prime Iranian target. Almost as important were the tankers carrying Iranian crude oil. No wonder that between 23 June and 25 July the Iraqis staged four series of air raids against Iranian shipping in the Gulf. Tehran retaliated, but rather feebly. On 5 July it attacked a Liberian-registered tanker loaded with Saudi oil in the Lower Gulf.

The overall Iraqi purpose in initiating and sustaining the Tanker War

was to make oil shipments from the Gulf hazardous, thus internationalizing the conflict and drawing in the superpowers – and/or
getting Saudi Arabia and Kuwait to join the hostilities formally on
Baghdad's side. The latter development would have opened up a new
front against Iran, severely straining its already depleted air force and
torpedoing Iranian plans to mount land offensives against Iraq. In the
event, Baghdad failed to achieve either of its objectives.

In early July the much-awaited Iranian land offensive in the south was
deferred. The floods in the marshes, and the need to study a peace plan
conceived by Egypt and forwarded to Tehran by Indira Gandhi, chair-
person of the Non-Aligned Movement (NAM), led to the postponement.
The elements of the peace plan were: an immediate ceasefire; return to
international borders by the combatants; stationing of an international
force on the Iraqi side to supervise the ceasefire; an NAM commission to
determine who started the war and who prolonged it; and the setting up
of the Islamic Reconstruction Fund to finance reconstruction of the
war-damaged zones of both countries.

This breathing-space enabled Saddam Hussein to strengthen the Iraqi
war machine by fortifying the existing defence positions, increasing the
size of the armed forces, and consolidating the reorganization of the
military – signalled by the establishment of a new East of Tigris
command in February 1984, the change of the head of the air force in
March, and the setting up of the new Shatt al Arab command in May.

On the eve of the fourth anniversary of the Gulf War in September
1984 the Iraqi army, composed of 22 divisions, was 500,000 strong:
twice its size at the beginning of the hostilities, and three times its
strength in June 1982. The Popular Army was enlarged to an even greater
extent. Its members, given two months training, were charged mainly
with protecting the regime and strategic targets, but they were also
despatched to the rear areas of the front lines on a rota basis. The Popular
Army's strength of 560,000 in early 1984 was two-and-a-half times that
in September 1980. The government mounted a mobilization plan in
the summer to expand this force further. All university students were
required to enrol in a five-week course during summer holidays at
Popular Army training camps. Every so often police raided places
popular with young men, and pressed them into joining the Popular
Army. 'Iraq's ability to mobilize manpower is three times that of Iran,'
declared Tariq Aziz in August 1984. 'We are definitely not suffering
from lack of numbers [in the armed forces].'[3] This statement came

during the year which ended with record military imports of $7.7 billion, far above the previous year's $6 billion.

The Iraqis were particularly diligent in fortifying their four-tier defensive system in the south: minefields, barbed wire, anti-tank trenches and heavy artillery placed on high ground. Abundantly armed, the Iraqis were in high spirits. To block Iranian penetration, they had created from the waters of the Haur al Hawizeh marshes an artificial lake eight miles long and two to seven miles wide south of the marshland. On the south and west of the lake were hundreds of bunkers filled with regular soldiers and Popular Army militia. The Iraqis were as numerous as the Iranians in the area: 200,000.[4]

To be able to breach such defences, Tehran needed more men with better training, and more and better military hardware. Iranian leaders seemed to have concluded that for frontal infantry assaults on heavily fortified Iraqi positions to succeed they required greater mechanized mobility and air cover as well as more tanks and logistic stocks. A network of military roads and logistic storage areas was constructed along the border, particularly in the southern sector, and the procurement of heavy military hardware was accelerated. Among other things Tehran purchased trainer aircraft from Switzerland, Chieftain tank parts from Britain (for which orders had been placed before the revolution) and Soviet-made tanks from Syria and Libya, and placed orders for arms with Brazil through Libya.[5] Iran upgraded the training of its militia and junior officers, and reorganized and retrained its infantry units to improve their attacking abilities. The Iranian plans were aided by the improved co-ordination between the military and the Revolutionary Guards Corps, much in evidence in the Majnoon Islands offensives.

Politically, too, Iran was more cohesive than before. The composition of the Second Islamic Majlis, elected in April–May 1984, was an important indicator. Unlike its predecessor, it lacked any members of the opposition Freedom Movement, which had boycotted the elections. The new parliament confirmed Musavi as prime minister on 5 August by 163 votes to 21, an improvement on the 115 votes he had secured in the First Majlis. Rafsanjani was re-elected speaker by 181 votes to nil, an increase of 35 votes over his performance four years ago. Under his leadership parliament had emerged as the most important political institution. Its decision to allow its proceedings to be broadcast live on radio manifested the confidence that the Islamic regime felt.

Against this background Khomeini brushed aside the opinion that the nation was growing war-weary. 'Our revolutionary guards who lead a less than normal life do not fear war,' he said in his Eid al Fitr (the festival of 'Breaking the Fast') message. 'War would not do them any harm. It is those who have palaces and the like who should fear war, because they would lose out.'[6]

The result of these military and political changes became apparent in Tehran's minor but properly planned offensive in the Saif Saad area of the central sector on 18 October 1984. Its forces infiltrated the enemy lines at night along a 12-mile front, and recaptured an area that Iraq had seized in the early days of the war. The Iraqis counterattacked, but recovered only part of the lost territory.

At about the same time came an indication that the doctrine of military caution coupled with professionalism was being adopted officially. Khomeini appointed Brigadier-General Qasim Ali Zahir-Nejad as his second personal representative on the Supreme Defence Council for the duration of the war. Zahir-Nejad had resigned as chief of staff in July 1984 in response to the revolutionary guards commanders' criticism that he had failed to exploit the early gains of the Majnoon Islands offensive in February.

The general pattern of the armed conflict during 1984 was a compendium of the old pattern of the land war and air strikes on commercial shipping and population centres. The intermittent warfare was interspersed with ceasefire calls by Baghdad which were routinely rebuffed by Tehran. On land Iran retained the initiative with its actual and threatened offensives. In the skies and the Gulf waters, though, it was on the defensive, finding itself unable to match the size and efficiency of the Iraqi air force.

In early 1985 the Iraqis expected an Iranian offensive. To pre-empt it they attacked the enemy north and east of the Majnoon Islands on 28 January, but the Iranians were well-entrenched and repulsed the assault. Two days later the Iraqis mounted an offensive in the central sector to recapture the Saif Saad area, but failed.

THE WAR OF THE CITIES

On 5 March 1985 Iraq bombed a steel factory in Ahvaz and an unfinished nuclear power plant in Bushahr. By so doing, Iran argued, Baghdad had breached the June 1984 UN-sponsored agreement to refrain from hitting civilian targets. From this ensued the 'War of the Cities' which persisted until mid-June.

The Iranians shelled Basra. In return the Iraqis carried out air attacks on various Iranian cities and towns, including Isfahan, about 250 miles from the border. Iran retaliated with an air raid on a Baghdad suburb on 11 March, the day of a major Iranian land offensive. The next day Iraq hit 16 cities and towns of Iran, and gave one week's notice of treating Iranian airspace as a 'war zone', which implied that civilian aircraft might be shot down. Iran responded by hitting Kirkuk on 14 March with a surface-to-surface missile, probably a Soviet-made Scud-B with a 1000lb warhead and a range of 185 miles, reportedly obtained from Libya. The following day the Iraqis bombed Tehran, about 300 miles from the international border. Iran responded to the Iraqi air raids on its capital by firing four Scud-B missiles at Baghdad. It was at a disadvantage in engaging in aerial dogfights. Iraq not only used the advanced Mirage F-1s for bombing population centres but also armed them with the deadly infra-red Matra-530 and Magic-1 air-to-air missiles. It claimed to have shot down 12 Iranian F-14s.

On 31 March, when the UN secretary-general undertook a tour of four regional states, including Iran and Iraq, Tehran reported that Iraqi raids had killed 1450 civilians and injured more than 4000.[7] The reason for the Iraqi resumption of the War of the Cities was articulated by Major-General Thabit Sultan, commander of the Iraqi Fourth Corps. 'We want to bring the Iranian people into the front lines of the war,' he explained. 'We hope this will encourage the Iranian people to rebel against their government and bring the war to an end.'[8] This hope was unrealized, since the Islamic regime in Tehran successfully presented the Iraqi air strikes as further evidence of Saddam Hussein's inhumanity. Khomeini dismissed appeals by the opposition leader Bazargan for a ceasefire as defeatist and demoralizing to the armed forces. None the less, on 6 April both sides agreed to stop attacking each other's urban centres.

Taking advantage of the comparative lull in the fighting the Saudi foreign minister, Prince Saud al Faisal, visited Tehran to seek a cease-fire on the eve of Ramadan beginning on 20 May. Nothing came of it.

On 25 May 1985 a suicide bomber driving a car packed with explosives made an unsuccessful attempt to assassinate Shaikh Sabah al Sabah, the Kuwaiti ruler. Claiming that the action had been directed by Iran,[9] Saddam Hussein resumed air raids on Tehran, and intensified attacks on ships in the Gulf. On 30 May and again on 4 June 1985 Kharg Island was subjected to particularly severe air strikes. In return Iran deployed its F-4 fighters based on Lavan Island to strike ships trading with Kuwait or Saudi Arabia near the Qatari coast.

The Iranian government resolved to use the occasion of Jerusalem Day, celebrated since the revolution on the last Friday of Ramadan, to prove to the world that it had popular support to continue the war. Baghdad intervened. Its Farsi service radio warned that a massacre awaited those who congregated for the Friday prayer and sermons at Tehran University, mentioning the campus and certain streets and squares leading to it as specific targets for bombing. On 14 June Tehran witnessed a congregation variously estimated at between one and five million strong. There was no bombing by the Iraqis. The same day Baghdad announced a two-week halt in air raids to give the Iranian people 'the chance to pressure [their leaders] into accepting peace'.[10] As it did not resume them on 30 June 1985, or later, the rationale offered by Iranian leaders that the massive turnout of the people in Tehran on 14 June had convinced Iraq of the popularity of the Islamic regime's policy on the war gained credence.

During a seven-week period in March–April and May–June 1985, Iraqi planes hit Tehran 43 times. In contrast, 12 Iranian surface-to-surface missiles landed in Baghdad. Once the populations of these capitals got over the initial shock of the bombs or missiles, they found that the economic damage caused by them was limited and bearable. As such, Iraq's launching of the War of the Cities did not bring it any tangible military or psychological benefit.

Concurrent with the War of the Cities was the Iranian offensive, codenamed Badr (after the Prophet Muhammad's first victory over the unbelievers), mounted on 11 March 1985 in the Haur al Hawizeh marshland. Tehran committed over 60,000 soldiers and revolutionary guards to capture the lower reaches of the Tigris, about 8 miles from the starting point of the assault, cross the river, and sever the nearby Basra–Baghdad highway running parallel to the western bank. Over the past several months the Iranians had, through aggressive patrolling in small speedboats using narrow waterways flanked by tall reeds, flushed out the Iraqis from the marshes and pushed them back to fixed positions on dry land. They had also improved their logistics.

Once the offensive got going the swampy conditions again helped the Iranians to offset the Iraqi advantage in tanks as they negotiated the marshes in boats and along the narrow strips of dry land in the area. Once they reached the dry plain they waited to build up their forces before pushing 4 miles, through huge tracts of barbed wire and across minefields, to the Tigris under heavy fire from the Iraqi positions. A brigade of some 5000 Iranians set up two pontoon bridges across the river and captured the Basra–Baghdad highway on 17 March. The next day Tehran claimed that its forces controlled all of the Haur al Hawizeh marshes south of the Iraqi town of Amara.

The news that Iraq's defences, so painstakingly built up over four years, had been breached by the Iranians set alarm bells ringing in Baghdad. The Iraqis rallied. Using Uzayr in the north and Qurna in the south as two points of a pincer, they mounted a massive counter-offensive. They combined large artillery reinforcements with furious air force activity, staging up to 250 sorties a day. And, as in previous emergencies, they resorted to chemical weapons. Saddam Hussein despatched the elite Presidential Guard division to the front, bringing the total Iraqi forces engaged in the combat to 60,000. The deployment of Iraq's crack troops turned the tide.[11] Lacking sufficient armour, logistical backing or air power to resist the massive Iraqi onslaught, the Iranians failed to maintain their hold over the newly acquired territory. By 20 March they had been forced to retreat to the Haur al Hawizeh marshes. Both sides suffered heavy casualties, with some 20,000 Iranians and 14,000 Iraqis dead.[12]

Overall, both sides felt that their land war strategy and tactics had proved effective. The Badr offensive convinced Tehran that by employing certain tactics efficiently it could overcome Baghdad's superiority in military hardware. It showed the Iranian planners the virtue of depriving the Iraqis of full use of their more numerous armour, artillery and warplanes by attacking at night in marshes – or in mountainous terrain. They continued to stress the surprise element in their planning. 'In our various preparations, while we aim to avoid heavy casualties, we seek to surprise the enemy and wear him out psychologically,' stated Colonel Ismail Sohrabi, Iran's chief of staff. 'Our operations enable our men to fight an enemy with superior hardware.'[13] Though the Badr offensive failed to yield the prized Basra–Baghdad highway to the Iranians, its damage to the Iraqi war machine was deemed satisfactory in Tehran.

His success in repulsing the Iranian offensive made President Saddam Hussein feel satisfied with his overall strategy of static defence and heavy dependence on advanced military hardware. In May 1985 he awarded the medal of valour to each of the 14 members of the military high command. By now he had modified his policy of keeping the military leaders in the background.

Prominent among those who came to the fore were Major-General Hisham Sabah Fakhri and Major-General Mahir Abdul Rashid. As the commander of the Fourth Corps, Fakhri, a native of Mosul, played a crucial role in countering the February 1983 Iranian offensive and boosting the severely damaged Iraqi morale. About a year later he was appointed deputy chief of staff in charge of operations, a key military position. Abdul Rashid, a relative of Saddam Hussein, distinguished himself in 1983 as the commander of the First Corps posted in the north. Soon after his transfer to the Third Corps in the Basra region in January 1984, he had to face an Iranian offensive. His star rose when he succeeded in blunting that thrust too.

Such performances encouraged Saddam Hussein to give greater freedom to field commanders to conduct combat operations and assume responsibility for their decisions. On the whole he and other political leaders were now more amenable than before to considering seriously the views and wishes of senior military officers. With a new batch of commanders, promoted on the basis more of professional competence than political loyalty, the quality of military advice improved substantially. Therefore crucial war decisions now came to be made jointly by Saddam Hussein and the military high command. The state-run media publicized the Iraqi president's meetings with senior defence forces officers which were now more numerous than those with political or administrative officials.

At the same time Saddam Hussein continued his policy of consolidating the loyalty of officers and troops to himself. This task was performed by a specially trained corps of political officers who employed such means as regularly furnishing every soldier and militiaman with a series of paperbacks of Saddam Hussein's statements and speeches. (By late 1984 Saddam Hussein's speeches and statements had been compiled into 312 books.[14]) An extreme example of this was the Presidential Guard, composed largely of men from and around Tikrit – the native place of the president, and the origin of the family name of Tikriti which had gone into disuse following a government decree in 1976 banning the use of family names, often derived from towns or clans or sub-clans.[15] Under the command of Major-General Talie Khalil Duri, Saddam

Hussein expanded the Presidential Guard to a division, and transformed it into an elite unit of the army, now composed of seven corps.

In order to meet the pressure of the actual and potential Iranian offensives it became necessary for Iraq to maintain up to a million armed men on active duty. This created much political and economic strain. The number of deserters rose, and they swelled the ranks of the opposition.[16] The government revived the 1982 law which prescribed death penalty for desertion.

The inflated Popular Army had a negative effect on the economy. Production suffered as employees took time off to serve in the militia – as did the public treasury which reimbursed their employers. Labour scarcity compelled the authorities to recall pensioners to work. The proportion of women in administrative jobs rose to 51 per cent and in the public sector to 31 per cent. To increase the population of Iraqi nationals the government announced in August 1985 that any foreign Arab resident could hold dual nationality. This was meant to encourage particularly the over one million Egyptian workers to settle in Iraq – thereby increasing *inter alia* the proportion of Sunni Arabs in the country. Despite restrictions on sending remittances home the nearly two million expatriates were transferring $2 billion annually. With Baghdad's oil income running at only around $8 billion a year in 1984, this was a substantial burden on Iraq's current trade account.

As if this were not enough, there was drought in 1984 which reduced the wheat crop by two-thirds. This, combined with a drop in petroleum revenue and the falling value of the American dollar – in which all oil transactions were conducted – worsened the interrelated problems of inflation, hoarding, profiteering and smuggling. To stem hoarding the government decided, in January 1985, to imprison hoarders for 15 years and confiscate their property, awarding one-fifth of it to the informants.

Tehran faced equally daunting economic problems in the wake of the world oil glut, caused by falling consumption. In the fiscal year 1984–5 Iran earned $14.7 billion in oil revenue against the projected $21.2 billion, a drop of 30 per cent. The government responded by slashing its civilian expenditure by 40 per cent, and severely restricting imports, including industrial materials and spares. This, and the periodic power cuts due to the excess of demand over supply, had a debilitating effect on the economy. Industrial output during March–June 1985 fell by 17 per cent over the same period in the previous year.[17]

The war and import restrictions had distorted the economy and, with the rising budget deficit, fuelled inflation. The government claimed that by curtailing its expenditure – mainly on development projects – and reducing money supply growth from 23 per cent in 1981 to 6 per cent in 1984 it had halved the inflation rate from 21.5 per cent to 10.5 per cent. But in early 1985 the Paris-based Organization for Economic Co-operation and Development put the inflation rate around 30 per cent. Hoarding and profiteering persisted, despite the widely publicized efforts of the patrols of 'assistants of God' who brought many offenders to the economic crimes courts.

Those with fixed incomes felt the pinch, including the country's 1.5 million civil servants. The government encouraged people to complain, and ran a daily 'complaints slot' on its radio. Newspapers urged readers to send in complaints by letter or phone; and many did. They concerned erratic distribution of rationed goods, sharp increases in prices, power cuts, bribery and bureaucratic sloth. By so doing the officials and editors allowed the disgruntled to let off steam, and not to let dissatisfaction build up to explosive proportions.

Premier Musavi had his own frustrations to cope with. 'It is now two years since we sent to the Majlis bills on taxation, land distribution, foreign trade and the limits of the private sector,' he complained in December 1984.[18] These bills had been passed by parliament but vetoed by the conservative Guardians Council charged with vetting legislation in the light of Islamic principles and the Iranian constitution.

The exigencies of the Gulf War and the consequent rationing of basic necessities had brought most of the external trade and much of the internal commerce under official control through administrative decrees. But the government's effort to regularize the situation through legislation had been impeded by the Guardians Council. It judged in 1983 that such legislation was counter to the Islamic precept of freedom of commerce as well as the constitutional provision for economic freedom. On the other hand Article 44 of the constitution specifically put foreign trade in the public sector. In April 1984 parliament passed a modified bill which made concessions to private traders, but even this was rejected by the Guardians Council.

In late August Khomeini used the occasion of the swearing-in of the new cabinet, following the convening of the Second Islamic Majlis, to offer guidelines. It was the duty of the popular Islamic regime to enable its citizens to be active in all sectors of life, he stated. Therefore government monopoly of foreign trade was wrong. While the state was free to import goods it ought to focus on military and strategic materials. In any case, it was charged with the overall responsibility for economic planning, and that gave it the right to oversee the private sector. Khomeini's interpretation of Islamic principles satisfied the contradictory demands on the regime. It was required to maintain supplies and fair distribution of basic goods at reasonable prices to help preserve public morale in the face of a long war. It was also required to conciliate bazaar traders who felt threatened by continued charges of engaging in 'economic terrorism' by the authorities.

As it was, in 1984 the Islamic revolution was five years old and in a state of consolidation. Islamization had been instituted in all walks of life, with Islamic banking coming into effect on 21 March 1984. In the political sphere all opposition, present or potential, had been suppressed or enfeebled. All the revolutionary institutions were in place and functioning. It was the regime's aim to preserve unity within the clergy-dominated revolutionary Islamic camp, and mobilize the people behind a unified front led by Ayatollah Khomeini. In this process the war with Iraq came to play a dominant part. Khomeini continued to take a moral-religious view of the conflict. 'Those who criticize us and say "Why don't you compromise with these corrupt powers" analyse things from a materialistic viewpoint,' he told senior officials in his Eid al Fitr message. 'They do not know the views of God and prophets, how they dealt with oppressors . . . To compromise with oppressors is to oppress the oppressed.'[19]

From mid-July to early August the Iranians mounted a series of minor offensives, codenamed Quds and Ashura, in the northern, central and southern sectors. In the north they were aided by the Iraqi Kurdish rebels, and in the south by the contingents of exiled Iraqis armed and trained by Tehran, Al Mujahedin. By mid-August the Iranians had captured 120 square miles in the northern and central zones as well as several Iraqi positions in the Haur al Hawizeh marshes.

This was the background against which presidential elections were held in Iran on 16 August 1985. Among the 50 candidates who registered with the Guardians Council was Mahdi Bazargan. His party, the Freedom Movement, favoured opening talks with Iraq and combining diplomacy with fighting. It argued that Iran had wrongly rejected such an opportunity three times: in May 1982 at the time of the recapture of Khorramshahr; in March 1984 after the Majnoon Islands offensive; and in May 1985 when the Iraqi offer of a ceasefire during the month of

Ramadan was conveyed to Tehran through the Saudi foreign minister. War was in the interest of imperialism and Zionism, and lethal to Islam and the revolution, it concluded.[20] However, the Guardians Council rejected 47 candidates, including Bazargan, on the grounds of either a lack of genuinely Islamic credentials, or of administrative or managerial skills – or an unqualified acceptance of the doctrine of the Rule of the Just Faqih (Jurist), which underwrites the Iranian constitution. However, the main reason was that the Council did not wish the election campaign to provide an opportunity for concerted attacks on the government on the conduct of the war and the economy, or for the opposition forces to widen their base.

Of the two candidates allowed to run against Hojatalislam Ali Khamanei, the current president and the official favourite, was Habibollah Asghar-Owladi, a former commerce minister, who advocated a greater role for the private sector. The third candidate, Mahmoud Kashani, an eminent lawyer, criticized the administration for lacking a 'real economic policy', and the press for being under either the control of the government or 'the influence of unhealthy groups'.[21]

Political leaders and the media exhorted the electorate to vote, describing failure to do so as unIslamic and 'a betrayal of the martyrs who had joined Allah to consolidate the divine system [in Iran]'.[22] Yet, at 14,244,630 out of a total of 25,138,000 voters, the turnout of 57 per cent was much lower than the 73 per cent for the October 1981 presidential election. But since the previous poll had been held in the wake of President Rajai's assassination the circumstances were exceptional. This time the situation was comparatively normal.

Khamanei won. But, despite being a better-known figure than before, he secured 88 per cent of the vote as against the 95 per cent he had achieved in the previous election. His support fell from about 16 million votes to 12.6 million.[23] The regime's critics attributed the decline to the growing unpopularity of the official policies, particularly on the war and the management of the economy. Its supporters, on the other hand, argued that the fall in voter participation was a reflection of the prevailing stability and the confidence among citizens that Khamanei would be re-elected by a wide margin. In any case, they added, President Khamanei had secured much wider electoral support than most Western chief executives, and by Western standards the voter participation had been quite satisfactory.

Interestingly, by late 1984 the importance of the ruling Islamic

Republican Party within the revolutionary infrastructure had declined. Though a nominal IRP member, Premier Musavi declared that he could not function within the framework of one party. The IRP had become riven with factionalism. Referring to two camps within the party, each with different approaches to socio-economic issues, Rafsanjani stated that the infighting had paralysed the party and significantly impeded the executive and legislature.[24] These factions were popularly known as radical and conservative, with Premier Musavi identified with the former, and President Khamanei and the Guardians Council with the latter. Khamanei, the party general secretary, tended to downplay the internecine differences while Ayatollah Khomeini, recognizing the reality, periodically called for an end to factionalism.

Khamanei's re-election provided him with a chance to change the prime minister. He was widely known to be unhappy with the performance of the government of Musavi, his reluctant choice in October 1981. Musavi's supporters mounted a grassroots campaign for his re-selection. The atmosphere became so charged that 135 Majlis deputies sought Ayatollah Khomeini's guidance on the appointment of the next cabinet. In his reply Khomeini stated: 'I consider Mr Musavi to be a pious and dedicated Muslim, and his government to be a successful one under extremely complicated conditions prevailing in the country. I don't consider it advisable to replace the Musavi government, but the president and the Islamic Majlis are the final powers to choose.'[25] By so doing Khomeini opted for preserving revolutionary unity (by including both factions in the executive branch) and maintaining continuity in the state apparatus – with Musavi, Khamanei and Rafsanjani occupying the same leading positions they had done for the past several years.

The need for national unity was all the greater in view of the war which was being waged as much in the Gulf waters as on land. During the latter part of 1984 Baghdad's air superiority improved further. Its attacks on Iranian oil tankers increased in January 1985, and totalled 30 by the end of March. Tehran's score was seven. In one year of the Tanker War, which started in April 1984, Iraq had hit 65 ships versus Iran's 25.

While Baghdad continued to do better than Tehran in attacking oil tankers it failed to achieve its objective of demolishing the Kharg oil terminal. It had become apparent by now that the Iraqi air force lacked the aircraft, the munitions and the human skills to destroy Kharg.

Furthermore, Iraq operated under certain diplomatic limitations. The Gulf rulers, who funded the Iraqi war effort, cautioned Baghdad against driving Tehran to extremities by knocking out its Kharg oil facilities. Equally, the Western powers, intent on preserving navigational safety in the Gulf, urged caution on the Iraqis. Finally, as Saddam Hussein was to explain in mid-August 1985, Iraq had not tried to obliterate Kharg because he believed that Tehran might come round to having peace talks.[26]

As it was, the Iraqi president had considerably lowered his war aims. 'Iraq is now fighting only to prevent Iran from occupying Iraq,' he said in an interview with a Kuwait-based newspaper. 'Technically speaking, the war may also end by one side achieving a military victory and occupying the land of the other. However, only the first alternative is realistic – the one foiling the aim of the other. When one side fails to achieve its goals through war, it means defeat [for it].'[27]

Within this strategic thinking – which put primary stress on heavy, static defence – Saddam Hussein had some area of manoeuvre in intensifying Iraqi attacks on Kharg. Hitherto, he had reckoned that if Iraq destroyed the Kharg terminal then Tehran would retaliate by mounting a punishing land offensive against it. But once Baghdad had succeeded in blunting repeated Iranian assaults, the last one in March 1985, it lost its fear of Iranian reprisals on land. This, coupled with the failure of the Iraqi-initiated War of the Cities in June 1985 to compel Tehran to negotiate, led Saddam Hussein to plan devastating attacks on Kharg to give the Iranian regime a taste of the 'comprehensive war' it wished to conduct. Militarily, Baghdad was ready. It had by then obtained a squadron of an advanced version of the French Mirage F-1s capable of firing Exocet missiles and refuelling in the air: this allowed it to return the five Super-Etendard planes it had leased from Paris. French and Indian instructors had helped improve the Iraqi pilots' altitude attack training and planning. On the Iranian side the defence capacity of Kharg was reduced by the transfer of computers and other automatic equipment to Tehran in the spring of 1985 to protect the city from persistent enemy bombing.

Between 14 August and 5 October 1985 Iraq staged 21 air raids on Kharg. But only a few of these were effective – during the earlier period, particularly on 14 and 25 August – due to the surprise element and the innovative flight patterns of the Iraqi warplanes. The pilots started out at very low altitudes, thus evading the Iranian radar, and then rose sharply near the target. This enabled them to fly directly over the Iranian air defence equipment, take effective electronic countermeasures (such as jamming the radars of the enemy missiles), and direct their anti-radiation air-to-surface missiles with active radars at their targets. This was the task of the first wave of attacking Iraqi jet fighters. The succeeding wave(s) fired stand-off air-to-surface missiles at the range of 3.5 to 5 miles. The Iraqis followed this pattern for the second time on 25 August. The attacks damaged the main T-shaped jetty, and reduced Kharg's capacity by about a third.

However, the Iranians soon learned to identify the flight profiles of the Iraqi warplanes. They also reinforced their short range air defence (SHORAD) to compel the Iraqi attackers to stick to higher altitudes. They refurbished their electronic counter-countermeasures. And they adopted radar emission tactics which made it difficult for Iraqi anti-radiation missiles to home in on their targets. Adept at technical innovation, the Iranians had earlier modified some of the key oil facilities to reduce their radar emission, and used decoys or radar reflectors to mislead Exocet anti-ship missiles. Though the renewed Iranian effort shored up the defences at Kharg, it did not reach a point where Baghdad was forced to reconsider its tactics or cease its attacks. Its raids on 27 September and 3 October resulted in damage to loading berths. None the less, even at its lowest capacity Kharg was capable of handling 1.5 million b/d.[28]

The crude oil was now being ferried in Iranian tankers from Kharg to Sirri Island, 340 miles to the south and out of the range of Iraqi warplanes, where it was stored in 'mother' ships for transfer to the customers' tankers. To cushion the interruptions in supplies to Sirri, Iran purchased offshore mooring buoys to load 350,000 b/d at two locations north-west of Kharg. The commissioning of the Sirri terminal obviated the need for Iran's petroleum buyers to expose their tankers to Iraqi attacks by trading with Kharg. And the fact that Sirri had a reserve of 15 million barrels stored in its tank farm helped Iran to meet its contractual obligations to its customers without interruption. Also the oil terminal on Lavan Island 250 miles south of Kharg, with 400,000 b/d capacity, now served by a tanker shuttle from Kharg, remained operational.

By mid-October Iran had established that Iraq was incapable of destroying the Kharg oil facilities, and that any disruption in Iranian oil shipments could only be temporary. However, there was an overall reduction in exports, from an average of 1.5 million b/d in mid-1985 to 800,000 b/d in late 1985.[29] As a long-term solution to the problem, Iran announced a programme of constructing several floating jetties on the edge of the Gulf, and a string of fixed oil terminals at Taheri, 170 miles south of Kharg, and Bandar Asaluyeh, 30 miles further south. The aggregate loading capacity of these new facilities was to be 6.5 million b/d.

Iran continued its strategy of intermittent attacks on enemy soil. Its assault on 8 September 1985 in the north of the territory east of Rawandoz gained it a substantial area. In this it had the active backing of the insurgents of the Kurdish Democratic Party who claimed control of northern Iraqi teritory almost up to the Syrian border.

Tehran doggedly pursued its strategy of encircling Basra by establishing a firm toehold in the Haur al Hawizeh marshes, particularly in the Majnoon Islands. Having infiltrated the marshland and established their control over the intricate waterways, the Iranians mounted an offensive on 11 September 1985 to overrun the southern part of the larger Western Majnoon Island. They succeeded. Baghdad responded with a counteroffensive, deploying among others units of the elite Presidential Guard. It failed to retake the lost territory, but sufficiently damaged the enemy capability to frustrate its imminent plan to use the captured territory as a staging post for attacking Basra. In October Baghdad initiated a campaign to deprive the Iranians of natural cover by trimming the tall reeds in the wetlands and constructing 35-foot-high watchtowers armed with night vision equipment and acoustic sensors. But this had only a marginal impact on Iran's dominance of the marshes. Iran had by now established specialized amphibious commando units of about 1000 men. Further to the south, it had constructed a network of roads on the earth mounds scattered throughout the marshes and the flood areas of the Shatt al Arab south of Abadan. In short, by the end of 1985 Iran was well prepared to stage a new series of assaults in the southern sector.

In direct response to the Iraqi bombing of Kharg, the Iranians increased their air raids on the Iraqi oilfields in the north and their inspection of freighters in the Gulf suspected of carrying Iraq-bound arms or ammunition. On 11 November 1985 the Washington Post reported that since early September the Iranians had inspected 300 ships in the Gulf. Also Tehran improved its capability to hit vessels in the Lower Gulf by building a helicopter base on its offshore oil platform at

Reshadat (called Rustam before the revolution) 75 miles from the Qatari coast.

More importantly, in early October 1985 Tehran organized partial mobilization under the title 'Caravan to Karbala'. Estimates of the target figure varied from 300,000 to 1,000,000. Numerous towns and cities began sending their 'Caravan to Karbala' to the war front. Karbala was a particularly emotive warcry for Iranian Shias. It was where Imam Hussein had been killed in 680, along with 72 ill-equipped followers while fighting a well-armed enemy force of 4000. The event is re-enacted annually as a passion play by Shias in a ten-day ceremony, which is accompanied by mass flagellation. The mobilization was as much part of Tehran's psychological warfare to signal its will to fight on as it was to strengthen its military position on the ground. As Premier Musavi put it: 'This is a war in which the party which is more steadfast will win.'[30]

While Iran continued to hold the initiative in the land war, its military activities in the Gulf and its air force operations were no match for those of its enemy. In 1985 Iraq claimed to have staged 20,011 air sorties against Iran and 77 major raids against the Kharg oil terminal. It also claimed to have struck 124 'hostile' maritime targets, often meaning tankers.[31]

Generally speaking, the Baghdad regime weathered the events of 1984–5 well, and proved its stability, in contrast to what had happened in 1982–3 when each of the vital state institutions – the party, the presidency, the military and the intelligence – underwent serious crisis.

The security services had been the last to experience a shakeup in the autumn of 1983, the details of which leaked out only in the following spring. In mid-October 1983 Saddam Hussein dismissed Barzan Tikriti as intelligence chief. Observers offered a variety of reasons for this. Barzan Tikriti reportedly failed to inform the president of an assassination plot by senior military officers. According to another well-informed account, he wanted to plant his security men within the military hierarchy, and this was resented by senior officers. Finally, Saddam Hussein was believed to have been under pressure by Washington to distance his regime from international terrorism; and Barzan Tikriti was close to Abu Nidal, a Palestinian leader reputed to be deeply involved in terrorist actions. By dismissing his stepbrother, the Iraqi president countered the charge of nepotism directed at him by his critics, conciliated military leaders during the course of an Iranian offensive in the south, and checked the powers of a man in charge of one of the regime's prime mainstays. As the best organized and most efficient secret service in the Arab world, Iraqi intelligence employed an army of informers and agents, and diligently performed the job of keeping the citizenry in a condition of 'healthy' fright. Having sacked its chief, the Iraqi president purged the security apparatus. He established another intelligence service responsible directly to him, and appointed his 20-year-old son, Uday Hussein, as head of his two personal security services.[32]

The success in repulsing repeated Iranian offensives strengthened Saddam Hussein's power and prestige at home. One of the manifestations of the confidence he exuded was the holding of the elections to the Second National Assembly in October 1984. However, unlike in 1980, military personnel were barred from voting this time. Disenfranchizing a million voters, engaged in actively defending the country, was a curious decision, all the more so when the results showed that victorious candidates had played an active role in aiding the war effort. Nearly three-quarters of those elected were Baathists. About 40 per cent of the deputies, including the speaker of the Assembly, were Shia. The number of women deputies nearly doubled, from 17 to 33: a reflection of the increased importance of women in all walks of life during the war. Interestingly, the newly elected parliament formed a special committee to focus on citizens' complaints. Its overall role, however, remained marginal, with the major decisions, legislative and executive, being taken by the president and the Revolutionary Command Council.

Saddam Hussein continued to project himself as a pious Muslim – even more so when his regime faced an acute military threat from Tehran. He offered much-publicized prayers at Shia holy shrines before the October 1984 Iranian offensive and again after the successful repulse of Tehran's March 1985 assault. During Ramadan (in May–June) he decreed that government officials should hold public fast-breaking banquets, thus creating a symbiosis between the Baathist regime and Islam.

In late April he sponsored the Second Popular Islamic Conference in Baghdad attended by more than 300 clerics and laymen. As before, it sided with Iraq in the war. Describing the Iranian rulers as 'oppressive and cruel', it urged all Muslim countries to cut diplomatic, economic and cultural links with Iran. For the next three months Iraqi clergy and Baathist officials addressed rallies in the country to explain the conference resolutions. The overall purpose of the exercise was to show that the Iraqi regime revered Islam, and that the Muslim world was behind Iraq in its struggle against the heretical leaders of Iran.

These actions went hand in hand with the government's policy of eliminating the independent power-base of theological institutions, which had by late 1985 resulted in the closure of 86 religious centres and the banishment or execution of their leaders.[33] By then the ministry of waqfs and religious affairs had decided to set up the Islamic Higher Institute to train preachers, prayer leaders and theological students. It also continued its policy of restricting the hajj pilgrimage to men above 50 and blood relatives of the war dead. Thus it thwarted a channel for military personnel to desert or pick up revolutionary Islamic concepts during the pilgrimage.

Among those carrying out acts of sabotage Al Daawa was the most active. And the authorities were harsh in their policy towards its members and other militant Shias. Following the assassination on 1 March 1985 of an Iraqi diplomat and his son in Kuwait, the government executed without trial ten members of the Hakim family who had been detained in Najaf since May 1983, thus bringing the total to 16.

But the opposition force that really mattered to Baghdad was based in Kurdish areas and growing strong. However, in countering the Kurdish problem, Baghdad received enthusiastic co-operation from Ankara, with which it had in 1978 concluded a secret accord (made public six years later) allowing each side to pursue 'subversive elements' up to 9 miles inside each other's territory. In May 1983 Turkish troops infiltrated 18 miles into Iraqi Kurdistan to destroy the bases of its Kurdish guerrillas in the KDP-occupied part of Iraq. Following this, Tariq Aziz visited Ankara to reinforce mutual security co-operation further. The outcome was the signing of an agreement in October 1984 permitting cross-border operations up to 18 miles into each other's territory. Saddam Hussein concluded this agreement at a time when he was conducting secret talks with Jalal Talabani, the leader of the Patriotic Union of Kurdistan. The PUK denounced the pact as anti-Kurdish, broke off the negotiations and resumed its armed struggle to achieve autonomy for Kurds.

With this all the Kurdish groups now lined up against the central government; and, aided by Iran, Syria and Libya, they escalated their guerrilla activities. By May 1985 it was estimated that the Kurdish insurgents controlled about a third of Kurdistan, consisting of the three Iraqi provinces of Dohak, Arbil and Suleimaniya. The KDP, commanding 10,000 fighters, occupied areas in the northern region along the 550-mile Iraqi–Turkish border, from Zakho to Barzan. The PUK, commanding 4000 militia, was entrenched in southern Kurdistan along the Kirkuk–Koy–Sanjak–Qala Diza axis. Until the summer of 1985 the Iranian government had been somewhat distrustful of the KDP because of its refusal to join the Supreme Assembly of the Islamic Revolution in Iraq due to its secular and nationalist character. However, Iran changed its stance in the wake of the Iraqi raids on Kharg in August 1985 and allowed the KDP a supply route for heavy weapons from Libya and Syria through its territory. The KDP rejected Tehran's advice to mount frontal attacks on the Iraqi positions, and stuck to its age-old guerrilla tactics. It and the PUK refrained from taking over towns and cities, and concentrated on retaining control of the countryside. The Baghdad government responded by bombing and depopulating Kurdish villages.

In its anti-Baathist drive the KDP had begun providing refuge to the Shia activists of Al Daawa in the territory it controlled. Al Daawa claimed that about a thousand of its members were active in Kurdistan.[34] More disturbingly for the Baghdad authorities, these parties had become magnets for army deserters. Fearful of execution, the deserters joined the KDP or Al Daawa, which organized them into armed autonomous units. They operated in rural areas, focusing on economic and military targets. Although membership of the Tehran-based SAIRI did not inhibit Al Daawa from pursuing its activities, independently, inside and outside Iraq, it was beholden to the Islamic Republic of Iran and its leader, Ayatollah Khomeini.

In marked contrast to Saddam Hussein, obsessed with cultivating the personality cult, in September 1985 Khomeini instructed his followers to remove his portraits from all mosques, and directed the state-run media to stop the practice of frequently invoking his name on radio and showing his face on television.

The question of succession was high on the agenda of the Experts Assembly, composed of 83 clerics elected in December 1982, when it began its third session in mid-November 1985. In line with Article 107 of the constitution, it chose Ayatollah Hussein Ali Montazeri as the future leader by a more than two-thirds majority of those present. But, oddly, it did not make its decision public. On 22 November Hojatal-islam Ahmad Barikbin, the Friday prayer leader of Qazvin, leaked it during his sermon. Four days later Rafsanjani explained that the Assembly had resolved that Montazeri was 'acceptable to an overwhelming majority of the people for future leadership', and because the decision referred to the future it was not meant for publication.[35]

Many observers saw this as a preventive measure to avoid a leadership vacuum should the 83-year-old Khomeini die suddenly. Also this was a clear signal to opposition forces that on Khomeini's demise there would be a smooth transition of power, and that the successor regime would be well prepared to meet any political-military campaign that major opposition groups might launch, singly or jointly.

Hussein Ali Montazeri was born in 1922 in a peasant family of Najafabad, 250 miles south of Tehran. He had his early theological education in Isfahan, and then went to Qom where he became a student of Khomeini. In the early 1960s he taught at the prestigious Faiziya seminary. He participated in the anti-Shah insurrection in June 1963 and was active in anti-Shah clerical circles. In 1971 Khomeini, then in exile, appointed him as his personal representative in Iran. Three years later Montazeri was arrested along with other prominent clerical opponents of the Shah. He was tortured in jail, and released in November 1978. On his return to Iran in early 1979 Khomeini appointed Montazeri the Friday prayer leader of Qom, a highly prestigious position. The next year Khomeini asked him to become the supreme guide of Iran's universities and theological colleges and began transferring to Montazeri some of his own religious-legal powers. He authorized him to appoint members to the Supreme Judicial Council. Montazeri also began overseeing the workings of the parliamentary committee on land distribution. Like Khomeini, Montazeri daily received various representatives, committees and delegations. They gave him reports of their actions, and he set out guidelines for their future activity. The media regularly reported his actions and statements. Thus a well-planned strategy was in place to prepare Iranians for transition of power to Montazeri on Khomeini's death.

All in all, 1985 was an important year for Iran. The issue of Khomeini's succession was settled. As for the war, now in its sixth year, Iraq had devised and implemented two new tactics – air raids on Iranian cities and intense bombing of Kharg – to break Tehran's resolve to continue fighting until Saddam Hussein's downfall, and bring it to the negotiating table. It failed. But the Iraqi regime had shown that it had the men, materials and morale to preserve the territorial integrity of the country, and this in turn made it feel that the period of peril to its own survival was truly over.

Ayatollah Khomeini
is greeted by the
people of Tehran;
February 1979

Left: The domineering figure of Ayatollah Khomeini in Tehran; October 1980

Left inset: President Saddam Hussein portrayed as a genial father figure; September 1980

Above: Fuel oil tanks aflame in Baghdad after an Iranian air strike; September 1980

Below: Oil pipelines in Abadan hit by Iraqi shells; September 1980

Above: An Iranian cleric in a street battle in Khorramshahr; October 1980

Right: Iranian refugees fleeing the fighting in the border town of Bostan; December 1981

Below: A devastated street in Abadan under siege; April 1981

Above: A mass grave for the dead left behind by the retreating Iraqis near Bostan; December 1981

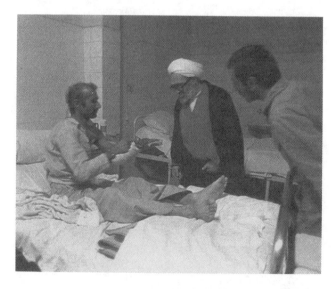

Left: Ayatollah Montazeri visit: a war casualty i Dezful; October 1980

Left: Iraqi victims of war in the Dezful-Shush area; March 1982

Below: Iraqi soldiers on the run as Iran recaptures Khorramshahr; May 1982

قتلت رستم وربت الكعبة

Above: A mural in Baghdad depicts the believer Saddam Hussein confronting the evil serpent representing Khomeini, Assad and Qadhafi; November 1983

Right: Kurdish guerrillas in action against the Iraqi government; July 1983

Below: Iranian forces mounting an attack in the Haur al Hawizeh marshes; February 1984

Left: Iranian victims of war near Amara (Iraq); February 1984

Below: This contingent of Iraqi prisoners of war shows a substantial proportion of non-Iraqi mercenaries; February 1984

Above: Iranian boys marching with their savings to fill the war chest; April 1984

Right: Iraqi boys march for peace in Baghdad; September 1986

Above: Iranian soldiers and dissident Iraqi fighters guard a position in the Haur al Hawizeh marshes; October 1985

Left: An air raid shelter in Dezful;
March 1985

Above: Iraqi soldiers near Fao
preparing to retake the port town
lost earlier to the Iranians; March
1986

Below: Weapons training for
Iranian women volunteers in
Tehran; June 1986

Above: A border post in the Haur al Hawizeh marshes

Left: The ubiquitous image of President Saddam Hussein in Iraq

Above: Iran's Kharg oil terminal under attack; October 1986

Below: Iranians conducting naval exercises codenamed 'Martyrdom' in the Gulf; August 1987

Above: A Cypriot supertanker after an Iranian strike in the Gulf; December 1987

Below: American warships destroy two Iranian offshore oil platforms in retaliation for an Iranian missile attack on a US-flagged supertanker in Kuwaiti waters; October 1987

Left: Victims of Iraqi chemical attacks in the Kurdish town of Halabja; March 1988

Below: President and Commander-in-Chief Saddam Hussein in a bunker in the southern sector; April 1988

7 INTERNATIONAL REPERCUSSIONS

The onset of the Tanker War had a direct impact on the Gulf states, particularly when Iranian retaliation took the (unacknowledged) form of attacks on ships trading with Kuwait or Saudi Arabia. Gulf Co-operation Council members succeeded in convincing the Arab League foreign ministers' conference in Tunis on 20 May 1984 that Tehran's attacks on Saudi or Kuwaiti vessels outside the Iraqi-declared war exclusion zone constituted acts of Iranian aggression.

A denouement between Tehran and Riyadh was reached on 5 June when the Saudis shot down an Iranian F-4 fighter which they claimed had intruded into Saudi airspace and had ignored two warnings. According to an account given by a top Saudi official to a group of Western journalists in Jiddah three years later, Tehran began sending up its warplanes after losing its F-4. 'The Iranians sent up eight, we sent up 15; then they had 20. By the end we had 25 F-15s and 18 F-5s in the air . . . Then we heard one command from the Iranians to their pilots – RTB – Return to Base.'[1] If true, this incident showed that neither party was willing to go over the brink and declare war against the other.

Iran did not wish to be diverted from its primary conflict with Iraq. As for Saudi Arabia and Kuwait, they had good reasons to refrain from joining the fray. They seemed to have heeded both friendly advice from Damascus and dire warnings from Tehran. 'The lifestyle of the littoral states of the Persian Gulf . . . depends on ports, installations and their oil pipelines,' said Rafsanjani. 'All of them could be destroyed by shelling, let alone air attacks.'[2] In any case these countries needed time, equipment and practice to make their defences effective. America came to their aid. Besides airlifting fresh weapons to Saudi Arabia, Washington sent military personnel to Kuwait to upgrade its US-made Hawk anti-aircraft missiles. The Pentagon extended the Awacs cover to Kuwaiti refineries and desalination plants.

Interestingly, Iran ended its protest note to Riyadh on the downing of its warplane with a renewal of 'our highest regards'. This, a swift mediation by Syria, and a temporary cessation of Iran's attacks on Saudi ships eased tensions between the two capitals. Reciprocating the

Iranian gesture, King Fahd's note to Tehran on 8 July expressed his intention to return to 'quiet diplomacy' with Iran.[3] In mid-July the Saudi hajj authorities invited Rafsanjani to make the pilgrimage. He welcomed the gesture; but, in the absence of approval by Ayatollah Khomeini, did not follow it up. Riyadh showed its goodwill by agreeing to a 50 per cent increase in Iranian pilgrims, who had numbered about 100,000 in 1983.

Having postponed the next major offensive in July, the Iranian leaders decided to give diplomacy a chance as they used the time to acquire more weapons. In early August Ayatollah Khomeini openly deplored the fact that Iran had only a few friends. 'We have no more friends than can be counted on the fingers of one hand,' he stated. Rafsanjani stressed that exporting the revolution did not imply the use of force. 'We [only] wish to provide the divine message to the deprived, meek people of the world,' he added. In late October, addressing a gathering of Iranian ambassadors, he referred to early Islam when the Prophet Muhammad sent envoys to all parts of the world to establish proper relations. 'We cannot sit idly by saying we have nothing to do with [other] governments,' he added. 'This is contrary to intellect and the Islamic law. We should have relations with all governments except a few with whom we have no relations at present.'[4]

By then President Khamanei had completed a successful tour of Syria, Libya and Algeria. In Damascus he was reportedly advised by President Assad not to mount a major land offensive against Iraq and not to alienate the Gulf states. However, Assad's mediating efforts were not enough to reassure the Gulf monarchies. At the fifth GCC summit in Kuwait in late November 1984 they decided to set up a Rapid Deployment Force of two brigades under a senior Saudi officer based in Riyadh: a decision disapproved of by Tehran.

A more meaningful change in the attitudes of GCC states and Iran occurred in the spring of 1985 after the failure of Tehran's March offensive. Lack of military success against Baghdad softened Tehran's stance towards the Gulf states. It led Iranian leaders to conclude that, in order to channel all their energies into achieving the overriding objective of ousting the Iraqi president, they needed to end these less significant feuds. They also seemed to have discovered merit in balancing their intransigence on the battlefield with flexibility in diplomatic and commercial links with their neighbours. On the other side, the confidence of the Gulf rulers in the durability of their dynasties, badly shaken in the wake of the Iranian revolution, was bolstered by the Iraqi success in repulsing a major Iranian offensive.

Having weathered the squalls of Islamic republicanism created by Tehran, the Gulf monarchs now felt secure enough to normalize relations with Iran. Also, much to their relief, the nightmarish prospect of Iran blocking the Hormuz Straits had not materialized. Moreover, they seemed to trust Tehran when it declared that it wanted to keep the waterway open, if only for its own economic survival.

The process of mutual acceptance, particularly by Iran and Saudi Arabia, was aided by the mediating efforts of President Assad as well as the ruler of the UAE. On 18 May 1985, responding to an invitation from his Iranian counterpart, Prince Saud al Faisal, the Saudi foreign minister, arrived in Tehran. Among those he met was President Khamanei, who declared that Iran proposed to 'coexist with them [its neighbours] in a spirit of unity and friendship'.[5] The subjects discussed included the Gulf War, Iranian–Saudi ties and Iranian–GCC relations. Their differences on the war were too wide to be bridged. Tehran viewed Prince Saud's visit as a successful move in their strategy of isolating Saddam Hussein from his erstwhile Arab allies. Prince Saud, on the other hand, saw his endeavour as paving the way for a negotiated peace. None the less, his meetings with Iran's top leaders established dialogue at the highest level, and augured well for improved relations in the future.

About a month before the sixth GCC summit in Muscat, Oman, in early November 1985, Ali Muhammad Besharati, Iran's vice-foreign minister, toured Bahrain, Qatar and the UAE. In each country he repeated Khomeini's statement: 'We want Arab countries to be dignified and glorious. We want to improve relations with them.'[6]

Tehran had reason to be mildly satisfied with the communiqué issued by the sixth GCC summit in early November 1985 in Muscat. For the first time since its formation in May 1981 the GCC refrained from mentioning Iraq's peace efforts and condemning Iran for continuing the Gulf War. Instead, it pledged to continue its efforts to end the war 'in a manner that safeguards the legitimate rights and interests of the two sides'.[7] Iranian leaders saw this as a small, but significant, move towards neutrality by the GCC, something they were aiming at.

But that did not mean alteration in the policies of Riyadh and Kuwait to provide financial and other aid to Baghdad. During 1984 and 1985 the two Gulf states supplied 300,000 b/d of oil to Iraq's customers, with Baghdad stating that this arrangement had emerged as a compensatory measure following the closure of the oil pipeline running through Syria to the Mediterranean. Saudi–Kuwaiti aid to Iraq in 1984 was estimated at \$4 billion.[8] In the spring of 1985 there was a reassessment by Riyadh and Kuwait of economic assistance to Baghdad due to Iraq's falling oil income, rising threats by Iran, and the imminence of the commissioning of the new pipeline to carry Iraqi oil through Saudi Arabia to the Red Sea. Once Saudi efforts to persuade Iran to talk peace had failed, the Gulf states accepted Baghdad's argument that the only way to bring Tehran to the negotiating table was by crippling its economy. This opened the way for serious and persistent Iraqi air raids on the Kharg oil terminal.

In this, Kuwait was the more enthusiastic supporter of Baghdad partly because it was more vulnerable to Iranian threats. For its water and electricity it was dependent on a few desalination and power plants. Their destruction by aerial bombing or internal sabotage would have caused a mass exodus from the country. On 18 December 1984 Iran demonstrated the vulnerability of the Kuwaiti and Saudi defences when its aircraft penetrated the Saudi air defence shield in the Upper Gulf and hit a Kuwait-bound freighter. Then, following the failed assassination attempt on the Kuwaiti ruler on 25 May 1985, relations between Kuwait and Tehran deteriorated sharply. Disclaiming any involvement in the incident, Iran accused Iraq of sponsoring such acts in order to sabotage the continuing process of rapprochement between Tehran and the Gulf capitals. But such statements were not taken seriously by Kuwait or other Gulf states.

The United Arab Emirates provided a contrast to Kuwait. It was the only Gulf state to have been described once by Tehran as 'a progressive country led by wise men'.[9] Since it came nearest to being neutral in the war, Tehran had close ties with it. Exchanges of ministerial visits were frequent. Dubai, an entrepôt of the UAE, benefited enormously from Iran's economic and diplomatic isolation. Its commercial links with Iran, the region's largest market, were both overt and clandestine. It became an ideal place for Iran to procure the food, industrial raw materials, machinery and spare parts it badly needed. In 1985 the two-way trade between Iran and the UAE was expected to reach a record level of \$1000 million a year.[10]

There was still another powerful reason why the UAE was trying to maintain good relations with Tehran. Nearly two-thirds of its oil was derived from offshore wells. These outlets were hard to protect from attacks by hostile naval forces. It was therefore in the UAE's economic interests not to arouse the ire of Iran, which commanded a strong navy. Sectarian considerations also entered the diplomatic equation formulated in Abu Dhabi. About one-fifth of the UAE's quarter-million nationals were Shia. Moreover, being mainly a commercial community based in Dubai, they had a larger influence on state policies than their numbers suggested. All told, therefore, the combined weight of geopolitical, sectarian and economic factors was such that the UAE could not afford to adopt the anti-Iranian stance often advocated by Saudi Arabia and Kuwait.

In the Arab world at large Syria continued to maintain its alliance with Iran while urging temperance on the Islamic Republic in its military policies. It did so in the summer of 1984 at the behest of GCC states, and again on the eve of the GCC summit in November. Assad withstood pressures from Gulf states to dissociate himself from Tehran by arguing that Syria's friendship with Iran was a better guarantee for the security of GCC states than the armed might of Iraq, and that Tehran had assured him that it had no designs on Arab territory either in Iraq or any of the Gulf states.

Assad's argument lost some force when Tehran mounted its major offensive against Iraq in March 1985. It accentuated divisions in the Arab world. The serious Iranian threat to the Iraqi regime brought the rulers of Egypt and Jordan to Baghdad on 16 March. The summit conference of Saddam Hussein, President Mubarak and King Hussein revived President Assad's paranoia about the rise of an anti-Syrian axis in the Arab world. His government welcomed the arrival of the Iranian foreign minister in Damascus on 19 March to attend a meeting of his counterparts from Syria, Libya, Algeria and South Yemen. The event reaffirmed the continuation of the Iranian–Syrian–Libyan alignment, with Libya agreeing to sell Tehran, *inter alia*, Soviet-made Scud-B surface-to-surface missiles. Following Rafsanjani's visit to Tripoli in late June 1985 – during which he and Colonel Qadhafi reaffirmed the strategic alliance between their countries – Iraq withdrew its recognition of the Qadhafi government 'as an Arab regime'. Syria continued its policy of staging air operations to divert the resources of Iraq's aerial defences during Iran's land offensives against Iraq.

In early August Iran's parliament overwhelmingly ratified legislation offering Syria an annual grant of one million tonnes of oil and selling it up to five million tonnes at a discount of $2.50 a barrel. This was in the context of the ten-year economic pact signed in 1982, mainly to compensate Damascus for its losses due to the closing of the Iraqi pipeline and the fall in the Gulf states' subsidies to it due to its alliance with Iran.

Later that month the foreign ministers of Syria, Iran and Libya met to co-ordinate their policies in the region. Rising tension between Libya and the United States, coupled with Western accusations that Libya, Iran and Syria were actively aiding international terrorism, further strengthened ties between these states.

Syria and Libya were joined by Algeria, South Yemen and Lebanon in their boycott of the summit of the Arab League which opened in Casablanca, Morocco, on 13 August 1985. Reaffirming the previous summit and foreign ministers' resolutions in favour of Iraq and against Iran, the remaining 16 members committed themselves to upholding the 1982 Fez summit resolution passed under the terms of the League's charter and the 1950 Joint Arab Defence Agreement. It was against this background that Baghdad mounted its effective air strikes against Kharg oil terminal.[11]

Outside the Arab League, Egypt continued to back Iraq solidly. It had emerged as the third most important arms supplier to Baghdad, after the Soviet Union and France, its shipments reportedly including chemical weapons. Its policy of charging Iraq the same price for military supplies as it did its own defence forces was particularly welcomed by the financially strained Baghdad. President Mubarak's arrival in Baghdad in the midst of a severe Iranian offensive boosted sagging Iraqi spirits. Saddam Hussein called on Arab League members to invite Egypt to the next summit.

The most important non-Arab neighbour of the belligerents, Turkey, remained neutral, and did flourishing business with both Iraq and Iran. This was as true of the military government as of the elected civilian administration, headed by Turgut Ozal, which followed in December 1983.

Four months later Ozal visited Tehran. In 1984–5 Turkish-Iranian trade amounted to $2300 million (compared to $22 million in 1978), making Turkey the Islamic Republic's third most important commercial partner after West Germany and Japan. Tehran balanced its trade with Ankara by selling 100,000 b/d of its oil to its neighbour. Iran took a pragmatic view of its relations with Turkey. It overlooked the fact that Turkey was close to the West and had Nato bases on its soil, and that its secular constitution banned mixing religion and politics. Instead it stressed the fact that Turkey was an important neighbour and a Third World state whose nationals were 99 per cent Muslim.

Despite the irritation caused by the Iraqi strikes in May and June 1985 against Turkish-owned oil tankers carrying Iranian oil from Kharg, Ankara's relations with Baghdad remained cordial. Turkey was one of the leading trading partners of Iraq. Both countries had a strong interest in maintaining military co-operation in suppressing Kurdish insurgency. In November 1985 Turkey concluded a contract for a second oil pipeline with an annual capacity of 71 million tonnes (1.4 million b/d), to be finished within two years. Initial Iraqi suspicions of Turkey as a member of Nato gave way to genuine warmth as Baghdad drew closer to the pro-Western Arab states of Saudi Arabia, Jordan and Egypt, and restored diplomatic links with Washington on 26 November 1984.

THE SUPERPOWERS

Commercial ties between Iraq and the US were already so close that, at $1 billion, Baghdad–Washington trade in 1983–4 was three times the size of Baghdad–Moscow commerce. In May 1984 Saddam Hussein publicly confirmed that Iraq had been receiving intelligence from the US-manned Awacs surveillance planes despatched to Saudi Arabia in October 1980.[12] Referring to the Iraqi-initiated Tanker War, President Reagan condemned Tehran for its attacks on neutral ships in the Gulf while declaring that Baghdad 'had not gone beyond bounds' in hitting Iranian vessels which were legitimate economic targets.[13] To assist Baghdad financially, Washington's Eximbank provisionally guaranteed $485 million of the estimated $570 million cost of constructing an Iraqi pipeline through Jordan to the Gulf of Aqaba.

The haste with which the US announced the resumption of diplomatic links with Iraq, within weeks of the re-election of Reagan to the White House on 7 November 1984, showed that the groundwork for this step had been done before the presidential election. It flowed from the overall American strategy to strengthen forces opposed to Islamic radicalism in the Middle East, which was considered as much of an enemy of Western interests in the region as Marxism or Soviet influence. The formalities of the renewal of diplomatic ties took place in Washington, where President Reagan received the Iraqi foreign minister

Tariq Aziz. Significantly, Baghdad did not pressure Washington to make any concessions on America's strategic links with Israel as part of the price for exchanging ambassadors, although the tight US–Israeli alliance had been the reason for Iraq's severing of ties with Washington during the June 1967 Arab–Israeli War.

The open rapprochement between America and Iraq caused no anger or surprise among Iranian leaders. It merely provided further evidence for their thesis that both superpowers were opposed to the Islamic revolution: the Soviet Union because of its own materialist, atheistic ideology; and the US because of the threat that the regeneration of Islam as a comprehensive social system, and the subsequent realization of true independence by the Muslim masses throughout the world, posed to the political and economic hold that Washington had over the resources and leadership of most Muslim countries.

Following the Reagan–Aziz meeting the US made its intelligence in the Gulf available to Iraq on a regular basis by setting up direct links between the Central Intelligence Agency headquarters in Langley, Virginia, and the American embassy in Baghdad. According to European intelligence sources, warnings of attacks by Iranian planes on ships in the busy Gulf lanes were relayed to the Iraqis 'within minutes' of the Iranian pilots' take-off, monitored by the American-piloted Awacs in the Gulf. These were supplemented by reports every 12 hours on the Iranian military activity on the ground – culled from the information gathered from the many American satellites orbiting the Gulf and from the American Awacs – which were passed on to Baghdad via Riyadh.[14] This information played a vital role in aiding the effectiveness of the operations mounted by Baghdad to defeat the massive Iranian offensive of March 1985. Iran's unexpected success in breaching the Iraqi lines caused as much alarm in Washington as it did in Baghdad. Equally, the Iraqi accomplishment in repulsing the Iranians brought as much relief in Washington as it did in Baghdad. Following this, American military specialists advised Iraq on establishing 'electronic walls' along the Iraqi-Iranian border.

In July 1985 a US official spokesman stated that being neutral in the Gulf War did not mean that 'We don't have sympathies'.[15] Certainly America's sympathies did not lie with Iran. As for Iraq, America manifested an unmistakable bias towards it in September, when it concluded a co-operation agreement with Baghdad concerning trade, industry, agriculture, energy, health and telecommunications. The US continued its policy of offering credits to Iraq to buy American food-grains, the sum in 1985 amounting to $675 million.

One of the reasons for Baghdad's resumption of diplomatic links with Washington was to pressure the US to urge its allies to bar weapons sales to Tehran. As it was, following its January 1984 decision to put Iran on the list of the countries that support international terrorism, the US State Department had in March appointed a special ambassador to implement 'Operation Staunch' designed to stop the arms flow into Iran. In September America imposed further restrictions on exports to Iran. These drove the Iranians further into exploring private channels for procurement of arms and spares. They were particularly keen on purchasing US-made Tow anti-tank missiles in order to neutralize the Iraqi superiority in tanks used against their infantry assaults.

In June 1985 a Trans-World Airways plane with 145 passengers, flying out of Athens, was hijacked by pro-Iranian Lebanese Shias and taken to Beirut. The 17-day hijack, in which an American navy diver was killed, increased American hostility towards Iran at both popular and official levels.

Washington tightened up on those trying to smuggle arms and spares from the US to Iran. According to the reports published in the *New York Times* and *Washington Post* in August 1985, during the previous year the Federal Bureau of Investigation had secured 14 indictments against 44 individuals and eight companies – twice the total of the past three years. Among those arrested was a deputy chief of staff of army materials command: he was reported to be working on an arms deal worth $140 million. The smugglers were aided by the fact that every year about one per cent of the total US arms and spares stockpiles worth $80 billion 'disappeared', often due to misplacement.[16] The American authorities claimed to have broken up five weapons-exporting groups using London as their shipping and financing centre. They allegedly met orders emanating from the National Iranian Oil Company building in London, which was shared by the Iranian air force's logistical support centre in Europe. Washington pressured London to restrict the activities of the dealers selling military goods to Iran.

While the US State Department was pursuing 'Operation Staunch' with great vigour, the CIA, the National Security Council and the White House were engaged in a secret revision of America's policy towards Iran and the supply of arms and spares. The starting-point was a memo-randum written in early 1985 by Graham Fuller, vice-chairman of the

National Intelligence Council. In it he warned of the possibility of Moscow making serious inroads in Iran following Khomeini's death, and suggested that the US should establish contacts with moderate elements within the Iranian regime. The update of this memorandum on 20 May 1985 predicted that serious factional fighting could erupt even before Khomeini's death and that the Soviet Union was well-placed to take advantage of the chaotic conditions in Iran. These two documents became the starting-point for internal discussions at the highest level in the Reagan administration, and finally led to the secret American arms deals with Iran between August 1985 and November 1986.[17]

Interestingly, in the summer of 1985 there were reports of secret contacts between Iran and the Soviet Union regarding a possible arms deal. *Le Monde* of 18 December claimed that direct military co-operation between Tehran and Moscow had been in progress 'for some months'.

In public, however, the Soviet presence in Afghanistan continued to be the main barrier to close ties between Tehran and Moscow. Their bilateral trade in 1984, at $493 million, was only half the level of the previous year.[18] Relations deteriorated when, in the wake of the Iraqi air raids on the Soviet-aided industrial projects in Ahvaz and Isfahan in March 1985, Moscow withdrew all its 1200 specialists working in Iran on the grounds of lack of safety. Tehran protested, but to no avail.

On the other hand, following the suspension of flights to Iran by international airlines, the Soviet Union allowed Iran Air to use its airspace for flights between Europe and Tehran. Iran sensed a potential for better relations with the arrival of a new leader, Mikhail Gorbachev, in the Kremlin.

An Iranian delegation led by Kazem Ardebili, deputy foreign minister, visited Moscow in April to improve political and technical co-operation. He was the highest-ranking official to visit Moscow in three years. As Iraqi aerial raids on Kharg became more frequent and intense during the summer – thus increasing the possibility of Tehran blocking the Hormuz Straits and causing an American intervention – Iran felt a tactical need to improve ties with Moscow. In early October Rafsanjani reminded a Friday prayer audience in Tehran that the Soviets had said that they would not stand by if the US were to intervene militarily in the Gulf.[19] Two months later, on the eve of Saddam Hussein's arrival in

Moscow, the Kremlin sent a message to Tehran reaffirming its neutrality in the war: a gesture made public once again by Rafsanjani.

The Soviet Union, the source of 70 per cent of arms transfer to Iraq in late 1984, was displeased by the resumption of diplomatic ties between Baghdad and Washington. It suspended talks on the sale of advanced jet fighters to Iraq, while other Warsaw Pact nations slowed their weapons supplies to Baghdad. In January 1985 the Iraqi deputy premier, Ramadan, reproached Moscow for continuing to ship weapons to Syria which delivered 'the greater part of them to Tehran in exchange for oil'. However, Baghdad could not afford to be too critical of Moscow which supplied it not only with weapons but also with 1500–6000 military advisers.[20] It feared that the Kremlin might respond to persistently harsh criticism in public by adopting a pro-Iran tilt.

Tehran's March 1985 offensive, when the Iranians broke the Iraqi defence lines, created a favourable climate for Baghdad. Tariq Aziz flew to Moscow to urge the Kremlin to airlift ammunition, spare parts and various types of missiles including SS-12s, and received a positive response. In mid-May he declared that the Soviets had supplied Iraq's military needs, and added that there was no possibility of Baghdad purchasing weapons from the US due to the 'difficult and humiliating conditions' attached to such sales.[21] Thus reassured, in September Moscow concluded a co-operation agreement with Baghdad to develop Iraqi oilfields. A year earlier Moscow had given Iraq $2 billion in soft loans for economic projects including a nuclear power station and oilfield development.

Saddam Hussein's visit to Moscow in mid-December 1985 was his first since he assumed supreme power in 1979. Among other things it was meant to balance Iraq's growing friendliness with the US. More specifically, the Iraqi leader wanted to urge his Soviet counterpart to intensify the diplomatic process to end the Gulf War, and in the meanwhile provide advanced weapons to Baghdad for conducting the conflict effectively. Press reports indicated that Moscow agreed to Saddam Hussein's request for weapons – but not the Scud-B surface-to-surface missiles that the Iraqis had used against the Iranian cities, a tactic much criticized by the Kremlin.[22]

Over the years China came to play a substantial role in the supply of arms and ammunition to the belligerents in the Gulf War, using North Korea as a conduit for its shipments to Iran so as not to alienate its friends in the Arab world, particularly Egypt. China's entry into the international arms market stemmed from the decision of its leaders to implement military industrialization at a huge cost; and the arms factories were encouraged to sell their wares abroad and raise foreign exchange for modernization. Press reports in March 1985 that Tehran and Peking had entered into a $1.6 billion arms deal involving tanks, fighter jets and surface-to-air missiles were met with official denials. They were, however, indicative of the cordial relations between the two states on the eve of Rafsanjani's visit to Peking in late June. The political reasons for Sino–Iranian amity were expressed by Rafsanjani thus: 'We consider China to be really independent and without domineering intentions. It pursues a policy of support for the oppressed, and is opposed to superpower domination.'[23] But this did not stop China from letting Egypt divert to Iraq the warplanes it had purchased from Peking, and supplying contract labour to Baghdad.

From the Iranian viewpoint Japan offered much potential for active co-operation. It required oil that Iran possessed, and offered high technology that Tehran sought. It had no political or military ambitions in the region. But Japan was equally intent on maintaining friendly relations with Iraq – if only because Iraq's Gulf backers were a major source of oil for Japan. Indeed, Tokyo had tried to mediate between Iran and Iraq, an effort that Rafsanjani, during his visit to Japan in early July 1985, tried to discourage.

THE EUROPEANS

West Germany had taken a bold step towards cultivating Iran. In July 1984 its foreign minister, Hans Dietrich Genscher, became the first senior West European politician to visit Tehran. During his stay he stated that the Western attempt to isolate an important country like Iran was 'one of the biggest mistakes made by Western powers'.[24]

At the other end of the West European spectrum was France. Its diplomatic and military relations with Iran remained poor; but this had no adverse impact on commercial links which were healthy, with French companies buying up a substantial amount of Iranian oil. Tehran objected to the refusal of France to repay a $1 billion loan made by the Shah to fund a French nuclear project and to its continued policy of being a leading supplier of advanced weaponry and ammunition to Iraq. In March 1985 Paris agreed in principle to 'balance' its links with the warring sides. Two months later its new chargé d'affaires in Tehran inaugurated his term with the statement that France had made some mistakes in its Middle East policy which were regrettable.[25] But, apparently, selling weaponry to Iraq was not one of them.

The outflow of French arms and ammunition to Iraq reached a new peak in 1985. At 4332 tonnes, military shipments to Iraq from Châteauroux-Delos airport in that year were 14 times the figure for 1975, and included lethal air-to-surface missiles and anti-personnel bombs. In the autumn of 1985 the customs authorities at the airport estimated the value of military exports to Iraq at $40 million a week – $2100 million a year. By then Iraq had become the largest importer of military goods in the world, beating its closest rival, Saudi Arabia, by a margin of 3:1, the actual value of the imports in 1984 being $9500 million and $3100 million respectively.[26]

On the Iranian side, by 1985 the clandestine supply of arms and ammunition from West European sources had become routine. Luchaire-SNPE, a state-owned company in France, had secured an order to supply Iran with 500,000 shells of 105mm and 155mm. Like other firms in a similar situation the nominal destinations of Luchaire's shipments were such countries as Brazil, Ecuador, Greece, Pakistan, Thailand and Yugoslavia. In 1985 Nobel Chemie of Sweden signed a contract with Iran (through a front company set up in Switzerland and via its Yugoslav subsidiary) to supply 1300 tonnes of explosives. It then farmed out the contract to three other members of the cartel, as mentioned in Chapter Five.[27] In March 1985 Swedish customs discovered through the documents seized at an arms factory that weapons and ammunition were being sold clandestinely to Iran from several West European countries. Besides such deals, a scheme to establish an ammunition factory in Isfahan by Karl Eric Schmitz, managing director of a Swedish company – involving machinery, equipment and industrial materials worth $800 million – went into operation in 1984.[28]

In contrast to Iran, Iraq had an easy run in procuring arms and ammunition in Western Europe outside France. For instance, in the first half of 1984 it concluded a weapons contract worth 'several billion lire' with Tirrena Industriale of Italy with a clause forbidding sale of arms or ammunition to Iran. As a member of the European cartel clandestinely selling ammunition to Iran, this company had also obtained an order for supplying explosives to Tehran. Later that year, as a result of pressure by Washington on the Italian government to stop sales of military goods to

Iran, Tirrena Industriale reneged on its sub-contract with the European cartel.

All in all, therefore, as the conflict dragged on Tehran found itself more and more isolated.

Contrary to the situation elsewhere in the world, the two superpowers did not take opposite positions. While sympathetic to Iraq, Moscow and Washington desisted from active intervention in the conflict. In the wake of the Tanker War the two superpowers held top-level consultations and reached a limited understanding that the Gulf must remain a free waterway. In June 1984 US Secretary of State George Shultz publicly declared that the Soviet Union and the US had 'a shared concern' about the Gulf War, and that it had not become a hostage to East–West rivalry. From early 1985 the two superpowers began including the war and its consequences in their continuing talks about Third World conflicts. If nothing else, this implied that they would not let the Gulf War escalate.

8 IRAN'S FAO OFFENSIVE AND AFTER

In early 1986 Iran mobilized about half of its regular army and two-thirds of its Revolutionary Guards Corps. On the night of 9 February it mounted a three-pronged offensive codenamed Wa al Fajr-Eight – two prongs focused on areas about 25 miles north and south of Basra, with the remaining one directed at the Fao peninsula further south. The marsh-infested peninsula, lying between the Shatt al Arab and Kuwait's offshore Bubiyan Island, was administered from the southernmost port town of Fao connected by a 75-mile road to Basra.

The Iranians were repulsed north of Basra in the Haur al Hawizeh marshes, but managed to capture Umm Rassas Island in the Shatt al Arab south-east of the city. Their major success, however, came in the Fao peninsula. In driving rain and gusty winds they crossed the 1000-yard-wide Shatt al Arab at six points, and started advancing along a long front. They had perfected their amphibious tactics over the past year with practice runs in the mountain lakes and rivers in northern Iran. Now, in Fao and elsewhere, the Iraqi troops, who were asleep, were taken by surprise. Later they were unable to cope with multiple landings by the enemy who swiftly strengthened the bridgeheads and set up a pontoon bridge. The net result was panic, and the loss within two days of Fao as well as much weaponry and ammunition to the invading Iranians.

To divert the Iraqis, Tehran staged another assault in the marshes north of Basra on the night of 11 February. This engaged the immediate attention of Iraq's high command, and the Iraqi counteroffensive in the Fao peninsula did not come until 14 February. Baghdad pressed into action three armoured columns down the centre and sides of the peninsula, backed up by heavy artillery. By then two divisions of Iranians had seized 320 square miles of Iraqi territory, as well as many fortified enemy positions and large quantities of its arms including heavy weaponry, and dug in. They offered stiff resistance to the counter-attacking Iraqi columns. By then they had achieved their short-term objectives of virtually cutting off Iraq from the Gulf, destroying or capturing large numbers of Iraqi troops and weapons, taking over the missile station in the area, and seizing a radar station which gave cover to the Iraqi planes on their raiding missions in the Gulf.

Saddam Hussein strengthened the local Seventh Army Corps with units from the elite Presidential Guard and the battle-experienced Third Army Corps from the Haur al Hawizeh area, in order to expel the Iranians from the Fao peninsula. But due to the soft, marshy soil the armoured columns could only use the narrow roads. As they did so, they encountered every 300 yards the defensive positions of the Iranians, who were entrenched and well-supplied with anti-tank missiles. The Iraqi tactic of intense artillery fire proved ineffective against widely scattered Iranian infantry targets. Also, they faced an enemy now armed with the tanks and armoured personnel carriers it had captured earlier from their own ranks. Furthermore, the Iranians had by then set up successful supply lines by making combined use of the pontoon bridge and boats at night or during unsettled weather in daylight.

As for the superior Iraqi air power, its effectiveness was compromised by poor weather as well as by the Iranian tactics and equipment. On an average Baghdad daily staged 355 warplane and 134 helicopter sorties; but heavy rains reduced their efficacy and good targets were hard to come by. The Iranian infantry had by now mastered the art of dispersing quickly, digging in and taking cover – as well as moving military supplies and equipment in small quantities at night. Finally, the Iraqis had to cope with one, or possibly two, air defence systems of American and/or Chinese origin that the Iranians had managed to transport across the Shatt al Arab. Also, following their success in clandestinely procuring US-made spare parts, the Iranians had made 24 F-14 interceptor aircraft airworthy, so doubling the previous total. In their determination to compel the Iranian infantry to cease daytime assaults and end hostile military activity in the rear – as well as to overcome the barrier of cloudy skies – the Iraqi air force resorted to attacks at unusually low altitudes. This made its machines vulnerable to enemy anti-aircraft guns and missiles, leading to a loss of 55 planes and helicopters within a fortnight of the offensive.[1]

On the whole, however, by finally achieving an optimal combination of armour, artillery and warplanes, Iraq began stabilizing the frontline by 18 February. In contrast, Tehran found itself unable to support its infantry with enough tanks and firepower. On 21 February the Iraqi troops, bolstered by more units from the Third Army Corps, used chemical weapons, but rain and humid conditions diluted the effect of poison gases.[2] Also there was a limit to the contribution that the Third Army Corps could make to the Fao campaign, given that the Iranians maintained a high military profile north of Basra, particularly after they had withdrawn from their freshly captured Umm Rassas Island. Having stabilized the front line, the Iraqis launched an infantry assault on the night of 23 February. They failed, and in the process lost two battalions.

To ensure that the Iraqi high command did not move more troops to Fao from elsewhere, on the night of 24 February Tehran mounted an offensive – codenamed Wa al Fajr-Nine – in Iraqi Kurdistan 14 miles from Suleimaniya. A fortnight earlier Tehran had encouraged the Kurdish insurgents to commence attacks on the government troops to pin them down in the north. Their joint operations brought 130 square miles of Iraqi territory under Iranian control by early March, and led to heavy fighting near the dam on Darbandi Khan Lake, the main source of electricity for Baghdad. Iraq retaliated by keeping up air attacks on Iran's economic targets, including oil tankers in the Gulf, where in late February it extended the maritime exclusion zone from 50 miles west of Kharg to 70 miles.

Saddam Hussein was not prepared to cede Iraqi land to Iran, and assigned his top generals – Abdul Rashid and Fakhri – to eject the invader from the Fao peninsula. By early March their forces had succeeded in setting up new defensive positions, building up superior firepower and storing large ammunition stocks. But an attempt to outflank the Iranians with amphibious landings on 9–10 March ended in a costly failure. Having stabilized the front lines by mid-March, the Iraqi commanders pressed their forces forward during the next fortnight, only to suffer unacceptable levels of casualties.

Iraq's total manpower losses were put at 8000–12,000 dead.[3] The corresponding figure for Iran was 20,000. This ratio was unacceptable to Baghdad, partly because its losses included many skilled soldiers and airmen who could not be replaced immediately, and partly because of the demographic disadvantage it had vis-à-vis Tehran. Having weighed the military gain of recovering Iraqi soil against the steep political cost of high casualties, Saddam Hussein called off the counteroffensives.

The extent of Saddam Hussein's resolve to retake the Fao peninsula can be gauged by the number of sorties the Iraqi air force carried out. Between 9 February and 25 March 1986 Iraq staged 18,648 missions[4] – compared to 20,011 missions in the whole of 1985.

Despite the scale of its casualties, Tehran maintained two divisions in the peninsula with a back-up of five more across the Shatt al Arab. On the other hand the Iranians, lacking enough tanks and artillery to take advantage of their strategic position and highly motivated infantry, had to be content with consolidating what they had gained, and abandon their earlier plans of using the Fao foothold to advance on Basra to the north or the Kuwait–Basra highway 35 miles to the west.

For the first time in two years the Iranians had captured and retained Iraqi land, disproving the prevalent perception among local and foreign observers that Iran was incapable of breaking the military stalemate. More importantly, the Iranian achievement lent credibility to Tehran's threats of a 'final offensive' to end the war on its terms, and created tension and consternation in Baghdad as well as in Arab Gulf capitals.

From a military viewpoint, Iran showed that it was quite capable of mounting simultaneous offensives, a strategy it had not effectively implemented before. Secondly, the success of this plan derived from the flexibility that Iranian commanders showed in pouring their forces into the penetration they managed to obtain on a certain front. Surprise played an important role in these campaigns. And so did the weather. The Iraqis, who depended on the intelligence supplied by the US, were later to blame Washington for the fiasco in the Fao peninsula. The American documents and analysis, they revealed, showed concentrations of Iranian troops north of Basra, and only there. But Washington, it seemed, had not deliberately withheld information from Baghdad. It was simply that foul weather conditions in the Fao peninsula militated against the US satellites gathering information on the ground. Moreover, the Iranians employed certain means to deceive and circumvent the American intelligence-gathering equipment. For instance, they used open trucks to transport troops: the intelligence analysts concluded that these vehicles were carrying goods rather than men. Also Iranian field headquarters sent messages to field commanders by couriers using motorcycles, and not by coded messages over radio telephone, thus depriving the American and Iraqi monitoring devices of the opportunity to pick up these messages.[5]

The military successes were all the more welcome in Tehran in view of the gloom created by a crash in oil prices. Buoyed up by these Iranian achievements, Khomeini declared on the eve of the Iranian New Year, 21 March 1986, that the coming year would be the 'Year of Victory'. Then on the eve of the anniversary of the founding of the Islamic Republic on 1 April, Khomeini gave one of his strongest calls for the mobilization of all able-bodied men and the continuation of the war until the fall of Saddam Hussein. Premier Musavi announced a plan for military training for the country's 1.6 million civil servants, and ruled that at any time up to 20 per cent of them would be allowed to go to the front. (Until then the figure had been 5–10 per cent.) The earlier decision to augment the armed forces by 500 battalions, or 300,000 men, was reaffirmed. Plans were announced to accept women volunteers in the Basij militia. This was a clever move, expected to encourage the un-decided male members of extended families to volunteer in the wake of their female relatives.

Khomeini appointed an eight-member Supreme Council for War Support which in turn set up 90 mobilization councils in the country and assigned them local quotas. Muhsin Rezai, the Revolutionary Guards Corps commander, summed up the official policy and the rationale behind it in a speech on 31 May 1986. 'So far in the imposed war only two per cent of the country's popular forces and 12 per cent of its economic forces have been utilized,' he said. 'It is sufficient for us to bring into the battlefield four times more infantry forces with light weapons than the Iraqis [to win] . . . We are on the threshold of a full-scale people's war, and this is the only path.'[6] The government invested the Revolutionary Guards Corps with exceptional authority to muster men and materials, a reflection of the unprecedented prestige that the Revolutionary Guards Corps had come to enjoy – a situation bolstered by the loss of Mehran by the Iranian military in mid-May 1986 to the Iraqis.

For Baghdad the Fao defeat had come at a time when it believed that its battered economy, which had suffered a 14 per cent drop in 1985, was on the mend. Saddam Hussein's failure to expel the Iranians from the peninsula even after the terrain had dried out by late April – thus allowing the Iraqis to manoeuvre their tanks freely – left him vulner-able. It was now all the more important for him to show his people that the armed forces were active, and not merely in defending the nation. In that context the successful Iraqi air strikes on the Isfahan and Tehran refineries in mid-March and early May respectively were significant. Together these installations accounted for two-thirds of the total Iranian output.[7]

But far more important was the major offensive that Saddam Hussein staged on 17 May 1986 with four divisions in the central sector which led to the seizure of 60 square miles of Iranian soil encompassing Mehran and surrounding villages. The town was lightly guarded by 5000 Iranian troops, who suffered heavy casualties. The Iraqi leader heralded the event as the beginning of the newly adopted strategy of 'dynamic defence', a departure from the static defence posture that Baghdad had adopted since June 1982. His government described it as 'a daring expression of the Iraqi leadership's political decision . . . to force the Iranian leaders to yield, preparing the way for peace'.[8] The victory boosted the morale of his forces. He then offered to exchange Mehran for Fao. Tehran rejected the proposal summarily.

Iraq had failed to remove the Iranians from the high ground surrounding their seized territory around Mehran. And it was there that the Iranians built up their forces, undetected. On the night of 30 June– 1 July they staged a successful offensive, codenamed Karbala-One, which caught the Iraqis off guard. On 3 July Baghdad conceded that Iran had retaken Mehran. Thus Tehran deprived Baghdad of its bargaining counter, and re-established its superiority on land fronts. It also demonstrated that it could rapidly move troops from one sector to another.

With his strategy of 'dynamic defence' in tatters, Saddam Hussein called an extraordinary congress of the Regional [i.e., Iraqi] Baath Party. As expected he was re-elected party general secretary. He expanded the Regional Command from 15 members to 17 after dropping Naim Haddad, a Shia. His three new appointees included Ali Hassan Majid, his cousin and director-general of public security. Another kinsman, Fadil Barrak Tikriti, director of intelligence, was appointed a reserve member of the Regional command. Hussein thus continued his policies of reinforcing his personal control over the party and state, and increasing the importance of the security apparatus in sustaining his regime. He portrayed the poor progress of the war as a result of a continuing international conspiracy intent on destroying the Iraqi nation and Baathist ideology. This was his way of disowning any responsibility for initiating the war and/or mishandling it.

The only military response the Iraqi president could give to Tehran's victory on the battlefront was to intensify the strategic air campaign. As it happened, the timing was propitious. The Iranian economy was in decline. By increasing its oil exports from 2 million to 4.5 million b/d within a few months during the winter of 1985–6, Saudi Arabia had depressed oil prices from $27 a barrel in December 1985 to below $10 a barrel in April 1986. It argued that sharply lower prices would hurt such non-OPEC producers as Britain and Norway, and make their petroleum industry uneconomic, thus compelling them to co-operate with OPEC in fixing prices and making them stick world-wide. Privately, however, both Saudi Arabia and Kuwait hoped that by depressing oil prices they would, *inter alia*, reduce Iran's oil income to the extent of seriously impairing its ability to prosecute the war. In the spring of 1986 Iran's monthly oil income was $500 million compared to $1250 million a year before. It was then that Baghdad, reportedly aided by expertise provided clandestinely by American specialists, extended its targets to include such Iranian economic and infrastructural targets as industrial factories, ammunition plants, power stations, communications centres, hydro-electric installations and bridges. As Iraq received advanced munitions and its pilots mastered more daring tactics, the accuracy of its air missions increased.

For instance, by 8 August 1986 the Iraqi air force had hit five of the 11 oil tankers comprising the Iranian fleet ferrying oil between Kharg and Sirri Island, where crude was stored in floating vessels for pumping into the customers' tankers, thus saving the latter the hazardous journey up the Gulf. A high point came on 12 August with an Iraqi raid on Sirri Island, when Exocet air-to-ship missiles hit three storage tankers. Since Sirri is 490 miles from Iraq's southernmost air base at Shuaiba, near Basra, this attack could have been staged only by arranging refuelling of the bombers either inflight or at an air base in a pro-Iraqi Gulf state.

The Iranians shifted the tanker transfer loading site about 15 miles north-east of Sirri, thus bringing it nearer to their coastal air defences, and moved three storage vessels 130 miles eastward to Larak Island. They also adopted such tanker protection devices as using dull, non-reflecting paint for crew quarters to weaken radar detection, fixing radar reflectors to the two ends of the vessel, acquiring launchers for canisters of aluminium chaff to deflect Exocet missiles, and using electronic countermeasures equipment to prevent a radar lock-on.[9] In addition, Iran dotted its coastline with tugs to rescue swiftly any ship that was struck.

In retaliation for Iraq's 12 August attack on Sirri, the Iranians staged air strikes on oil installations near Kirkuk, and aimed a Scud-B surface-to-surface missile at a refinery near Baghdad, which instead fell on a nearby residential area. In early September they destroyed radar facilities on Iraq's (disused) offshore Khor al Amaya and Mina al Bakr oil terminals. However, such actions as well as Iran's periodic artillery barrages against Basra were no match for the damage the frequent and heavy Iraqi bombardment caused to Iranian economic targets. In late

August, for example, Baghdad announced that over the past year its warplanes had staged 120 air missions against Kharg alone.

Baghdad's raids on the oil facilities of Lavan and Kharg Islands in the first half of September caused temporary cuts in Iranian oil liftings. Successful Iraqi strikes on Kharg on 29 September and 6 October 1986 reportedly shut down the remaining two tanker berths, reducing the total Iranian shipments – including those from its storage tankers at Larak – to 800,000 b/d, about half of the Iraqi exports. By then, Iran was obliged to reintroduce petrol rationing, having to import up to 200,000 b/d of refined oil products (amounting to about one-third of its total consumption) due to the damage to its refineries caused by frequent Iraqi bombardments.

It was obvious that Iran was unable to curtail the freedom of the skies that Iraq's air force enjoyed in its bombing of Iranian targets. The Islamic Republic failed to improve its air defences sufficiently to inflict a high cost on the Iraqi warplanes raiding such crucial targets as Kharg and strategic sites in Tehran and other cities. The only effective response Iran could, and did, offer to Iraq's relentless air campaign to enfeeble its economy was to mount periodic land offensives against Iraq – a prospect which worried Saddam Hussein enough to have him publicly appeal to Iran in August 1986 not to implement its threat of launching the 'final offensive'.

What resulted was an Iranian assault, codenamed Karbala-Two, on 1 September in the Hajj Umran region, which saw Iran's forces penetrate deep into Iraqi Kurdistan. Two days later Tehran launched another offensive, codenamed Karbala-Three, in the Fao peninsula. In its course it built a second pontoon bridge over the Shatt al Arab. However, the overall gains of the two attacks were modest.

On 10 October 1986 Iran carried out an airborne commando raid deep inside Iraq, targeting an oil pipeline near Kirkuk. The operation, in which the Iranians were aided by their Kurdish allies, was successful. This was the only new military tactic that Iran had introduced into the war in recent years.

But Iraq sprang a bigger surprise when its warplanes raided the Larak Island oil facilities on 25 November. This operation required the aircraft to travel, non-stop, a total distance of 1170 miles, and deliver, *inter alia*, laser-guided bombs. It was not certain whether Baghdad achieved this feat on its own or, as the Iranians alleged, with the assistance of Riyadh, which allowed the bombers to refuel at a Saudi air base. Determined to maintain oil shipments under all conditions, Iran bought a dozen very large and ultralarge tankers to bolster its ferrying and storage capacities.

That Baghdad was making the maximum use of its air force was obvious from the fact that on 25 November, as well as the ambitious attack on Larak, it staged 163 other sorties. On the other hand it was this level of activity which led Tehran to claim that it had shot down 10 Iraqi aircraft in November. This was also due to the improvement in the Iranian air defence capability, partly achieved by the clandestine deals it had made to procure US-manufactured missiles and spares.

In the Gulf, too, Iran's performance improved. In 1986 Tehran struck 41 naval targets compared with 14 in the previous year. (The corresponding figures for Iraq were 66 and 33.)[10] At the same time Iran actively pursued its policy of stopping and searching merchant ships bound for Gulf ports, first undertaken in August 1985, to check that they were not carrying arms or ammunition bound for Iraq. The rules of naval warfare traditionally accord a belligerent certain rights to ascertain whether neutral shipping is being used to provide contraband to its enemy.

The general pattern of the war in the second half of 1986 was well represented by the events of 6 and 8 December. At first Iraqi warplanes struck a power station on the coast of the Caspian Sea, the industrial city of Ahvaz in Khuzistan, and an Iranian oil tanker. Two days later Tehran responded by bombing Basra, and firing artillery salvoes at various Iraqi targets along a 150-mile front which included areas defended by Iraq's Third, Fourth, Fifth and Seventh Army Corps.[11]

At the end of six years of warfare, in September 1986, the estimates of the Iraqi dead were in the region of 100,000–120,000; those of the Iranian dead stood at twice that figure. Under this pressure, Baghdad conscripted its 125,000 male university students and teachers for the first time.[12] It extended the military draft to men aged up to 50 years and began accepting women volunteers for military training. Not to be seen to be falling behind, Tehran announced in late November that five divisions of women militia had marched past the parliament building.

Iran had considerable difficulty in financing its military and civilian imports following a steep fall in petroleum prices, which led to the lowest oil revenue, in the period March–December 1986, for the past 12 years. By mid-1986, for instance, it had picked up only one-fifth of the 1.5 million tonnes of iron and steel it had ordered from Turkey. Imports of food were drastically cut as well as military goods. Even then the only way it could get through the year was by dipping into its foreign reserves of $7492 million at the end of 1985 to the tune of some $3000 million.[13]

At home, the Iranian government shifted some of the burden of the war to the public at large by mobilizing different groups of towns and villages to feed and clothe their 'sponsored' units of the Basij militia at the front. It had already stopped initiating new development projects, and most of its expenditure now was on current account, with salaries and employee benefits consuming about 70 per cent of it. To meet the growing budget deficit it had the choice of raising loans either abroad or from the Central Bank. Given the parliament's annual renewal of a guideline forbidding the raising of external credits, the government had no option but to approach the Central Bank. This course led to increased money supply and fuelled inflation. It was opposed by the Central Bank governor, Muhsin Noorbaksh, who resigned in November 1986.[14]

Whereas differences between a technocrat and the political leadership could be resolved by the former's resignation, the solution to the more profound disagreements among policymakers on economic reform and management proved elusive. 'There are at present two relatively powerful factions in our country with differences on how the country should be run, and on the role of the government and that of the private sector in affairs,' stated Rafsanjani in mid-1986. 'These two tendencies also exist in the Majlis, in the government, within the clergy, within the universities and across society as a whole.'[15]

The mounting economic problems of the government, headed by Musavi, a proponent of the public sector and interventionist policies, provided an opportunity to the pro-private sector conservatives to attack the administration in parliament – and in the recently established newspaper Resalat (Mission). Their attacks became so vehement that, during 'Government Week' in late August, Khomeini warned 'certain gentlemen' to 'watch their pens'. This had the desired effect, and moderated the heated debate between radicals and conservatives. To help the government to overcome its economic crisis, reflected in the 12 per cent decline in the 1986 GDP,[16] Khomeini ruled that personal taxation over and above the Islamic taxes of zakat and khums was religiously legitimate.

The government decision to slash food imports from $2000 million a year to $800 million caused certain shortages and public grumbling. To ensure that popular criticism did not build up to violent proportions, the authorities had been encouraging voicing of grievances through the state-run radio as well as newspapers.

Within the leadership differences had emerged even on the war aims. The maximalists, to be found mainly in the Revolutionary Guards Corps, set their sights on liberating the Shia holy shrine cities of Najaf and Karbala, installing an Islamic regime in Baghdad, and moving on to liberate Jerusalem. The minimalists wanted the overthrow of Saddam Hussein, the appointment of an international commission to name the aggressor, and war reparations to Iran as the victim of aggression. Rafsanjani was a minimalist, who even tried to qualify Khomeini's declaration about 1986–7 being the Year of Victory. 'It does not mean that the war will come to an end,' he explained. 'We hope to gain more considerable victories this year ... And we believe that when all the supporters of Saddam Hussein have become disappointed ... then victory will be ours.' Some weeks later he expanded on the idea of an anti-Saddam Hussein coup in Iraq. The subsequent regime, he explained, could not be held responsible for the war. Moreover, he promised that Iran would not press for war compensation if the post-Saddam Hussein government proved to be 'Islamic' even if it were backed by America – just as the Saudi regime was.[17] However, minimalists were as committed to continuing the war as maximalists – if only for psychological reasons. 'If we lay down our arms [now], it would no longer be possible to pick them up again,' Rafsanjani explained.

At the same time the government allowed criticism of its war policies, albeit on a limited scale. The Freedom Movement, the only opposition group functioning within Iran, addressed an open letter to Khomeini in September 1986. The party argued that the Gulf War was not a fight between Islam and disbelief (as Khomeini insisted) but an internecine conflict between two 'oppressed Muslim nations'. Moreover, the letter said, the continuation of the hostilities was contrary to the Quran, the Islamic Sunna (Tradition), and the manner of the (Shia) Imams. The Quran states: 'If the enemy inclines towards peace, do thou [also] incline toward peace, and trust in God for He is the one that heareth and knoweth.'[18] Such a document received very limited circulation inside the country. But it was immediately picked up by the anti-regime radio stations functioning abroad and Western-based Farsi language broadcasting services, and beamed into Iran. Thus it gained wide currency.

This was in stark contrast to the situation prevailing within Iraq. There, criticism of war management was a capital offence. Among those executed on this count in June 1986 was General Umar Hazza, a close relative of Saddam Hussein. He reportedly attacked the conduct of the war openly when the Iraqi president visited him to express condolences on the death of his son in battle.[19]

Its failure to recover the Fao territory, and the loss of captured Mehran to the Iranians, increased the Baghdad regime's insecurity. The only way Iraq could withstand simultaneous Iranian offensives in more than one sector, its leaders concluded, was by expanding its military. As a result, by the sixth anniversary of the war in September 1986, the prestigious six-brigade Presidential Guard was enlarged into a force of 17 mechanized brigades of 25,000 elite troops. And each of the seven army corps was built up to a strength of about 100,000 troops. The Iraqi high command reinforced the front lines with earth barriers, barbed wire, minefields, entrenched tanks and additional artillery pieces.[20] It also maintained high standards of food and other supplies to the troops at the front as well as the practice of giving soldiers one week off after three weeks at the front.

These military aims were secured at a great cost to the financial standing of the country. Starting early in 1986, Iraq began defaulting on its foreign loan repayments and letters of credit. Between May and September it concluded agreements on loans rescheduling with its leading creditors – West Germany, France, Japan and Turkey – as well as with Yugoslavia and India. Baghdad was heavily indebted to its Arab allies. Jordan's credit to Iraq of $525 million, originating in supplies of food and consumer goods, was more than its own foreign reserves of $300 million. As for Baghdad's foreign holdings, these fluctuated between nil and $500 million. It managed to scrape through 1986 by curtailing imports by 40 per cent, and increasing its outstanding commercial loans from $10.1 billion to $12.8 billion.[21]

In the final analysis what reassured Baghdad's creditor nations was its enormous oil reserves, and the promise by Saddam Hussein that once the war had ended with his regime still intact, their commercial and financial establishments would be given preference in the awarding of lucrative contracts for reconstructing Iraq. For the time being they were impressed by the governmental resolve, which had resulted in the oil output rising to 1.7 million b/d in early 1986 and the commissioning of the pipeline through Saudi Arabia carrying 500,000 b/d. Another pipeline with the same capacity passing through Turkey was under construction.

There were inevitably ill-effects from the sharp cuts in civilian imports, including food, which increased shortages and profiteering. The paucity of foreign currencies caused problems for the expatriate workers wishing to remit their savings home. This led to blackmarketeering in foreign currencies, a practice which the government attacked vehemently as an economic crime. The punishment was severe. In August 1986 six businessmen were executed on charges of corruption.[22] In early November, the RCC imposed life sentence as the penalty for insulting it, the president, the Baath Party, the National Assembly or the government – and execution for doing so with a view to arousing public opinion against the authorities.

A similar severity was introduced in the observance of public morality and certain Islamic events. For the first time, on the eve of (holy) Ramadan in early May 1986, the Baathist authorities ordered strict observance of fasting between sunrise and sunset, the closure of all nightclubs during the month, and the deportation of about a thousand Thai and Filipino barmaids, initially brought in to entertain troops on leave.

None of these gestures made any impression on the Iraqi Islamists organized under the aegis of the Tehran-based Supreme Assembly of the Islamic Revolution in Iraq. Though the organization remained committed to founding an Islamic state in Iraq, it agreed to co-operate with other Iraqi opposition parties which did not share its Islamist goal. Prominent among these were Kurdish autonomist groups and the newly formed Umma Party. All these forces, represented by 400 delegates, were brought together in Tehran in late December 1986 by the SAIRI under the auspices of the Conference on Solidarity with the Iraqi People. It was inaugurated by President Khamanei, and attended among others by eminent Kurdish leaders such as Masud Barzani and Jalal Talabani. The conference decided to escalate the armed struggle against the Saddam Hussein regime and to form a joint military committee, including an Iranian representative, to co-ordinate their armed activities. The fact that secular or nationalist bodies of Iraqis were formally incorporated in this committee indicated that Tehran had by now given up its hope of seeing an Islamic regime installed in Baghdad.

At the same time there was no let-up in Iran's own military campaigns. By mid-December it had gathered 200,000 troops in the southern sector to match the enemy strength. On the night of 23 December Tehran staged an offensive, codenamed Karbala-Four, along a front between Abu Khasib, 10 miles south-east of Basra, and a string of islands in the Shatt al Arab near Khorramshahr. Four divisions of revolutionary guards and Basij militiamen crossed the waterway near Abu Khasib, and found themselves facing heavily fortified enemy troops, who were backed up by artillery and air power and had been forewarned by the intelligence reports supplied by the US. Poorly supported by their own artillery and air force, the Iranians fell victims to the superior Iraqi firepower and air strikes. A similar fate awaited the one division which tried to capture Umm Rassas and three smaller islands further south. Within two days the Iranians had to retreat, having suffered an estimated 8000 casualties versus Iraq's 3000.

But this reverse did not dent Tehran's resolve to achieve a major military victory in the southern sector.

1987: THE MAKE OR BREAK YEAR

1987 began with a major Iranian offensive, codenamed Karbala-Five, aimed at capturing Basra. It lasted from 6 January to 26 February – primarily because Tehran's forces failed to break through a series of elaborate defence rings constructed by the Iraqis over the past several years to protect their second largest city.

What favoured Baghdad's planners was the fact that about 12 miles south-east of Basra the international frontier swerves sharply from the fluvial border of the Shatt al Arab, and takes a straight north-south direction. Between the waterway and the land border, the Iraqis had by April 1981 dug a trench three yards deep, 18 miles long and three-quarters of a mile wide. By connecting it with the Shatt al Arab through a wide channel, called the Jasim Canal, and three narrow ones, and using giant pumps, they filled it with water. This moat proved to be an effective barrier to the invading Iranians in their July 1982 offensive, providing the Iraqis with killing fields to its east, north and south. By January 1983 the Iraqis had extended the water barrier by creating a trapezium-shaped reservoir, named Fish Lake, that was 6 miles long at its south-eastern end. And by August 1984 they had constructed two channels from the reservoir: one narrow outlet to the south-east towards Khorramshahr, and the other, 1.2 miles wide, heading north. It was a stupendous, expensive task – requiring the excavation of 400 million cubic metres of heavy clay at the cost of $1000 million – but well worth it, for the Iraqis used the canals as well as the lake to place their heavy weapons behind them.[23] Along with this they erected earth barriers to prevent the Iranians draining the marshes along the border. Thus they had two watery barriers for their enemy to cross. In addition, they fortified their forward land border defence positions north of the Shatt al Arab as well as their positions at Abu Khasib on the western bank of the river 10 miles downstream from Basra.

On the night of 6 January four Iranian divisions infiltrated the Iraqi lines along the southern edge of Fish Lake, and overran the poorly defended border town of Duaiji. Anticipating major Iraqi counterattacks from Basra, the Iranian high command simultaneously staged a flanking move to the north of the northern offshoot of Fish Lake. Its forces broke through two of the four Iraqi defence lines there. As for the main offensive, within hours of the capture of Duaiji, the Iranians gained the Iraqi town of Shalamche on the eastern bank of the Shatt al Arab. They expanded their bridgehead at Shalamche to about 35,000 men, and began occupying the territory between Fish Lake and the Shatt al Arab.

The Iraqis staged infantry counterattacks supported by air sorties and artillery fire, which were less effective than before. This time the Iranian forces contained a high proportion of battle-experienced revolutionary guards who, as well being properly armed and led, pursued specific field objectives. Tehran had succeeded in obtaining large quantities of anti-tank weapons and spare parts for its US-made Hawk anti-aircraft missiles. In the hands of well-trained troops these took a heavy toll of the Iraqi tanks and aircraft. Also the marshy and watery terrain reduced the effectiveness of Iraqi artillery and fragmentation bombs by absorbing most of the impact of their explosion and speed. The Iranians succeeded in expelling the enemy from many of its secondary defensive positions, but not from the primary ones, consisting of massive earth ledges, bunkers and huge arsenals of arms and ammunition. They lacked the firepower and mobility required to overwhelm their adversaries. Their net gain by mid-January was 26 square miles of Iraqi soil between Fish Lake and the Shatt al Arab, with their forces installed in positions 7–10 miles from Basra.

To relieve the pressure of continuing Iraqi counterassaults, Tehran staged an offensive, codenamed Karbala-Six, on 13 January in the central sector near Qasr-e Shirin, using regular army troops. It claimed to have regained 100 square miles of Iranian territory from the Iraqis.

In the south, Tehran mounted a major offensive on 19 January and again a week later. These moves caused a major flight of people from Basra, but did not gain much terrain for the attackers, now about seven miles from Basra and two miles from the town of Abu Khasib. However, Iranian pressure compelled Baghdad to fortify its front-line troops with more units of the Seventh Army Corps and the elite Presidential Guard. By so doing the Iraqi high command reduced its reserves to such a low level that, had the Iranians achieved a major breakthrough, it would have found itself short of reserve forces to stop the enemy.

Having failed to expel the foe from its soil, Iraq resorted to attacking Iranian cities with aerial bombardment and long-range surface-to-surface missiles. It made a point of hitting Tehran, Qom and Isfahan, the urban centres with religious or political significance – Qom being a holy Shia place and Isfahan, the second largest Iranian city, being in the forefront of providing war volunteers. By the end of January, these air raids had caused 1800 deaths and injuries to 6200 persons.[24] This was the Baathist regime's dramatic way of weakening the will of Iran's clerical rulers to pursue the war. They in turn responded by hitting Baghdad with long-range missiles, and Basra with a combination of locally manufactured short-range missiles, called Oghab (Eagle), and artillery shells, turning Basra into a besieged city.

Tehran stated that its chief aim was to destroy as much of the Iraqi war machine as possible and demoralize the Baghdad regime. By planning to turn most of the one million residents of Basra into refugees, Iran's leaders wished to strain the Iraqi economy to breaking point. Militarily, the prospect of a ghost city of Basra opened up the possibility of the Iranian troops bypassing it on their way to the Kuwait–Basra road, with a view to blocking the highway and cutting off the single most important inlet for civilian and military imports into Iraq. Diplomatically, an empty city was seen as providing a chance of letting many of the 500,000 Iraqi exiles and refugees in Iran occupy it as the first step towards founding the Islamic Republic of Iraq under the leadership of Hojatalislam Baqir Hakim.

On his part, Saddam Hussein combined aerial raids on Iranian population centres with efforts to divide a wedge between ruler and ruled in the Islamic Republic. In his 21 January 'Letter to the Iranian People' he encouraged them to challenge Khomeini's claim of divine sanction for his rule and for the war, which had been unsuccessful. Iran's failure to break through the Iraqi defences, he argued, 'was the means by which

God wants his judgement to be clear'.[25] It was to rebut this argument among others that, in his speech on the eve of the eighth anniversary of the Islamic revolution on 11 February 1987, Khomeini explained that the waging of the war needed to be seen as 'a divine cause' rather than 'a single final offensive'.[26]

In fact, despite repeated attempts, the Iranians had failed to seize more Iraqi territory – a situation which allowed the Kremlin to engage in a fruitful mediating role, aided by the presence in Moscow of Iran's foreign minister, Ali Akbar Velayati, on 14 February. The Soviets had always strongly disapproved of the Iraqi tactic of bombing population centres. The Iraqis agreed to stop raiding Iranian cities if the Kremlin would promise to replace their substantial losses of warplanes with advanced MiG-27s and MiG-29s. Once this pledge was forthcoming, and Baghdad felt confident that it had virtually blunted the Iranian thrusts, the stage was set for a fortnight-long 'suspension' by Iraq of the War of the Cities on 18 February 1987. In casualties Iran had been the worse sufferer. This round of the War of the Cities had affected 35 Iranian urban centres, resulting in the deaths of 3000 people and injuries to 9000. In contrast, Iran's 11 long-range missiles directed at Baghdad, and massive artillery salvoes at Basra and many other Iraqi urban centres, had killed 300 Iraqis and injured 1000.[27]

While responding to the Iraqi gesture by discontinuing its missile and artillery attacks on Iraqi population centres, Iran did not abandon its Karbala-Five offensive. On the night of 22 February a two-pronged assault was staged from its bridgehead at Shalamche to overrun Iraqi positions along the Jasim Canal, gaining some ground but not enough to change the stalemate which had evolved over the past four weeks. Yielding to pressure from Moscow and Damascus, and concerned at the prospect of Baghdad's renewing the War of the Cities after its temporary suspension, Tehran finally called off the Karbala-Five offensive on 26 February.

This encouraged Saddam Hussein to retrieve the territory he had lost. On 1 March the Iraqi armour, assisted by artillery and air force, tried to overrun the Iranian positions around Fish Lake. But their joint arms operation failed to dislodge the enemy, mainly because of poor tank manoeuvring and inadequate air support. In a way this was a repeat of the Iraqi performance in the Fao peninsula a year before. And, just as in Fao, the Iranians demonstrated their ability to seize limited territory and retain it against heavy odds – as well as their inability to expand their small, strategic gains due to their continued inferiority in fire-power and air support combined with strained logistics.

All told the Karbala-Five offensive cost Iran the lives of 20,000 to 25,000 revolutionary guards, and severe injuries to an equal number, most of the casualties being war veterans. Of the more than half a million guards, only about 100,000 were battle-experienced, so the loss was quite damaging to Iran's war machine. The Iraqi dead and seriously wounded were half as numerous as the Iranians'; but they too included a large number of experienced officers and other ranks. Some of the battles were truly bloody, involving colossal use of artillery shells.[28]

The Karbala-Five campaign established that Iran's revolutionary guards had mastered the tactics of infiltration, small-scale operations, and amphibious attacks, and had ceased to be a human battering ram, as was the case in the offensives of the mid-1980s.[29]

It also showed that, thanks to the success that Tehran had had in procuring spares and ammunition for their US-made and other weaponry, the Iranians had made more warplanes and attack helicopters airworthy than before, and had greatly improved their air defences with anti-aircraft guns, Hawk missiles, the Chinese-made HQ2 surface-to-air missiles and the Swedish-origin short-range laser-guided RBS-70 surface-to-air missiles. Yet Iran used its improved air strength more for defensive than offensive purposes, limiting its daily air sorties to about a dozen. It exacted a hefty price from Baghdad for its high offensive activity in the skies: 50 warplanes, or about one-tenth of its total combat aircraft.[30] But a more serious blow to Iraq was the loss of its experienced pilots, who were so scarce that only about a quarter of the combat planes could be manned by them. Given this, and the $15 million-plus cost of a warplane, Baghdad had to reconsider critically the tactic of using these machines for close air support to the infantry or damaging an oil facility to the tune of a million dollars or so. On the other hand, given the poor state of the early warning radar stations in Iran, the Iraqis had virtual carte blanche in bombing Iranian cities and economic targets.

All in all, the Karbala-Five and Karbala-Six offensives reaffirmed Iran's superiority over Iraq on land fronts even though, by putting one million men under arms by early 1987, Iraq had achieved manpower parity with its adversary. On the other hand, Tehran's failure to achieve victory by the end of the current Iranian New Year on 20 March 1987

provided an occasion for Saddam Hussein to organize a massive demonstration in Baghdad on 21 March to celebrate the occasion. The fact
that his government regarded not being defeated as victory was a
testimony to the static defence to which it had become wedded over the
past five years. Aware of this, Tehran resolved to press its military and
psychological advantage with a view to ending the conflict on its
terms.

From March onwards Iran concentrated on slowly occupying areas in
Iraqi Kurdistan. On 4 March the Hajj Umran area east of Rawandoz
witnessed the staging of Iran's Karbala-Seven offensive, when soldiers
and revolutionary guards infiltrated Iraqi positions on snow-capped
mountains 8400 feet high, and then captured them. Repeated Iraqi
counterassaults failed to displace the Iranians. At a high-level meeting
of military and political leaders in Baghdad on 15 March, Saddam
Hussein warned against the eventuality of a slow defeat through attrition. To ensure that the Iraqi Fifth Army Corps in the Kurdish area
was not reinforced by troops in the south, the Iranians began draining
the water barriers defending Basra. They mounted an offensive, codenamed Karbala-Eight, on 3 April to overrun Iraqi positions. Despite
bloody battles they made only modest gains; but the move was serious
enough to rule out the transfer of units from Iraq's south-bound Third
and Seventh Army Corps to the north.

Early spring saw the emergence of a grand coalition of all Iraqi Kurdish
rebel groups. With this Tehran intensified its military operations in the
northern sector in conjunction with the Kurdish insurgents. Together,
the Iranian troops and Kurdish guerrillas mounted the Karbala-Nine
offensive on 13 April and captured strategic heights near Suleimaniya.
Two days later, in a desperate move to reverse the rebel gains, the
Baghdad government used chemical weapons against 20 Kurdish villages. On 27 April the anti-Baghdad forces staged the Karbala-Ten
offensive from Iran's Sardasht area with the aim of capturing the Iraqi
towns of Mawet to the south and Qala Diza to the north. They claimed
to have occupied 100 square miles of Iraqi territory and caused 4000
enemy casualties. Rafsanjani said that these gains were as important as
Fao because, as he put it, 'Suleimaniya province is a gate of entrance to
other parts of Iraq.'[31] Baghdad's grave concern at the prevailing situation
became obvious when in mid-May Saddam Hussein held an urgent
meeting with the commanders of the Iraqi troops in Kurdistan.

In late May and June the anti-Baghdad forces launched a series of offensives – codenamed Nasr, Victory – with the overall aim of expanding their areas of control in the Mawet and Suleimaniya regions and capturing territory further south in the Khurmal–Halabja area east of the hydro-electric dam along the southern tip of Darbandi Khan Lake, the main source of electricity for Baghdad. Iranian claims included the capture of Mawet in the north, 22 square miles of land near Suleimaniya, several Iraqi posts near Khurmal, and the Iraqi command base at Arabit, north-west of Darbandi Khan Lake.[32]

Iran's sustained and successful initiative in Iraqi Kurdistan was in contrast to the developments in the Gulf. There, much against its will, Iran found itself expending military energy in diversionary activity against Kuwaiti moves which increased Washington's naval presence and its pro-Iraqi tilt.

Like Iran, but unlike Iraq, Kuwait was totally dependent on tankers to export its oil. In order to get even with Iraq for persistently hitting its tankers, Tehran had resorted to attacking the ships trading with this crucial ally of Iraq. In September 1986 Kuwait initiated moves to secure superpower protection for its vessels. Moscow's willingness to help was translated into the leasing of three Soviet tankers to Kuwait in mid-March 1987. Two months later, in order to comply with American law, Kuwait agreed to transfer the ownership of half of its 22 tankers to the US-based Chesapeake Shipping Incorporated so as to secure American naval escort.

Ironically, the matter acquired urgency by virtue of an Iraqi action against the US. On 17 May 1987 two Exocet missiles fired by an Iraqi warplane hit an American frigate, USS *Stark*, about 85 miles north-east of Bahrain, killing 37 crewmen. Saddam Hussein apologized for the attack which, he claimed, was accidental. But an Iranian official described it as 'a serious and dangerous trap' laid by Baghdad to draw both superpowers into the war. Washington put its naval force on high alert and authorized it to fire on any craft believed to be of 'hostile intent'. The incident raised tensions in the Gulf, with the US reaffirming its decision to go ahead with the reflagging of the Kuwaiti tankers, and Richard Armitage, assistant defence secretary, publicly stating on 29 May: 'We can't stand to see Iraq defeated'.[33]

On 16 May and again on 19 June two tankers carrying Kuwaiti oil – one of them Soviet-registered – were hit by sea mines off the coast of Kuwait. By mid-June mines, allegedly laid by Iran, had been detected at the approaches to the channel leading to the Mina Ahmadi oil terminal in Kuwait. It took the US and Saudi navies about a month to clear the channel and the approaches of mines. On 7 July Iraq attacked Kharg as Tehran fortified its strategically placed islands of Abu Musa and Greater and Lesser Tunb near the Hormuz Straits.

Four months earlier US intelligence had noticed Iran deploying a battery of powerful shore-to-ship missiles near Hormuz. The weapon was thought to be an improved Chinese version of the Soviet Styx anti-ship missile with a range of 25–50 miles, designated as HY-2 and popularly known as Silkworm. With a maximum payload of 1100 pounds, it was three times more deadly than an Exocet and gave Iran the capacity to sink vessels rather than merely damage them. By mid-April Iran had reportedly assembled a dozen launchers and at least 36 Silkworm missiles. The Iranian navy continued its stop and search operations in the Gulf. On 1 May, for instance, it intercepted 14 ships in the Hormuz Straits carrying goods intended for Iraq, and detained one. On its part Iraq continued its periodic attacks on enemy targets in the Gulf, hitting Iran's Cyrus, Nowruz and Ardeshir offshore oilfields in late March, and on 14 July bombing Farsi Island in the Upper Gulf, from where Iranian speedboats, manned by revolutionary guards, attacked ships trading with Saudi Arabia or Kuwait.

It was against this background that on 22 July two reflagged Kuwaiti tankers, escorted by three US warships, started their 550-mile journey from Hormuz to Kuwait. Two days later *Bridgeton*, the 410,000-tonne tanker, hit a mine about 120 miles from Kuwait and near the Iranian offshore island of Farsi. Though the vessel, made of heavy plate, received minor damage and continued its journey, the incident opened a chapter of direct US–Iran naval confrontation in the Gulf. After three years of striving, Iraq had finally succeeded, through its ally Kuwait, in internationalizing the conflict, with one superpower poised firmly against Iran.

For domestic and ideological reasons the Khomeini regime could not afford to be seen to be overawed by Washington. To demonstrate its defiance, three-day naval manoeuvres in the Gulf, codenamed Shehadat, Martyrdom, commenced on 5 August. These involved test-firing a shore-to-ship missile and ramming a speedboat loaded with explosives into a dummy naval target.

At the same time Tehran was reluctant to open a new major front in the Gulf, and thus deflect its resources from pursuing the war against Iraq on which, according to Rafsanjani's interview with the *Ittilaat*

(Information) on 23 July 1987, the leadership was unanimous – provided the country's domestic administration could be maintained normally. Tehran had the means and determination to persist in its present strategy of steadily seizing Iraqi territory with a view to securing its ultimate objective of Saddam Hussein's overthrow, he added. But there was a snag. 'A war of attrition can be dangerous as our enemies can use time against us,' he warned. 'However, a direct involvement of third parties in the conflict is unlikely.' None the less, should this happen and endanger the country, then Iran would unveil the next phase of its military plans. This would involve occupying strategic points between Basra and Baghdad with a view to cutting off southern Iraq from the capital, a task which would require a large mobilization. Referring to the 500 battalions raised in the past year, he added: 'We have the capacity to raise 2000 others, and to provide them with logistical support. It is a political choice, and there are differences on making it.' Stating that over the past year the war had cost Iran $3 billion, he warned that pursuing a policy of 'all-out war' could aggravate the economic crisis and provoke popular discontent. 'The high cost of the war could discourage the families of the *mustazafin* – the deprived – who supply most of the troops,' he concluded. 'I have asked myself if it was opportune to ask people to tighten their belts further.'

This assessment was remarkable on two counts. It was extraordinarily honest and frank; and a leader of Rafsanjani's stature had taken the Iranian public into his confidence and outlined the contours of strategic policy thinking and debate at the top.

Not surprisingly, Rafsanjani was instrumental in the despatch of a high-powered mission to Kuwait to persuade its government in secret talks to suspend the US reflagging of its tanker fleet in return for an Iranian guarantee to end attacks on Kuwaiti shipping.[34] Kuwait turned down the offer, and reflagged the remaining nine tankers. This confirmed Iran's earlier assessment of Kuwait, as summarized by its foreign minister, that Kuwait had 'virtually turned [itself] into an Iraqi province' having placed its resources 'at the disposal of France, America and the Soviet Union'. He had then stated in his letter to the UN secretary-general that 'As long as Iran's oil exports are threatened by Iraq, Iran cannot allow Iraq to receive guaranteed oil [income] in order to beef up its war machine through Kuwaiti tankers flying whatever flag.'[35] By attacking a Kuwaiti freighter outside the Hormuz Straits on 31 August, Tehran gave vent to its anger at Kuwait's stance.

Faced with the US warning in mid-July that Iran's Silkworm missile batteries would be destroyed if it showed 'hostile intent' towards reflagged Kuwaiti tankers under American escort, Tehran devised a plan to hit either these vessels when *not* under US protection or other vital economic targets in Kuwait. It used its Fao foothold to fire Silkworms at Kuwaiti targets. The first such attack came on 4 September when a missile fell into the coastal waters of Kuwait. During the next three days the Iranians fired two more missiles. One of these, directed at the Mina Abdullah refinery, hit nearby houses. Kuwait responded by expelling six of its seven Iranian diplomats.

On the night of 21 September the US navy attacked an Iranian landing ship, the *Iran Ajr*, which, it alleged, was laying mines 50 miles northeast of Bahrain. American helicopter gunship operators, equipped with night vision goggles, first fired machine-guns and then rockets, and immobilized the *Iran Ajr*, killing three sailors. The US navy claimed to have found 10 mines aboard. At first Tehran declared that the vessel was carrying food, then changed the story, saying that the ship – loaned to the Iranian navy by its owner, the Islamic Republic of Iran Shipping Company – was ferrying military supplies from Bandar Abbas to Bushahr. Whatever the truth, the incident embarrassed Iran, and dented its strategy of avoiding armed conflict with America by keeping it off balance, and concentrating its main energies on preparing the next major land offensive against Iraq in late autumn or early winter. In a way Washington's action was a belated response to the damage to the US-flagged tanker *Bridgeton*, by an Iranian mine two months earlier. The score was now even.

As the war entered its seventh year on 22 September 1987, Iran found itself willy-nilly facing the combined strength of the Iraqi air force, now possessing 400 combat aircraft, and the US naval force of some 40 warships. A lack of clarity on the military strategy was once again aired by Rafsanjani in an interview with the *Tehran Times* on 30 August. There were two options, he said: either mobilize the full resources of the nation to launch a long, multi-pronged offensive to end the conflict with victory, or continue with the present war of attrition. 'Perhaps there is a third way between the two which would mean lessening facilities for the public and giving more to the war.' Apparently the government in Tehran was unable to make up its mind.

On the Iraqi side, too, there was confusion about military strategy. In his survey of the war Saddam Hussein described it as something beyond the control of human beings. 'If God wants this war to continue for more than seven years, we must perform our national duty as dictated by our conscience and our responsibility,' he stated. On the other hand he claimed: 'The Iraqi people can defeat them [the Iranians] any time, whether they like it or not.'[36] But overall, given that Baghdad was wedded to the concept of static defence on land, Saddam Hussein's task was easier than his enemy's. All he had to do was to maintain the land defences intact, keep up the attacks on Iran's economic targets in the Gulf and on the mainland, and wait for the hostility between Tehran and Washington to escalate to Tehran's growing disadvantage. On the diplomatic front, Iraq further improved its standing by accepting the latest ceasefire call by the UN Security Council under the unanimously passed Resolution 598 of 20 July 1987. Iran prevaricated.

With the US naval presence at an all-time high, and increased activity in Iranian and American quarters, tension mounted. Aware of a build-up of Iran's naval forces in the Upper Gulf, US warships had taken to monitoring the Iranian side. Its naval manoeuvres near Farsi Island on 3 October had drawn a few US warships in the area, causing tempers to rise. The Iraqis chose this time to stage an aerial attack on the distant Larak oil facilities on 5 October, hitting three tankers.

It was against this background that a clash occurred in the area on the night of 8 October in which the Americans destroyed three Iranian patrol boats and killed three sailors. According to Washington, the Iranians fired at its patrol helicopter which called up helicopter gunships. Tehran claimed that the American helicopters fired first, and that its sailors had downed one of them with Stinger anti-aircraft missiles.

A few days later the Iranian Revolutionary Guards Corps commander promised a 'heavy blow' against the US 'in due course', and added: 'The best response to America is to continue the war because Saddam's fall means an end to all wishful hopes of America in the region.'[37] Iran lobbed two long-range missiles at Baghdad.

On 16 October the Iranians fired a Silkworm missile at an American-flagged supertanker, *Sea Isle City*, docked at Mina Ahmadi in Kuwaiti waters, injuring 18 crewmen. The immediate American response came from Secretary of State George Shultz, who said that the tanker was not under US escort when hit, and that the incident constituted an attack on Kuwait.

Such an assessment went down badly with Kuwait and Saudi Arabia.

They reportedly pressured Washington to retaliate for, they argued, failure to do so would encourage Tehran to act more boldly next time. President Reagan consented. Of the options before him – destroying the Silkworm sites in Fao and/or near the Hormuz Straits; attacking Iran's mainland oil facilities; hitting some Iranian offshore oil installations – he chose the third. These facilities were away from the Iranian mainland and unlikely to jeopardize American lives. On 19 October the US navy destroyed two offshore oil rigs at Reshadat and Resalat (called Rakhsh before the revolution) in the Lower Gulf, one of them equipped with radar and anti-aircraft guns against Iraqi air raids. Washington described its action as 'a measured response', and considered the matter closed. Tehran, which estimated the damage at $500 million, denounced it as a violation of its sovereignty, and vowed retaliation.[38]

On 22 October Iran hit Kuwait's Sea Island oil terminal 10 miles from the port of Mina Ahmadi, from where the country exported about a third of its total oil outflow of 600,000 b/d. Tehran thus felt that it had got even with the US–Kuwait–Iraq combine.

All along Iran had kept up pressure on the Iraqi army, particularly in the northern sector. In June the Kurdish rebels mounted a series of offensives, codenamed Fatah, Victory, in Suleimaniya province, where they claimed to have captured Sayyid Sadiq, north of Darbandi Khan Lake. At the same time various Kurdish parties tried to hammer out a common political aim which was more than provincial autonomy and less than complete independence. In early September 1987 they agreed to fight for a future Kurdish state in 'confederation with a future democratic Iraq'.[39] This reassured Tehran, which had been suspicious of the idea of 'self-determination' for Iraqi Kurds, being opposed to the same demand by Iranian Kurdish rebels. In early October Iraqi Kurds, armed and equipped by Tehran and Damascus, staged offensives in the Kirkuk area against Iraqi forces.

That the Iranians were active in the southern sector as well became known in late October when Iraq's deputy premier, Ramadan, referred to the massed Iranian troops on the border reportedly poised to attack. But Tehran was inhibited from launching a major offensive on the eve of the extraordinary Arab League summit on the Gulf War on 8 November.

Once the summit finished on 11 November with a condemnation of Iran for its refusal to end the war, Tehran adopted a tough stance. Khomeini alluded to a modified strategy of the war which stressed the continuation of offensives in order to 'deprive the enemy of respite'. Referring to the Karbala-Five offensive earlier in the year in his sermon to the Friday prayer congregation on 13 November, Rafsanjani said: 'Another Karbala operation with the same force and extent would lead to developments into the unknown'.[40] The Iraqi high command put its forces on maximum alert all along the Iranian border.

On 16 November Tehran's gunboats attacked three tankers carrying Saudi oil. But, responding to behind-the-scenes pressure by Damascus, Iran refrained from attacking targets in Kuwait. Instead, on 17 November, its forces carried out minor assaults in the central sector, and heavily shelled Basra, where 90 per cent of the houses had been damaged by the 61,979 shells received so far.[41] Iraq retaliated by raiding Iran's unfinished nuclear power station at Bushahr.

The next month witnessed Iran staging probing attacks against Iraq's defence lines in the Fakeh area north of Basra – coupled with a declaration that the Islamic Republic was pursuing a strategy of inflicting 'repeated blows' that would give the enemy no respite. This was a clear indication that the dilemma facing the regime articulated by Rafsanjani in July and August remained unresolved. Militarily, the government wanted to engage in a massive and broad offensive; politically and financially, it could not afford it.

The recovery that the country had made from its acute economic recession of 1986 was fragile. With petroleum prices stabilizing around the range of $15–18 a barrel in early 1987, Tehran's oil income during the first quarter was twice the total of $900 million for the corresponding period of 1986. During 1987 Iran maintained its output near its OPEC quota, which varied between 2.3 million and 2.6 million b/d; and during the periods of lull in the Gulf, such as the one that followed the passing of the UN ceasefire resolution on 20 July, it exported 2 million b/d. But towards the end of the year, it found itself with as much as 750,000 b/d of petroleum in hand due to the boycott of its oil imposed first by Paris and then Washington. As a result of oil customer resistance and depressed oil revenue, Iran was forced to save foreign exchange by curtailing importation of industrial raw materials. This in turn led to full or part-closure of factories, and a sharp rise in unemployment officially put at 14 per cent in October 1986.

The rising budget deficit, coupled with the discarding of the prudent policy of linking local currency expenditure with foreign earnings, had fuelled inflationary pressure. The official figure of 20 per cent inflation for the year ended 20 March 1987 was widely regarded to be about half of the actual rate. The subsequent hardship caused to a vast majority of Iranians engaged the attention of Khomeini, who also had to grapple with the problem of the ailing Islamic Republican Party.

The main reason for establishing the party a few weeks after the revolution was to provide a formal organization for Islamic activists which could compete with the existing, mainly secular parties, and which could become the primary vehicle for imparting Islamic consciousness to the public at large. However, by mid-1983 all secular parties had been banned, and so the Islamists lost the raison d'être for an organization of their own. Moreover, other post-Pahlavi institutions – the Revolutionary Guards Corps, the Basij, the Revolutionary Komitehs, the Reconstruction Crusade and so on – had become established and popular, while Friday prayer sermons were now the main vehicle for cultivating and sustaining Islamic consciousness. Many radical Islamists left the IRP and became active in one or more of the other revolutionary institutions. In the 1984 parliamentary elections the candidates backed by the revolutionary guards did better than those supported by the IRP. The differences between the conservative and radical elements within the party and elsewhere became so acute as to warrant a public statement by Rafsanjani in mid-1986. To rectify the situation Ayatollah Khomeini appointed a mediation council to conciliate factional differences. It failed in the task. In his internal report the party general secretary, President Khamanei, explained that the mediation council's failure stemmed from the ideological nature of the differences prevailing between the factions. He noted that the party's performance had been tawdry, and the output of its political and ideological units negligible. In his internal report, Rafsanjani noted that 'different sections with different tastes' were confronting one another, and wondered if it was right to have a party at all. Having noted the contents of both reports, Khomeini decided on the dissolution of the Islamic Republican Party, which took effect on 2 June 1987.[42] With this the parliament, the Majlis, became the only forum for political manoeuvring by different factions.

Rafsanjani immediately appealed to Khomeini for 'precise and clear intervention and help' to the Islamic Majlis in its legislative programme concerning 'fundamental and essential issues'. These related to property rights in land, industry and trade. In a statement issued in mid-July, on the eve of the hajj pilgrimage, Khomeini stressed the need for a 'planned economy' in an Islamic state. He underlined Islam's regard for 'the bare-foot' and the building of 'a just economy', with the interests of the oppressed taking precedence over those of the rich. He declared, 'The rich should never influence the Islamic state and its rules simply because of their wealth.'[43]

Khomeini's guidelines on the economy were so much in tune with Premier Musavi's interventionist thinking that the latter tried to recover the ground he had conceded to businessmen and traders over the past three years following Khomeini's edict against excessive state interference in managing the economy. More specifically, the government issued firm guidelines to its 12,000 price control inspectors, responsible for checking the prices of 37 basic goods and services, and announced the penalty of withdrawal of a trading licence from the overcharging merchant or businessman. It claimed to have reduced prices by seven per cent in two months.

To restrain defence expenditure in the face of increased mobilization, the government launched 'financial jihad' in November 1987. It called on those unable to fight to sponsor one soldier at the front for three months at a cost of $2800. This was a way of directly involving in the war effort the rich whose financial security was being guaranteed by the actions of those at the front – as Rafsanjani explained.

The other important way in which the government economized on scarce foreign exchange was by building up its military industry. It claimed to have saved $1 billion in hard currencies in the first nine months of 1986–7 thanks to increased domestic arms output. The new year saw Iran producing an unmanned reconnaissance plane, successfully testing its locally made fighter aircraft, and introducing prototypes of combat and support helicopters. It had begun manufacturing its own version of the Swiss trainer aircraft PC-7 and planned to produce a battle tank adapted from American and Soviet models. It was already engaged in making 122mm field guns and rocket-propelled grenades with launchers.

Among the missiles that Iran was reportedly manufacturing were the local versions of the Chinese Type 83 artillery rocket and the Soviet surface-to-surface missile Scud-B. Also mass production of an Iranian version of the US-made Tow anti-tank missile had begun. Rafsanjani claimed that Iran had seized Silkworm anti-ship missiles from Iraq in Fao, and then produced its own weapon based on Silkworm. The Islamic Republic was self-sufficient in small arms and ammunition. It produced mortars of various calibres. Its output of 6 million artillery shells in 1986 was expected to double in 1987. The scale of the military industry run by the ministries of defence, the Revolutionary Guards Corps, and the Reconstruction Crusade could be gauged by the fact that half of the factories belonging to the ministry of heavy industry had been converted to defence production, and a further 12,000 workshops were engaged in subcontracted work. Of Iran's 200 universities and colleges, 115 were engaged in military research and development.[44]

Iraq too was pursuing a policy of self-sufficiency in defence equipment. This task was assigned to the Military Industries Commission. It claimed to be meeting fully the country's needs in light weapons. It also produced not only light and heavy ammunition but also mortars, rocket launchers, artillery guns, armoured personnel carriers and guided bombs. Additionally, it had sponsored weapons development projects in Egypt concerned mainly with surface-to-surface missiles, including an extension of the range of the Soviet-made Scud-B. The success of this project came on 3 August 1987, when Baghdad announced the test-firing of a missile which achieved a range of 380 miles, twice that of Scud-B.

By late 1987 Iraq had nearly 400 combat aircraft, six times the strength of Iran's airworthy warplanes, although at 193, Iraq's attack helicopters were less numerous than Iran's 341. On the ground Baghdad possessed 4500 tanks and 3200 armoured fighting vehicles versus Tehran's respective totals of 1570 and 1800. Iraq owned 2800 major artillery pieces whereas Iran had only 1750. Baghdad had managed to replace its substantial losses in warplanes and other military hardware by continuing to borrow large sums. Its total foreign credits – excluding $45–55 billion in economic and military loans and grants from GCC members – amounted to $50.5 billion, or nearly three times its Gross Domestic Product. By continually extending its conscription rules Baghdad had increased its professional military troops to 955,000, far above Tehran's 655,000. Iraq's Popular Army (with some female units), estimated to be 650,000 strong, was slightly larger than Iran's Revolutionary Guards Corps at 620,000. Thus the Baathist regime had put under arms nearly 1.6 million men in a country with a total of 2.7 million males aged 18 to 45. Its achievement looked all the more impressive in contrast to the Iranian total of approximately 1.28 million men under arms out of a total of some 9 million males aged 18 to 45.[45]

Achieving the target of putting 60 per cent of Iraqi males aged 18 to 54 years into military uniform meant worsening the labour shortage that already existed. The only solution lay in dramatically increasing productivity in farms, factories and offices. Two decrees issued in late February 1987 tried to do this by reducing administrative bureaucracy and raising output. One disbanded the organizations mediating between the industry ministry and public enterprises; the other empowered ministers and state company directors to take immediate steps unilaterally to augment production.

In mid-March the Revolutionary Command Council issued decrees which put civil servants and industrial workers in public sector companies on a par, and prohibited state employees from forming trade unions. *Al Thawra* (The Revolution), the Baath Party newspaper, of 13 March described the measures as 'transforming the so-called class struggle into a positive and constructive one'. In practical terms the new decrees abrogated the 1970 Labour Code – and with it, the regulations concerning fixed working hours and overtime payment. 'The purpose [of these measures] is plain: it is to increase production,' said Saddam Hussein. 'For example, we want 12 hours of work every day. We'll say everybody works 12 hours per day, and there would not be people who work eight hours.' His resolve to boost output at all costs was underlined by a warning he issued in early July. Referring to the complaints he had received from some enterprises about meddling by party and security service officials which adversely affected production, he warned: 'It has been decided that the party and the security services shall not interfere in the essential work and tasks of productive enterprises.' He emphasized the importance of increased output when he directed all officials to 'pay as much attention to economic affairs as to political ideology'.[46] The dramatic impact of these decrees and statements could be judged by the industry minister's claim early next year that Iraq had reduced its foreign labour in 1987 by a third.[47]

The immediate impact of the official measures was to reassure the numerous foreign creditors, who were pleasantly surprised to hear the finance minister say that Iraq had balanced its current trade account for the first half of 1987. Iraqi oil exports in the middle of the year were running at 2.3 million b/d, a record since the war – and far above the Iranian shipments of 1.8 million b/d. Baghdad's oil income for the year was expected to be about $11.3 billion, a big jump from the $7 billion earned in 1986.[48]

The improvement in the oil income reflected well on the Iraqi president and reinforced his position as the sole source of authority in the republic. He continued his policy of further tightening his grip on the state and the party by installing his relatives or henchmen in important positions. In April 1987 he appointed a cousin, Ali Hassan Majid, as the general military commander of the Kurdistan region with full powers to conduct military, intelligence and party affairs in order to defeat Tehran's strategy of steadily expanding its area of control in the northern sector. The media gave much prominence to the president's two sons – Uday and Qusay[49] – who, it seemed, were being groomed for senior state or party positions. In early August Saddam Hussein replaced Sadoun Shakir (Tikriti), an old party stalwart, as interior minister with Abdul Wahhab, a member of the Regional Command since June 1982, known for his total loyalty to the Iraqi president.

How far Saddam Hussein wished to mould Iraqi society and state in his own image became obvious in his July 1987 speech to mayors of provincial towns. 'I wanted the people to make use of my words and my conduct so that nobody would come to tell me the opposite, or act in a contradictory manner, claiming that is the line adopted by the party,' he declared. So while he drew his power from being the general secretary of the Baath Party, in reality he placed himself above and beyond the organization. He cleverly wrapped up his action in a populist garb. 'In this way,' he explained, 'we are activating the people's control and its role in society.'[50]

He remained the prime objective for extermination by his sworn enemies. On 9 April 1987 his motorcade was ambushed on the outskirts of Mosul by Al Daawa militants. Six of them were reportedly killed – and so were 10 presidential bodyguards. Saddam Hussein was unhurt. The assassination attempt was timed to commemorate the execution of Ayatollah Baqir Sadr, an eminent Shia cleric, seven years earlier.[51]

Besides such sensational attempts Al Daawa continued its occasional acts of sabotage. A car bomb planted by it in Baghdad on 12 August, for instance, caused 20 deaths. But more serious to Baghdad was the news in late 1987 that the Tehran-based Supreme Assembly of the Islamic Revolution in Iraq planned to set up a government in exile. The assassination on 17 January 1988 in Khartoum, Sudan, of Hojatalislam Mahdi Hakim – a brother of the SAIRI leader, who had been selected as 'foreign minister' in the proposed government – almost certainly carried out by Iraqi agents – showed that Baghdad's security services were performing efficiently.

All in all, therefore, 1987 ended with Iraq in a better economic and political state than before. Diplomatically, too, the Baathist regime was doing well. It had accepted the UN Security Council Resolution 598 in contrast to the continued prevarication of its adversary.

In its official response to the resolution on 12 August, Iran criticized the US for imposing its will on the Security Council in order to regain credibility among pro-American Arab states lost in the wake of the Irangate revelations. But it did not reject the document. Later its deputy foreign minister invited the secretary-general, Javier Pérez de Cuellar, to Tehran for consultations on the implementation of the resolution. During his visit, Iranian leaders insisted that Clause Six of the resolution, regarding the establishment of an impartial commission to inquire into the responsibility for the conflict, be given precedence over Clause One, concerning an immediate ceasefire. If the impartial panel found Iraq the aggressor, then Iran would postpone its demands for the overthrow of Saddam Hussein and war reparations.[52]

After his visits to the Iranian and Iraqi capitals Pérez de Cuellar submitted a report to the Security Council. In it he noted that the Iranian leaders insisted on the importance of linking the ceasefire with the naming of the party responsible for starting the war, and that they would accept a formal truce only after the process of determining war guilt had been put into train. As for the Iraqi authorities, they wanted to see the resolution implemented in the order in which the clauses were written – i.e., with a full ceasefire and withdrawal of forces to the international frontier preceding an investigation into responsibility for the conflict.[53]

During his visit to the United Nations, primarily to address the General Assembly, President Khamanei submitted a seven-point plan to implement Resolution 598 to Pérez de Cuellar. It included a de facto ceasefire to coincide with the appointment of an impartial body to inquire into the origins of the war. After the publication of the commission's findings Iran would accept a formal ceasefire. As for the withdrawal of troops to the international border, Iran refused to commit itself to an automatic withdrawal while Iraq insisted on such a move 'without delay' after the truce.

On 15 October Pérez de Cuellar submitted a four-paragraph document to the Security Council which linked a truce with other peace moves.

Though secret, the adopted document was believed to contain a 'D-Day' for a ceasefire: the day UN observers would be despatched to monitor the truce. After that date both sides would pull back to the internationally recognized border. On 'D-Day or another day to be agreed upon' an impartial panel would start work on determining responsibility for the war. The Council seemingly accepted the Iranian idea of linking the truce with setting up an impartial inquiry into the origins of the war while conceding the Iraqi demand that a troop withdrawal should take place 'without delay' after the ceasefire. It commended the UN secretary-general's timetable, and authorized him to set up machinery to implement Resolution 598.[54]

Thus Iran ended a tumultuous 1987 without provoking either direct military involvement of third parties or a damaging international embargo stemming from the rejection of the UN Resolution 598.

THE BEGINNING OF THE END

The onset of winter raised expectations of a major Iranian offensive in the south. But unlike in previous years, this time the signs were ambivalent. The Iranian mobilization in the southern sector was of medium size, more suited for a series of probes than a single major assault. That the government had fallen short of its manpower target became obvious when in January 1988 it extended conscription from 24 months to 28. There were reports too of the authorities failing to build up sufficient stocks of ammunition, supplies and military hardware. Their efforts were adversely affected by the ceaseless Iraqi bombing of bridges, factories and power plants. They were aware of the fact that over the past year the Iraqis had bolstered their defences, and had thus raised the already high cost of frontal assaults on their positions. On top of that was the new diplomatic factor. By staging an all-out land offensive against Iraq, Tehran was bound to alienate the UN Security Council, thus inviting an international arms embargo, which would make its task of importing arms, ammunition and spares even more expensive and time-consuming than at present.

So Iran fell back on its war of attrition strategy, propounding a policy of limited but constant pressure along the entire border. The only significant move Tehran made in January was a minor offensive, code-named Bait al Muqaddas-Two, near Mawet in Kurdistan. And the only noteworthy development during the next month was that Iranian warplanes engaged Iraqi Mirages in a dogfight over the Gulf on 9 February, downing three. On the same day, at a different location, an Iraqi Exocet missile narrowly missed a US warship. Fearing a repetition of the May 1987 accident involving USS *Stark*, Washington pressured Baghdad to cease air activity in the Gulf. Baghdad complied, but soon became impatient.

The lull in fighting did not suit Iraq. Much to its chagrin, the diplomatic activity at the United Nations had ground to a halt. An uprising against Israel by the Palestinians in the West Bank and Gaza, which had emerged in December, had grabbed international attention. Baghdad wanted to see the Gulf War return to centre-stage at the UN. Confident of blunting any Iranian offensive against Basra, the Iraqi leadership wanted to provoke Iran into mounting an all-out assault in the south. Such a move by Tehran was also bound to revive the stalled UN intervention for a ceasefire, which was the ultimate objective of Baghdad.

During the last week of February Iraqi authorities carried out 'an experimental evacuation' of Baghdad. On 27 February Iraq renewed the War of the Cities by attacking the Iranian town of Saqqez in the northern sector, killing 26 civilians. Tehran responded by firing three Scud-B missiles at the Iraqi capital at dawn on 29 February.

Iraq retaliated by delivering 16 long-range missiles at Tehran between the evening of 29 February and the night of 1 March. This shook the residents. They were at the receiving end of a missile – named Al Hussein, after a most revered Shia figure – which was a modified version of Scud-B, with an additional tonne of rocket fuel and a payload reduced from 1760 lbs to 440 lbs, which doubled its normal range to 370 miles. Since Tehran is about 340 miles from the Iraqi border along the line that joins it with Baghdad, it was now within the range of an Al Hussein missile. This version of the War of the Cities lasted until 20 April, with short gaps in mid-March and in early April, during the visit to Baghdad of the Turkish premier Turgut Ozal. Iraq fired up to 200 Al Hussein missiles at Iranian cities, principally Tehran, and caused 2000 deaths. Iran's score was 77 Scud-Bs, most of them directed at the Iraqi capital.[55]

The truce in the War of the Cities on 11 March – resulting from Ozal's public appeal to both parties and Moscow's behind-the-scenes pressure on Baghdad – broke down when on the night of 13 March Iran mounted its Zafar-Seven offensive near Khurmal and Bait al

Muqaddas-Three offensive north of Suleimaniya in Kurdistan, capturing several villages. Two days later Iran and its Iraqi Kurdish allies staged a major offensive, codenamed Wa Al Fajr-Ten, and captured Halabja, a town of 70,000 people, situated 15 miles inside Iraq. On 16 March the Iraqi air force attacked the town with bombs of cyanide or nerve gas, and killed at least 4000 people, mainly civilians.[56]

Baghdad's action in Halabja provided a propaganda opportunity to Tehran, which was used effectively both at home and abroad. The pictures of men, women, children and animals frozen to instant death shocked the world. Coupled with this was the fact that the Iraqi government had killed its own unarmed citizens with poison gases – an unprecedented event. But by giving wide publicity to Iraq's chemical bombardment of Halabja, Tehran engendered a heightened fear among Iranians that Baghdad would mount poison gas attacks on Iran's cities using their surface-to-surface missiles. Indeed, on 1 April Iranian radio demonstrated the new alert tone in case of a chemical attack, and gave instructions on how to avoid its worst effects. This was a prudent move, but inevitably it demoralized the public, already made depressingly conscious of the scale of death that poison gas had caused in Halabja.

At the policy-making level the Iraqi action made Tehran worryingly aware that if Baghdad found itself in a desperate situation in the face of a major Iranian ground offensive, it would load its long-range missiles with chemical warheads and fire them at Iran's urban centres. In December 1986 Premier Musavi had stated that Iran had developed its own chemical warfare technology. A year later he informed the Majlis that the government had started producing 'sophisticated offensive chemical weapons', but added: 'Iran will not use chemical weapons as long as it is not forced to, and will respect international conventions.' In mid-March 1988 the London *Observer* reported that a fortnight earlier Iran had tested a chemical warhead for a missile near Semnan.

But chemical arms could not be deployed until and unless Ayatollah Khomeini, the commander-in-chief, gave permission. When he was approached on the subject by top officials, he reportedly reiterated his earlier refusal based on the argument that Islam prohibits its fighters from polluting the atmosphere even in the course of a jihad, holy war.[57] However, neither this reasoning nor Khomeini's refusal was publicized: that would have given Saddam Hussein carte blanche and defeated Tehran's strategy of keeping the Iraqi president guessing, and would also have precluded Iran from using poison gases in the future. For the present, however, given that chemical weapons were not to be deployed, Iran felt inhibited about staging an all-out offensive against Iraq in the south.

Meanwhile, Tehran's policy of progressively seizing Iraqi land in Kurdistan continued. By late March it claimed to have captured 540 square miles of Kurdistan, including the eastern shore of the Darbandi Khan Lake. This was apart from the 4000 square miles of rural Kurdistan reportedly controlled by Kurdish rebels, mainly along the Iraqi-Turkish border.

Iraq responded by activating the National Liberation Army set up in June 1987 by the Baghdad-based Mujahedin-e Khalq. On the night of 27 March the NLA, composed entirely of anti-Khomeini Iranians, launched an offensive in the Fakeh region along the highway to Dezful. They claimed to have overrun 370 square miles of Iranian soil. Though Iran expelled the NLA forces quickly from its territory, Iraq had established that it now had the NLA card to play against the Iraqi Kurdish card held by Tehran.

Iran kept up its pressure on Iraqi Kurdistan by staging on 10 April yet another offensive, codenamed Bait al Muqaddas-Five, in the Panjwin area. It reckoned that a major breakthrough in the north would compel the Iraqi high command to transfer troops from other regions to Kurdistan to protect the roads leading southward to Baghdad and westward to the Kirkuk oilfields, thus weakening the defences in the southern and central sectors. Indeed a widely publicized visit just then by Adnan Khairallah, Iraq's defence minister, to the northern sector confirmed the view prevalent in Tehran. But, as it turned out later, this was a ruse. Saddam Hussein had decided earlier to focus on retaking the Iranian foothold on the Fao peninsula.

After an interval of four weeks, on 10 February Baghdad had resumed its attacks on Iranian tankers, provoking Tehran to retaliate in kind. During the next fortnight there was a flare-up in the strikes on ships in the Gulf, with an average of one hit a day. On 14 April a 120-pound mine struck *Samuel B. Roberts*, an American frigate, 70 miles east of Bahrain – an area that had been cleared of sea mines in December 1987 – injuring 10 sailors and severely damaging the vessel. US officials claimed that the mine was newly laid and that the two others found nearby had Iranian serial markings. Tehran denied the allegations, and blamed 'Iraqi agents' for planting the mines. Anticipating American reprisals,

Iranian leaders concentrated on how best to meet them. Among the steps they seemingly took was to withdraw their meagre air force to the bases deep into the interior.

It was against this background that the Iraqis mounted an offensive in the Fao peninsula on the night of 16 April. They attacked the Iranians from the north with massive artillery barrages, mixing their regular ammunition with shells containing cyanide gas or nerve agents. With the Iranian defence positions facing north (towards Basra) and north-west (towards Umm Qasr) the southern coast was undefended; and it was on this shoreline that the Iraqi commandos landed in helicopters and boats. With his forward forces collapsing under the impact of poison gases, and the Iraqis advancing unhindered from the rear, the Iranian field commander decided to withdraw quickly across the Shatt al Arab. The battle was over by the morning of 18 April.

While Tehran had clearly not expected an Iraqi assault on its 180-square-mile foothold in the Fao peninsula, it had judged earlier that it would be hard to retain it in the face of a massive offensive by Baghdad. Evidence of this could be deduced from the missile silos in the occupied area emptied of their Silkworms, the weapons used earlier against Kuwait. The depleted forces, amounting to no more than a brigade of 5000 men (who found themselves facing up to 40,000 Iraqis), was another indication of a comparative loss of Iranian interest in the territory.

None the less, Tehran was doubly surprised to see the enemy – which had for years stuck strictly to a defensive strategy – adopt an offensive policy and implement it successfully. Khomeini was reliably known to have upbraided the armed forces leaders for having become 'too arrogant'. And Muhsin Rezai, the Revolutionary Guards Corps commander, publicly admitted having made 'mistakes'.[58]

Baghdad greeted the recapture of Fao with mass celebrations. The victory was of tremendous psychological importance to the Iraqi regime, notwithstanding its lack of military significance. It badly needed a morale booster – and a dramatic break from its defensive posture of the past several years. Not surprisingly, it unilaterally halted missile attacks on Iranian cities.

Saddam Hussein had chosen his timing well, just when Iranian leaders were engaged in planning a strategy to face a probable US military riposte in the wake of severe damage to an American warship. In fact Adel Darwish, a London-based Arab journalist, having visited Fao and Baghdad, alluded to the suggestion (in Iraq) that 'Saddam Hussein was tipped off by the Americans about their willingness to mount their own attack on Iran following the discovery of a fresh batch of floating mines in the Gulf.'[59] Subsequent events lend credence to this proposition.

At dawn on 18 April the US navy destroyed an Iranian oil rig off Sirri Island and another at Salman (called Sassan before the revolution) 80 miles south-west of Sirri. In the course of the destruction of the Sirri oil platform by a cruiser and two frigates, an Iranian missile boat allegedly approached the American warships 'with obvious hostile intent'. It was sunk by US ships. This was part of 'a measured response' by Washington to the mine damage to its warship on 14 April. But a more serious event was to occur seven hours later. According to the American journalists on board USS *Jack Williams*, when the Iranian frigate *Sahand* was detected sailing out of Bandar Abbas, an order went forth to 'get it'. This occurred 10 miles south-west of Larak Island when, alleging that the *Sahand* had fired at three American planes, USS *Enterprise*, an aircraft carrier, retaliated with missiles and laser-guided bombs at the Iranian frigate, and set it on fire. An hour later, a US warplane dropped a laser-guided bomb on the Iranian frigate *Sablan*, after it had allegedly fired at the plane, and immobilized it.[60]

This meant that two of Iran's four frigates were put out of action. Tehran was in no state to confront the American fleet of some 30 ships. Its strength lay in a force of many hundred armed speedboats based along the coast and several strategic islands. It responded by ordering a group of its speedboats to attack an oil rig in the UAE's Mubarak oilfield 30 miles north of Sharjah – as well as a nearby tanker and freighter. While the boats were engaged in this operation they were hit by US warplanes. One vessel sank and another was damaged. The news of these skirmishes, which further highlighted the bloody hostility existing between Iran and America, was received enthusiastically in Baghdad.

The Iranian mood was well expressed by President Khamanei, who threatened attacks on 'US interests throughout the world for criminal America's all-out war [against Iran]'. Both he and Rafsanjani urged all trained volunteers to rush to the battlefields for military operations on several fronts. 'The anti-Islamic arrogant powers have decided to make a serious attempt to save Saddam [Hussein] and tie our hands,' said Rafsanjani.[61] But the response to official calls for mobilization was lukewarm. The news of Iraq's liberal employment of chemical weapons in Fao had considerably dampened the volunteers' usual enthusiasm for combat.

Tehran wanted to show that it was unbowed, and determined not to yield to American pressure. On 24 April its gunboats attacked a Saudi-owned tanker off Dubai. Washington was in an equally uncompromising mood. On 29 April the Pentagon announced a change in the rules of engagement so that neutral ships under attack could call on the US fleet for protection.

The Iranians were in the midst of their unfinished parliamentary elections. On the eve of the first round on 8 April Khomeini expressed his preference. He urged votes for the candidates 'who are committed to Islam and loyal to the people, who have tasted the bitter taste of poverty and support the Islam of the deprived of the earth in words and deeds'. He called on voters to 'isolate and expose' those who stand for 'Islam of capitalists, Islam of the arrogant, of the insensitive rich, of the hypocrites – in short, American Islam'.[62]

This was in line with the stance he had adopted over the past several months when, for instance, he had in July 1987 authorized the government to deal with inflation by punishing hoarders and profiteers without going to court. Following President Khamanei's statement on 1 January 1988 that the government could exercise its authority only within the ordinance of the Sharia, Islamic law, Khomeini contradicted him publicly. The Ayatollah stated that the present Islamic government in the form of 'the God-given absolute mandate' was 'the most important of the divine commandments and has priority over all other derivative commandments – even prayer, fasting and pilgrimage to Mecca'.[63]

Having thus established the supremacy of the Islamic government, Khomeini took a practical step to dissipate the legislative impasse created by the rejection of important economic reform bills by the conservative-dominated Guardians Council. On 6 February he appointed a 13-member Council for the Expediency of Islamic Order, composed of the six clerics on the Guardians Council and seven other nominees including the president, the premier, the parliamentary speaker, and the chief justice. It was assigned the specific task of settling the fate of the parliamentary bills rejected by the Guardians Council in the past or future. By so doing Khomeini in effect modified the veto power of the Guardians Council which, he felt, had in its rulings failed to take fully into account the social environment prevalent in the Islamic community at large. This was a sign that Khomeini had decided to get on with implementing measures for an equitable distribution of wealth for the benefit of the needy rather than hold them in abeyance until a victorious end to the Gulf War.

With Khomeini's bias against conservative traditionalists now more apparent than before, electors favoured radical and reformist candidates. They emerged as the dominant group among the 191 of the 270 seats decided in the first round. The turnout of 68 per cent was 15 per cent higher than in the previous poll. In the run-up to the second round on 13 May tempers rose so sharply against conservatives that the offices of their mouthpiece, the *Resalat*, in Tehran and Shiraz were attacked. Their poor performance in the last round raised tensions. The radical and reformist groups, including revolutionary guards, planned a mass demonstration in support of Khomeini on 24 May. But he advised its cancellation and called for cool tempers.

There was an urgent need for national unity in Iran in view of Baghdad's new resolve to recapture all the territories it had lost. Starting on 23 May, Iraq mounted offensives in the northern and central sectors, then finally in the south, in the Shalamche region east of Basra.

On 25 May, the Iraqis overpowered the Iranians in a ferocious artillery and rocket barrage, mixing conventional shells with the ones filled with cyanide gas or deadly nerve gases, and expelled them from the Shalamche bridgehead. They also introduced a new, awesome weapon: a surface-to-surface cluster missile with a range of 35 miles, which exploded about 500 feet above the target, releasing 200 bomblets. Just as in Fao, the Iranians discovered that in the searing temperatures of 45°C prevalent on the fronts, it was virtually impossible to wear their protective clothing and masks. As quick-acting agents, cyanide gas and nerve agents put the Iranians on the run, but permitted the advancing Iraqis to undertake mopping-up actions, unhindered, in an atmosphere free of the quickly dissipating poison gases. Furthermore, the Iranian units were undermanned and under-equipped to withstand a massive Iraqi onslaught by the local Third Army Corps bolstered by the elite Presidential Guard units used earlier in Fao. Baghdad had by now learnt to deploy Presidential Guard and commando units to achieve breakthroughs which were then quickly exploited by tank units. In this offensive Iraq regained its territory up to the Kut Suwadi and Bubyan border posts 25 miles from Basra. Just as in the Fao peninsula, by bombing the Iranian rear area with slow-acting mustard gas, the Iraqis frustrated Tehran's plans of immediate counterattacks.[64]

Once again Saddam Hussein chose the timing correctly. On 21 May Iran had commenced a ten-day combined forces exercise, codenamed Zulfikar (Sword of Imam Ali) Three in the Persian Gulf and the Gulf of Oman, involving 50 frigates, destroyers, landing craft and minesweeping, anti-submarine and logistic vessels. The Iranian navy was complemented by army and navy aviation units, air force units, ground forces, marines and an airborne brigade. An Iranian source was quoted as saying that the exercises were aimed at disproving Washington's claims that it had crippled half of the Iranian naval hardware in its April encounter.[65] So once again the US ended up, by chance or design, diverting Iranian attention and military equipment to the benefit of Iraq.

The loss of the Shalamche salient, secured at a heavy cost in men and materials to Iran, deserved a response at the highest level. It came in Khomeini's message to the newly convened Third Islamic Majlis on 28 May. 'The combatants must continue their fight by depending on their faith in God and their weapons,' he said. 'The outcome of the war will be decided on the battlefields, not through negotiations.'[66]

Five days later he issued a seven-point decree, appointing Rafsanjani acting commander-in-chief in place of President Khamanei, and instructed him to create the general command headquarters and fully co-ordinate the military, Revolutionary Guards Corps, volunteer forces and internal security forces. This was his way of conceding that all was not well with the country's armed forces coupled with a promise that a determined effort would be made imminently to overcome the hesitation that had paralysed the military and political hierarchy ever since the Americans had actively joined an anti-Iranian front in the Gulf. (Privately, however, Khomeini directed Rafsanjani to seek the views of Iran's political and military leaders on the conflict as well as to carry out a thorough survey of the war machine.)

Rafsanjani set up a unified command under himself. For the longer term he seriously considered a merger of the military and the Revolutionary Guards Corps, but rejected it. The military, he stated, is 'a long-established and classical organization' whereas the Revolutionary Guards Corps is 'revolutionary and self-motivated'. This was the root cause of the difficulty in achieving total harmony between the two. He envisaged partial merger of some functions like military research and development, and rationalization of military industry divided between the military, the Revolutionary Guards Corps and the Reconstruction Crusade.

To make a dramatic impact on Iranians, Rafsanjani ordered on 13 June a thrust into the recently lost Shalamche region. Tehran claimed a penetration of 7 miles into Iraq and the inflicting of 18,000 casualties on the enemy troops before a voluntary withdrawal. This was a spoiling operation, designed to delay Iraqi consolidation and show that Iran was quite capable of mounting assaults. But for a major land offensive the Khomeini government required at least several months of preparations; and Iraq was in no mood to let it have that breathing-space.

Interestingly, the elevation of Rafsanjani as the highest military official also saw an intensification of efforts by Iran's foreign ministry to seek a diplomatic solution to the conflict. 'If the UN, the Security Council and the world are sincere in dealing with this issue [of finding a solution to the Gulf War], it will be done,' said Rafsanjani on 3 June. 'But we do not trust them . . . While we have the door open and have given our foreign ministry permission to pursue that course of action, if we relax for one moment in the war, God forbid, our initiatives and leverages will be taken away from us.'[67] In short, Iran was now publicly following the twin policy of 'fight and talk'.

Part of the reason why Tehran had kept up diplomatic dialogue was that it wanted to counter the American and British pressure on the Security Council to impose a weapons embargo on Iran for failing to comply with its ceasefire resolution. In late February Iran had informed the UN secretary-general that since it accepted the 10-point implementation plan for Resolution 598 there was no ground for arms sanctions against it.

It transpired later that Khomeini appointed Rafsanjani acting commander-in-chief partly because he thought that the popular and charismatic Rafsanjani would be in a better position to rein in Revolutionary Guards Corps leaders in case they objected vehemently to the Ayatollah's unconditional acceptance of the UN ceasefire resolution. After all, Rafsanjani had a high standing among the rank and file of the Revolutionary Guards Corps.

Over the years Rafsanjani had emerged as one of the most trusted lieutenants of Khomeini. A son of a pistachio farmer, Ali Akbar Hashemi Rafsanjani was born on 25 August 1934 in Bahraman, a village near Rafsanjan in south-east Iran. After his early education in Rafsanjan, Ali Akbar went to Qom for religious education, and became a student of Khomeini. Later he taught at Faiziya seminary in Qom. He was drafted into the army in 1962, but discharged shortly afterwards because of the influence he gained over fellow conscripts in his unit. He participated in the anti-Shah insurrection of June 1963 and underwent a jail sentence. Between then and the 1977–8 revolutionary movement, he was gaoled four times. After the revolution he was appointed by Khomeini to the 13-member Islamic Revolutionary Council. Following his election to the First Majlis in 1980, he was elected speaker of the house, a post to which he has been re-elected every year since. Under his leadership parliament emerged as a most vigorous and powerful institution. An outstanding public speaker, he has a talent for explaining complex subjects – including Khomeini's views on the running of an Islamic state and society – simply and entertainingly. Soon after the Gulf War erupted, Khomeini appointed him his personal representative to the Supreme Defence Council, which in turn named him its official spokesman. As the only cleric with some military experience he had much say in the conduct of the war.

His elevation to the post of acting commander-in-chief came in the wake of reverses suffered by the Revolutionary Guards Corps, primarily responsible for the defence of Fao and the Shalamche bridgehead. With the Corps' prestige at a low point, Rafsanjani had little difficulty in sidelining its commander, Muhsin Rezai, in charge of operations, and its minister, Muhsin Rafiqdust, in charge of military production. By setting up a unified command under himself, Rafsanjani improved co-ordination between the military and the Revolutionary Guards Corps: a development which deeply disturbed the military high command in Iraq.

On 19 June the Iraqis used their previously successful tactic of firing artillery shells of cyanide gas and nerve gases at the Iranian front lines and dropping mustard gas bombs at the rear in the Mehran region. They captured the town and the surrounding area, and then handed them over to the Mujahedin-e Khalq's National Liberation Army, stating that the fighting was strictly between anti-Khomeini Iranian forces and Tehran. But this combat only lasted three days and resulted in the NLA's withdrawal from the territory.

Far more seriously, at dawn on 25 June the Iraqis staged a lightning offensive on the Majnoon Islands. They overpowered the Iranians with ferocious firepower combined with poison gas attacks, and surprised the enemy troops by encircling them from the rear and cutting off their supply lines. For the first time in the war Iraq used paratroops, with a brigade dropping inside Iran east of the islands. Elite Presidential Guard units mounted an amphibious attack using, *inter alia*, hovercraft. They were backed by the Third Army Corps posted to the west of the islands and equipped with some 2000 tanks (about half the national total) and 600 artillery pieces, heavily outgunning the Iranian revolutionary guards units which included Iraqi dissidents. In a frontal attack Iraq's Third Army Corps infantry elements advanced along the embankments, and were supported by the infantry units of the Sixth Army Corps.[68] The result was an Iraqi victory within a day.

The achievement set off celebratory marches and rallies in Baghdad. The recovery of the Majnoon Islands – with their estimated reserves of some seven billion barrels of oil in eleven fields scattered over a distance of 36 miles – was the last in a series of lightning victories that Iraq had scored in the south.

On 30 June Iran's Supreme Council for War Support conceded military reverses, and went on to explain that the Iranian forces had been obliged to 'step back' due to 'the unholy alliance' between America, the Soviet Union and Arab reactionaries aimed at saving the Iraqi president from 'certain downfall'. More specifically, the Council blamed Moscow for its recent supplies of long-range missiles to Iraq and Washington for its increasingly aggressive actions against the Iranian navy. It called for volunteers to rush to the battlefields. But the response was poor mainly because of the prominence given in the Iranian media to Iraq's extensive use of poison gas weapons at the fronts in explaining Iran's poor military performance.

Yet, oddly, the Islamic Republic's political life continued normally. On 30 June Mir Hussein Musavi, a radical, was confirmed as prime minister by all but 13 of the 217 Majlis deputies present. This was in contrast to the last such vote in October 1985 when 99 parliamentarians had either abstained or voted against him. The vote reflected the dominance of radicals and reformists in the house, with their strength put at about two-thirds of the total. The Majlis went on to exempt him from presenting his cabinet for a vote of confidence. Whatever the state of the troops at the fronts, the government and parliament were more cohesive than before.

Ever since its strikes against Iran's war vessels in mid-April, the US fleet in the Gulf had been on alert against possible Iranian reprisals. American warships (as well as the two supply barges that the Pentagon had anchored in Kuwaiti territorial waters) were under constant Iranian surveillance, while the Americans busily monitored the movements of major Iranian craft. They were apprehensive that Tehran would take some dramatic action – such as ramming a warship with one or more speedboats loaded with explosives – against the US navy around 4 July, American Independence Day.

It was against this backcloth that at dawn on 3 July a minor skirmish occurred between the two sides in the Hormuz Straits. Having sent out reconnaissance helicopters to track Iranian speedboats in the vicinity, an American cruiser, USS *Vincennes*, and its sister ship, USS *Elmer Montgomery*, hit and sank two of them for allegedly firing at a US helicopter. In this charged atmosphere an Iranian airbus with 290 people aboard commenced its scheduled flight from Bandar Abbas airport, used for both civilian and military planes, to Dubai. It was mistaken by the USS *Vincennes* for an F-14 warplane and shot down. The American cruiser happened to be where it was – under the air corridor allotted to civilian flights between Bandar Abbas and Dubai – because it was keeping watch on the Iranian port of Kuhestak, where a fixed site for Silkworm missiles was being built.

Initially Washington denied shooting down the aircraft, then it partly blamed Tehran, and finally admitted that its cruiser crew may have overreacted. Iran accused the US of deliberately attacking the plane. Its air force commander pointed out that Iraqi warplanes, loaded with bombs, flew regularly in the Gulf at low altitudes, without drawing any adverse response from the US navy.

Khomeini directed Rafsanjani to prepare and implement the Iranian response to the airbus disaster. Ayatollah Montazeri, the heir-apparent to Khomeini, said, 'If the great leader of the revolution gives the order for the forces of the revolution and resistance, the cells at home and abroad will make the material, political, economic and military interests of the US the targets of their struggle . . . now that in addition to its surrogates, the main enemy, America, has entered the field openly.' In reply Khomeini said that Montazeri should 'lend support' to Rafsanjani.[69] This was his way of subtly favouring diplomacy above rising confrontation with the US.

On 5 July Iran called for an urgent meeting of the UN Security Council. It was the first time since October 1980 (when the Islamic

Republic began boycotting Security Council meetings in protest against its anti-Iran bias) that Tehran had turned to the world body.

This was to prove the curtainraiser to something more profound: Iran's acceptance of Security Council Resolution 598 – the beginning of the end of the Gulf War.

9 INTERNATIONALIZATION
OF THE WAR

Part of the reason for Tehran's Fao offensive in February 1986 had been to break what it described as 'the oil conspiracy' against the Islamic Republic hatched by Iraq, Saudi Arabia and Kuwait. Following the unsuccessful October 1985 OPEC conference, where Iraq failed to secure a quota equal to Iran's, Baghdad resorted to unilateral action in its oil production. Saudi Arabia decided to regain its past share of the market by any means. Between late 1985 and early 1986 it increased its petroleum exports from an average of 2 million to 4.5 million b/d. This drove the oil price down from $27 a barrel to $15. Riyadh's strategy was meant to hurt non-OPEC producers to the extent that they felt compelled to co-ordinate their production with OPEC and make a common price hold internationally. Above and beyond that, Saudi Arabia and Kuwait expected the steep fall in petroleum price to curtail Tehran's oil revenue to the point of seriously injuring its ability to conduct the Gulf War.[1] Iran responded by attempting to reduce Iraq's oil output by mounting offensives in the south with a view to disrupting its petroleum facilities there and bombing its oilfields in the Kurdish region.

Kuwait felt seriously threatened by Tehran's successful offensives in Fao in February 1986. It condemned these and put its forces on alert. Reversing its policy of excluding Gulf War footage from its television screens, the Kuwaiti government began transmitting material supplied by Iraqi television. The Kuwaiti press adopted a blatantly pro-Baghdad stance, highlighting among others the news of private donations for Iraq's war effort. By late March these were to reach a total of $525 million.[2] The government renewed its countersale petroleum contract with Baghdad.

Riyadh was equally concerned. On 12 February King Fahd reportedly telephoned Saddam Hussein to inquire about the Iranian offensive; and over the next fortnight there were four high-level contacts between Riyadh and Baghdad. Saudi and Kuwaiti foreign ministers flew to Damascus to urge President Assad to warn Tehran against invading Kuwait, adding that if he failed to restrain Iran he would lose the Gulf states' subsidies to his government.

Tehran repeated its public disapproval of the aid that Saddam Hussein's Arab neighbours were providing him. 'These countries should remember that we are now on their borders,' Rafsanjani said on 28 February. 'Iran will no longer accept that your ports should receive arms shipments for Iraq, that your roads should be used to strengthen the Iraqi army, and that Iraqi oil should pass across your territory.'[3]

But such tactics proved counterproductive. At their meeting in Riyadh from 1 to 3 March 1986, GCC foreign ministers combined their condemnation of Iran's occupation of Fao and its threats against their countries with praise for Iraq for its readiness to end the conflict peacefully. Following this, the GCC chiefs of staff decided to despatch the GCC Rapid Deployment Force, consisting of two brigades made up chiefly of Saudi and Kuwaiti troops, from Hafar al Batin, Saudi Arabia, to the Saudi–Kuwaiti border.[4]

In early March Iran hit four ships leaving or approaching the western side of the Gulf in as many days in retaliation for Iraq's attacks on four Iranian tankers plying between Kharg and Sirri Islands during the previous week. Thus Iran proved its potential for enforcing its threats against Iraq's allies.

Kuwait was the more vulnerable: unlike Saudi Arabia (and like Iran), it was totally dependent on tankers for exporting its petroleum. So, in response to Iraqi attacks on Iranian tankers, Tehran began concentrating on Kuwaiti tankers. As for its oil facilities at home, in mid-June 1986 Kuwait's petroleum complex at Mina Ahmadi suffered major fires. The saboteurs claimed to belong to the Revolutionary Organization: Force of the Prophet Muhammad. They were almost certainly local Shia. This action further increased tension between Shias and Sunnis, which had been building up since the December 1983 bombings. As a result of this, and pressure from Riyadh, the ruler of Kuwait dissolved parliament – the only forum for open debate on current national problems – in July 1986.

While publicly condemning Iran's military actions, Riyadh tried to keep its lines of communication with Tehran open at the highest level. Indeed, for a change, it mediated between Syria and Iran. Due to payment arrears and disagreement on oil charges in the wake of the price crash during the winter of 1985–6, Tehran had suspended its petroleum exports to Syria in March 1986. Riyadh intervened successfully, and Iran resumed its shipments in June. Soon after, Tehran began receiving 100,000 b/d of Saudi refined oil products through intermediaries. These imports helped Iran to overcome shortages caused by Iraq's attacks on its Tehran and Isfahan refineries.[5]

At the OPEC conference in early August 1986 the Saudis abandoned their price-war strategy, partly because they had failed to secure the co-operation of Britain and Norway in aligning non-OPEC and OPEC oil outputs and prices, and partly because the pressures on them by other OPEC members, suffering huge losses in oil income, became unbearable. They agreed to an OPEC production pact on an interim basis, which raised the price by about a third, and placed it in the range of $14–16 a barrel. While this improved relations between Tehran and Riyadh, those between Tehran and Kuwait remained tense.

Later in August, following the Iraqi air raid on the Sirri oil terminal, Tehran stepped up its attacks on Kuwaiti oil tankers. The next month Kuwait secretly approached Washington and Moscow to protect its fleet of 22 oil tankers. This was the first step, inadvertent or otherwise, which was to mature into the internationalization of the Gulf War by the following summer.

Before the OPEC conference on 9 October the Iranian oil minister visited Riyadh and had 'brotherly talks' with top dignitaries including the king. OPEC agreed to a total output of 17 million b/d, a mere 200,000 b/d above the figure proposed by Iran. A further sign of improved Tehran-Riyadh relations came on 29 October when King Fahd dismissed Ahmad Zaki Yamani, the Saudi oil minister for 24 years, because of his lack of support for a fixed price of $18 a barrel favoured by the Saudi monarch and Tehran.

While Saudi Arabia was steadily mending its ties with Iran it received a shock when revelations about clandestine contacts between Tehran and Washington erupted in early November. This episode, to become popularly known as the Irangate or Iran–Contra scandal, shook the whole region as well as America's European allies and the Soviet Union.

THE IRANGATE AFFAIR AND ITS AFTERMATH

On 3 November 1986 *Al Shiraa* (The Sail), a Beirut-based magazine, disclosed that America had sold arms to Iran clandestinely and that Robert McFarlane, former US National Security Adviser, had visited Tehran earlier in the year to meet Iranian officials. The news stunned the world.

Two elements were involved. Aware of the geostrategic importance of Iran, Washington wanted to end the extreme hostility that Tehran showed towards it. Secondly, at a more mundane level, it was intent on securing the release of the American hostages taken by pro-Tehran groups in Lebanon.

Significantly, the first abduction of a US citizen, William Buckley, the CIA station chief in Beirut, occurred on 16 March 1984 – two months after the US State Department included Iran in its list of nations supporting international terrorism and vigorously pursued its policy of blocking arms supplies to Tehran. The Islamic Jihad Organization, which kidnapped Buckley, coupled its demand for the release of 17 men convicted in Kuwait on charges of bombing the US and French embassies with a call on Washington and Paris to alter their policies towards Tehran, including ending their arms embargo against Iran.

By 20 May – when Graham Fuller, vice-chairman of the National Intelligence Council, updated his earlier assessment of Iran for discussion by top American policymakers[6] – pro-Iranian groups in Lebanon had taken a total of five American hostages.

With the help of Ibrahim Yazdi, a former Iranian foreign minister, who was visiting Washington, McFarlane, then still National Security Adviser (who had in August 1984 asked various government agencies to reassess US policy towards Iran) set up 'backchannel' communication with some 'moderate' members of the Iranian government. What gave further impetus to these contacts was the hijacking of a Trans-World Airlines jet to Beirut in June 1985. Intervention by the Syrian president was not enough to bring about the release of all the 39 American passengers. The last four were released on 30 June only after a prominent emissary had arrived from Tehran, acting at the behest of Rafsanjani, the official spokesman of the Supreme Defence Council.

President Reagan sent a secret message to Rafsanjani, then on a visit to Tokyo, via the Japanese Premier Yasuhiro Nakasone. In it he thanked Rafsanjani for the release of the American hostages on the TWA flight and expressed hope for better American–Iranian relations. About then, the first week of July, Reagan allowed McFarlane to explore the proposal that Tehran might influence the Lebanese Islamic Jihad Organization to free their American hostages (now numbering seven) in 'probable' return for American weapons. The proposition had been offered to McFarlane by the director-general of Israel's foreign ministry: he had been in touch with an expatriate Iranian arms dealer, Manuchehr Ghorbanifar.

In early August 1985, after McFarlane had briefed Reagan on the Israeli proposal to sell US-made Tow anti-tank missiles to Iran through Israel, he secured the president's approval. On 30 August 508 Tows left Israel for a third country, and arrived in Iran on 13 September. The next day one American hostage was freed.

In the second deal on 22 November, involving an exchange of 120 Hawk anti-aircraft missiles for the remaining five American hostages (the sixth, Buckley, having been killed by then), US officials were directly involved. It went awry. Three days later the CIA arranged for a shipment of 18 Hawk missiles from Israel to Iran aboard a plane of one of its front companies. The Iranians rejected the consignment within days after test-firing a missile and finding it unsuitable for their purpose.

On 5 December Reagan signed a Presidential Finding retroactively authorizing the supply of US weapons to Iran. The next day at a high-level meeting in the White House – where the participants included Vice-Admiral John Poindexter, appointed to succeed McFarlane in January – it was decided to end arms sales to Iran but to continue exploring diplomatic and other contacts.

However, on 17 January 1986 Reagan reversed his stance. He signed an order authorizing the CIA to purchase 4000 Tows from the Defense Department and sell them to Iran, with Israel making the necessary arrangements for the transaction. Thus the US became a direct supplier of weapons to Iran. Concurrently, dissatisfied with the use of an intermediary, Ghorbanifar, for contacting the Tehran government, Poindexter, the new National Security Adviser, demanded a meeting with responsible Iranian officials.

On 15–16 February Washington shipped 1000 Tows to Israel. By the end of the month Israel had arranged to transfer these missiles to Iran. Though no American hostage was released and no meeting between senior US and Iranian officials took place, Washington continued to pursue the initiative. On its part Tehran now insisted on receiving Hawk missile spare parts and radars to activate their inoperational Hawks.

The Americans were anxious to hold high-level talks with the Iranian government. Poindexter appointed McFarlane to pursue the matter along with Lieutenant-Colonel Oliver North, deputy-director for political-military affairs on the National Security Council. On 15 May

President Reagan authorized a secret visit to Iran by American officials and approved a document outlining US policy towards Iran to be delivered to their Iranian counterparts. It was based on North's memorandum to Poindexter in early April. 'We have convinced the Iranians of a significant near term and long range threat from the Soviet Union,' it stated. 'We have real and deceptive intelligence to demonstrate this threat during our visit. They have shown considerable interest in this matter as part of the longer term relationship.' Elsewhere the memorandum stated: 'We have no interest in an Iraqi victory over Iran. We are seeking an end to this conflict and want to use an improved relationship with Iran to further that end.'[7]

On 23 May the US shipped 508 Tow missiles and Hawk spares to Israel. The same day an American delegation led by McFarlane flew to Israel on its way to Tehran, arriving there on 25 May. His plane carried about a fifth of the Hawk spares that the Iranians had asked for.

McFarlane had been given to understand that two American hostages would be freed on his arrival and the other two shortly thereafter (the fifth having been killed in retaliation for the American air raids on Libya on 15 April 1986). But nobody was released during his four-day stay. McFarlane had arrived hoping to confer with either Rafsanjani or President Khamanei. In the event he met no one higher than a senior civil servant. He had rejected Ghorbanifar's suggestion that he and North should go first to Tehran and prepare the ground for McFarlane's visit. But McFarlane, who had served under Henry Kissinger, a former US National Security Adviser and Secretary of State, had a vision of achieving something of the magnitude of the rapprochement that Kissinger brought about between Communist China and America through his secret visit to Peking in 1971. He therefore rushed to Tehran.[8] Not surprisingly, in his talks with an Iranian official he stressed Moscow's evil designs on Iran in order to lure Tehran back into Washington's orbit.

In June 1986 the US solicited Israel's assistance in securing the release of the American hostages. On 3–4 July seven tonnes of US-made arms and spares were delivered to Iran via Spain and Yugoslavia, most probably by Israeli agents. This shipment contained spare parts for the US-manufactured warplanes and tanks in use in Iran. On 26 July the Revd Lawrence Jenco, an American, was released in Beirut. On 3 August Iran received the remainder of the Hawk spares it had asked for.

It was obvious that the United States was getting nowhere in achieving its objective of improving relations with Iran, and that its dealings with the Khomeini regime through an Iranian intermediary had ended up as straight 'arms for hostages' swaps. This ran contrary to America's much trumpeted policy of not dealing with hostage-takers and terrorists. Moreover, it encouraged the pro-Iranian groups in Lebanon to engage in hostage-taking. In mid-September they kidnapped two more Americans.

Meanwhile US officials succeeded in establishing a 'second channel' to the Tehran regime, the new contact being a 'relative' of Rafsanjani. North and his team met the new Iranian contact in West Germany in early October. He offered to help secure the release of one American hostage if the US would send 500 Tows to Iran. On 29 October these weapons were shipped from Israel to Iran through a third country. Four days later, on the eve of Congressional elections, an American hostage, David Jacobsen, was released in Beirut. The Islamic Jihad Organization, his captor, said that it was releasing him in response to 'overtures' by the US.[9] On the whole the Iranians had managed to make their American negotiators appear poor bargainers in private as they were to do later in public, by extracting more than they gave in return.

The disclosure of clandestine US arms sales to Iran had a devastating impact upon American public and world opinion. It showed Washington acting against its professed policy of 'no deals' with terrorist individuals or states, and dramatically undermined the popular standing of President Reagan. His approval rating dropped by a third, from 67 per cent to 46 per cent. It demonstrated acute schizophrenia in the American government with the state, defence, justice and customs departments actively pursuing anti-Iran policies, and the White House, the National Security Council and the CIA trying to woo the Khomeini government. The net result was a severe blow to the credibility of the Reagan administration among its Arab and European allies.

Reagan mounted a damage control strategy. In a television broadcast on 13 November he justified his action in order to achieve the objectives of an end to the Gulf War and the release of American hostages. 'Iran encompasses some of the most critical geography in the world,' he stated. 'Iran's geography gives it a critical position from which adversaries could interfere with oil flows from the Arab states that border the Persian Gulf. Apart from geography, Iran's oil deposits are important to the long term health of the world economy.' Turning to the political aspect, he said, 'Iranian revolution is a fact of history; [and] between American and Iranian basic national interests there need be no permanent conflict.'[10]

The mood in Tehran was celebratory. Iranian leaders interpreted the episode as signifying victory for their country. Here was their most powerful adversary, the United States, on public record as recognizing the Islamic revolution and having negotiated with the revolutionary government. 'America has accepted that Iran is standing invincibly on its own feet,' said Rafsanjani. Speaking on the Prophet Muhammad's birthday on 20 November, Khomeini described the episode as 'an issue greater than all our [previous] victories'. He added: 'Those who broke relations with Iran have come back, presenting themselves meekly and humbly at the door of the nation wishing to establish relations and making apologies.' He advised Reagan to mourn over what had happened, which was a disgrace for the Americans.[11]

Khomeini might as well have advised the Gulf rulers to mourn. They were reportedly in a state of shock and disbelief. At the very least, they felt, America had shown disregard for their security. It seemed to them that the US had reckoned that Iran would prevail in the Gulf War and had therefore taken steps to restore ties with the imminent victor. If this was the practised policy of Washington, they might as well follow suit. Also, implicit in the clandestine episode was Washington's wish to recreate the strategic alliance that had existed between it, Israel and Pahlavi Iran. The continued revelations detailing shipments of arms to Iran from Israel provided Gulf Arab states much cause for concern.

According to the Danish Seamen's Union, the Danish ship *Else-HT* carried at least 3600 tonnes of military materials, mainly US-made, in four journeys in May and June 1986 between the Israeli port of Eilat and Bandar Abbas. Another Danish freighter delivered arms and ammunition from Israel to Iran in mid-October.[12] Israel's basic interest was to see that Iran did not lose to Iraq, which it regarded as an implacable foe – both as a militant practitioner of Arab nationalism and a strategic ally of the Soviet Union.

Israelis were deeply involved in two big weapons deals for Iran which fell through because of the vigilance of the US justice and customs departments. The linchpin was Cyrus Hashemi, an expatriate Iranian weapons dealer, who had first tried to set up, unsuccessfully, an arms for hostages deal during the Carter presidency.[13] He co-operated with the American justice and customs authorities by fronting a phoney company interested in buying military hardware for Tehran, in return for a promise by the US government to drop charges against him for having sold embargoed items to Iran earlier.

The project got going in November 1985, and involved two packages of arms and ammunition. The first deal, worth $1180 million, included 18 F-4 fighters, 13 F-5 warplanes, 46 Skyhawk fighter-bombers, five C-130 transport planes, Tows, guided bombs, Hawks, tanks and other lesser weaponry. The other package was worth $1200 million. The arms and ammunition were to be obtained from stocks held in Israel and West European countries. On 22 April US law enforcement officials, working in conjunction with the Bermudan government, arrested in Bermuda and New York 10 of the 18 Americans, Israelis and West Europeans involved in the two Hashemi deals. Among those arrested was Avraham Bar-Am, a retired Israeli general possessing a routine Israeli defence ministry document authorizing him to seek sales of Israeli weapons abroad.[14]

By thwarting these enormous deals the US delivered a severe blow to Iran's military plans and did a tremendous service to Iraq. It is quite possible that if these contracts had been executed Iran would have turned 1986–7 into the 'Year of Victory', as promised by Khomeini on the eve of the Iranian New Year on 21 March 1986.

Baghdad was quick to pick on the Israeli involvement in arms supplies. Its official communiqué referred to 'the shady deals aimed . . . at continuing the threat to the security and stability of the area so as to achieve the Zionists' aggressive and expansionist objectives in the region'.[15] Iraq's deputy premier, Ramadan, argued that Washington's clandestine arms sales to Tehran were designed to serve two main purposes. One was to regain its lost influence in Iran. The other was to prolong the Gulf War in order to use the Iranian threat to scare the Arab Gulf states into accepting US intervention and letting it establish military bases in the region.[16]

These were also the conclusions that Moscow drew from the Irangate scandal. The Soviets regarded the prospect of the return of US influence in Tehran with foreboding, and were pleased to see the Iranian-American attempts at a rapprochement fail dismally. In order to underline their potential military value to Tehran they reportedly supplied it with a shipment of advanced weapons of a defensive nature worth $18 million.[17] This gesture came at the end of the year which had begun with the visit to Tehran of Georgi Kornienko, first deputy foreign minister of the USSR, when a decision was taken to revive the Permanent

Commission for Soviet-Iranian Economic Co-operation after its six-year hibernation. In August the Iranian oil minister said in Moscow that his country would resume its natural gas supplies to the Soviet Union – a trade it had terminated after the Islamic revolution. More importantly, in September, Rafsanjani stated that the Soviets had declared that they would not stand idly by if the US were to intervene militarily in the Gulf.[18]

At the same time Moscow continued to advise Tehran to end its war with Baghdad. It supported Security Council Resolution 582, passed unanimously on 24 February 1986 during the battles in the Fao peninsula. The resolution deplored 'the initial acts which gave rise to the conflict and the continuation of hostilities'; and repeated calls made in earlier resolutions for an end to the fighting and withdrawal to the international boundary. For Tehran the reference to 'the initial acts' was a move in the right direction, but was not enough.

A month later the Security Council adopted the report of a UN team of experts which concluded, after examining over 700 casualties of chemical weapons in Tehran and Ahvaz, that Iraq had used mustard and nerve gases against the Iranian forces on many occasions. 'It is our impression that the use of chemical weapons in 1986 appears to be more extensive than in 1984,' the report concluded. While condemning Iraq by name (for the first time) for resorting to chemical weapons, the Security Council unanimously registered its disapproval of 'the prolongation of the conflict which continues to take a heavy toll of human lives'. Iran stated that mere condemnation was not enough and that the Council should take steps to punish 'the aggressor'.[19]

On 8 October 1986 the Security Council unanimously approved Resolution 588 which called upon the warring parties to implement Resolution 582, and requested the UN secretary-general to intensify his mediation efforts. Iran rejected it because it contained no reference to Iraq as the invader.

Addressing the Islamic Conference Organization summit in Kuwait on 26 January 1987, the UN secretary-general, Pérez de Cuellar, called for the setting up of an international panel to determine which country was responsible for the war. This was seen as a concession to Tehran's demand that Iraq should be publicly blamed for starting the war. It improved Pérez de Cuellar's personal standing in Tehran. As for the call by the ICO summit, boycotted by Iran, for a ceasefire, Tehran described it as 'meaningless'.

Interestingly, the United States moved its whole fleet of six warships assigned to the Gulf (and using the port facilities of Bahrain) to the Upper Gulf to provide naval cover to the ICO summit in Kuwait. This occurred against the backdrop of Kuwait and Washington moving closer after the government-owned Kuwait Tanker Campany had agreed in December 1986 to have its ships placed under the American flag, and the oil minister had submitted a formal request to Washington in January 1987.

For the Reagan administration at home there was the acute problem of countering the negative impact produced by the burgeoning evidence that officials in the National Security Council, the White House and the CIA had been formulating and executing their own set of foreign policy decisions, and in the process breaking the law. In early 1987, as the Congressional committees and the President's Special Review Board, chaired by former Senator John Tower, began collecting embarrassing evidence in the Irangate affair, the Reagan administration clutched at the discovery of Silkworm shore-to-ship missiles mounted by Iran at the mouth of the Hormuz Straits. It launched a barrage of anti-Tehran propaganda to divert public attention away from the unsavoury aspects of the Irangate scandal and reassure its Gulf allies of its commitment to their welfare. George Shultz and Caspar Weinberger, secretaries of state and defence respectively, who had disapproved of arms dealings with Tehran, were prominent in implementing an anti-Iran and pro-Arab Gulf policy.

Iran's anti-ship missiles, however, were directed specifically at Iraq. In 1980 Baghdad had placed a $1500 million order with Italy for six corvettes, four frigates and one support ship. In January 1987 two corvettes and a support ship were delivered. These vessels sailed for Alexandria, Egypt, on their way to the Iraqi port of Umm Qasr. Iran was determined to attack these warships as they entered Hormuz. To get its message across to Baghdad it mounted Silkworm missiles. The tactic worked. Iraq's newly acquired naval ships returned to Italy.[20]

Given the disarray in which the Reagan administration found itself in early 1987, it was unable to respond positively to the Kuwaiti request for providing a naval escort for its reflagged oil tankers. But the situation changed when Washington learnt on 2 March that Moscow had agreed to lease three of its own tankers to Kuwait. This was widely publicized in the American media – but not the interconnected fact that a few weeks earlier Kuwait had allowed the Soviet Foreign Trade Bank to raise a $150 million loan through a Kuwaiti investment company.[21] The

Kuwait–Moscow deal provided the US administration with a rationale to meet the Kuwaiti request as well as secure Congressional and popular support for it by raising the Soviet bogey.

On 7 March Washington informed Kuwait that it would escort Kuwaiti oil tankers once these had been put under the American flag. Weinberger explained later that rejection of the Kuwaiti request would have either 'created a vacuum in the Gulf into which Soviet power would shortly have been projected' or turned the Gulf into 'a monument to Iranian intimidation and indiscriminate attacks on shipping'. The latter part of the argument was false. Only one per cent of the vessels using the Gulf had been struck, and among these twice as many had been hit by Iraq – 266 in the first seven years of the conflict – than the 138 fired on by Iran.[22] There was no public mention in Washington of the threat by Saudi Arabia and Kuwait that they would sell their very considerable holdings in US Treasury bonds if America refused to protect Kuwaiti oil carriers.

In any event, Washington was now firmly committed to an anti-Iranian stance. In late February, towards the end of Iran's Basra offensive, Reagan denounced Iran for its intransigence in the war and for 'its efforts to subvert its neighbours through terrorism and intimidation'.[23] Iraq, which had pressed for such a declaration by a top US official in the wake of the Irangate affair, welcomed Reagan's statement.

In Washington's view Kuwait and Saudi Arabia were the prime candidates for subversion by Iran. Not surprisingly, as the US began to forge ahead with escorting Kuwaiti tankers it implemented a joint Saudi-American plan to extend the Awacs surveillance to the Lower Gulf. In June Riyadh agreed to hunt mines off the Kuwaiti coast and designated certain Saudi hospitals for use by the American troops in the region.

With *Bridgeton*, a reflagged Kuwaiti tanker, hitting a mine in the Upper Gulf on 24 July 1987, the temperature rose sharply. In his guidelines to 155,000 Iranian pilgrims to Mecca for the annual hajj – a six-day ritual – Khomeini combined the political message of 'Islamic unity against the superpowers' with the religious theme of 'disavowal of the infidels', which the believer is enjoined to practise during the hajj. He urged the pilgrims to bear witness to 'the disavowal of the infidels headed by criminal America' in the form of demonstrations and marches.

On 31 July, the first day of the hajj, a demonstration by about 100,000

Iranians and non-Iranians in Mecca started peacefully. But when the vanguard of the procession was about 500 yards from the previously agreed termination point, it was blocked by Saudi police. Tempers flared and a riot broke out. During the hour it lasted the marchers were subjected to electrified batons, tear gas, rubber bullets and live ammunition. As a result of the police action and the stampede caused by it, 402 people, mostly pilgrims, died.[24] The Mecca killings severed the high-level communications channel between Iran and Saudi Arabia. A spontaneous demonstration in Tehran on 1 August ended in attacks on the Saudi and Kuwaiti embassies.

Khomeini saw the hand of America behind the actions of 'those devious people, the ringleaders of [Saudi] Arabia, the traitors to the holy shrines', thus holding the US ultimately responsible for the massacre. For the past three years demonstrations by the Iranian pilgrims in Mecca, staged with the co-operation of Saudi authorities, had passed off peacefully. The difference this time was the heightened presence of the American navy in the Gulf, which had encouraged the Saudi authorities, angered and exasperated by having to cede the streets to the Iranians, however briefly, to teach the disruptive Iranians a lesson. Small wonder that the Pentagon put its fleet in the Gulf on the highest state of alert.

A few weeks later Riyadh and Washington agreed to expand landing rights and refuelling support for US forces. Also Kuwait offered refuelling facilities for the American planes involved in the US naval escort for its reflagged tankers.[25] It had earlier rebuffed a secret offer by Tehran to end its attacks on Kuwaiti shipping in return for Kuwait's suspension of the reflagging of its tanker fleet to be escorted by the US navy.

Saudi hostility towards Iran reached a point where its interior minister, Prince Nayif ibn Abdul Aziz, said on 25 August: 'The [Saudi] Kingdom hopes to remove from Iran the authority which sends the people of Iran to their deaths.' Since Iraq was best equipped to bring about the overthrow of the Khomeini regime, Riyadh redoubled its efforts to aid Saddam Hussein. It gave Iraq an outright grant of $2 billion.[26]

It was obvious that the Iran–Iraq War had become internationalized, with the US siding with Iraq and its Gulf allies. Intent on keeping America out of the fray, and yet unable and unwilling to confront it and other powers, Iran had in the spring of 1987 adopted the least confrontationist tactic available: planting sea mines at certain strategic places along the shipping lanes of the Gulf.

THE SOVIET STANCE

The first superpower to have one of its ships damaged by an Iranian mine was in fact the Soviet Union. It happened on 6 May 1987 to the *Ivan Koroteyev*, and again on 16 May to the *Marshal Zhukov*, one of the three Soviet tankers leased to Kuwait. Since Moscow had no political interest in building up international opinion against the Khomeini regime, its response was limited to despatching three minesweepers to the Gulf to hunt mines. This action was coupled with a statement that the Soviet Union had no intention of increasing its naval presence beyond the two frigates and one intelligence-gathering ship already in the area.

As the US began its naval build-up in the Gulf relations between Tehran and Moscow became friendlier. In mid-June, after a visit to Tehran, Yuli Vorontsov, Soviet deputy foreign minister, said that the US military had no business in the Gulf. Following a meeting with Vorontsov in the Iranian capital, Rafsanjani stated that Moscow regretted its decision to lease three tankers to Kuwait, implying thereby that the Soviets would not lease any more ships to Kuwait if so requested. This was confirmed by an official spokesman in Moscow in early July. He added that the Soviet Union would withdraw its five warships and minesweepers from the Gulf if the US and its Western allies did the same with their 32 warships and minehunters.[27]

In late June Iran began preparing emergency plans for exporting its petroleum – in case the Kharg oil terminal was destroyed and/or the Hormuz Straits blocked – in which the already existing overland gas pipeline to the Soviet Union (which could easily be converted to carry oil) figured prominently. An Iranian deputy foreign minister broached the subject during his meetings in mid-July with Soviet officials in Moscow, and got a positive response. Premier Musavi declared that Iran and the Soviet Union had held 'positive talks' on a plan to ship Iranian oil across Soviet territory and via the Black Sea.[28]

This was a clear signal to the Reagan administration that were the US to destroy the Kharg terminal and bring about the blocking of the Hormuz Straits (as an Iranian retaliation), the Soviets would step in to enable Iran to continue selling oil abroad and thus financing its war machine. What was more, by making Kharg redundant the Soviets would rob Iraq of the only trump card it possessed: its ability to hit Kharg and the associated Iranian oil tankers with virtual impunity.

The Kremlin pursued this policy without altering its basic stance on the need to end the war. It offered to host an international conference on the Gulf War in Moscow where the belligerents could reach an agreement. The idea was accepted by Iraq in late April 1987, but rejected by Tehran. Undeterred, Moscow explained to Iran that it was the continuation of hostilities which was being exploited by Washington to implement its grand design to establish land bases in the Gulf states and draw GCC countries, singly or jointly, into a tight military alliance. So the best strategy, from Iran's viewpoint, was to cease fighting. The Soviets worked actively for the adoption of ceasefire Resolution 598 at the Security Council.

In its official response to Resolution 598, passed on 20 July 1987, Iran asked the UN secretary-general to prevail upon the US to stop its naval build-up in the Gulf, and upon France to stop its arms supplies to Iraq. This, Tehran argued, was in line with the resolution's Clause Five which calls upon 'all other states to exercise the utmost restraint and to refrain from any act which may lead to further escalation and widening of the conflict'.

Significantly, Iran made no reference to the Soviet Union, which was the principal source of weapons for Iraq. Indeed, following the Iraqi reverses in Fao in early 1986, the Soviets had begun a massive military resupply operation to shore up Baghdad's defence capacity, raising its military import bill for the year to $4900 million from the previous year's $4000 million.[29] Their commitment to Baghdad had increased in the wake of the Irangate revelations which raised (at least theoretically) the spectre of an Iran–US alignment against the USSR. In the winter of 1986–7 there was much speculation in Washington and some Arab capitals about ending the Gulf War through a change of government in Baghdad. This had alarmed Moscow, which believed that removing Saddam Hussein from high office would lead to a downfall of the Iraqi regime. There was therefore much ground for strained relations between Moscow and Tehran, which protested vehemently at the Soviet arming of Baghdad. It was only in the spring of 1987, when the US initiated a policy of high profile in the Gulf, that the situation changed.

As confrontation between Tehran and Washington began to build up, Moscow saw a good opportunity to improve its economic and diplomatic ties with Iran. In early August the two sides signed a series of economic agreements covering the building of a new oil pipeline, power plants, steel mills, oil exploration in the Caspian Sea and a second railway link. They reached a preliminary agreement on converting a gas pipeline to carry 700,000 b/d of oil, about half of Iran's average export figure. In mid-October Moscow started buying 100,000 b/d of Iranian oil and supplying in return refined petroleum products which were in short supply in Iran.

Part of the reason for Moscow's strengthening of ties with Tehran lay in its diplomatic rivalry with Peking. Both China and Iran deplored the dominance of the globe by the USA and the Soviet Union, and by insisting that the security of the Gulf was the sole responsibility of the region's countries, Iran was trying to undermine the dominance of the superpowers. During the Iranian foreign minister's visit to Peking in mid-June 1987 the Chinese president, Li Xiannian, said that China viewed the superpower involvement in the Gulf with 'great concern'. A few weeks earlier the two countries had concluded a deal whereby China agreed to build four arms and ammunition factories in Iran in exchange for Iranian oil. It also required Peking to supply Tehran with arms, including HQ-2 surface-to-air missiles, and spares for Soviet-made weapons. Over the past couple of years groups of Iranian revolutionary guards had been going regularly to China for arms training. The decision in early August 1987 by the two capitals to increase bilateral trade from the current $300 million to $500 million annually showed their intention to reinforce economic links.[30]

However, Peking was unwilling to strengthen ties with Tehran at the expense of its relations with Baghdad. Indeed, it had maintained its arms sales to Iraq, endowed with much larger sums of cash than Iran, at a far higher level than to Iran. According to the US Arms Control and Disarmament Commission, between 1981 and 1985 China sold $3100 millions-worth of weapons to Iraq against only $575 millions-worth to Iran.[31] But the situation changed during the next two years to the extent that, according to Richard Murphy, US assistant secretary of state, in 1987 China had supplied well over half of Iran's weapons imports including anti-aircraft missiles, artillery and ammunition. Part of the reason was that the Western sources of weapons for Iran had almost dried up due to America's pressure on its allies, with six West European nations in 1987 supplying no more than a total of $200 millions-worth of arms and ammunition to Tehran.[32]

At the UN Security Council the USSR and the US were unanimous in their support for Resolution 598 having mandatory force under Chapter 7 of the UN Charter, but differed on implementing it. While Washington interpreted the absence of unqualified Iranian acceptance of the resolution as rejection, and pressed for imposing an arms embargo against Iran, Moscow counselled patience as it urged Tehran to continue talking with the UN secretary-general about implementing the document. As the only superpower with direct lines to both belligerents, the Soviet Union was in a unique position to influence events.

Given the size of the US fleet in the Gulf and its clashes with the Iranians, and the proximity of these actions to the Soviet borders, Moscow was as committed to reducing the American military presence in the area as Tehran. The gravity of the situation was underlined in mid-October 1987 by the Soviet leader, Mikhail Gorbachev, when he warned the visiting American Secretary of State, George Shultz, that US policy in the Gulf could endanger relations between the superpowers.

At the Security Council the Soviet Union backed the UN secretary-general's 15 October 1987 plan to implement Resolution 598 which partially incorporated the Iranian idea of a de facto ceasefire to be in place while an impartial commission of inquiry determined the origins of the war and also backed Baghdad's demand that a troops withdrawal should occur 'without delay' after the ceasefire. The belligerents were given until 30 October to respond to the secretary-general's plan. Moscow pressured Baghdad to accept this document. Baghdad refused, noticing in the new document an incorporation of the principle of simultaneous implementation of certain clauses of Resolution 598, and insisting that Resolution 598 should be executed in the strict order in which it was drawn and that nothing should be subtracted from or added to it.

When the deadline passed without any progress the Reagan administration mounted a campaign for weapons sanctions against Iran. This was partly to boost the popular standing of the president in the light of American public opinion, which was overwhelmingly anti-Iranian. The Pentagon's retaliatory attack on Iran's two oil rigs on 19 October received an approval rating of 76 per cent. The Senate, while deeply concerned about growing American involvement in the Gulf, temporized. While expressing 'reservations' on the reflagging of Kuwaiti tankers it supported the US naval presence in the Gulf. It called on the president to report on the American involvement in the Gulf within two months – with a view to the Senate voting on his policy after a month-long deliberation.

Abroad, the US administration pressured the Soviets to endorse its plan for arms sanctions against Iran. In reply Moscow suggested a weapons embargo against both Iran and Iraq, to be enforced by a naval blockade created by a United Nations force formed by bringing the various national fleets in the Gulf under the UN flag. This would have meant placing under the international flag 48 warships and mine-hunters: six Soviet vessels, 17 American and 25 West European.[33] Washington rejected the Soviet plan summarily. Thus Moscow's diplomatic manoeuvring shielded Tehran from American designs and provided it with time to refine its responses to Resolution 598 and its implementation.

Iran had good reason to be thankful to Moscow, for it had felt increasingly isolated during the summer and autumn of 1987 when its relations with France and Britain had soured.

THE EUROPEANS

On 28 May Edward Chaplin, Britain's second-ranking diplomat, was beaten and arrested in Tehran. This event was linked to the police assault in Manchester, England, on an Iranian diplomat, Ahmad Qasimi, who in response to a charge of shoplifting had claimed diplo-matic immunity. Chaplin was released the next day. On 18 June the British government ordered 15 of its 16 Iranian diplomats to leave by the end of the month. It also withdrew its head of mission in Tehran, thus reducing each country's representation to a single diplomat.

Following an Iranian attack on a British-flagged ship in the Gulf on 23 September, Britain ordered the closure of Iran's military procurement office in London which had functioned unofficially from the offices of the National Iranian Oil Company. In contrast, Kuwait was encouraged to register its tankers in Britain and thus entitle them to British naval protection in the Gulf. Also, Britain's relations with Iraq remained strong. It was Baghdad's second largest non-military supplier, with British exports in 1986 amounting to $665 million.[34]

France remained firmly committed to Iraq's welfare. Given that in mid-1987 French loans to Baghdad amounted to $7 billion, Paris could not afford to see Saddam Hussein fall.[35] Any major default by Baghdad would have struck a severe blow to the French arms industry, which had been exporting a substantial part of its output to Iraq.

However, French animosity towards Tehran lessened in the wake of the defeat of the ruling Socialists in the March 1986 parliamentary elections. Following a visit by Iran's deputy prime minister, the new centre-right French government, led by Jacques Chirac, agreed to expel the Iranian Mujahedin-e Khalq leader, Masud Rajavi. In June he left for Baghdad. The government also agreed to repay the first third of the $1000 million lent to France by the Shah's regime in 1975. The loan was Iran's contribution towards establishing a European uranium enrichment consortium to supply fuel to two nuclear power plants in Iran to be built by French companies: these projects had been cancelled by the Khomeini government.

In late June 1987, however, relations deteriorated suddenly when the French police insisted on interviewing Wahid Gordji, an interpreter at the Iranian embassy, concerning bombings in Paris nine months earlier. When he refused to leave the Iranian mission, the police surrounded the building. The Iranian government retaliated by blockading the French embassy in Tehran. On 17 July the two countries severed diplomatic links. French ships in the Gulf were put on alert. A fortnight later the state oil firms in France stopped buying Iranian oil, and the government instructed private companies to follow suit. In 1986 France had lifted $372 millions-worth of Iranian crude.[36] Thus, in the final analysis, the centre-right government in Paris proved to be as unfriendly to Tehran as its predecessor.

But frosty relations did not preclude clandestine weapons sales emanating from the need for the French authorities to keep afloat state-owned arms factories. In early November 1987 it was disclosed by *Le Figaro*, a Paris-based newspaper, that according to the French army's comptroller-general, the ruling Socialist Party workers had received commissions of about 4 per cent on $120 millions-worth of illegal sales of 450,000 artillery shells to Iran between 1983 and 1986 by Luchaire-SNPE, a state-owned company.[37] The revelation was compared to the Irangate scandal in America.

Two months earlier the discovery of weapons and drugs on a Beirut-registered ship in the Italian port of Bari had led to the arrest of 32 people including certain executives of Valsella Meccanotecnica for selling anti-personnel mines and other arms to Iran. Between 1981 and 1984 Valsella had produced 250,000 anti-personnel mines for Iran in conjunction with Bofors-Nobelkrut of Sweden. In 1984 the Italian government had declared itself in favour of an arms embargo on both Iran and Iraq; but because it did not pass legislation to that effect there was no legal sanction behind its decision. Indeed, between then and mid-1987, when the government acted under pressure from Washington to close the legal loophole, an official committee had renewed or issued 39 authorizations for arms sales to Iran and Iraq. With the Middle East accounting for more than half of Italy's annual arms exports of $2.2–2.93 billion, the shipments to Iran and Iraq were substantial.[38] On the other hand, Iran was the third most important oil source for Italy, after Libya and Saudi Arabia.

The one European country which was not tarred with any illegal arms sales scandal, and which continued to maintain consistently friendly relations with Iran, was West Germany. In 1986, with bilateral trade running at $2025 million, West Germany was Iran's top trading partner. The corresponding figure for Iraq was $626 million. In early 1987 a foreign ministry official visiting the Iranian capital backed Iran's call for identifying the aggressor in the Gulf War.

As it happened, West Germany was the president of the UN Security Council in July when a ceasefire resolution was being finalized. Its officials publicly stated that the resolution was 'too harshly worded' against Iran. Indeed, it was on their initiative that the paragraph concerning a commission of inquiry to establish responsibility for the war was incorporated into the final draft of Resolution 598, and it was primarily due to this provision that Tehran did not reject the document. The secondary reason was that the resolution had been passed under the mandatory powers of the Security Council, meaning that the Council was expected to punish the non-complying party or parties.

A few days after the adoption of Resolution 598 on 20 July, Iran's foreign minister, Velayati, visited Bonn. In a radio interview his West German counterpart, Hans Dietrich Genscher, said that Iraq was responsible for starting the war, and criticized it for using chemical weapons against Iran. He added that the war was 'terrible' and that West Germany was doing everything possible to free 'the two civilized nations from it'.[39] Such statements established Genscher as a man of independent judgement: a quality regarded by Tehran as essential in a potential mediator. So far the main barrier to a diplomatic solution to the Gulf War had been that virtually all the individuals or institutions offering to mediate were seen by Iranian leaders as lacking integrity and impartiality. (They made a distinction between the Security Council as a body – dominated by the superpowers, and therefore unworthy of trust – and the UN secretary-general, Pérez de Cuellar, a man of integrity.)

Not surprisingly, Genscher's stance upset Baghdad and led to a three-month postponement of the meeting of the Iraqi and West German economic commissions scheduled for August. To ease the situation Genscher visited Baghdad in mid-November 1987 and met President Saddam Hussein. Deeply indebted to Bonn, Iraq could not afford to alienate it. Relations thawed when West Germany agreed to reschedule $2053 million credit to Iraq. The Iraqi president knew that Genscher wished to see the war end, something he too wanted. Iranian leaders were aware that he had economic leverage over Iraq and, as the most senior foreign minister in the European Economic Community, commanded respect in both Washington and Moscow.

THE ARAB WORLD

Just as Genscher had proved his value to Iran as a mediator in the international arena President Assad had done so in the Arab world, particularly with the Gulf monarchs.

To the surprise of most observers, Assad had a secret meeting with his arch-rival, Saddam Hussein, in north Jordan in late April 1987 on his way back to Damascus from Moscow. He agreed to this under pressure from the Kremlin and King Hussein of Jordan, who was host at the meeting. The news leaked out in early May. Soon after, Assad despatched his foreign minister to Tehran to reassure the Iranian president of Syria's continued backing for Iran in the Gulf War. The action was timely. On 30 April Tehran and Damascus had announced an annual oil agreement involving a grant of one million tonnes of Iranian oil to Syria and the sale of two million tonnes at the official OPEC price. The reduction from the past annual sale of five million tonnes was due to the rise in Syria's own output of light crude.

In an interview with the *Washington Post*, published on the seventh anniversary of the outbreak of the Gulf War, Assad stated that he had no intention of reducing Syrian support for Iran in its war with Iraq, and argued that Syria's refusal to break with Tehran had played 'a major role in preventing the expansion of the war'.[40] This was the argument the Syrian foreign minister had offered at the Arab League foreign ministers' conference held on 25 August in the wake of the passage of a ceasefire resolution by the Security Council and the rioting in Mecca. But most of the conferees were unimpressed. The assembly passed a resolution which condemned Iran's occupation of Iraqi territory, denounced mine-laying in the Gulf, and approved Kuwait's actions to protect its security as well as its economic interests. It called on Tehran to accept Security Council Resolution 598 by 20 September.

At the Arab League summit in Amman from 8 to 11 November, President Assad was a major player. He advocated amending UN Resolution 598 to appoint immediately a commission of inquiry to establish war guilt, and called for the withdrawal of all non-regional powers from the Gulf. His opponents urged that Arab League members should sever links with Tehran and support an arms embargo against it at the United Nations. The most ardent supporter of this line was of course Saddam Hussein. Finding his colleagues half-hearted in their resolve to punish Iran for the wrongs it had committed against Iraq, Kuwait and Saudi Arabia, he threatened to stage a walk-out. This led to a closed door session when King Hussein of Jordan and others mediated. In exchange for dropping the demand for cutting relations with Iran, and the promise by the Gulf states to pay up their arrears in financial subsidies to Syria as a front-line state facing Israel (agreed in 1978),[41] Assad agreed to endorse a compromise resolution. It condemned Iran's occupation of Iraqi territory and its procrastination in accepting Security Council Resolution 598, and urged Iran to accept the UN document and implement it in accordance with its operative paragraphs.

The summit decided that diplomatic relations between Arab League members and Egypt were 'a sovereign matter to be decided by each state'. Within days Saddam Hussein restored diplomatic ties with Cairo, which had backed him in the war with arms and manpower. The upgrading of links with Baghdad was bound to benefit Egypt's arms industry and its exports, then running at $500 million a year. It emerged later that Iraq had been funding a military project in Egypt to modify the Soviet-made Scud-B surface-to-surface missile to increase its range by reducing its payload and boosting its thrust with extra fuel tanks, and that in the first quarter of 1988 Egypt sold Iraq 120 modified Scud-B missiles.[42]

Iran's prime minister described the Arab League summit as 'a failure' which, he predicted, would turn 'devout Muslims' against their reactionary rulers. Privately, Iranian officials were disappointed to see Assad endorse the main resolution, but they could not afford to upset their only ally among major Arab leaders. The other Arab figure of substance, Muammar al Qadhafi of Libya, had abandoned their cause and restored diplomatic links with Baghdad in late October after a gap of nearly two and a half years.

Assad was under considerable pressure from the two sides he was trying to conciliate: Iran and the GCC states, particularly Kuwait and Saudi Arabia. Since Syria owed up to $1.5 billion in unpaid bills for Iranian oil, there was a limit to its ability to put pressure on Tehran. Assad had also to speak up for the security of Saudi Arabia and Kuwait so that they would meet their financial commitments to Syria and, more importantly, renew such pledges in 1988 when their previous agreement ended. It was therefore essential for Assad to show success in moderating Iran's military stance in the war.

In mid-January 1988 the Syrian press reported that the government had received a conciliatory letter from the Iranian foreign minister, and commented that it was necessary to remove tension and solve the current problems through talks between the countries of the Gulf region. The groundwork for a GCC–Iran meeting to be held in Damascus, Abu Dhabi or Muscat was being laid by Syria. The Assad government urged Tehran to declare that it harboured no hostile plans against such non-combatant Gulf countries as Kuwait and Saudi Arabia. And it called on the GCC states to try to persuade Baghdad to end its strikes against Iran's oil installations and tankers as well as industrial plants. Damascus formalized its proposals into a seven-point peace plan which included the formation of a mediation committee and a six-month moratorium on attacks on shipping as well as on Iranian and Iraqi urban centres and strategic targets.[43]

While these talks were in progress Damascus urged Tehran to refrain from mounting a large ground offensive. This was a major diplomatic damper on Iran's military planners, the other being the fear of triggering a United Nations arms embargo by actively defying Security Council Resolution 598. This was a serious possibility, as a leak by a Security Council source to *Al Ittihad* (The Unity), the official organ of the UAE, in mid-February 1988 indicated. A draft resolution on an arms embargo naming Iran as the non-complying party had been agreed by the five permanent Security Council members, with Britain acting as the co-ordinator, the newspaper reported. On 28 February Tehran informed the UN secretary-general that in view of Iran's acceptance of the 10-point plan to implement Resolution 598 there was no basis for a weapons embargo against it.[44]

As for the Syrian peace plan, the main hurdle was to secure Baghdad's agreement to suspend air raids on Iran's strategic oil and non-oil targets, thus abandoning its unchallenged mastery of the skies. When Iraq reopened the War of the Cities in late February it signalled the death of Syria's peace package.

The confidence of GCC states, particularly Kuwait, was enhanced by the visits to the region in mid-January by the US defence secretary, Frank Carlucci, and the Egyptian president, Hosni Mubarak. Carlucci announced that there were no plans to reduce the US naval presence in the Gulf. This news was well received by Kuwait which had by now allowed the US to anchor two supply barges within its territorial waters to act as floating bases, and re-registered 17 of its original 22 tankers under the American and British flags.[45] Mubarak promised to help Kuwait improve its air defences. Both Kuwait and Saudi Arabia had renewed for one more year their oil countersale agreement with Iraq.

In mid-April 1988 Iraq's recapture of its territory in the Fao peninsula, followed by America's mauling of the Iranian navy, boosted the confidence of Kuwait and Saudi Arabia. They noticed that the Reagan administration reacted sharply to the damage caused by a mine to one of its warships by knocking out two Iranian oil rigs, and that it responded to the subsequent moves by Tehran with unexpected speed and vigour, in the process sinking or damaging five Iranian vessels. Most importantly, the administration's actions received enthusiastic backing from both the US Congress and public opinion. They felt reassured of the American resolve to checkmate Iran militarily in the Gulf.

It was against this backdrop that Saudi Arabia severed its links with Iran on 27 April 1988. The immediate reason was Tehran's refusal to accept Riyadh's curtailment of Iranian pilgrims for the hajj from 155,000 to 45,000, based on the newly adopted formula of 1000 pilgrims per million Muslims in a country, which had earlier been approved by the Islamic Conference Organization. Riyadh accused Tehran of an 'enemy-like stand towards Saudi Arabia and intentional harm to its basic interests'. While disputing Riyadh's right to limit the numbers of pilgrims and impose conditions on the hajj, Iran stated that a major factor in the Saudi decision was its co-ordination with the US policies to help Iraq.[46]

Riyadh's unilateral action had come after its repeated failure to get either the GCC or the Arab League to approve severing ties with Tehran. In the GCC the Saudi plan was thwarted by Oman and the United Arab Emirates. Due to their opposition to a tough anti-Iran line at the GCC summit in late December 1987 the conference confined itself to expressing deep regret at 'the destructive war' between Iran and Iraq, and urging the UN Security Council to implement Resolution 598 as soon as possible.

Given that the territorial waters of Oman and Iran touch at the narrowest point of the Hormuz Straits, Oman had no choice but to co-operate with Iran in patrolling the waterway; and it was therefore in Oman's national interests to maintain cordial relations. Also, unlike elsewhere in the Arabian Peninsula, there was no sectarian tension between the Omani ruler Sultan Qaboos – belonging to the Ibadhi school within the Kharaji sect, which is quite apart from Sunnism and Shiaism – and the Shia regime of Iran. By late 1987 Omani-Iranian cordiality had grown to the extent that the two governments decided to set up ministerial commissions to boost mutual relations.

In the UAE's case, its major port, Dubai, had become an important source of supplies to Iran, which accounted for about a third of Dubai's booming re-export trade. Its re-exports to Iran in the first half of 1987 at $218 million exceeded those for the whole of the previous year.[47] Iran–UAE trade was running at over $1000 million a year, and the trend was upwards. Due to the growing risk to neutral shipping in the Gulf – with attacks rising from 41 in 1986 to 87 in the following year[48] – an increasing number of traders in Saudi Arabia resorted to using the Lower Gulf ports, such as Dubai, for their imports and then having them transported overland. The rising conflict in the Gulf thus brought an upsurge in the UAE's trading activity.

Both the UAE and Oman were against imposing arms sanctions on Iran. Their position found widespread support at the UN Security Council in the wake of US attacks on the Iranian navy in mid-April 1988. Moscow and Peking criticized Washington's armed intervention against Iran. Similar sentiments were expressed by other Security Council members including West Germany, Japan, Italy and Brazil. Given the veto power of the Soviet Union and China as permanent members of the Security Council (the others being America, Britain and France), there was now virtually no chance of an arms embargo against Tehran being imposed.

Behind the scenes Iran's foreign ministry, working in conjunction with the parliamentary speaker Rafsanjani, had been engaged in secret peace-seeking diplomacy through the UN secretary-general. Intriguingly, in a confidential memorandum he despatched to Tehran in late April,

Pérez de Cuellar, reportedly stated that his 'implementation plan had been accepted by the parties', implying thereby that the Iranian foreign ministry had opted for terminating the conflict.[49] But the final decision in Tehran could not be taken until the second round of parliamentary elections, due on 13 May, was over – setting the scene for the formation of a new government.

It was probably during this brief hiatus that Iran's foreign ministry activated the mediating role of Hans Dietrich Genscher in Bonn. According to one version, published in the London-based *The Middle East*, the 'understanding' that reportedly emerged between the warring parties – designed to lead to disengagement and de-escalation – was that if Baghdad's offensive succeeded in pushing the Iranians out of any Iraqi territory, then Tehran would not mount counterattacks to retake the area. In return Iraq promised not to occupy Iranian soil.

The first trial of this formula came with the successful Iraqi assault of 25 May in the Shalamche area. The Iranians did not mount immediate counteroffensives to regain the territory (partly because the Iraqis' use of mustard gas weapons made troop-gathering operations by Tehran extremely difficult). Iran's foray into the area on 13 June was a spoiling operation, and ended with voluntary withdrawal. It was meant to herald the appointment of Rafsanjani as acting commander-in-chief, and reassure Iranians that their armed forces had not lost their capacity to stage offensives. Significantly, Rafsanjani stated in June that 'total victory' was no longer the 'only path to victory'. On their part when, in the course of the Majnoon Islands offensive on 25 June, the Iraqis captured Iranian territory, they withdrew from it quickly. Thus the two sides established trust of a sort.

Iran left the Halabja territory on 12 July, and Iraq withdrew from the Iranian enclave in the Naft-e Shah region in the central sector. More significantly, the Iraqis withdrew from the 2260 square miles of Iranian land they had overrun in the Dehloran–Musian area in their campaign to regain the lost Iraqi land in the region.[50]

Public confirmation of the crucial role played by Genscher came with the news that, on the eve of Tehran's unqualified acceptance of Resolution 598, the Iranian ambassador in Bonn had flown to Greece to meet Genscher, then on holiday there.

The Iranian foreign ministry's fence-mending had by now led to restoration of diplomatic ties with France. A major break came in early May 1988 on the eve of the French presidential election, with Prime

Minister Chirac running against the Socialist incumbent, François Mitterrand. The Chirac government agreed to return the last third of the Iranian loan of $1 billion, end the embargo on Iranian oil and resume diplomatic links. Though Chirac lost the presidential contest to Mitterrand, and his government was replaced by a Socialist-led one following fresh parliamentary elections, Paris implemented its promises to Tehran. Full diplomatic relations were resumed on 15 June 1988.

But there was no slackening of ties between Paris and Baghdad. President Mitterrand reaffirmed that France's military relationship with Iraq would continue. France remained the second most important source of weapons for Iraq, after the Soviet Union.

THE SUPERPOWERS

Iran's first deputy premier, Ali Muhammad Besharati, claimed that during the first half of 1988 Moscow had supplied Baghdad with 5000 tanks and 300 long-range missiles. Going by the published figures it was obvious that economic ties between Baghdad and Moscow had grown stronger in 1987. During that year their bilateral trade reached a record $1200 million, up 46 per cent by volume over 1986.[51]

Not to lag behind, the US had offered a record $961 million to Iraq in agricultural commodity credits for the fiscal year beginning on 1 October 1987. Foodgrains, sold at bargain prices and purchased by Baghdad with American loans, were a vital prop to the war-torn economy of Iraq, particularly in the spring of 1986, when a steep fall in the oil price had created an economic crisis. Baghdad's response to America's latest financial gesture was to praise its benefactor for 'its positive efforts to keep the military balance in the Gulf'.[52] In reality this meant America trying to frustrate Tehran's strikes against the ships of Baghdad's allies in response to the Iraqi attacks on its oil tankers. Later, in April 1988, this 'balancing act' brought Baghdad and Washington together to co-ordinate their military operations against Tehran.[53]

Not surprisingly, the official Soviet newsagency, Tass, described the US naval attacks against Iran in mid-April as 'banditry' in the Gulf. Equally expectedly, a Moscow Radio commentator referred to the shooting down of Iran's civilian airliner by the US navy on 3 July as 'deliberate mass murder in cold blood'. The Supreme Soviet in Moscow passed a resolution of condolences for the victims.

In contrast, no sympathy was expressed in America for the Iranian dead by either government officials or legislators: they were too absorbed in their plans to celebrate Independence Day on 4 July to care. Washington laid part of the blame on Iran for letting a civilian airliner take off from an airfield also used by military aircraft, and fly over an area in the Gulf where combat had taken place recently. American public reaction was in tune with the official stance: 75 per cent of those questioned by the *Washington Post* blamed Iran more than they did the US; and, more significantly, 61 per cent rejected the suggestion that compensation should be paid to the families of those killed.

These findings, along with others over the past year, established conclusively that the Reagan administration had strong popular backing for its anti-Iran policy. Deeply embarrassed by the Irangate revelations, it had widened and deepened its actions against Tehran. For instance, in 1987 it made 40 formal approaches to 20 countries to prevent arms sales to Iran. Following an oil embargo against Iran due to its 'increasingly bellicose behaviour' in late October 1987, the US pressed its Western allies and Japan to follow suit.[54] It succeeded in pressuring China to cease selling Silkworm anti-ship missiles to Iran.

Increasingly, Tehran found itself unable to withstand the diplomatic, military and economic campaign that Washington had mounted against it in the wake of the Irangate affair. It discovered, too, that its tactic of using the Soviet card to unsettle the US could not yield much. For the plain fact was that the Kremlin was steadfast in its support for Saddam Hussein and his regime, and was as committed to warding off an Iranian victory as the White House. The most it could do for Iran militarily was to supply anti-aircraft missiles periodically. The most it could do diplomatically for Tehran at the UN was to hold off US pressure for an arms embargo. Its own diplomatic initiative centred on the idea of arranging a meeting between the Iranian and Iraqi foreign ministers in Moscow. In early March 1988, in the midst of the War of the Cities, it once again suggested such a conference. But Iran rejected the proposal because it did not regard the Soviet Union as impartial.

Thus, in the wake of the Iranian airbus disaster, Tehran had two stark choices: either to escalate confrontation with America in the Gulf and/or elsewhere, or to accept unconditionally Security Council Resolution 598. It chose the latter.

10 THE END

Between 5 July, when Iran lodged a complaint with the UN Security Council against the US for shooting down its civilian aircraft, and 20 July, when the Council expressed regret and welcomed the International Civil Aviation Organization's decision to investigate the incident, a lot happened in diplomatic and military spheres.

Signalling a definite shift in Iran's foreign policy stance, Rafsanjani told the Friday prayer audience in Tehran on 8 July: 'America is trying to push us into committing a crime as bad as its attack on the [Iranian] airbus. We are trying not to do that . . . world opinion would turn against us [if we did].'[1]

Iraq kept up its campaigns to recover its lost territories. Having regained the Kurdish town of Mawet on 30 June, Baghdad claimed on 9 July to have regained 23 mountain peaks in the area. The next day it announced the recapture of 14 mountain peaks in the Panjwin district. On 12 July its Fourth Army Corps and the Presidential Guard succeeded in expelling the Iranians from the occupied Iraqi territory in the Musian border region in the south-central sector. In the course of this offensive the Iraqis drove 30 miles into Iran and captured Dehloran. But, having cleared the area of enemy forces, they withdrew to the international border on 16 July. Just as in the diplomatic arena, so in the military field Iran began to play a different tune. Portraying its setback in the Musian area as a 'tactical retreat', Tehran stated that the war was not about territory, but was 'a continuous confrontation between the righteous and the wicked'.[2]

It was a confident Saddam Hussein who delivered the main speech on 17 July 1988 to celebrate the twentieth anniversary of the Baathist seizure of power. Stating that the recent Iraqi victories could pave the way for a peaceful settlement, he urged Iranian leaders to draw 'genuine lessons from their defeats and abortive adventures against Iraq and [other] countries in the Gulf'. He repeated his five-point peace plan: a ceasefire and return to the international frontier; exchange of prisoners of war; the signing of a peace treaty and a non-aggression pact; a mutual agreement not to meddle in each other's domestic affairs; and a commitment by both parties to strive for stability and security in the region.[3]

Unknown to the world, a conclave of top political, military and theological leaders of Iran at the presidential residence in Tehran on Thursday 14 July discussed the war, and came out in favour of accepting the Security Council Resolution 598 unconditionally. The next day, Friday, an extraordinary meeting of the cabinet, attended by Rafsanjani and the chairmen of important Majlis committees, endorsed this decision. That evening a delegation of top leaders had an audience with Khomeini to convey the general consensus to him. The following day, 16 July, the Assembly of Experts, a popularly elected permanent constitutional body composed solely of clerics, already gathered in Tehran for its annual session, formally adopted a resolution to recommend the ceasefire to Khomeini. As vice-chairman of the Assembly of Experts, speaker of the Majlis and acting commander-in-chief Rafsanjani conveyed the Assembly's resolution to Khomeini, who alone as supreme leader and commander-in-chief had the constitutional power to decide matters of war and peace.

Once Khomeini had given his consent, reportedly in writing, both Rafsanjani and President Khamanei acted to implement his decision. The Iranian president opened his letter to the UN secretary-general with the statement that 'The fire of the war . . . has gained unprecedented dimensions, bringing other countries into the war and even engulfing innocent civilians. The killing of 290 innocent human beings [in the Iranian airbus] . . . is a clear manifestation of this contention.' He concluded with the acceptance of Security Council Resolution 598. His letter was delivered to Pérez de Cuellar in New York at midnight on Sunday 17 July, and made public some hours later. Iran had finally accepted Resolution 598, two days less than a year after it was passed unanimously by the Security Council on 20 July 1987.

In Tehran the authorities faced the tricky task of explaining this volte-face to the general public. 'Even as the blows of the Muslim combatants on the battered body of Iraq became more deadly, so . . . the imperialists and reactionaries came to Iraq's aid with all their might, sparing no criminal act and seeking to uphold the Baghdad regime through massive military, financial, political and propaganda aids,' said Iran's Armed Forces General Command Headquarters. 'They were trying to present Iraq as a peace-loving regime. So it is natural for us to try to expose the aggressor to prevent the enemies of Iran from taking the initiative internationally.'[4] This well-worn argument failed to convince most Iranians. Indeed, by all accounts, the news of Tehran's acceptance of the ceasefire resolution was received in Iran with astonishment and disbelief. Nothing had prepared the people for the dramatic decision taken by their government.

Iranians awaited a word from Khomeini. This came on 20 July, the first anniversary (by the Islamic calendar) of the massacre of Iranian pilgrims in Mecca, in the form of a 90-minute-long statement read on Tehran Radio. 'Because of the events and factors which I will not discuss for the time being, and considering the advice of all ranking political and military experts of the country ... I agreed to accept the ceasefire resolution,' he said. 'I consider it to be in the interest of the revolution and the system at this juncture. God knows that, were it not that all our honour and prestige should be sacrificed for Islam, I would never have consented [to the ceasefire].' In other words, as he put it elsewhere: 'The new decision was made only on the basis of expediency. I renounced whatever I had said [in the past] only in the hope of God's blessing and satisfaction.' Khomeini was well aware of the confusion and discontent his decision was likely to create among those who had admired and followed his uncompromising stance throughout the war. 'Some people, led by emotions, might talk about the whys and wherefores of the decision, which is a beautiful thing in itself, but now is not the time to deal with it,' he stated. 'I repeat that accepting this [resolution] was more deadly for me than taking poison. I submit[ted] myself to God's will and drank this drink for His satisfaction.' He appealed to his 'revolutionary sons' to show understanding and patience. 'I know it is hard on you – but isn't it hard on your old father?' he asked. 'Be patient . . . Do not scold the officials for the decision they have taken, because making this proposal was hard on them too.' Finally, he cautioned the nation against complacency. 'Accepting the UN resolution does not mean that the question of war has been solved,' he said. 'We should be prepared for jihad to deflect possible aggression by the enemy. Our nation should not consider the matter closed.'[5]

Khomeini was understandably reluctant to outline the events and factors that culminated in his reversal of position. But a drift towards a negotiated peace could be traced to March 1988 when the Budget and Planning ministry, required by law to produce outlines of the budget for the following two years, concluded that given the continued low revenue from oil sales, the government would have to cut social expenditure by at least a quarter. This brought into focus the political dilemma Rafsanjani had mentioned many months earlier about imposing further austerity on the *mustazafin*, the needy, which could alienate them. While the foreign ministry was encouraged to keep its talks with the UN secretary-general going, no decisive action could be taken because of the impending parliamentary elections and the subsequent formation of a new government.

Following the elections and the convening of the Third Islamic Majlis in late May came Khomeini's appointment of Rafsanjani as acting commander-in-chief. This was a damage limitation operation meant to defuse any opposition to a ceasefire that might arise from militant revolutionary guards commanders. Rafsanjani used the firebrand rhetoric of continuing the holy war for twenty years as a ploy to achieve complete control over the Revolutionary Guards Corps. By so doing he minimized the chance of armed hardliners opposing any peace move to be made by the political leadership. Two other factors helped him in this objective. The defeats suffered recently by the revolutionary guards in Fao and Shalamche had lowered their stature in the public eye and put their commanders on the defensive. Secondly, a quick survey by Rafsanjani revealed mismanagement and malpractice in the domestic military supplies system which had been entrusted to the Revolutionary Guards Corps.

Mismanagement in providing defence equipment to the armed forces had emerged, on top of the mounting difficulties Iran experienced in its foreign military procurements. It found itself unable to replace the losses it had suffered in the course of the 1987 Basra offensive in such crucial items as engines and guns for its tanks and artillery shells. Washington's attempts to stem the flow of arms and spares to Iran had proved increasingly effective in depriving it of sophisticated weaponry and ammunition. Matters were made worse by the financial stringency imposed on Tehran, whose oil revenue in 1988 was running at about three-fifths of Iraq's.

According to Rafsanjani, the US and Iraq had made it crystal clear that they would resort to any means to prevent an Iranian victory, and that Iraq had been given 'the green light to commit any crime', including large-scale deployment of chemical weapons in its offensives.[6]

Iran found itself unable to counter this shift in the military balance by bolstering its military manpower and morale. If anything, the volunteers for active duty in early summer of 1988 were about one-third down on the previous year. Part of the reason was that those who did their three-month stint at the front found no major activity there. This discouraged their friends and colleagues in civilian life from volunteering to take up front-line duties. The political indecisiveness, in turn, stemmed from the formidable firepower that Iraq had built up since the spring of 1987, the reluctance of the international community to penalize Baghdad for its continued and extensive deployment of poison gases, the heavy diplomatic price that Iran would have to pay at the United Nations for launching a major offensive, and the Iranian leaders' unwillingness to impose further austerity on the people.

They were indeed being sensitive to the popular mood, which they constantly monitored through the network of clerics who were in daily touch with the public. Even the families of the war dead – who should have been vociferous in calling for revenge on the Baghdad regime – were reportedly expressing conciliatory sentiments in their encounters with the head of the Martyrs Foundation, Hojatalislam Mahdi Karoubi.

In short, Iran was no longer able to overcome its inferiority in arms, financial strength and diplomatic backing with manpower and high motivation. By late June its leaders had let the military initiative slip to Baghdad to the extent that they had the option of either accepting Resolution 598 voluntarily or having a peace settlement imposed on them: a prospect so humiliating as to threaten the very future of the Islamic Republic. Hence, Khomeini's repeated stress in his 20 July statement on 'expediency' to save 'the revolution and the system at this juncture'.

Aware of the military and political predicament Iranian officials faced, Baghdad offered a tough response to their conciliatory decision. In his 20 July letter to the UN secretary-general the Iraqi foreign minister, Tariq Aziz, coupled his insistence on direct talks between the two parties on implementing Resolution 598 according to the sequence of its 'operative paragraphs' with three more conditions. The UN should clear the Shatt al Arab and prepare it for navigation by Iraq and Iran. Secondly, Iraq's right to navigate in the Gulf and the Hormuz Straits should be guaranteed. Thirdly, in case of failure by Tehran and Baghdad to conclude a comprehensive peace settlement, the UN should play an active role in the restoration of direct official talks. The next day Iraq's ambassador at the United Nations declared that 'all issues' must first be settled through direct negotiations before a ceasefire could come into effect, with UN observers being allowed to enter Iraqi territory.

These demands were a façade and a delaying tactic behind which Saddam Hussein wanted to press home the military superiority Iraq had acquired over Iran. On 22 July the Iraqis mounted offensives in the northern, central and southern sectors. Tehran claimed to have blunted the Iraqi assaults in the Kurdish north. But, in the face of chemical attacks on Qasr-e Shirin and Sar-e Pol-e Zahab in the central sector, it evacuated these towns. In the southern sector, the Iranians apparently repelled the Iraqi offensive in the Shalamche area. But further south, the Iraqis penetrated 40 miles into Iran and came within 15 miles of the Khuzistani capital, Ahvaz. On 23 July Khomeini urged all able-bodied men to volunteer for the fronts, and warned: 'Hesitation today means slavery tomorrow.'[7] This time Iranians responded enthusiastically and in large numbers. A surge of patriotism swept the country. Parliament closed to allow its members to fight. Tens of thousands of civil servants, students and clerics rushed to the fronts.

Since the Iraqi threat to Ahvaz was the more ominous, Tehran concentrated first on this region. Fierce skirmishes, including hand-to-hand fighting, ensued. By 25 July Iran's forces had recovered the 230 square miles they had lost earlier.

But the fighting in the central sector lasted longer. Baghdad's capture of two Iranian border towns provided a salient to the anti-Khomeini National Liberation Army (of Iran) to implement a joint Iraqi-NLA plan. This visualized concurrent offensives in the central and southern sectors designed to create confusion in the already demoralized Iranian ranks, and a march by the NLA on the provincial capital of Bakhtaran. Its fall was expected to induce a popular uprising in Tehran against the Islamic regime, whose downfall was to be followed by the founding of the Popular Democratic Republic of Iran. (This plan was similar to the one that had been hatched eight years before in Baghdad to overthrow the Khomeini regime, the only difference being the substitution of the monarchist generals and politicians by Mujahedin-e Khalq leaders.) Part of the reason why the Iraqi president activated the NLA was that he wanted to impress on Tehran that he had a viable anti-Khomeini Iranian force to counterbalance the anti-Saddam Hussein force of Kurdish guerrillas that Iran had been backing for many years.

On 26 July the NLA, advancing under heavy Iraqi air cover, seized Karand and Islamabad-e Gharb on the Baghdad-Tehran highway. A town of 15,000 people, Islamabad-e Gharb, situated 60 miles from the frontier, was razed to the ground. The NLA's next target was Bakhtaran. The Iranians let the 7000-strong NLA forces, including a substantial number of ill-trained women, advance to this city of half a million 100 miles from the frontier. Then they cut off the NLA's supply lines and counter-attacked under cover of fighter planes and helicopter gunships. The Iraqi air force did not venture beyond Islamabad-e Gharb. The inexperienced NLA forces could not stand the pressure. On 29 July they announced a voluntary withdrawal from Islamabad-e Gharb and Karand. By the time the fighting was over and the NLA and Iraqi forces had been pushed back to the international border, Tehran claimed to have killed 4500 NLA and Iraqi troops.[8]

Leaving aside the objective of aiding the NLA to implement a highly unrealistic military-political plan, Saddam Hussein had various reasons to mount a series of major offensives. The official explanation that Iraq was making its military moves to enhance its number of Iranian war prisoners was patently unconvincing. It made no difference whether Iraq held 2000 prisoners or 20,000 when it came to exchanging them with Tehran's stock of 50,000–70,000 Iraqi captives.

In reality, the Iraqi president wanted to test Iran's commitment to a peaceful resolution of the war while putting pressure on its armed forces. There was a feeling in Baghdad that Khomeini's acceptance of Resolution 598 was a ploy to give his country a breathing-space of a few months to escape from the tight corner it had found itself in. Saddam Hussein wanted to impress on his own people and others that Iraq was militarily superior, and concurrently to enhance Baghdad's strategic position before the ceasefire. In a sense he wished to transform what was, by most accounts, a military draw into an outright victory.

But in the event Saddam Hussein's actions aided the Khomeini regime politically and, by implication, militarily. By again unleashing his forces on Iran all along the border, he reminded the Iranians – made complacent by six years of military superiority – that it was he who had started the war by invading the Islamic Republic eight years ago. With this, Khomeini's warning of 20 July that Iran must remain vigilant acquired fresh meaning. Iranians responded to the Iraqi invasion in July 1988 in the same way as they had done in September 1980. And this time they were better armed and trained.

So, by early August, the Iraqi leader's military ploy had basically failed. The peace process at the United Nations was stalled by his insistence that direct negotiations with Iran must precede a ceasefire. By engaging Iranian representatives in face-to-face talks with their Iraqi counterparts Saddam Hussein meant to extract from the Khomeini government an acceptance of the legitimacy of his own regime. He and his top aides reportedly believed that Khomeini accepted Resolution 598 only after his lieutenants had assured him that there was no realistic prospect of signing a peace treaty with an Iraqi government headed by Saddam Hussein, and that they would obtain a verdict from the United Nations blaming Iraq for starting the war.

Following Iran's acceptance of the resolution Khomeini rejected a proposal to appoint a special committee to conduct talks at the United Nations. Instead he gave carte blanche to the foreign ministry, headed by Ali Akbar Velayati, to carry out these negotiations. Velayati rejected the Iraqi demand for direct talks because it amounted to a unilateral addition to Resolution 598. His stand had the approval of almost all Security Council members. Iran's acceptance of a truce – welcomed unanimously by the countries of the region as well as the leading members of the American and Soviet blocs – had overnight transformed international opinion in its favour. To break the deadlock the Security Council's permanent members and, more importantly, Iraq's close allies, particularly Saudi Arabia, pressured Saddam Hussein to drop his demand for direct talks before a ceasefire. The Saudi and other Arab Gulf rulers seemingly advised the Iraqi president to join the peace process immediately or face the prospect of a humiliated Iran striking back at Iraq at an opportune moment in the future to avenge its honour.

Yielding to these pressures – and also, reportedly, having secured assurances from the Security Council's permanent members that in the case of Tehran's reviving hostilities they would back Baghdad – Saddam Hussein withdrew his demand on 6 August. He stated that his country was ready for a truce on condition that 'Iran announces clearly, unequivocally and formally its acceptance to enter into direct negotiations with Iraq immediately after a ceasefire takes place.'[9] Tehran agreed.

On 8 August the Security Council unanimously approved the implementation details of Resolution 598. The UN secretary-general announced 0300 hours on Saturday 20 August 1988 as the time for a truce. He planned to have an observer force of 350 drawn from 25 countries, and named the United Nations Iran–Iraq Military Observer Group (UNIIMOG) to be in place by the ceasefire date.

Saddam Hussein declared a three-day holiday on Tuesday 9 August to celebrate 'this great victory'. People in the capital and elsewhere took to the streets in a great burst of joy and relief. Baghdad, which until a year ago was a glum city, was now transformed into a relaxed, self-assured metropolis, with its shops full of consumer goods and its residents filled with euphoric pride. The popularity of Saddam Hussein soared. He was now seen by most Iraqis as the national saviour who had preserved the honour and territorial integrity of the homeland.

The mood in Tehran and elsewhere in Iran was sceptical relief. Rafsanjani ordered his troops on 9 August not to start any military action against Iraq. The next day more than a million people marched in Tehran in support of Khomeini's acceptance of the ceasefire. The rationale popularized by the leadership was that at this juncture of their Islamic struggle peace was to their benefit, and that accepting Resolution 598 did not mean they had given up their holy mission.

As for the outcome of the war there was little doubt in Tehran. 'Today the Iranian nation understands that the enemy has been defeated because it has not been able to achieve its ominous aims of weakening Iran or turning its people against the leadership after eight years,' stated President Khamanei in his Friday prayer address on 12 August. Allied to this assessment was the idea that Iran had won a moral victory by refusing to abandon its principles even though it had meant having to fight with 'one hand tied behind its back'. 'The Iraqis violated every accepted principle of warfare including using chemical weapons,' said Rafsanjani. 'But Iran staved off the aggression without compromising Islamic principles.' These included refraining from the use of poison gases even though Iran had the facilities to manufacture and deploy them.[10]

In general Khomeini's decision was well received. Many among the upper and middle classes had wished to see the war ended earlier. And the working and lower middle classes were too loyal to Khomeini to question his judgement. The prospect of some revolutionary guards officers defying the government receded abruptly when the Revolutionary Guards Corps commander, Muhsin Rezai, in the course of his meeting with Khomeini on 22 July handed him a letter accepting the ceasefire decision and reaffirming his loyalty to him.[11]

The overnight improvement in the exchange rate of the Iranian Rial in the free market of Tehran from IR 1450 to IR 700 to the US dollar (the official rate was IR 70) was a sign of a dramatic rise in the confidence of rich Iranians in the future of the Islamic Republic. However, the actuality was far from rosy. In the first half of 1988 Tehran's oil income, at $3.7 billion, was nearly a quarter down on the previous year, and it was producing less than its OPEC quota of 2.4 million b/d. More seriously, Iraqi bombings had reduced the country's petroleum production capacity by half, from 5.7 million to 3 million b/d.[12]

In contrast, Iraq's oil revenue in the first half of 1988 was up by a quarter on the previous year. And, despite the war, Baghdad had increased its petroleum production capacity from 3.5 million b/d before the hostilities to four million b/d. Its exports were running at 2.3 million b/d, only marginally lower than the pre-war average. On the other hand, Iraq had emerged as a cripplingly indebted nation. Its debts to the West and Japan alone amounted to $25 billion. Then there were the Soviet credits, believed to be in the range of $6–9 billion. This meant that even if the loans from the Gulf states – estimated to be between $50 and $55 billion[13] – were to be converted into grants, Iraq would still have to repay $31–34 billion, equal to its 1986 Gross Domestic Product. Iran began 1988 with foreign reserves of $5.8 billion. In addition, its foreign assets and loans to such countries as Syria and North Korea amounted to another $5 billion. It owed only $500 million abroad.[14]

Iraq therefore had more pressing material reasons to celebrate the start of a ceasefire in the early hours of 20 August with a 101-gun salute. Its citizens danced in the streets when the war that their president had started finally ended after 95 months.

AFTER THE CEASEFIRE

It had been a bloody and expensive conflict. Conservative Western estimates put the total number of war dead at 367,000 – Iran accounting for 262,000 and Iraq 105,000. With more than 700,000 injured, the total casualties were put at over one million. The official figures, given a month later by Iran's minister of Islamic guidance in a radio interview, put the Iranian dead at 123,220 combatants, and another 60,711 missing in action. In addition 11,000 civilians had lost their lives. Tehran's total of nearly 200,000 troops and civilians killed was in stark contrast to Baghdad's estimate of 800,000 Iranians dead.[15]

According to the Stockholm International Peace Research Institute, excluding weapons imports, at current prices Iran spent between $74 and $91 billion to conduct the war, and Iraq between $94 and $112 billion. Their aggregate military imports bill amounted to $53.2 billion, divided into $41.94 billion for Baghdad, and $11.26 billion for Tehran.[16] If the direct damage caused by the warfare and the indirect loss of income from oil and agricultural produce were added to the cost of conducting the war then the totals became astronomical. An estimate by Kamran Mofid, a British-based economist, put the aggregate direct and indirect cost of war to Tehran at $627 billion, and to Baghdad at $561 billion.[17] There was thus vast scope for war reconstruction. But it could not be seriously undertaken until and unless there was a comprehensive peace between the two neighbours. That seemed a long way off, judging by the wrangling in which they became embroiled at their talks in Geneva on 25 August 1988.

These negotiations started with a 'face-to-face' meeting. In reality, at Iran's insistence, the Iranian and Iraqi delegations sat along two sides of a triangle with the secretary-general and his aides taking up the third. That is, the negotiators did not literally face one another, and they communicated indirectly through the UN secretary-general. After this opening session the two delegations conducted talks from separate rooms. None the less, it was remarkable that two adversaries locked into bitter combat for so long had at last chosen to cease fighting. This was a matter of great relief and even pride not only to the UN secretary-general but also to the Security Council's permanent members.

The Soviet Union had a particular reason to be pleased. Its advice to fellow permanent Council members to show patience towards Iran had paid off. The Kremlin had all along been careful not to pressure Tehran too much, or impose peace on it and thus have to deal with a sulking neighbour in the future. In mid-August the Soviet foreign minister told Iran's deputy foreign minister at the United Nations that with the end of the war relations between their countries would expand.

Washington claimed Tehran's acceptance of the ceasefire resolution as a success which had stemmed from its determination to stay the course and follow 'a firm and consistent policy' in the Gulf War. It offered high-level official talks to Tehran. Rafsanjani spurned the offer, stating that a 'tangible gesture' of American goodwill would be the unfreezing of the $500 millions-worth of arms and spares that Tehran had already paid for before the revolution.[18] Still, with the cessation of Iranian attacks on shipping in the Gulf, tension between Tehran and Washington eased to the point where the US defence secretary said on 9 August that the Pentagon would reduce its fleet of 27 warships in the Gulf to the pre-war level of four or five.

Just then France let it be known that it was seriously considering lifting its ban on Iranian oil purchases. Britain's relations with Iran had thawed following its official protest to Iraq on the latter's chemical attacks on Halabja in March 1988. Steady progress was then made towards normalizing diplomatic relations, a process which received a boost by Iran's acceptance of Resolution 598. After all, Britain had been co-ordinating the stands of the permanent Security Council members since early 1988. Iran's improvement of relations with the two West European Security Council permanent members reassured it that it could expect even-handed treatment from the Council. This was important, as the Council provided general guidelines to the secretary-general as he presided over peace negotiations between Tehran and Baghdad.

The talks in Geneva became bogged down as Iraq's Tariq Aziz insisted on tackling the issues of the clearance of the Shatt al Arab and a guarantee of free navigation for Iraqi vessels in the Gulf and the Hormuz Straits. He wanted the UN to supervise the clearance of the Shatt al Arab and ensure safe navigation. And he insisted that Iran must cease its inspection of Iraqi ships in the Gulf for arms. He made these demands in the context of Clause One of Resolution 598, which called on the parties to 'discontinue all military actions on land, at sea and in the air'.

Iran's foreign minister, Velayati, argued that there was no reference to the Shatt al Arab in the Security Council resolution. So long as there was no formal peace treaty between the two countries they were technically at war. As such Iran had the right, by international law, to search ships it suspected of carrying weapons to its enemy. Tehran also blocked any United Nations moves to survey the Shatt al Arab to assess the work needed to clear it of sunken vessels and unexploded bombs, arguing that according to the 1975 Iran–Iraq Treaty cleaning up the waterway was a joint responsibility of the signatories.

Aziz stated that Iraq considered the Iran–Iraq Treaty null and void, and had said so on 17 September 1980. His deputy, Nizar Hamdoon, explained in a BBC interview that the 1975 Treaty contained four principles: non-interference in the internal affairs of the signatories; cessation of Iranian aid to the Iraqi Kurds; return by Iran of the border territories it had retained in contravention of its 1913 accord with Ottoman Turkey; and delineation of the fluvial border along the mid-channel of the Shatt al Arab. The violation of any one of these principles – such as gross interference by Iran in Iraq's internal affairs after the 1979 revolution – invalidated the whole treaty. Velayati retorted that the document was basically a border treaty and that, according to international law, such documents were permanent and non-changing. In any event, he added, the 1975 Treaty could not be abrogated unilaterally.[19]

To break the impasse the secretary-general suggested that Iran should suspend its practice of searching shipping in the Gulf while Iraq dropped its demand for immediate clearance of the Shatt al Arab. Once they agreed on this then their governments should withdraw to the international border within 15 days. Iran consented because, if nothing else, it wanted to retrieve the 400 square miles of its territory that Iraq occupied on the ceasefire day. Iraq was not too enthusiastic about the compromise.

Obviously, by pressing demands which were outside the provisions of Resolution 598, Saddam Hussein was impeding the peace process. He had his reasons. He wanted to salvage some concrete benefit from the war he had initiated. By tearing up the 1975 Treaty on television he had convinced Iraqis that he had restored Iraq's sovereignty over the whole of the Shatt al Arab, and he wanted to postpone the day when he had to concede, directly or indirectly, that this was not so. Secondly, by employing delaying tactics, he was trying to postpone the implementation of Clause Six pertaining to an impartial commission to decide responsibility for starting the war.[20] Were the commission to name Iraq as the guilty party, which seemed very likely, there was every chance that Iran would demand war reparations, putting Saddam Hussein in an indefensible position.

In late October the Security Council unanimously expressed concern at the slow pace of the peace talks. While the ceasefire was holding, it did not seem very stable: at one point, for instance, the Iranian and Iraqi forces were only 10 yards apart.

Yet there was no serious risk of the hostilities erupting again. Both nations were truly exhausted. Steeply indebted to the Gulf states, several Western nations and Japan, and the Soviet Union, Iraq simply did not have the freedom of action it had enjoyed eight years before. As for Khomeini, he had not initiated hostilities in the past, nor was he likely to do so now, given his advanced age and poor health, and the war-weariness of his country.

While a peace treaty between Tehran and Baghdad was still a long way off, there was little prospect of war breaking out again.

11   CONCLUSIONS

Wars are expected to produce clear winners and losers. The Gulf conflict failed to do so, chiefly because the combatants continually raised and lowered their military and political objectives in the light of their performance on the battlefield.

Baghdad's initial, declared military aim was to seize the remaining half of the Shatt al Arab along its fluvial frontier with Iran and some 190 square miles of disputed border territory. But within two months of the hostilities Iraq's deputy premier vowed to continue capturing cities of Khuzistan and appropriating Iranian oil, with the Iraqi press routinely portraying Khuzistan/Arabistan as a province of Iraq. Politically, the aim was to create a division between the Iranian people and their clerical rulers, thus preparing the ground for the monarchical politicians and generals to seize power. From disavowing any ambition to cause the dismemberment of Iran by encouraging the secessionist activities of its ethnic minorities, Baghdad moved in spring 1981 to the position of unconcern if Iran were to disintegrate. In contrast, four years later, reflecting the Iraqi weakness on land fronts, Saddam Hussein defined 'victory' for Iraq merely as 'defending ourselves until the other side gives up'.[1]

Tehran underwent similar changes. Starting with the basic defensive objective of expelling the invading Iraqis, it went on to demand the removal of President Saddam Hussein's regime. The exact nature of this requirement varied from wholesale replacement of the Baathist state with an Islamic one to the mere resignation of Saddam Hussein from the presidency. Following Tehran's victory in Fao early in 1986, the Iranian 'maximalists' visualized liberating the Shia holy shrine cities of Najaf and Karbala, and installing an Islamic regime in Baghdad, as a stepping-stone to freeing Jerusalem from Zionist control. In contrast the 'minimalists' limited their objectives to toppling Saddam Hussein, getting an inquiry commission appointed to determine war guilt and receiving substantial war reparations from the aggressor and its Arab allies.

In the end Tehran failed to achieve its minimalist aims which were political in nature. Equally, Baghdad failed to drive a wedge between ruler and ruled in the Islamic Republic, or cause dismemberment of Iran.

Territorially, at the time of the 1988 ceasefire, Iraq possessed about twice the border land it had claimed from Iran in 1980. Militarily, Baghdad sounded as bullish at the end as it did at the start of the war. But the Iranian regime and society were stronger and far more cohesive, militarily and politically, than they were eight years earlier. So the overall conclusion can only be that the Gulf War was a draw. This assessment sits well with the fact that the conflict started and ended with the same regimes in power: a secular Baathist one in Baghdad and an Islamic revolutionary one in Tehran.

The Iranian revolution was a result of specific national conditions, as was the Bolshevik revolution in Russia. Just as the Bolsheviks tried to present their overthrow of the autocratic Tsar as something of global importance and applicability, so too did the Iranian revolutionaries. Arguing that their revolution had stemmed from the universalist ideology of Islam, they saw the change in Iran as the first step towards the recreation of the Domain of Islam of the seventh century. If nothing else, such an appraisal provided them with a rationale for spreading their revolutionary doctrine in the neighbouring Muslim states. They considered Iraqis to be most receptive to it. Their attempts to stoke revolutionary fervour among Iraqi Muslims, particularly the Shia majority, aroused the anger and alarm of the Baathist government. This, and the power vacuum created by the disappearance of the strong, centralized Iranian state under the Shah, led to the outbreak of the Iran–Iraq War.

Baghdad's invasion came at a time when revolutionary ardour was waning in Iran. It provided the clerical rulers with a platform from which to rejuvenate the drive for national unity and Islamic revolution. Defending the Islamic base of Iran and expelling the aggressor became highly effective rallying cries. The war inhibited fractious debate and dispute. It engendered an environment conducive to a dramatic rise in the strength and importance of the ideologically oriented Revolutionary Guards Corps. Moreover, it created conditions which were in tune with the essence of Shiaism, imbued with the concepts of moral rectitude, struggle and renewal through suffering. As a society which had been in virtual turmoil since the autumn of 1977, Iran took warfare in its stride. Years of revolutionary upheaval had transformed Iranians into a highly politicized community, given to making sacrifices and adopting an ethic of social co-operation, so essential to waging a long war.

In Iraq, by contrast, society, economy and regime were all stable and thriving. While Saddam Hussein set much store by his military move, he also visualized it as nothing more than a limited war to be finished within weeks on his terms.

Iraq's president considered the new Iranian regime to be weak and disunited, both militarily and politically. It seemed incapable of mustering enough will and resources to suppress the divisive forces that were trying actively to undermine it. At the same time the Tehran regime had the potential for inspiring Iraqi Shias with a steady diet of revolutionary Islamic doctrine, to the point of causing a major insurrection in Iraq. Here then was a rare chance for Iraq to strike at Iran with a dual purpose: to end its dangerously subversive role; and to retrieve a major Iraqi concession on the strategic Shatt al Arab and so formalize a new balance of forces in the region.

The misreading of the nature of the Iranian polity and the war did not lead to a major reassessment by Saddam Hussein and his close aides of the nature of the Iraqi state and its relationship with the supreme leader. In fact the desperate need to conduct a defensive war to safeguard the territorial integrity of Iraq overshadowed all else. Such a struggle intensified the phenomenon of the personality cult and the identification of Saddam Hussein with the Iraqi state, further allowing him to tighten his control over major levers of power.

If nothing else, the Gulf War proved once again the old adage that safeguarding one's own land is easier than acquiring enemy territory. Most of the battlefield successes came in the wake of surprise attacks against a poorly prepared, or retreating, foe. And most of the assaults against well-prepared opponents ended in failure.

Once Iran had firmly seized the military initiative in mid-1982 it started deploying the revolutionary guards' human wave tactic by itself – a change from the previous practice of incorporating it into combined-services operations. Time and again the Iranian endeavour failed to breach Iraqi defence lines. It was not until early 1984 that Tehran managed to upgrade the training and organization of the Revolutionary Guards Corps and improve its co-operation with the professional military, thus enhancing its chances of success.

By then the war had turned into a prolonged conflict between national wills, an armed contest – military, politico-ideological and economic – between rival social systems. It came to dominate society and politics in both countries; and its progress became bound up with the future of the two regimes.

While the military gains achieved by Tehran by early 1985 were unimpressive, the socio-political value of the armed conflict to the regime was quite substantial. 'We have been able to use the war to awaken the people and to fight the problems that threaten the revolution,' said Rafsanjani on the eve of the sixth anniversary of the Islamic revolution.[2]

A defensive struggle against an Iran on the offensive helped Saddam Hussein to forge national unity to a degree he had not thought possible before. Most Iraqi Shias remained loyal to the state. Their failure to respond to repeated calls by Khomeini to revolt against the Baathist regime stemmed from three major causes. Divided by clan and tribe, they had failed to evolve a corporate sectarian identity; with an enemy at the frontier, nationalist feeling took precedence over sectarianism; and most Shias shared with their fellow Sunni citizens fear of a violent disruption of their lives in the wake of an Iranian victory. Whatever the reasons, the Shias' behaviour reassured the Iraqi leader who, reversing the earlier neglect of the religious question by the Baath Party, enthusiastically and publicly adopted Islamic symbols and rituals, and inducted the clergy, Sunni and Shia, into the war propaganda machine.

However, Kurdish nationalists remained unreconciled. But the fact of their being confined to a certain area proved to be both their strength and weakness. While their geographical specificity allowed the regime to isolate them, as inhabitants of mountainous terrain, they proved difficult to subdue and equally difficult to integrate into the Iraqi mainstream.

The long conflict militarized Iraqi society. Under the pressures of warfare Saddam Hussein, a politician initially determined to keep the armed forces under strict civilian control, let military service and soldierly values dominate society and the ruling party. The Iraqi media widely publicized Saddam Hussein's conferences with senior defence officers, which far outnumbered his meetings with high political or administrative officials. It was significant that most of the deputies elected to the Second National Assembly in October 1984 had been active in the war effort. With the size of the regular military approaching one million, and the Popular Army well past the half-million mark, Saddam Hussein realized that the armed forces were a far more effective tool to integrate society and state than the Baath Party. Not surprisingly, he instructed party cadres to imbibe military values and uphold discipline, patriotism and martyrdom.

In the course of the conflict the Iraqi leader upgraded the professional expertise of the military while downgrading the importance of Baathist ideology among the officers. This lessened the interest of the armed forces hierarchy in domestic politics and increased their commitment to defending the country.

The war brought about a marked change in the Baath Party itself. In the name of increasing production, the importance of Baathist socialism was played down and the private sector encouraged to grow at the expense of the public sector. The concept of Arabism was made subservient to the idea of Iraqi nationalism, which was used as the paramount force to motivate citizens to join the war effort.

In contrast, there was little change in the Islamic ideology of Iran. This was so partly because no firm blueprint of the application of Islamic principles to administering a modern state and society had emerged by the time the hostilities broke out. Then the Iranian government used the war as a reason to postpone decisions on major socio-economic issues of land reform, the ownership of foreign trade, personal taxation, labour relations and the role of the private sector. Meanwhile, Khomeini and his lieutenants continued to reiterate the commitment of the Islamic regime to the relief of the needy, 'the bare-foot' – for they were in the forefront to provide recruits for the Revolutionary Guards Corps and its auxiliary, the Basij militia, composed entirely of volunteers. But improvement in the living standards of ordinary Iranians could not occur so long as the war had unquestioned priority over development projects.

The economic predicament of Tehran was all the more acute because it was decided to fund the war machine strictly out of current resources, which dwindled dramatically in the wake of a crash in oil prices in the winter of 1985–6. Jealous of its newly-won independence, the revolutionary government refused to borrow money abroad.

This was in stark contrast to the policies of Baghdad. Given the enormous foreign loans and grants raised by Iraq, and the importation of 1.5 to 2 million foreign workers, it could be argued that Iraq fought the war on borrowed money and manpower.

Iran's leaders portrayed war and the restrictions imposed by it as providing an incentive to accelerate the process of self-dependence and self-realization. The innovation and improvization displayed by Iranians on and off the battlefield, particularly in making the best of the civilian and military technology available to them, impressed observers. The conflict gave rise to many new local industries in defence and non-defence fields.

Military industry in Iran registered an impressive growth both in the output of old products and the starting of production of new and sophisticated hardware. In the later stages of the war Tehran claimed to be saving $1–2 billion a year in foreign currencies due to the rise in its defence equipment. Iraq too underwent a similar process.

This was a good example of how the Iranian leadership viewed the war in relation to the revolution – as a means of consolidating it and achieving such revolutionary objectives as self-reliance. All along, its primary concern was to deepen and broaden the Islamic revolution. So long as the conflict served that purpose, repeated offers of a ceasefire by Iraq or the United Nations or the Islamic Conference Organization were spurned. Only when Khomeini realized, through his close contact with the widespread religious network functioning under him, that ordinary Iranians were becoming war-weary, did he accept a truce. He realized that imposing further economic austerity on the people, combined with a measure of coercion to prosecute the war effectively, would erode the mass base that his regime enjoyed. That is, a stage had been reached when continuing hostilities would damage the revolution rather than buttress it.[3] In the final analysis, therefore, only a change of situation within Iran itself had an impact on Khomeini: he remained impervious to the pressures exerted on his regime by such diverse forces as Saudi Arabia, Libya, the Soviet Union, the United States, the Islamic Conference Organization and the UN Security Council. Significantly, in his 20 July 1988 statement he specifically said: 'Iranian officials independently made the decision to accept the [UN] resolution; and no other person or country had a role in this.'[4]

With Iraq, the direct opposite was the case. While Saddam Hussein was the main player in mounting the invasion of Iran, he seemingly acted in collusion with his close neighbours in the Gulf. As the war dragged on, he became more dependent on his Arab and non-Arab allies. Only by borrowing enormous sums could he continue the conflict and concurrently provide consumer and other goods to his countrymen. By the time the war ended, with Iraq heavily indebted, he had compromised his independence. This became obvious when he could not withstand the pressure from Saudi Arabia as well as the US and the USSR to drop his precondition for direct talks with Iran and accept Resolution 598.

On the other hand only by internationalizing the conflict – specifi-cally, getting the American navy involved in the Gulf shipping – did the Iraqi president finally achieve an end to the armed conflict, something he had been pursuing for the better part of eight years.

In this he was helped actively by Kuwait, with the latter approaching both superpowers to provide naval escort to its oil tankers. Kuwait was merely an extreme example of the wariness and alienation that the Gulf monarchies felt towards the Islamic Republic. During the early days of the Khomeini regime the pro-Western rulers of these states were the main targets of revolutionary, republican propaganda emanating from Tehran.

Once Iran had become embroiled in hostilities with Iraq the diplo-matic stance of these states became an important ingredient in the progress of the war. Their pan-Arabism, combined with a fear of an anti-Western revolutionary Islam in power in Iran, led them to side with Iraq – with Kuwait and Saudi Arabia providing not only funds but also the crucial use of their ports and highways for the transport of civilian and military imports into Iraq. The best Tehran could hope for was genuine neutrality by these countries. To achieve this it softened its definition of exporting the revolution, doing no more than winning converts to its cause through example. By 1984–5 there was a marked change in its public and private stance towards the Gulf capitals. It was thus that it succeeded in persuading Oman and the United Arab Emirates to adopt a neutral stand. But from Iraq's viewpoint what really mattered was the position taken by Saudi Arabia and Kuwait. During the eight years of the conflict, despite a barrage of blandishments and threats emanating from Tehran, they did not loosen their alliance with Iraq.

Saudi Arabia played a crucial role in bringing about a rapprochement between Baghdad and Washington, strengthening Iraq's hand very con-siderably. But for the timely intervention by the US in 1983 and again in 1986 to help it financially, Iraq would have been in dire economic straits. Then there was the long-term arrangement to provide US-Saudi intelligence to Baghdad, which proved invaluable to the Iraqi high command in forging advance plans to blunt the many offensives Tehran mounted.

America had no particular affinity, political or economic, for Iraq. It was chiefly its hostility towards the Islamic revolution in Iran that drove it to court Baghdad. The outbreak of the Gulf War in September 1980 was clearly linked with the events in Iran (the failed monarchist coup in July 1980) and America (the presidential election in early November 1980). Like many other countries the US was surprised by the spirited resistance that Iran offered to the invading Iraqis and the success it had in expelling them.

So long as stalemate prevailed on the front lines Washington was content to maintain a semblance of neutrality in the conflict. But as the scales began to tilt increasingly in Iran's favour in late 1983, the US changed its position and stated that Iraq's defeat would be against its interests.

With every Iranian military success – from the Majnoon Islands in 1984 to Fao in 1986 and Shalamche a year later – Washington increased its backing for Baghdad, culminating in an unprecedented naval build-up in the Gulf and, for all practical purposes, the opening of a second front against the Islamic Republic.

There are compelling historical and ideological reasons for deep animosity between Washington and revolutionary Tehran. The dominance of America over Pahlavi Iran after the 1953 CIA-backed counter-coup was so overwhelming that the post-Pahlavi regime felt that Iran could recover its independence only by purging American influence in all its facets: military, political, economic, technological, educational and cultural. On its part, Washington could not stomach the fact that it had lost the most prized strategic asset in the region – hence its repeated attempts to destabilize and overthrow the Islamic regime through the very considerable contacts it maintained with the monarchist and other anti-Khomeini forces. The invasion of Iran by Iraq, although carried out by Saddam Hussein, can be seen as the last desperate attempt by the US to, at least, seriously weaken the Khomeini regime in the process of securing the release of American hostages on the eve of the presidential poll.

There was a deep-seated antipathy between the two countries at the popular level, which persists. The long ordeal of the American hostages in Iran in 1979–80, played up day after day in the US media, left a deep mark on the American population. This became obvious when President Reagan's tough stance against Iran in the Gulf during the last year of the war – which resulted in considerable loss of Iranian fighters and civilians as well as oil rigs and naval craft – received overwhelming backing from the public and legislators. (Failure to cause division between the American government and its citizenry on the issue of Reagan's naval intervention in the Gulf was one of the main reasons for

Tehran's accepting the ceasefire.) Equally, the Pentagon's actions in the Gulf stoked up anti-American feeling in Iran, even among the middle and upper classes.

In addition there was intense ideological antipathy between the two states which continues. Puritanical Iranian revolutionaries regarded America as the prime source of moral corruption on earth, as indicated by the high incidence there of sexual promiscuity and venereal diseases, divorce, broken families, drug abuse and serious crime. They portrayed the United States as the largest devourer of the resources of the Third World, including Muslim states: a superpower which exercised over-whelming political, economic and cultural control over many Muslim countries and their ruling elites.

More specifically, Iran was concerned with the power equation in the Gulf. Given its large area and population, it visualized itself as the regional superpower. The adoption of Islam as its political ideology was seen by Iran as a powerful tool to gather the states on the western side of the Gulf under an Islamic umbrella, since their ruling elites too claimed to derive their legitimacy from this faith. But Tehran experienced strong opposition to the realization of this scenario. Firstly, there was histori-cal animosity and distrust between Arabs and Persians. Secondly, there was the Shia–Sunni schism, with all the Arab Gulf rulers being Sunni and having poor regard for Shias. Finally, and most importantly, all these states had strong military, economic and political ties with the US.

It soon became obvious to revolutionary Tehran that it could gain influence in the Arab Gulf capitals only at the expense of Washington. This exacerbated relations between the Western superpower and the Islamic Republic.

As the leader of the West, the United States is only too aware of the significance of the Gulf as the leading (as well as the most concentrated) source of petroleum, essential for the healthy growth of the economies of the West and Japan. Possessing 420.9 billion barrels of oil out of the world total of 795.4 billion,[5] the eight states bordering the Gulf are in a unique position to control the oil market either directly or through OPEC.

It was this potential that Iran wished to see realized under its leader-ship which would have stemmed from its victory in the Gulf War. At the very least a victorious Iran would have pressured the Gulf monarchs to fall in line with its professed policy of cutting oil output to raise the price as a means of transforming the region into a hub of industry and high-level technology, and setting up a Gulf Common Market as a stepping stone to a larger Islamic Common Market. This prospect was much dreaded by the West, particularly the US which, through Saudi Arabia, exercises crucial influence on the rate of extraction and price of petroleum.

While the recent oil price level and output have been reassuring to the West, the prospects for the near future are not. At the current production rate the proven reserves of North America would be exhausted within 20 years. And, on present trends, by 1995 the West would be dependent on the Gulf oilfields for 30–45 per cent of its petroleum needs.[6] For the welfare of the Western economic system, therefore, the US simply could not afford to let Iran prevail in the Gulf War. It could not allow the ultimate power to fix the rate of extraction and price of oil to slip from the hands of its close ally, Saudi Arabia, to revolutionary Iran.

Moscow had equally compelling reasons to deprive Tehran of victory. As a Marxist, atheist state, it was, and remains, antithetical to the religious regime of Khomeini. It disapproved of the repression un-leashed by the Iranian government on the Tudeh Party in 1983. It disapproved, too, of the Islamic propaganda beamed by Tehran at the central Asian Soviet republics populated by some 40 million people with a Muslim background. Iran's victory in the war would have given greater stridency and appeal to its Islamic mission, and thus improved the chance of Muslim fundamentalism spilling over into the southern Soviet republics. Finally, there was the issue of Afghanistan, where the Moscow-backed Marxist regime was engaged in a mortal struggle with the Islamic resistance. Had Iran defeated Iraq, it would have diverted part of its enhanced energies into backing Muslim fundamentalists in Afghanistan – an enterprise the Kremlin was determined to thwart.

In any case, the Kremlin was required by its Friendship Treaty with Baghdad to help in the defence of Iraq, a country with whose official ideology of secular socialism, albeit of the Baathist variety, it had much sympathy. In the absence of common borders, what held the two states together was the sharing of certain socio-political values. Moscow's unwavering commitment to safeguard the territorial integrity of Iraq established it as a reliable friend in the Arab world, something that could not be said of the US in the light of the Irangate affair.

While the Soviet Union appreciated Iran's strident anti-American policies and actions, it could not overlook the basic politico-ideological differences that existed between it and the Islamic Republic. At the same time it enjoyed a geostrategic advantage over its southerly neighbour. If it wanted, it could have diverted Tehran's military effort by massing troops along its border with Iran. That it never did so showed that Moscow did not want its commitment to help Iraq defend itself to be transformed into anti-Iranian actions – such as those taken by the US during the last year of the conflict. Quite simply, the Soviet Union did not want a sulking regime along its southern border harbouring a deep grievance against it – particularly when that regime had severed a very strong American connection and broken the chain of anti-Soviet forces surrounding the USSR.

Within these limitations the Kremlin helped Iraq militarily and economically. Equally, Washington aided Baghdad financially, diplomatically and through intelligence while mouthing its rhetoric about American neutrality in the war. At crucial moments both superpowers reached tacit understandings: firstly, to ensure that the Iran–Iraq War did not get drawn into the larger East–West conflict; and secondly, to guarantee free navigation to and from the Gulf ports.

The net result of these policies was to make an Iranian victory increasingly unattainable. Every battlefront gain by Tehran after 1984 resulted in substantial diplomatic loss to itself and a corresponding increase in the military and economic backing for Iraq by both the superpowers and its regional allies. Iran needed periodic battlefield victories to maintain the morale of fighters as well as civilians, and to keep on fighting. But once the coalition of regional and international powers made the price of each gain increasingly high – and the crash in oil prices in the winter of 1985–6 severely limited the cash available for essential military and civilian needs – there came a point when the Islamic Republic considered it prudent to cease fighting. By then, however, the new Iranian system had become so established that it could absorb a dramatic reversal of war policy.

Overall, the conflict provided Khomeini with an opportunity to consolidate the Islamic revolution; and he made an effective use of it. Equally, the Iraqi nation emerged from the war as more united and cohesive than before. Thirdly, the Iraqi effort to destabilize and overthrow the Iranian regime through the invasion misfired. Equally, the Iranian attempt to turn the warfare into a prime instrument for exporting the revolution failed. This, and the loss of Iraqi interest in pursuing its radical, republican cause in the Gulf states, made the Gulf monarchies feel secure. Fifthly, the Baath Party emerged as a much changed entity as a result of the war in both its domestic and foreign policies, virtually shedding its socialism, radical Arab nationalism and militant anti-Zionism. In Iran the impact of the conflict on the Islamic ideology was minimal in so far as its socio-economic applicability was still being worked out when the war erupted. The hostilities led the authorities to postpone major socio-economic decisions.

Seventhly, by encouraging Iraq to invade, the US and its Gulf allies succeeded in ending the special relationship between Baghdad and Moscow. In the Arab world Baghdad now belongs to the same column of moderate pro-Western capitals as Amman and Cairo when it comes to taking a position on the Israeli-Palestinian problem. Eighthly, Iraq has ended up as a dependent state, heavily indebted to its Gulf allies, the West and the USSR. In contrast, Iran has lost none of its independence as a consequence of the Gulf War. Indeed, having diversified its sources of arms procurement in the course of the conflict, it has enhanced its independence. Tenthly, both countries have built up their defence industries, and the Gulf War will be remembered as having provided much impetus to the arms factories of such Third World countries as Egypt, Brazil, China and North Korea. Finally, with the Saddam Hussein regime firmly in power in Iraq, it must be conceded that revolutionary Islamic fundamentalism has been contained – a result welcomed as much by the superpowers as by the regional states.

In a general sense, the Gulf War was an outgrowth of the Islamic revolution in Iran. While its instigator, Iraq, succeeded in containing the revolution, the conflict enabled the Khomeini regime to consolidate itself and become rooted in the Iranian soil. In the absence of a foreign invasion, there was an even chance that Iran would have slipped into a debilitating civil war.

Now that the Khomeini government of Iran has been deprived of the chance to export its revolution through force of arms, it has no option but to develop revolutionary Islamic fundamentalism socially and economically in one country to provide a model to other Muslim states.

As for Iraq, its leader, Saddam Hussein, continues to apply the vastly increased military and intelligence machines of the state to root out Kurdish insurgency, the only discordant element in an otherwise united nation. Abroad, he has been trying to punish President Assad for his alliance with Iran by supporting anti-Assad forces among the Lebanese and the Palestinians. In general, bolstered by a huge standing army and a confident populace at home, he has turned his attention to such pan-Arab issues as the Palestinian–Israeli problem, projecting himself as someone on a par with the leaders of the more populous and strategic Egypt and the much larger and more affluent Saudi Arabia.

EPILOGUE*

The tenth anniversary of Iran's Islamic revolution in February 1989 provided an opportunity for the leadership to assess the achievements and failures of the revolution as well as the impact of the war on its course. Among those who expressed doubts about the outcome of the Gulf War was Ayatollah Montazeri. 'Did we succeed in doing well during the imposed war, or did the enemies who imposed it turn out to be the winners?' he asked.[1]

This did not go unnoticed by Ayatollah Khomeini. In a long state-ment, issued on 22 February and ostensibly addressed to the country's clerics and theological students, he addressed the question posed (pub-licly) by Montazeri and (privately) by others. 'How short-sighted are those who think that, because we did not reach the final victory on the front, martyrdom and sacrifice are worthless,' Khomeini stated. 'We exported our revolution to the world through the war; we proved our oppression and the aggressor's tyranny through the war . . . It was during the war that we concluded that we must stand on our feet. It was through the war . . . that we consolidated the roots of our fruitful Islamic revolution . . . [that] we nurtured a sense of fraternity and patriotism in the spirit of all the people . . . that we showed the people of the world – in particular the people of the region – that one can fight against all the powers and superpowers for several years . . . [and] that our military industries enjoyed such momentum of growth.'[2]

Such a robust rejoinder to Montazeri in a public statement indicated that Khomeini disapproved of his assessment of the war and the rev-olution. Clearly, the situation was untenable, and could not last long. The resolution came on 28 March, when Montazeri submitted his resignation as the successor-designate. Khomeini accepted it immediately. This left the republic without a successor to the highest office.

In mid-April, responding to a letter from 130 MPs calling for changes to the constitution, Khomeini appointed a Constitutional Review Council. The Council was hard at work when Khomeini, aged

---

* Notes are at the end of the chapter.

eighty-six, fell seriously ill, and underwent a major operation on his cancer-ridden digestive system on 24 May.

He did not recover from it, and died on 3 June.

The ten days that Khomeini spent in hospital before his death provided the leadership with enough time to devise a plan to ensure a smooth transition of power. The task fell on the shoulders of the Assembly of Experts, a permanent constitutional body. During an eight-hour session the Experts rejected the alternative of a collegiate leadership (of three or five), and voted President Ali Khamanei as the Supreme Leader, while elevating his religious rank from hojatalislam to ayatollah.[3] Immediately Rafsanjani and Prime Minister Musavi pledged their loyalty to Ayatollah Khamanei.

Khomeini's funeral brought vast crowds (estimated to be two to five million strong) out on to the streets of Tehran, thus restressing the immense popularity of the Ayatollah to the world at large. The unity displayed by Khamanei, Rafsanjani, Musavi and Ahmad Khomeini (the Ayatollah's only surviving son) in public was exemplary. The scenario of a bloody power struggle after Khomeini's death, entertained by many foreign analysts, failed to materialize. The orderly transfer of power to forty-nine-year-old Khamanei proved that the revolutionary institutions had struck roots – a process much facilitated by the eight-year war with Iraq.

The Baghdad-based Mujahedin-e Khalq, the one anti-Khomeini organization capable of causing disorder in Iran, failed to act. For reasons best known to himself, the Iraqi president halted all anti-Iranian activities, including radio broadcasts, of the Mujahedin-e Khalq.[4]

Possibly, Saddam Hussein wanted to encourage the post-Khomeini regime to break the seven-month deadlock in the peace talks. Such an initiative was needed since the UN-mediated negotiations had reached a dead-end – with Tehran insisting that Iraq must relinquish forthwith the 920 square miles of Iranian territory it occupied, and Iraq demanding an immediate exchange of about 100,000 prisoners of war held by the two sides.

The Iraqi president pressed his country's claims wherever he could. In mid-June he secured the backing of three Arab countries outside of the Gulf region – Egypt, Jordan and North Yemen – under the aegis of the Arab Cooperation Council, in his on-going dispute with Iran on the fluvial boundary. The first summit of the four-month-old Arab Cooperation Council, held in Alexandria, Egypt, combined its backing for the

Iraqi claim to both banks of the Shatt al Arab with a call to the United Nations to clear the waterway of the debris of the Gulf War.

Iraq attached paramount importance to preserving and enhancing its access to the Gulf for economic and diplomatic reasons. It combined its reconstruction of war-damaged Basra with the expansion of facilities at Umm Qasr and Zubair ports. The re-opening of the Basra oil refinery, with half its pre-war capacity, in February 1989 was followed by the shipment of oil products from Zubair to Dubai.

Overall, though, Baghdad's reconstruction plans were hamstrung by the urgent demands of debt servicing and high defence expenditure. Its income was limited by the OPEC quota of 2.64 million b/d of oil. Little wonder that the government decided to extend the austerity programme it had introduced in 1983. Within four months of the ceasefire it began demobilizing its standing army, which had earlier reached the peak strength of 1,250,000. The first to be released were the troops who had served the longest, and the oldest reservists, aged forty-two and forty-three. By the end of 1989 Iraq had reduced its army by 200,000.[5]

Iran too faced similar problems. Its OPEC quota was pegged to the same level as Iraq's. And after a fairly long debate, its leadership decided against raising large credits from the West, primarily because Khomeini issued a strong anti-Western statement on 22 February 1989. Such loans were seen as a step towards economic dependence on the West, leading to the erosion of Iran's freshly won political independence, widely regarded as one of the most popular results of the Islamic revolution.

However, following the election of Rafsanjani as president, with enhanced powers, in late July, with 94.5% of the total votes, there was expectation abroad that Iran would build bridges with the West. This was not to be. Given the continued strength of the radicals in parliament and the mosque, Rafsanjani was not in a position to alter the direction of Iran's foreign policy.

On their part, the three permanent Western members of the UN Security Council seemed to have lost interest in advancing peace in the region. While the Gulf War was in progress, they had all pressured Iran to stop fighting. Now, when Iraq was stalling the peace talks by refusing to implement the last provision of Clause One of Resolution 598 – 'withdraw all forces to the internationally recognized boundaries without delay' – they did nothing.

Inside Iraq there was no pressure on Saddam Hussein to break the logjam in the peace negotiations. He was more entrenched in office than ever before; and there was no challenger on the horizon. Within nine months of the ceasefire the country's three most senior and popular generals had met their deaths in mysterious aircraft/helicopter accidents, the latest victim being General Adnan Khairallah, the defence minister.[6] Saddam Hussein's regime was secure and stable. The elections to the Third National Assembly went smoothly forward on 1 April 1989, with 160 of the newly elected 250 deputies belonging to the Baath Socialist Party.

Saddam Hussein was therefore in no mood to listen to the periodic warnings issued by Tehran that if the Iraqi troops did not vacate the Iranian territory they occupied they would be expelled by force. Nor did he respond to the concession made by the Iranian foreign minister in mid-November, when he proposed concurrent implementation of Clause One and Clause Three of Resolution 598: an immediate exchange of prisoners of war along with a simultaneous withdrawal of the two armies to the international border.[7]

So a situation of 'No war, no peace' persists. How durable is it? It could go on for a long time. There are several factors against a revival of the armed conflict. Neither Iranians nor Iraqis are in a mood to start fighting again. Given that neither side gained anything tangible from the eight years of warfare, it would be an uphill task for the regimes in Baghdad and Tehran to motivate the populace to pick up arms again. In fact, having suffered large losses, human and material, the two peoples are going to nurse bitter memories of the war for at least a decade or so. The Gulf conflict established unequivocally that the armies of Iran and Iraq were far more effective in defending their home ground than seizing the enemy's. Were the regime in Tehran or Baghdad to try mobilizing its military for an offensive, it would find it difficult to sustain its assault, thus putting its own survival in jeopardy. Iran no longer has at its helm the charismatic Khomeini to boost the morale of its embattled citizens. As for Iraq, it does not have the political and economic independence it enjoyed in 1980, when the oil boom boosted its foreign cash deposits to over $35 billion. Now, as a state burdened with heavy external debts, Iraq is vulnerable to pressures not only from Saudi Arabia and Kuwait but also from the Soviet Union, France, West Germany and Japan.

But this does not mean that either Iraq or Iran has lost momentum in building up its military industry and buying sophisticated weaponry. There were persistent reports in 1989 that Iraq was pursuing a crash programme to build a nuclear warhead for a new strategic missile,[8] and that it proposed to place a surveillance satellite of its own in orbit. On 7 December Baghdad claimed that two days earlier it had launched its first locally manufactured space rocket, named Al Abid (literally, The Worshipper). It also claimed to have developed two missiles with a range of 1,110 miles.[9] This can only accelerate Tehran's plans to acquire a nuclear weapon and a delivery system, and place a spy satellite in space – probably by using a Chinese rocket.

So, while the Gulf War is over, the arms race between Iran and Iraq is not.

NOTES

1. *Guardian*, 11 February 1989.
2. Ibid., 6 March 1989.
3. Later Ayatollah Abol Qasim Ghazali, a member of the Assembly of Experts, told a Tehran newspaper that Khomeini had informed his son, Ahmad, of his wish to see Khamanei installed as the Supreme Leader.
4. *Independent*, 8 June 1989.
5. *Guardian*, 5 December 1989; and *The Middle East*, December 1989, p. 30.
6. *Sunday Times*, 7 May 1989; and *The Middle East*, July 1989, p. 10.
7. *International Herald Tribune*, 17 November 1989.
8. *Independent*, 1 April 1989.
9. *Sunday Times*, 10 December 1989; and *Guardian*, 18 December 1989.

NOTES

1 ROOTS OF CONFLICT

1. There are three branches of Shia Islam: Zaidi or Fivers; Ismailis or Seveners; and Imamis, Jaafaris or Twelvers. Fivers believe in five Imams, religious leaders; Seveners in seven, and Twelvers (the largest branch) in twelve.

2. Jasim M. Abdulghani, *Iran and Iraq: The Years of Crisis*, Croom Helm, London, 1984, p. 3.

3. *My Memories: Half a Century of the History of Iraq and the Arab Question* (in Arabic), Dar al Kitab al Arabi, Beirut, 1969, pp. 216–21.

4. Cited in Shahram Chubin and Sepehr Zabih, *The Foreign Relations of Iran: A Developing State in a Zone of Great Power Conflict*, University of California Press, Berkeley, CA, 1974, p. 183.

5. Edmund Ghareeb, *The Kurdish Question in Iraq*, Syracuse University Press, Syracuse, NY, 1981, p. 133.

6. *New Middle East*, July 1970, p. 25.

7. *New Times*, no. 16, 1972, pp. 4–5, cited in Dilip Hiro, *Inside the Middle East*, Routledge & Kegan Paul, London, and McGraw-Hill, New York, 1982, p. 281.

8. *New Republic*, 1 December 1973.

9. Martin Short and Anthony McDermott, *The Kurds*, Minority Rights Group, London, 1977, p. 19.

10. Amir Taheri, 'Politics of Iran in the Persian Gulf' in Abbas Amirie (ed.), *Persian Gulf and Indian Ocean in International Politics*, Institute of International and Economic Studies, Tehran, 1975, p. 257.

11. Christine Moss Helms, *Iraq: Eastern Flank of the Arab World*, Brookings Institution, Washington, DC, 1984, p. 118.

12. Saddam Hussein, *Iraqi Policies in Perspective*, Translation and Foreign Languages Publishing House, Baghdad, 1981, p. 55.

13. Tareq Y. Ismail, *Iraq and Iran: Roots of Conflict*, Syracuse University Press, Syracuse, NY, 1982, p. 66.

14. Cited in *The Middle East*, March 1977, p. 42.

15. Committee Against Repression and For Democratic Rights in Iraq, *Saddam's Iraq: Revolution or Reaction?*, Zed Press, London, 1986, p. 66.

16. Marion Farouk-Sluglett, '"Socialist Iraq" 1963–1978 – Towards a Reappraisal', *Orient*, no. 2, 1982, p. 213.

17. Cited in Hanna Batatu, 'Iraq's Underground Shia Movements: Characteristics, Causes and Prospects', *Middle East Journal*, Autumn 1981, p. 587. Since Islam enjoins the believer to allocate part of his property for the benefit of the community, the size of religious endowments has increased over the centuries.

18. *Socialist Iraq: A Study in Iraqi Politics since 1968*, The Middle East Institute, Washington, DC, 1978, p. 65.

19. *Al Hawadith*, 20 December 1974.

20. Dilip Hiro, *Inside the Middle East*, p. 144.

21. *Le Monde*, 26 March 1988.

22. *Guardian*, 28 February 1979.

23. Article 154 of the 1979 constitution of Iran incorporated this principle thus: 'The Islamic Republic of Iran . . . considers the attainment of independence, freedom and just government to be the right of all people of the world. While scrupulously refraining from all forms of aggressive intervention in the internal affairs of other nations, it therefore protects the just struggle of the oppressed and deprived in every corner of the globe'. Hamid Algar (trans.), *Constitution of the Islamic Republic of Iran*, Mizan Press, Berkeley, CA, 1980, pp. 82–3.

24. *Iranvoice*, 30 July 1979.

25. *Observer*, 24 June 1979.

26. Ofra Bengio, 'Shias and Politics in Baathi Iraq', *Middle Eastern Studies*,

January 1985, pp. 6–7.

27. *Al Jumhuriya*, 10 January 1980.

28. Cited in Elyas Farah, *Evolution of Arab Revolutionary Ideology*, Arab Baath Socialist Party, Madrid, 1979, p. 124.

29. 'A View of Religion and Heritage' in Saddam Hussein, *The Arab Heritage and Contemporary Life*, (in Arabic), Dar al Hurriya li al Tibaa, Baghdad, 1978, pp. 5–17.

30. Ruh Allah Khumayni, *Islamic Government: Rule of the Faqih* (in Farsi), Najaf, 1971, p. 75. An English translation of this book appears in Ruh Allah Khumayni, *Islam and Revolution*, Hamid Algar (trans.), Mizan Press, Berkeley, CA, 1981, pp. 27–166.

31. Cited in *The Iranian Revolution and the Islamic Republic: Conference Proceedings*, The Middle East Institute, Washington, DC, 1982, p. 196.

32. The least influential among Shia clergy are pious men addressed as *thiqatalislam*, trust of Islam; then come the ones addressed as *hojatalislam wa al muslimeen*, proof of Islam and Muslims; then *ayatollah fi al almin*, sign of Allah in the world; and finally *ayatollah al uzma*, great sign of Allah, also addressed as *marji*, authority.

33. Robert Graham, *Iran: The Illusion of Power*, Croom Helm, London, 1978, p. 243, n. 43.

34. *Jumhouri-ye Islami*, 2 January 1980.

35. Asked to name his enemies, Khomeini replied: 'First, the Shah; then the American Satan; then Saddam Hussein and his infidel Baath Party'. Cited in *The Middle East*, 26 July 1982, p. 25.

36. *Foreign Broadcast Information Service*, 17 October 1979.

37. *Al Hawadith*, 4 January 1980.

38. *Foreign Broadcast Information Service*, 18 April 1980; *Washington Post*, 18 April 1980.

39. Dilip Hiro, *Iran Under the Ayatollahs*, Routledge & Kegan Paul, London and New York, 1985, pp. 154–6.

40. *Foreign Report*, 1 August 1980.

41. According to the Baathist doctrine the Arab Nation consists of the territories of the Arab League members – and Palestine/Israel, Cilcia and Alexandretta (in Turkey) and Khuzistan (in Iran).

42. *MERIP Reports*, July–September 1981, pp. 3–4. According to a well-informed source, on the eve of the war the Iraqi president sent word to the Kuwaiti ruler that General Oveissi could be in Tehran 'within days'. Patrick Seale, *Asad: The Struggle for the Middle East*, I. B. Tauris, London, 1988, pp. 361–2.

43. Just before the Iranian revolution the joint Iran–Iraq Delimitation Commission had demarcated the borders according to the 1975 Algiers Accord except for the area around the Zain al Qaws–Saif Saad area where Iran had agreed to cede territory in exchange for the concession won on the Shatt al Arab border. Due to the administrative breakdown in Tehran, caused by the revolution, the border commission stopped working before implementing the change in this region.

44. Cited in R. K. Ramazani, *Revolutionary Iran: Challenge and Response in the Middle East*, The Johns Hopkins University Press, Baltimore and London, 1986, p. 61.

45. Shahram Chubin, 'Reflections on the Gulf War', *Survival*, July–August 1986, p. 308.

2 EMBATTLED IRAN

1. *New York Times*, 3 October 1980.

2. Dilip Hiro, *Iran Under the Ayatollahs*, p. 168.

3. Baghdad Radio, 28 September 1980.

4. *Ibid*, 18 October 1980.

5. Daniel Dishon, Colin Legum and Haim Shaked (eds), *Middle East Contemporary Survey: Volume V, 1980–81*, Holmes & Meier, New York and London, 1983, pp. 26–7.

6. Baghdad Radio, 18 October 1980.

7. *Ittilaat*, 7 November 1980.

8. Baghdad Radio, 4 November 1980.

9. *Kayhan International*, 24 September 1986.

10. Iraqi News Agency, 11 November 1980.

11. *New York Times*, 22 October 1980.

12. *Selected Messages of Imam Khomeini Concerning Iraq and the War*

Iraq Imposed Upon Iran, Ministry of Islamic Guidance, Tehran, 1981, p. 68.

13. Daniel Dishon *et al.* (eds), *op. cit.*, p. 601.

14. *Daily Telegraph*, 18 June 1980.

15. *Marine Corps Gazette*, February 1982, p. 49.

16. *New York Times*, 2 March 1981.

17. *Ibid*, 8 March 1981.

18. *Strategy Week*, 13 April 1981, p. 6; 20 April 1981, p. 2.

19. *Washington Post*, 19 April 1981.

20. *Foreign Report*, 23 July 1981. On 27 July 12 officers and 200 soldiers were executed as members of this network.

21. *Economist*, 8 May 1981; *New York Times*, 7 July 1981.

22. Tehran Radio, 24 and 27 September 1980; *New York Times*, 1 October 1980.

23. *Baghdad Observer*, 18 December 1980; *Iraq*, 15 July 1981.

24. *Baghdad Observer*, 8 August 1981. However, such declarations by Saddam Hussein, a layman, did not have the same authority as those of a much revered Islamic figure like Khomeini.

25. Anthony H. Cordesman, *The Gulf and the Search for Strategic Stability: Saudi Arabia, the Military Balance in the Gulf, and Trends in the Arab–Israeli Military Balance*, Mansell, London; Westview Press, Boulder, Colo., 1984, p. 670.

26. *Strategy Week*, 24 August 1981. To the 35,000 Iranians mentioned in this publication another 3000 have been added to take into account the Abadan battle. Iraq claimed that 41,779 Iranians were killed in the first year of the war ending on 3 September 1981: Iraqi News Agency, 3 September 1981. To the Iraqi figure of 20,000 dead, given in *Le Monde* of 17 July 1981, another 2000 have been added.

27. Arthur J. Arberry (trans.), *The Koran Interpreted*, Oxford University Press, Oxford and New York, 1964, 3:164.

28. Interviews with Martyrs Foundation officials in Tehran, April 1983.

29. *Financial Times*, 10 November 1981 and 28 January 1982; Dilip Hiro, *Iran under the Ayatollahs*, pp. 150, 206.

30. *New York Times*, 30 March and 1 April 1982; *Economist*, 24 April 1982.

31. *New York Times*, 8 April 1982.

32. Iraqi News Agency, 29 March 1982.

33. Keith McLachlan and George Joffé, *The Gulf War: A Survey of Political Issues and Economic Consequences*, The Economist Intelligence Unit, London, 1984, p. 71.

34. *Ibid.*, pp. 71, 75.

35. *Ibid.*, p. 80.

36. Iraqi News Agency, 17 June 1981.

37. *Wall Street Journal*, 6 May 1982.

38. The main purpose of this pact, signed in June 1950 by five of the six founder-members of the Arab League – Egypt, Syria, Jordan, Lebanon, Iraq and Saudi Arabia – was to provide mutual aid in case of aggression by Israel. When Egypt concluded a peace treaty with the common enemy, Israel, in March 1979 it was suspended from the League.

39. *New York Times*, 29 May 1982.

40. *Le Monde*, 30 July 1980.

41. *Christian Science Monitor*, 27 May 1982.

42. *Al Thawra*, 17 April 1981.

43. *Sunday Times*, 24 May 1981; *International Herald Tribune*, 23 June 1981.

44. Ayatollah Khoei's son, Abbas, exiled in London, stated that in his telephone conversations his father had declared himself against the war and Saddam Hussein. *Guardian*, 30 October 1980.

45. *Al Thawra*, 4 November 1981.

46. This statement is incorrect. Khomeini carries the title of Sayyid, which is applied to male descendants of Imam Hussein, a son of Imam Ali. Khomeini's second name, Musavi, shows him to be a descendant of Imam Musa al Kazim, a Shia Arab.

47. *Guardian*, 31 May 1982.

48. *Ibid.*, 7 March 1983.

49. *Economist*, 31 July 1982. Bakr died a natural death on 4 October 1982. Later two of these ministers, Riyad Ibrahim Hussein and Tayih Abdul Karim, were to be executed.

50. Tehran Radio, 21 June 1982.

51. Baghdad Radio, 27 June 1982.

52. *Foreign Broadcast Information Service*, 29 June 1982; Amazia Baram, 'The June 1980 Elections to the National

Assembly: An Experiment in Controlled Democracy', *Orient*, September 1981, pp. 391–412. Twelve per cent of the deputies were Kurdish.

53. *Economist*, 4 December 1982 and 29 January 1983; and an interview with an Iraqi opposition leader in London, April 1988.

54. Baghdad Radio, 27 June 1982.

55. *Ibid.*, 27 June 1982.

56. *Ibid.*, 20 June 1982.

57. *Time*, 19 July 1982.

58. Baghdad Radio, 20 June 1982.

3 OUTSIDE POWERS

1. *Le Monde*, 8 October 1980. Some weeks before the eruption of the Gulf War, President Carter's National Security Adviser, Zbigniew Brzezinski, lost interest in the arms-for-hostages talks that were being conducted by Washington with Tehran through Cyrus and Muhammad Ali Hashemi, expatriate Iranian arms dealers. Brzezinski apparently had foreknowledge of the war and had placed his hopes in it rather than in striking a deal with Tehran. Patrick Seale, *Asad: The Struggle for the Middle East*, p. 363.

2. *New York Times*, 19, 20 and 24 October 1980.

3. *In These Times*, 24 June 1987 and 12 October 1988; *New York Times*, 3 August 1987. Among the three emissaries from Reagan's campaign office who met a representative of the Iranian government in a Washington hotel in October 1980 was Robert McFarlane, who six years later was to emerge as a principal actor in the Irangate affair.

4. *Nation*, 8 August 1981, p. 97.

5. *The Times*, 6 October 1980. Before the 1979 revolution the Soviets had sold small arms, artillery, surface-to-surface missiles and military transport equipment to Iran. Dilip Hiro, *Iran Under the Ayatollahs*, p. 281.

6. *Kayhan*, 11 November 1980.

7. *New York Times*, 4 February 1981.

8. *Washington Post*, 19 April 1981; *Izvestia*, 24 April 1981.

9. *Pravda*, 19 June 1981.

10. *Middle East Economic Survey*, 11 August 1980.

11. 'Islam is fundamentally opposed to the whole notion of monarchy,' Khomeini stated in October 1971 on the eve of the celebration of 2500 years of monarchy in Iran. 'Anyone who studies the manner in which the Prophet established the government of Islam will realize that Islam came in order to destroy these palaces of tyranny. Monarchy is one of the most shameful and disgraceful reactionary manifestations.' Ruh Allah Khumayni, *Islam and Revolution*, p. 202.

12. Claudia Wright, 'Implications of the Iran–Iraq War', *Foreign Affairs*, Issue 59, 1980–81, pp. 282–3.

13. *Daily Telegraph*, 4 February 1981. In the fourth quarter of 1980 Saudi Arabia raised its output by 440,000 b/d to fulfil Iraq's oil supply contracts to save Baghdad from losing its customers or having to pay penalties. *Petroleum Economist*, January 1982, pp. 23–4.

14. CBS Television, 5 October 1980; *Time*, 13 October 1980.

15. *Middle East Economic Digest*, 2 April 1982.

16. *Al Rai al Aam*, 10 December 1980; and *Al Siyasa*, 10 December 1980. Between 1979 and 1982 the cargo bound from Kuwait to Iraq increased almost threefold to 3.5 million tonnes a year. Christine Moss Helms, *Iraq: Eastern Flank of the Arab World*, p. 49.

17. Gerd Nonneman, *Iraq, the Gulf States and the War: A Changing Relationship 1980–86 and Beyond*, Ithaca Press, London and Atlantic Highlands, 1986, p. 96.

18. *Strategy Week*, 12 October 1980.

19. *Daily Telegraph*, 19 January 1983.

20. Baghdad Radio, 19 January 1981.

21. *Ibid.*, 21 July 1981.

22. The members of the Front of Steadfastness and Confrontation were: Algeria, Libya, the Palestine Liberation Organization, South Yemen and Syria.

23. *BBC Summary of World Broadcasts*, 26 September 1980.

24. *Ibid.*, 11 October 1980.

25. *New York Times*, 19 April 1982.

26. Tripoli Radio, 9 October 1980.

27. *Observer*, 12 July 1981.

28. *Middle East Newsletter*, 6 October 1980. France could have applied the same reasoning if it wished to sell arms to Iran.

29. Daniel Dishon *et al.* (eds), *Middle East Contemporary Survey: Volume VI, 1981–2*, Holmes & Meier, New York and London, 1984, p. 610. During 1980–81 Iraq signed military co-operation agreements with Italy and Spain.

30. William O. Staudenmaier, 'A Strategic Analysis' in Shirin Tahir-Kheli and Shaheen Ayubi (eds), *The Iran–Iraq War: New Weapons, Old Conflicts*, Praeger, New York, 1983, p. 44.

31. *Time*, 25 July 1982, p. 20.

32. Of the five Arab nations which declared war against Israel in 1948 all except Iraq signed a ceasefire agreement with the Jewish state.

33. *Defence and Foreign Affairs Daily*, 20 January 1983; *New York Times*, 8 March 1982; *Time*, 25 July 1983, pp. 26–8. These shipments included the ones most probably authorized by President Reagan in early 1981 as a trade-off with Iran for delaying the release of the American hostages until after the November 1980 presidential election.

34. Islamic Republic News Agency, 28 December 1981.

35. *Tehran Times*, 12 February 1982.

36. *Time*, 19 July 1982.

37. For instance, the *Pravda* of 9 March 1982 complained bitterly about Iran referring to the Soviet Union as a threat equal to that of America.

38. *Middle East Economic Digest*, 4 March 1983.

4 EMBATTLED IRAQ

1. Another contributory factor which underlined the unsuitability of Baghdad as the venue for the conference was the truck-bombing of the planning ministry building by a pro-Iranian group in early August 1982 which left 69 people dead.

2. *Financial Times*, 16 August 1982; Islamic Republic News Agency, 16 February 1984.

3. Anthony H. Cordesman, *The Gulf and the Search for Strategic Stability*, p. 684.

4. Iraqi News Agency, 16 November 1982.

5. Voice of the Masses Radio, 8 July 1982.

6. *Foreign Broadcast Information Service*, 12 November 1982. Later Tayih Abdul Karim, former oil minister and a fervent supporter of Bakr, was executed. *Le Monde*, 6 February 1983.

7. *Economist*, 4 September 1982.

8. Baghdad tried to overcome its skilled manpower problem by recruiting 40 to 60 Egyptian pilots in April 1982. *Al Nahar*, 24 May 1982.

9. *Tehran Times*, 2 November 1982.

10. Baghdad Radio, 10 November 1982.

11. *Washington Post*, 17 November 1982.

12. Daniel Dishon *et al.* (eds), *Middle East Contemporary Survey: Volume VI, 1981–2*, p. 309; *Kayhan*, 18 October 1982.

13. Baghdad Radio, 10 September 1982.

14. *Washington Post*, 2 February 1983.

15. *Foreign Broadcast Information Service*, 16 March 1983.

16. *The Middle East*, April 1983, p. 4.

17. *BBC Summary of World Broadcasts*, 11 June 1983.

18. *Financial Times*, 13 April 1983.

19. Tehran Radio, 19 September 1983.

20. *Kayhan*, 13 and 15 August 1983.

21. *BBC Summary of World Broadcasts*, 1 and 12 November 1983.

22. David McDowall, *The Kurds*, Minority Rights Group, London, 1985, p. 24; *BBC Summary of World Broadcasts*, 14 February 1983.

23. A visit by the author to Dezful after an Iraqi missile attack in April 1983 showed a quarter of the city's adult male population joining the funeral procession of the victims.

24. In early 1984 Iran said that Iraqi air and missile attacks on civilian areas during the war had left 4700 civilians dead and 22,000 injured. *Financial Times*, 7 February 1984.

25. *Sunday Times*, 11 March 1984.

26. *Jane's Defence Weekly*, 25 January 1984; *Sunday Times*, 18 March 1984;

Dilip Hiro, *Iran Under the Ayatollahs*,
p. 235.

27. *Sunday Times*, 29 April 1984; Dilip
Hiro, *op. cit.*, p. 236.

28. *Tehran Times*, 21 April 1983.

29. Kadhimain is the burial place of a
Shia Imam.

30. *Guardian*, 16 February 1984.

31. Baghdad Radio, 5 November 1983.

32. *Al Thawra*, 17 April 1983.

33. *Middle East Insight*, April–May
1984.

34. *Al Thawra*, 17 April 1983.

35. Baghdad Radio, 28 February 1984.

36. *Newsweek*, 19 March 1984.

37. *Al Thawra*, 6 September 1983;
Middle East Report, March–April 1988,
p. 36. Between September 1980 and April
1984, Saddam Hussein sacked more than
300 generals and other commissioned
officers for incompetence in combat.
Daniel Dishon *et al.* (eds), *Middle East
Contemporary Survey: Volume VIII,
1983–4*, Holmes & Meier, New York and
London, 1986, p. 471.

38. *Financial Times*, 9 February 1983.

39. McLachlan and Joffé, *The Gulf War*,
p. 69.

40. McLachlan and Joffé, *op. cit.*, pp. 71,
72.

41. *Kayhan*, 15 March 1984.

42. *BBC Summary of World Broadcasts*,
16 March and 14 July 1983.

43. Islamic Republic News Agency,
8 August 1983.

44. McLachlan and Joffé, *op cit.*, p. 57.

45. *Ibid.*, p. 55; Dilip Hiro, *op. cit.*, p. 239

46. Dilip Hiro, *op. cit.*, p. 239.

5 IMPACT OF THE WAR ABROAD

1. *International Herald Tribune*,
4 October 1982; *Economist*, 9 October
1982.

2. *Foreign Broadcast Information
Service*, 23 March 1983.

3. *Kayhan*, 2 and 3 February 1983.

4. *Ibid.*, 24 June 1983; *BBC Summary of
World Broadcasts*, 24 June 1983.

5. Baghdad Radio, 9 December 1982.

6. Christine Moss Helms, *Iraq: Eastern
Flank of the Arab World*, p. 185.

7. Zbigniew Brzezinski, *Power and
Principle: Memoirs of the National
Security Adviser*, Weidenfeld & Nicolson,
London, 1983, p. 504; *In These Times*, 12
October 1988.

8. *Washington Post*, 27 and 28 July
1982; *Time*, 25 July 1983.

9. Iraqi News Agency, 2 January 1983.

10. Richard M. Preece, *United
States–Iraqi Relations*, Congressional
Research Service, Library of Congress,
Government Printing Office, Washington,
DC, July 1986, p. 12; *New York Times*,
11 January 1984.

11. *Newsday*, 22 May 1984.

12. To satisfy Washington, Saddam
Hussein expelled the extremist
Palestinian leader Abu Nidal from
Baghdad, and in October 1983 sacked his
stepbrother, Barzan Tikriti, as intelligence
chief partly because of the latter's close
contacts with Abu Nidal. See also Chapter
6, p. 147.

13. *Washington Post*, 4 January 1984.

14. *Guardian*, 22 July 1983; *New York
Times*, 29 March 1984.

15. *Time*, 25 July 1983. At least in one
instance the Iranian troops in Bandar
Abbas, on discovering crates marked
'Made in the USA', prevented a Danish
ship from unloading its full cargo of 90,000
grenades and 2000 detonators supplied by
an American company, Western
Dynamics. Agence France-Presse,
6 February 1987.

16. *New York Times*, 22 November
1982.

17. *Kayhan*, 13 August 1983.

18. *Guardian*, 28 November 1983 and
20 March 1984.

19. Tehran Radio, 17 January 1984.

20. The National Security Archive, *The
Chronology: The Documented
Day-by-Day Account of the Secret
Military Assistance to Iran and the
Contras*, Warner Books, New York, 1987,
p. 22. In view of the comparatively modest
sums now known to have been spent by
Iran on arms imports, the higher figure of
$3000 million seems unrealistic.

21. *Le Monde*, 8 January 1983.

22. *The Times*, 4 October 1983;
Economist, 15 October 1983.

23. Walter De Bock and Jean-Charles Deniau, *Des Armes pour l'Iran: L'Irangate Européen*, Gallimard, Paris, 1988; see particularly Chapters 7, 8 and 9, and Appendix I.

24. *International Herald Tribune*, 3 June 1987; *Guardian*, 31 July 1987.

6 TOTAL WARFARE: TANKERS AND CITIES

1. *Washington Post*, 9 June 1984.

2. *New York Times*, 21 June 1984.

3. *Al Hawadith*, 10 August 1984.

4. *Guardian*, 28 June 1984; *Washington Post*, 21 July 1984.

5. *Guardian*, 12 August 1984; *The Middle East*, December 1984, p. 26.

6. *BBC Summary of World Broadcasts*, 14 August 1984.

7. *Newsweek*, 1 April 1985, p. 16. Since the beginning of the Gulf War some 7000 Iranian civilians were killed and over 30,000 injured in air raids. *Guardian*, 9 April 1985.

8. *Sunday Times*, 7 April 1985.

9. The Beirut-based Islamic Jihad Organization claimed responsibility for the attack and demanded the release of the 17 people arrested in connection with the December 1983 bombings in Kuwait, six of whom had been sentenced to death in March 1984.

10. *Financial Times*, 15 June 1985; *Arabia: The Islamic World Review*, August 1985, p. 46.

11. A military communiqué in Baghdad stated that the Presidential Guard division 'assumed the major burden in the honourable battle'. Baghdad Radio, 18 March 1985.

12. *Sunday Times*, 7 April 1985; *The Times*, 31 July 1985.

13. *Middle East Review*, World Almanac Publications, London, 1986, p. 111.

14. *Al Thawra*, 27 November 1984.

15. Other prominent examples of the dropping of the family name were Taha Yassin Ramadan (Jazrawi), Izzat Ibrahim (Duri), deputy general secretary of the Iraqi Baath Party, and Adnan Khairallah (Talfa),

defence minister. The idea was to mask the predominance of Tikritis at the top.

16. Iraqi opposition sources put the number of deserters at 120,000. *Foreign Report*, 30 May 1985.

17. Dilip Hiro, *Iran Under the Ayatollahs*, p. 376.

18. Cited in *The Middle East*, April 1985, p. 51.

19. *BBC Summary of World Broadcasts*, 14 August 1984.

20. *Iran Press Digest*, 25 July 1985. During the March 1985 offensive Bazargan and 60 of his followers sent a cable to the UN secretary-general in which they described the war as unIslamic and illegal since June 1982.

21. *Iran Press Digest*, 12 August 1985.

22. *Kayhan*, 13 August 1985; *Jumhouri-ye Islami*, 15 August 1985.

23. Kashani obtained 10 per cent of the total vote, and Asghar-Owladi 2 per cent. *Guardian*, 20 August 1985.

24. *Jumhouri-ye Islami*, 3 and 25 December 1984.

25. *Kayhan*, 25 September 1985.

26. *Al Khaleej*, 18 August 1985.

27. *Al Siyasa*, 2 August 1985.

28. *Guardian*, 5 October 1985.

29. *Economist*, 22 February 1986.

30. *Toronto Star*, 26 January 1986.

31. *Jane's Defence Weekly*, 19 January 1986, p. 43. But the actual attacks numbered only 33. The International Institute for Strategic Studies, *Strategic Survey 1987–1988*, London, 1988, p. 131.

32. *Guardian*, 7 November 1983; *Financial Times*, 9 December 1983.

33. *Le Monde*, 8 March 1986.

34. Juan R. I. Cole and Nikki R. Keddie (eds), *Shi'ism and Social Protest*, Yale University Press, New Haven, Conn., and London, 1986, p. 197.

35. Tehran Radio, 26 November 1985.

7 INTERNATIONAL REPERCUSSIONS

1. *Guardian*, 28 August 1987. The unnamed Saudi official was identified by a British journalist present at the briefing as Prince Badar, the Saudi ambassador to the US.

2. Tehran Radio, 31 May 1984.

3. *Al Riyadh*, 9 July 1984.

4. *BBC Summary of World Broadcasts*, 11 August 1984; Tehran Radio, 17 August 1984; *Foreign Broadcast Information Service*, 30 October 1984.

5. *Foreign Broadcast Information Service*, 20 May 1985.

6. *Jumhouri-ye Islami*, 14 October 1985.

7. *Foreign Broadcast Information Service*, 6 November 1985.

8. *Jeune Afrique*, 2 January 1985.

9. *Khaleej Times*, 19 November 1982.

10. *Jumhouri-ye Islami*, 14 October 1985.

11. On the other hand, according to the London-based pro-Iraqi publication *Al Dastur*, Baghdad was disappointed that the summit did not take steps to transform prior Arab collective commitments into specific actions. 19 August 1985.

12. *Financial Times*, 12 May 1984.

13. Interview with BBC Television, 31 May 1984.

14. *Sunday Times*, 16 March 1985.

15. *The Times*, 31 July 1985.

16. *Iran Press Digest*, 3 September 1985; *New York Times*, 29 September 1985.

17. National Security Archive, *The Chronology*, pp. 78, 104–5.

18. *Iran Press Digest*, 15 July 1985.

19. *Ibid.*, 8 October 1985.

20. *Foreign Broadcast Information Service*, 28 January 1985; *Economist*, 25 November 1985.

21. *Iran Times*, 28 June 1985.

22. *MERIP Middle East Report*, September–October 1987, p. 10.

23. *Iran Times*, 28 June 1985.

24. *BBC Summary of World Broadcasts*, 28 July 1984.

25. *Kayhan*, 2 May 1985.

26. De Bock and Deniau, *Des Armes pour l'Iran*, p. 231; US Arms Control and Disarmament Agency, *World Military Expenditures and Arms Transfers 1987*, Government Printing Office, Washington, DC, 1988, pp. 105 and 117.

27. De Bock and Deniau, *op. cit.*, p. 263; *International Herald Tribune*, 3 June 1987.

28. *Sunday Times*, 4 October 1987.

8 IRAN'S FAO OFFENSIVE AND AFTER

1. *Observer*, 23 February 1986; *Guardian*, 24 February, 1986.

2. While some 8500 Iranians were affected by chemical weapons, only 700 were killed or seriously wounded. John L. Laffin, *War Annual I*, Brassey's Publishers, London, 1986, p. 87.

3. Anthony H. Cordesman, *The Iran–Iraq War and Western Security 1984–87: Strategic Implications and Policy Options*, Jane's Publishing Company, London, 1987, p. 99. Another estimate put the number of dead at 10,000: *The Middle East*, April 1986, p. 7.

4. *Washington Post*, 26 March 1986.

5. Interviews in Tehran, September 1986. 'The American Awacs [based] in Saudi Arabia are watching us, but we have devised a technique so that they cannot find out what our forces are doing,' said Rafsanjani in the midst of the Fao offensive. *Guardian*, 21 February 1986.

6. Tehran Radio, 31 May 1986.

7. The capacity of the Isfahan and Tehran refineries was 200,000 b/d each, or two-thirds of the national aggregate. But their actual aggregate output at 512,000 b/d was about three-quarters of the total. *Middle East Economic Digest*, 3 October 1987, p. 17.

8. *Al Anaba*, 24 March 1986.

9. Defence Analysts, a British consulting firm, was foremost in providing this service to Iran. Of the four specially equipped Iranian tankers by the end of 1986, two were hit once by Iraqi Exocets. But the damage was slight compared to the effect of earlier attacks on unprotected oil tankers. *Jane's Defence Weekly*, 25 October 1986; *International Defence Review*, vol. 20, no. 3, 1987, p. 297. Another technique, developed by Marconi of Great Britain, was to have a tanker tow a decoy boat 200–300 yards behind it to deflect Exocet missiles. BBC World Service, 11 September 1987.

10. The International Institute for Strategic Studies, *Strategic Survey 1987–1988*, London, 1988, p. 131, citing Committee on Foreign Relations, US

Senate, *War in the Persian Gulf: The US Takes Sides*, Washington, DC, November 1987.

11. *Washington Post*, 6 December 1986; *New York Times*, 9 December 1986.

12. *Jane's Defence Weekly*, 1 November 1986.

13. *The Middle East*, July 1986, p. 9; *Middle East Economic Digest*, 16 May 1987, p. 13.

14. By 1985 the national debt stood at $38 billion, or a quarter of the annual Gross Domestic Product. *The Middle East and North Africa 1987*, Europa Publications, London, 1987, p. 414; The International Institute for Strategic Studies, *The Military Balance 1987–1988*, London, 1987, p. 98.

15. *Foreign Broadcast Information Service*, 11 June 1986.

16. The International Institute for Strategic Studies, *The Military Balance 1987–1988*, p. 98.

17. *Foreign Broadcast Information Service*, 1 August 1986; *The Middle East*, October 1986, p. 7.

18. *Arabia: The Islamic World Review*, July 1987, p. 21.

19. Cordesman, *op. cit.*, p. 110.

20. *New York Times*, 26 September and 12 October 1986.

21. Cordesman, *op. cit.*, p. 110; *The Middle East and North Africa 1987*, p. 448; *Middle East Economic Digest*, 29 August 1987, p. 4, and 10 October 1987, p. 16.

22. *Foreign Broadcast Information Service*, 26 June 1986; *Middle East Reporter*, 3 October 1986.

23. *New Scientist*, 17 January 1985, p. 10.

24. *Washington Post*, 28 January 1987.

25. *BBC Summary of World Broadcasts*, 21 January 1987.

26. *New York Times*, 11 February 1987.

27. *Washington Post*, 20 February 1987

28. R. K. Ramazani, 'The Iran–Iraq War and the Persian Gulf Crisis', *Current History*, February 1988, p. 62.

29. The Revolutionary Guards Corps developed a tactic by which small groups of well-trained ranks first penetrated gaps

or weak positions in the Iraqi front line to prepare the ground for an assault. If the attack succeeded the forces strengthened at the infiltration point. If it failed, the elite unit withdrew and tried the same tactic elsewhere. Among other things such tactics reduced the drain on the strained logistics of Iran.

30. Iraqi officials told the visiting US Congressman Robert Torricelli that their country had lost 10 per cent of its air force since 24 December 1986. *Washington Post*, 22 February 1987. Iran claimed to have shot down 77 Iraqi warplanes between 6 January and 7 February 1987. *Arab News*, 8 February 1987.

31. *Guardian*, 2 May 1987.

32. Islamic Republic News Agency, 23 May, 22 and 23 June 1987; and *Foreign Broadcast Information Service*, 24 June 1987.

33. Cited in *MERIP Middle East Report*, September–October 1987, p. 4.

34. *Independent*, 6 August 1987.

35. *Keesing's Record of World Events*, vol. XXXIII, p. 35598.

36. *Foreign Broadcast Information Service*, 31 August 1987.

37. *Middle East Economic Digest*, 17 October 1987, p. 20.

38. *Guardian*, 20 and 21 October 1987.

39. *Financial Times*, 4 September 1987.

40. *Middle East Economic Digest*, 21 November 1987, p. 33.

41. *Guardian*, 2 December 1987.

42. *Ibid.*, 3 June 1987; *The Middle East*, August 1987, p. 6.

43. *Middle East Economic Digest*, 13 June, p. 10, and 15 August 1987, p. 10.

44. *Independent*, 23 September 1987; *Middle East Economic Digest*, 21 November 1987, p. 12.

45. *Mednews: Middle East Defence News*, 22 February 1988, p. 1; The International Institute for Strategic Studies, *The Military Balance 1987–1988*, pp. 98, 100, 101. The armed forces figures included both the active and reserve personnel. Only Iran's (active) Basij militia of 350,000 was far stronger than the Iraqi volunteer force of 120,000.

46. *Al Thawra*, 11 March and 2 July

1987; *BBC Summary of World Broadcasts*, 16 July 1987.

47. *New York Times*, 7 February 1988.

48. *Middle East Economic Digest*, 10 October 1987, p. 16, 30 January 1988, p. 12.

49. Qusay Hussein was married to a daughter of General Mahir Abdul Rashid, commander of the Seventh Army Corps, and Uday was later to be engaged to a daughter of the Iraqi vice-president Izzat Ibrahim. However, in November 1988, Uday Hussein was arrested for allegedly murdering Kamal Hanna Jajjo – a food-taster and personal bodyguard of Saddam Hussein – during a drunken bout. *Observer*, 27 November 1988.

50. *BBC Summary of World Broadcasts*, 16 July 1987.

51. *Observer*, 10 May 1987.

52. *Guardian*, 18 September 1987.

53. *Al Khaleej*, 18 September 1987.

54. *Guardian*, 16 October 1987.

55. *Middle East Economic Digest*, 6 May 1988, pp. 1, 9; *Jane's Defence Weekly*, 23 July 1988, p. 130.

56. The speed of deaths in Halabja suggested something quick-acting – nerve agents or one of the cyanide-based gases affecting blood circulation. Among the documents captured by Kurdish Democratic Party guerrillas at Deralok in January 1988 was a letter sent on 3 August 1986 to various unit officers by General Deah Abdul Wahhab Izzat at Arbil, headed 'Control over distribution of biological and chemical materials'; the general required half-yearly stocktaking of all biological and chemical materials 'at the disposal of the units'. *Observer*, 27 March 1988.

57. *Independent*, 28 December 1987 and 2 August 1988; *Middle East Economic Digest*, 2 January 1988, pp. 4, 12; *Observer*, 13 March 1988.

58. *Financial Times*, 29 June 1988.

59. *The Middle East*, June 1988, p. 6.

60. *The Times*, 19 April 1988; *Middle East Economic Digest*, 29 April 1988, p. 20.

61. *Guardian*, 20 April 1988.

62. *Middle East Economic Digest*, 9 April 1988, p. 5.

63. *Jumhouri-ye Islami*, 11 January 1988.

64. *Daily Telegraph*, 28 May 1988; *Independent*, 2 August 1988; *Guardian*, 6 October 1988.

65. *Jane's Defence Weekly*, 4 June 1988, p. 1091. Earlier Iran had claimed that the American warships jammed its radars on 14 May when two Iraqi warplanes dropped parachute bombs on its four storage supertankers on Larak Island, severely damaging two vessels and killing 30 people. According to Tehran, the US navy had been jamming its radars in the Gulf since December 1987. As early as September 1987 it complained of US naval aircraft interfering with its coastal patrol planes. BBC World Service, 14 September 1987.

66. *Guardian*, 30 May 1988.

67. *Ibid.*, 24 June 1988.

68. *Independent*, 27 and 28 June 1988; *Jane's Defence Weekly*, 9 July 1988, p. 14.

69. *The Times*, 6 July 1988.

9 INTERNATIONALIZATION OF THE WAR

1. *Observer*, 20 April 1986.

2. *Middle East Economic Digest*, 19 April 1986, p. 20.

3. *Middle East Economic Survey*, 3 March 1986.

4. Laura Guazzone, 'Gulf Co-operation Council: The Security Policies', *Survival*, March–April 1988, p. 143.

5. Joseph Kostiner, 'Counterproductive Mediation: Saudi Arabia and the Iran Arms Deal', *Middle East Review*, Summer 1987, p. 45.

6. See Chapter 7, pp. 161–2.

7. *Nation*, 6 December 1986, pp. 625, 640–42; The National Security Archive, *The Chronology: The Documented Day-by-Day Account of the Secret Military Assistance to Iran and the Contras*, pp. 123, 148, 176, 181, 205, 261, 330 and 333.

8. High officials in Tehran had not expected someone of the stature of McFarlane to arrive, and they could not settle on their response. They therefore

approached Ayatollah Khomeini, who instructed them to find out what the special American envoy had to say, and nothing more. They sent senior English-speaking employees in the intelligence department of Premier Musavi to talk to McFarlane, making sure that the talks were tape-recorded. Interviews with well-placed sources in Tehran, January 1987.

9. *Nation*, 6 December 1986, pp. 625, 640–42; and The National Security Archive, *op. cit.*, pp. 495, 507, 531 and 536. So anxious was President Reagan to free the American hostages in Lebanon that in June 1986 he sanctioned military plans to rescue them. Nothing came of these secret schemes – described as 'hare-brained' in a confidential testimony by the CIA's chief of covert operations, Clair George. *Evening Standard*, 26 October 1988.

10. *International Herald Tribune*, 14 November 1986.

11. Tehran Radio, 7 November 1986; *Foreign Broadcast Information Service*, 20 November 1986. A mid-January 1987 meeting between US and Iranian representatives in Frankfurt, where the Americans unfolded a 'plan' to improve mutual relations, ended in failure when the Iranians (reported to be military purchasing agents) refused to discuss any 'plan' until Washington had released the $500 millions-worth of military spares paid for by the Shah. *Middle East Economic Digest*, 31 January 1987, p. 11.

12. *Philadelphia Inquirer*, 26 November 1986; *Nation*, 6 December 1986, pp. 625, 640–42. Most of the Israel–Iran arms trade was indirect, involving two or three intermediaries and liberal use of false end-user certificates. Physically, most of the shipments passed through Portugal where, after the necessary doctoring of documents, military goods were re-exported to Bandar Abbas.

13. See Chapter 3, n. 1.

14. *Observer*, 27 April 1986; The National Security Archive, *op. cit.*, pp. 291, 340 and 348–9.

15. Cited in Shahram Chubin and Charles Tripp, *Iran and Iraq at War*, I. B. Tauris, London, 1988, p. 281, n. 42.

16. *International Herald Tribune*, 20 January 1987.

17. *New York Times*, 18 December 1986; Stockholm International Peace Research Institute, *SIPRI Yearbook 1988: World Armaments and Disarmament*, Oxford University Press, Oxford and New York, 1988, p. 191. This was denied by Moscow. But the Iranians said that they had received arms from Moscow indirectly 'several times'. These included surface-to-air missiles and launchers.

18. *Los Angeles Times*, 26 December 1986.

19. *Guardian*, 15 March 1986; Associated Press, 24 March 1986.

20. *Wall Street Journal*, 5 January 1987; *Middle East Economic Digest*, 31 January 1987, p. 13.

21. *Keesing's Record of World Events*, vol. XXXIII, p. 35546.

22. *Washington Post*, 24 May and 13 October 1987; and United States Department of State, *Policy in the Persian Gulf: Special Report No. 166*, Government Printing Office, Washington, DC, July 1987, p. 10.

23. Cited in *Middle East International*, 17 April 1987, p. 12.

24. Dilip Hiro, *Islamic Fundamentalism*, Paladin Books, London, 1988, pp. 217–19.

25. *Washington Post*, 22 August 1987.

26. *Keesing's Record of World Events*, vol. XXXIV, p. 35677; *Observer*, 27 September 1987.

27. *Washington Post*, 8 July 1987; The International Institute for Strategic Studies, *Strategic Survey 1987–1988*, p. 130.

28. *Wall Street Journal*, 29 June 1987; *Independent*, 20 July 1987.

29. US Arms Control and Disarmament Agency, *World Military Expenditures and Arms Transfer 1987*, Government Printing Office, Washington, DC, 1988, p. 105.

30. *Arab News*, 2 June 1987; *Wall Street Journal*, 6 June 1987; *Observer*, 21 June 1987; *Keesing's Record of World Events*, vol. XXXIII, p. 35545.

31. US Arms Control and Disarmament Agency, *World Military Expenditures and Arms Transfer 1986*, 1987, Table III,

p. 144. Peking's military supplies to Baghdad included Chinese-made Badger bombers.

32. *Middle East Economic Digest*, 19 March 1987, p. 10.

33. Additionally, in November 1987, there were 15 American and three West European warships in the Arabian Sea. The International Institute for Strategic Studies, *op. cit.*, p. 130. This was the largest collection of Western navies since the 1950–53 Korean War.

34. *Guardian*, 11 August 1987.

35. Stockholm International Peace Research Institute, *op. cit.*, p. 195.

36. *Middle East Economic Digest*, 1 August 1987, p. 9.

37. *Le Figaro*, 4 November 1987; *Guardian*, 5 November 1987. See Chapter 5, pp. 125–7, and Chapter 7, pp. 165–6.

38. *Guardian*, 14 August 1987; *Independent*, 18 August 1987; *Middle East Economic Digest*, 12 September 1987, pp. 9–10. In April 1988 the Italian police seized 30 tonnes of unassembled armour-piercing bombs being put aboard an Iraqi Airways plane at Rome airport. It was discovered that since the ban on arms sales to Iraq and Iran in mid-1987 an Iraqi trading company had despatched 150 tonnes of weapons from Italy. *Middle East Economic Digest*, 29 April 1988, p. 21.

39. *Guardian*, 25 July 1987.

40. *Washington Post*, 22 September 1987.

41. Following Egypt's decision in September 1978 to sign a peace treaty with Israel, the Gulf states promised to pay financial subsidies to the front-line states of Syria, Jordan and Lebanon for 10 years. Saudi Arabia's annual subsidy to Syria amounted to $800 million; and Kuwait's $200 million. But they had all been erratic in fulfilling their pledges. By mid-1987 Syria was owed $1.8 billion by the Gulf states. *International Herald Tribune*, 18–19 July 1987; *Middle East International*, 7 November 1987.

42. The story leaked in June 1988 when some Egyptian military officers were caught attempting to smuggle out of America hi-tech materials to improve the accuracy of the modified surface-to-surface missile named Badr-2000 by the Egyptians and Al Hussein by the Iraqis. *Independent*, 27 June 1987; *The Middle East*, August 1988, p. 14.

43. Kuwait News Agency, 11 February 1988.

44. *The Middle East*, March 1988, p. 28; *Washington Post*, 5 March 1988.

45. BBC World Service, 30 November 1987; *Arab News*, 9 February 1988.

46. *Guardian*, 28 April 1988; *Middle East Economic Digest*, 6 May 1988, p. 8.

47. *Ibid.*, 17 October 1987, p. 22.

48. The International Institute for Strategic Studies, *op. cit.*, p. 131.

49. *Guardian*, 19 July 1988.

50. *Ibid.*, 13 July 1988; *Independent*, 18 July 1988; *The Middle East*, December 1988, pp. 20–2.

51. *Middle East Economic Digest*, 20 February 1988, p. 22; *Guardian*, 29 July 1988.

52. *Independent*, 24 October and 1 December 1987.

53. See Chapter 8, pp. 203–4.

54. Among the countries which resisted the US pressure were West Germany, Italy and Japan.

10 THE END

1. *Guardian*, 9 July 1988.

2. *Independent*, 18 July 1988.

3. *Middle East Economic Digest*, 29 July 1988, p. 12.

4. *Guardian*, 19 July 1988. An example of US financial aid to Baghdad was the sixfold increase in the American purchase of Iraqi oil: from 56,000 b/d in the first half of 1987 to 323,000 b/d in the following year. *Middle East Economic Digest*, 26 August 1988, p. 2.

5. BBC World Service, 20 July 1988; *Independent*, 21 July 1988.

6. *Middle East Economic Digest*, 29 July 1988, pp. 13–14.

7. *Sunday Times*, 24 July 1988.

8. *Independent*, 27 and 30 July 1988; *Guardian*, 27 and 30 July, and 5 September 1988. Among the NLA dead were leading military and political figures of the Mujahedin-e Khalq.

9. *Observer*, 7 August 1988.

10. Tehran Radio, 12 August 1988; *Guardian*, 20 August 1988.

11. Tehran Radio, 22 July 1988.

12. *Middle East Economic Digest*, 19 and 26 August 1988.

13. After the financial assistance of $1 billion a month that Saudi Arabia and Kuwait provided Iraq during the first two years of the conflict, this settled down to an average of $300 million a month for the rest of the war—consisting of such items as oil countersales, payments for weapons bought in the Soviet bloc or France, and deposits made to Western companies doing business with Iraq. To this sum of $45,300 million must be added the grants and loans of some $5000-7000 million by Quatar and the UAE. See Chapter 3, p. 77. See also Kamran, Mofid, *The Economic Consequences of the Gulf War*, Routledge, 1990, Chapter 10. These figures exclude the donations, running into hundreds of millions of US dollars, that Kuwaiti and Saudi citizens made to Iraq. See Chapter 9, p. 213.

14. *Middle East Economic Digest*, 12 August 1988, p. 11.

15. *The Times*, 19 July 1987, Tehran Radio, 19 September 1988. Of the 123,220 combatants killed, 79,644 belonged to the Revolutionary Guards Corps, 35,170 to the military and the rest to the gendarmerie, the Reconstruction Crusade, police and the Revolutionary Komitehs.

16. Stockholm International Peace Research Institute, *SIPRI Yearbook 1988*, p. 178; US Arms Control and Disarmament Agency, *Military Expenditures and Arms Transfers 1987*, p. 105. The military imports statistics have been obtained by adding the figures for 1987, published in *SIPRI Yearbook 1988*, to the totals for 1980-6 in *Military Expenditures and Arms Transfers 1987*.

17. *Independent*, 20 July 1988.

18. *Guardian*, 20 July 1988, *Middle East Economic Digest*, 5 August 1988, p. 25.

19. BBC World Service, 22 September 1988; *Independent*, 8 October 1988.

20. Unconfirmed reports say that Iran and Iraq have agreed informally on the composition and terms of the impartial commission to determine the origin of the Gulf War. It is to consist of three judges—including an Indian and a Yugoslav—presided over by a judge from the International Court of Justice and two liaison officers from Iran and Iraq. And it is to examine evidence starting 18 months before the outbreak of the war.

11 CONCLUSIONS

1. *International Herald Tribune*, 13 June 1985.

2. Tehran Radio, 8 February 1985. Premier Musavi echoed a similar sentiment. 'The pressure from the imposed war has in all honesty made Iran and its people a better nation,' he said. Tehran Radio, 5 December 1985.

3. Another main reason for adopting the Security Council resolution was a realization by Khomeini that following his death his successor, Montazeri, would not be able to tackle the twin problems of the war and the power vacuum created by his departure. He therefore decided to end the conflict and thus ensure the future of the Islamic revolution while he was still alive.

4. *Independent*, 21 July 1988.

5. These were the figures valid in January 1985. At the 1985 production rate of 4.2 billion barrels a year the Gulf reserves will last 100 years. In contrast, at the current production rate the petroleum reserves North America will be exhausted in 1ͅ years. *Middle East Economic Digest*, 16 ᴍ; 1987, p. 17.

6. *Ibid.*, 16 May 1987, p. 17; *Nation*, 19 September 1987, p. 262.

APPENDIX I:

Chronology

1968
July
17   A Baathist-led coup in Iraq.

1972
April
9   The Iraqi-Soviet Treaty of
Friendship and Co-operation is
signed.

1974
March
Iraqi Kurdish guerrillas, assisted
by Iranian, American and Israeli
weapons and expertise, mount an
escalating armed struggle against
the central government.

1975
March
6   An accord is signed in Algiers
between the Shah of Iran and
Saddam Hussein, vice-chairman
of the Revolutionary Command
Council of Iraq, to demarcate their
countries' river boundaries
according to the thalweg line, and
end all infiltrations of a
subversive nature (see Appendix
IV).
June
13   The Treaty concerning the
Frontier and Neighbourly
Relations between Iran and Iraq,
which defines the Shatt al Arab
border along the thalweg, is signed
(see Appendix V).

1977
February
Anti-government riots by Iraqi
Shias in Najaf and Karbala.

1978
October
The Shah of Iran is seriously
threatened by a revolutionary
movement guided by Ayatollah
Ruhollah Khomeini living in exile
in Najaf, Iraq. He is expelled by
the Iraqi government.

1979
February
11   An Islamic revolutionary regime
headed by Khomeini assumes
power in Iran.
June
Anti-government riots by Shias in
southern Iraqi cities and Baghdad.
July
16   Saddam Hussein becomes
president of Iraq, chairman of the
Revolutionary Command Council
and general secretary of the
Regional Command of the Baath
Party.
August
Executions of senior party and
state officials in Iraq, and a
widespread purge in the RCC,
Baath Party Regional Command
and provincial and local
governments.
Iran cancels $10 billions-worth
of arms contracts signed by the
Shah's regime with the US.
October
30   Iraq demands a revision of the
1975 border treaty.
November
4   Iranian students occupy US
embassy in Tehran and seize
documents and diplomats.
5   Iran abrogates the March 1959
mutual military agreement with
the US.

December

1   Iranians approve the new Islamic constitution in a referendum.

14   Tehran announces an Iraqi incursion into Iran which is repulsed.

1980

January

26   Abol Hassan Bani-Sadr is elected president of the Islamic Republic of Iran.

February

Periodic border clashes between Iran and Iraq against a background of hostile propaganda, which continue until the outbreak of war.

March

14   The first round of parliamentary elections in Iran.

April

1   An unsuccessful attempt to assassinate Tariq Aziz, deputy premier of Iraq.

8   Ayatollah Muhammad Baqir Sadr, an eminent leader of Iraqi Shias, is executed.

17   Khomeini urges the Iraqi people and military to overthrow the Baathist regime.

May

9   The second round of parliamentary elections in Iran.

June

20   Elections are held for the First National Assembly in Iraq.

July

9–10   A military coup by monarchist officers is thwarted in Iran.

August

5   President Saddam Hussein visits Riyadh and consults the Saudi monarch on his plans for war with Iran.

September

4   Iran shells the Iraqi towns of Khanaqin and Mandali. Later Iraq describes 4 September as the starting date of the war.

10   Baghdad claims to have liberated the disputed border territory in the central sector.

17   Saddam Hussein abrogates the 1975 Treaty with Iran and claims full sovereignty over the Shatt al Arab.

20   Iran calls up military reservists.

THE IRAN–IRAQ WAR

1980

September

22   Iraq invades Iran at eight points on land, and bombs Iranian airfields, military installations and economic targets.

23   Iran retaliates with bombing of Iraqi military and economic targets.

28   UN Security Council Resolution 479 urges cessation of hostilities. Iraq announces its readiness to cease fire if Iran accepts its complete rights over the Shatt al Arab. Tehran rejects the Security Council call.

30   America sends Awacs reconnaissance planes to Saudi Arabia.

October

13   Khomeini appoints President Bani-Sadr chairman of Iran's Supreme Defence Council.

November

10   Iraq captures Khorramshahr.

14–17   The Iraqis fail to gain Susangard.

December

Military stalemate caused by wet winter.

1981

January

1   Tehran merges the Basij-e Mustazafin militia with the Revolutionary Guards Corps.

5–10   Iran's counteroffensive in the Dezful–Susangard area is unsuccessful.

March

1–7   Mediation by the Islamic Conference Organization delegation fails.

May
25   Gulf Co-operation Council is established.

June
7   Israeli warplanes destroy a nuclear installation near Baghdad.
21   Khomeini dismisses President Bani-Sadr following his impeachment by parliament for incompetence.

July–August
    Iran mounts a series of small attacks in the area adjoining Abadan which is under siege.

September
27–29   The Iranians regain Abadan.

October
5   Hojatalislam Ali Hussein Khamanei is elected president of Iran.

November–December
    Iran retakes territories around Abadan and north of Susangard in a series of minor attacks.

1982

January
    Iraqi Kurdish guerrillas sabotage the oil pipeline to Turkey.

March
19–30   The Iranians expel the Iraqis from the Dezful–Shush area.

April
    Kurdish insurgency in Iraq intensifies.
10   Syria shuts off the pipeline carrying Iraqi oil to the Mediterranean.
12   Saddam Hussein states that Iraq will withdraw from Iran if it is assured that this would end the conflict.
29   Iran stages a major offensive, codenamed Bait al Muqaddas, in the southern sector.

May
24   The end of Iran's Bait al Muqaddas offensive, culminating in the retaking of Khorramshahr and driving the Iraqis back to the international border.
30   Anti-government riots in Shia-majority cities of southern Iraq.

June
5–6   Israel invades Lebanon.
7   The ICO appeals to Iran and Iraq to stop fighting.
9   After its meeting (not attended by Saddam Hussein) the RCC says that Iraq is ready for a ceasefire. Iran rejects the offer.
20   Saddam Hussein declares that Iraq's voluntary withdrawal from Iran will be completed by 30 June.
24–27   At the Ninth Regional Congress of the Baath Party, Saddam Hussein reasserts his total control, and institutes major reshuffles of the RCC, the party Regional Command and the cabinet.
30   Baghdad announces evacuation of Iran, but still holds some pockets of Iranian territory.

July
11   An attempt to assassinate Saddam Hussein in Dujayal fails.
13   Iran rejects UN Security Council Resolution 514 calling for a ceasefire and a withdrawal of the warring forces to the international border.
13–28   The Iranian offensive to capture Basra fails.

August
12   Iraq declares a maritime exclusion zone around Iran's Kharg Island oil terminal in the Gulf, making any vessel entering it liable to attack.

October
1–10   Iran's attempts to capture Mandali are unsuccessful.

November
1–11   Iranian offensives in the Musian area yield some gains.
17   The Supreme Assembly of Islamic Revolution in Iraq is formed in Tehran with the aim of overthrowing the Baathist regime in Baghdad.

1983

February
7–16   The Iranian offensive in the Fakeh

region of Khuzistan to capture the Basra–Baghdad road near Amara is unsuccessful. It scores only limited gains.

March

Iraq strikes Iran's Nowruz oilfield in the Gulf.

April
10–17   Iran stages an offensive in the Ein Khosh area to reach the Basra–Baghdad highway, but fails.

20–21   Iraq fires surface-to-surface missiles at Dezful.

May
4   The Iranian government dissolves the pro-Moscow Tudeh Party, and expels 18 Soviet diplomats.

July
22–29   Iran's offensive in Kurdistan yields it the garrison town of Hajj Umran.

30   Tehran stages an offensive west of Mehran in the central sector which achieves limited gains.

October

France delivers to Iraq five Super-Etendard fighter aircraft capable of firing Exocet anti-ship missiles.

20   Iran mounts an offensive in Kurdistan near Panjwin and makes modest gains.

1984

February
10–18   The Iraqi missiles fired at Dezful – and the Iranian shelling of Basra, Khanaqin and Mandali – start a round of attacks on civilian targets. These end with a UN-mediated agreement not to attack population centres.

16–24   The Iranian attempt to march from Dehloran into Iraq to cut off the Basra–Baghdad highway fails.

22   Tehran mounts a major offensive, codenamed Khaibar, in the Haur al Hawizeh marshes.

March
16   By the end of the Khaibar offensive Iran has retained control of Iraq's oil-rich Majnoon Islands

in the Haur al Hawizeh marshland.

21   UN experts conclude that chemical weapons were used against the Iranians.

27   Iraq uses the Super-Etendard–Exocet combination for the first time in its attacks on ships.

April
18   Iraq escalates the Tanker War.

April–May
Elections to the Second Islamic Majlis are held in Iran.

May
13   Iran retaliates by hitting ships serving Saudi and Kuwaiti ports in the Lower Gulf.

22   The naval units of the Revolutionary Guards Corps become operational.

June
1   The UN Security Council condemns attacks on ships trading with Saudi Arabia and Kuwait, and urges all states to respect free navigation in the Gulf.

5   Saudi Arabia shoots down an Iranian jet fighter allegedly violating its airspace.

12   A UN-sponsored ceasefire of attacks on population centres goes into effect with UN observers posted in Baghdad and Tehran to monitor breaches.

July
22   Hans Dietrich Genscher, the West German Foreign Minister, becomes the first senior Western leader to visit the Islamic Republic of Iran.

August
In response to continued Iraqi raids on Kharg and Iranian tankers, Tehran sets up a tanker shuttle between Kharg and the Sirri Island oil terminal in the Lower Gulf.

October
18–25   Iran retakes part of the disputed border territory in the central sector lost to Iraq just before the war.

20   General elections to the Second National Assembly of Iraq are held.

29   Khomeini calls for relations with all governments 'except a few'.

December

31   The year ends with 53 Iraqi attacks on shipping in the Gulf (against 16 in 1983) to Iran's 18 (none in the previous year).

1985

January–March

Baghdad claims to have hit 30 Iranian oil tankers in three months.

March

5   Iraq's bombing of Ahvaz and Bushahr starts another War of the Cities, with Iran firing surface-to-surface missiles at Baghdad and shelling Iraqi border towns.

11–20   Iran mounts an offensive in the Haur al Hawizeh marshes to seize the Basra–Baghdad road. An Iranian brigade reaches the highway on 17 March, but is unable to withstand the Iraqi counterattacks, which drive the invading forces back to their base.

April

6   A ceasefire in the War of the Cities.

May

18   Saudi foreign minister, Prince Saud al Faisal, visits Tehran. He fails to arrange a ceasefire in the Gulf War during the forthcoming month of Ramadan.

25   An attempt to assassinate the ruler of Kuwait fails.

26   Iraq resumes the War of the Cities and intensifies the Tanker War and strikes on Kharg.

June

14   A pro-government rally of between one and five million people is held in Tehran.

15   Baghdad announces a two-week suspension of aerial attacks on urban centres, and in fact fails to resume them.

July

14   Iran warns that it will stop and search ships in the Gulf suspected of carrying contraband or military goods to Iraq.

August

14–25   Intense and effective Iraqi air strikes against Kharg.

17   Khamanei is re-elected president of Iran.

September

8   The Iranian attack in the Rawandoz area in Kurdistan achieves a modest gain.

11   Tehran's plan to attack Basra after consolidating its hold over the Haur al Hawizeh is thwarted by strong Iraqi counterassaults.

13   Iran receives 508 US-made Tow missiles in a secret arms-for-hostages deal with the Reagan administration.

October

5   Since 14 August Iraq has staged 21 air sorties against Kharg.

November

11   Iran has inspected 300 ships in the Gulf since 4 September.

22   The Assembly of Experts names Ayatollah Hussein Ali Montazeri as the successor to Khomeini.

December

31   During 1985 Iraq hit 33 ships in the Gulf, and Iran 14.

1986

January

17   President Reagan authorizes the CIA to purchase 4000 Tow missiles from the Defense Department and sell them to Iran through Israel.

February

9–25   Of the three offensives mounted simultaneously by Iran, the southernmost, in the Fao peninsula, proves successful, providing a strategic foothold to Iranian forces and rekindling hopes of military victory over Iraq.

24   UN Security Council Resolution 582 deplores 'the initial acts

which gave rise to the conflict and the continuation of hostilities', and repeats earlier calls for an immediate truce.

24   Iran's offensive in the Suleimaniya region of Kurdistan, which ends in early March, brings the area near the Darbandi Khan Lake under its control.

1000 US-made Tow missiles are delivered to Iran through Israel.

March

9–10   Iraqi attempts to retake Fao fail.

24   Following a report by UN experts on the use of poison gases, the UN Security Council combines its condemnation of Iraq for deploying chemical weapons with its disapproval of the prolongation of the conflict.

April

Increased Kurdish guerrilla activity in northern Iraq. Oil price falls to below $10 a barrel from $27 a barrel in December.

22   US law enforcement officers arrest 10 of the 18 Americans, Israelis and West Europeans involved in two arms deals, worth $2380 million, concerning supply of US-made combat aircraft, transport planes, Tow and Hawk missiles, guided bombs and tanks to Iran.

May

Following Iraqi air raids on refineries in Tehran (in early May) and Isfahan (in mid-March), Iran starts importing refined oil products.

17   Iraq captures Mehran. Its offer to exchange Mehran for Fao is rejected by Tehran.

25   Robert McFarlane, former US National Security Adviser, arrives in Tehran on an official visit to bring about rapprochement between Iran and the US. His mission is a fiasco.

June

11   Hojatalislam Ali Akbar Hashemi Rafsanjani, the Majlis speaker, refers to the existence of 'two

relatively powerful factions' in Iranian politics with differences on the roles of the government and the private sector in the affairs of society.

July

Iraq intensifies its air strikes against Iran's economic and infrastructural targets.

1–9   Iran retakes Mehran.

3–4   Seven tonnes of US-made arms and spares are delivered to Iran via Spain and Yugoslavia.

At the extraordinary Congress of the Baath Party, Saddam Hussein tightens control by reshuffling the RCC, the party Regional Command and the cabinet.

August

An agreement between Iran and Saudi Arabia within OPEC lifts oil prices to the $14–16 a barrel range.

12   Iraq carries out a successful long-range air raid on Iran's Sirri Island oil terminal.

18   Iran states that it will resume gas exports to the Soviet Union, suspended since April 1980.

By late August Iraq has mounted a total of 120 air sorties against Kharg over the preceding twelve months.

September

1   Iran mounts a successful limited offensive in the Hajj Umran area of Kurdistan.

3   During an offensive in the Fao region the Iranians build another pontoon bridge across the Shatt al Arab.

16   Baghdad stages a successful air raid on Lavan oil terminal south of Kharg.

October

8   UN Security Council urges the warring nations to implement Resolution 582 and requests the secretary-general, Pérez de Cuellar, to intensify his mediation efforts.

9   Announcing fuel and power shortages, Tehran urges

conservation by consumers.

10 Assisted by Kurdish guerrillas, Iran carries out a commando raid on an oil pipeline near Kirkuk.

November

3 An article in the Beirut-based *Al Shiraa* reveals clandestine US weapons sales to Iran, and engenders a scandal of international proportions.

13 President Reagan states that the Iranian revolution is 'a fact of history', and that between American and Iranian national interests there need be 'no permanent conflict'.

20 Khomeini describes the Irangate affair as 'an issue greater than all our [previous] victories'.

25 Iraq stages its furthest air raid yet, and strikes Iran's Larak Island oil facilities.

December

23–25 Iran launches a major offensive, codenamed Karbala-Four, against the Iraqi forces near Basra. It fails.

27–28 A Conference on Solidarity with the Iraqi People, sponsored in Tehran by the SAIRI, decides to escalate the armed struggle against the Saddam Hussein regime.

31 During 1986 Iraq strikes 66 ships in the Gulf, twice the total for 1985; and Iran 41, nearly three times the previous year's figure.

1987

January

6 Iran launches a major offensive, codenamed Karbala-Five, to capture Basra.

13 The Iranians stage another offensive in the central sector near Qasr-e Shirin.

17–25 Iraq attacks Tehran and other Iranian cities with bombs and long-range surface-to-surface missiles. Iran retaliates with artillery and surface-to-surface missiles.

19–26 Iran mounts two more offensives in the south, and its forces reach

about seven miles from Basra, which is being progressively abandoned by its inhabitants.

25 Rafsanjani states that his country has no interest in expanding the war to other Gulf states, and calls on them to withdraw support from Iraq.

26 Addressing the Islamic Conference Organization summit in Kuwait, the UN secretary-general calls for the setting up of an international panel to decide which country was responsible for the war.

February

11 Khomeini explains that waging the war should be seen as 'a divine cause' rather than 'a single final offensive'.

18 At the behest of Moscow, Baghdad suspends the War of the Cities.

26 Iran declares the end of Karbala-Five offensive, which has brought it nearer to Basra and caused considerable loss to the Iraqi air force.

March

2 The Soviet Union agrees to lease three of its oil tankers to Kuwait.

4 Iran scores limited gains in an offensive in the Hajj Umran basin of Kurdistan.

7 The United States informs Kuwait that it will escort its oil carriers once these have been put under the American flag.

15 Saddam Hussein warns against 'a slow defeat through attrition'.

21 A massive demonstration is held in Baghdad to celebrate the failure of Khomeini to deliver his promise of turning the past year into the Iranian 'Year of Victory'.

23 Washington expresses concern at the prospect of Iran testing Silkworm anti-ship missiles in the Straits of Hormuz.

April

3 To prevent the transfer of Iraqi troops from the south to the north, the Iranians start draining water barriers protecting Basra

and mount an offensive.

9   An attempt to assassinate Saddam Hussein near Mosul fails.

13   The Iranians and their Kurdish allies capture strategic heights near Suleimaniya.

27   Iran gains ground near the Iraqi Kurdish towns of Mawet and Qala Diza.

May

6   The Iranians turn Farsi Island into a naval base.

    A Soviet freighter is hit by a mine in the Gulf.

16   A Kuwaiti-chartered Soviet tanker strikes a mine off Kuwait.

17   Two Iraqi Exocet missiles hit an American frigate in the Gulf and kill 37 crewmen.

June

    Iran gains more territory in Kurdistan near Suleimaniya and the hydro-electric dam on Darbandi Khan Lake.

2   Khomeini dissolves Iran's ruling Islamic Republican Party.

15   President Reagan explains that if the US did not protect shipping in the Gulf the Soviets would intervene.

20   Iraqi Kurdish guerrillas mount a series of minor offensives in Suleimaniya province.

July

20   The UN Security Council unanimously passes Resolution 598 calling for a ceasefire and withdrawal of warring forces. The ten-article text is comprehensive, and includes a clause for an impartial commission to determine war responsibility (see Appendix VI). Iraq accepts the resolution on the condition that Iran does the same.

24   A reflagged Kuwaiti supertanker, *Bridgeton*, escorted by US warships on the first Gulf convoy, hits a mine.

September

    America and Western Europe send warships including minehunters to the Gulf.

    Tehran fails to provide an unequivocal reply to Resolution 598, and states that its precondition for acceptance is the identification and condemnation of the invader. Meanwhile, it can offer a *de facto* ceasefire. Its demand that foreign fleets be withdrawn from the Gulf is backed by Moscow.

21   US naval helicopters destroy *Iran Ajr*, an Iranian ship, allegedly caught in the act of laying mines.

October

2   Iran and Iraq close down their diplomatic missions

7   US Congress votes to impose an embargo on all imports from Iran.

8   The Americans destroy three Iranian patrol boats near Farsi Island after claims that the Iranians fired on a US patrol helicopter.

16   An Iranian Silkworm missile hits an American-flagged supertanker in Kuwaiti waters and injures 18 crewmen.

19   US warships destroy two Iranian offshore oil platforms in retaliation for attacks on the supertanker.

22   Iran hits Kuwait's Sea Island oil terminal.

November

12   Khomeini refers to a modified strategy of the war which stresses the continuation of offensives in order to 'deprive the enemy of respite'.

December

    Iran stages probing attacks in the Fakeh area north of Basra.

31   During 1987 Iraq strikes 76 ships in the Gulf; and Iran 87, more than twice the previous year's total.

1988

January

    A minor offensive by Iran near Mawet in Kurdistan.

February

6   Khomeini appoints the Council for the Expediency of Islamic Order to resolve the legislative impasse.

27 Iraq renews the War of the Cities by bombing Saqqez in northern Iran. When Iran responds with missile attacks on Baghdad, Iraq hits Tehran with long-range surface-to-surface missiles for the first time.

March

13 Iran launches offensives in two areas in Kurdistan.

15 Assisted by its Kurdish allies, Iran captures Halabja in Kurdistan.

16 The Iraqi air force drops chemical bombs on Halabja, killing at least 4000 people.

    In late March Iran claims to be occupying 540 square miles in Kurdistan. And Kurdish rebels reportedly control 4000 square miles of rural Kurdistan.

April

8   The first round of parliamentary elections in Iran.

10 Iran launches an offensive in the Panjwin area of Kurdistan.

14 An American frigate strikes a mine in international waters off Bahrain.

16–18 The Iraqis recapture the Fao peninsula. They use chemical weapons.

18 US warships blow up two Iranian oil rigs, destroy an Iranian frigate and immobilize another, and sink an Iranian missile boat.

20 Iraq ends the War of the Cities having fired 200 long-range missiles at Iranian cities against Iran's 77.

May

13 The second round of parliamentary elections in Iran.

23–25 Iraq mounts offensives in the northern and central sectors, and then in the Shalamche region in the south. It retakes Shalamche, using chemical weapons.

28 The Third Islamic Majlis assembles in Tehran.

June

3   Khomeini appoints Rafsanjani as acting commander-in-chief of the armed forces in place of President Khamanei.

13 The Iranians penetrate the Shalamche area, then withdraw.

19–22 Iraq captures Mehran, using poison gases, and then hands it over to the anti-Khomeini National Liberation Army of Iran. The NLA is expelled by the Iranians.

25 The Iraqis recapture the Majnoon Islands.

30 Baghdad retakes Mawet in Kurdistan.

July

3   An American cruiser shoots down an Iran Air airbus with 290 people on board, mistaking it for an F-14 warplane.

9–10 The Iraqis regain territory in the Panjwin district.

12 Baghdad retakes the Iraqi territory in the Musian border region.

17 On the twentieth anniversary of the Baathist coup Saddam Hussein repeats his five-point peace plan, including a ceasefire and return to the international frontier, the signing of a peace treaty and a non-aggression pact, and a mutual agreement not to meddle in each other's domestic affairs.

18 Iran accepts UN Security Council Resolution 598 unconditionally.

20 Khomeini states that acceptance of a truce is 'in the interest of the revolution and the system at this juncture'. Iraq insists on direct negotiations with Iran, which the latter refuses.

22–29 The Iraqis mount offensives in the northern, central and southern sectors. They fail in the north, but advance elsewhere. The Iranians soon retake the territory lost in the south near Ahvaz. But it is another week before they regain the lost ground in the central sector from the occupying NLA forces.

August

1   A United Nations investigation concludes that Iraq made intensified use of chemical weapons in its military operations in the spring and summer.

6   Iraq withdraws its demand for direct talks with Iran.

20   A ceasefire comes into effect.

AFTER THE TRUCE

1988

August

25   Iran and Iraq commence talks in Geneva under the chairmanship of the UN secretary-general.

September–October

Negotiations stall. Baghdad demands the immediate clearance of the Shatt al Arab under the UN aegis while Tehran insists that, according to the 1975 Treaty, clearing the waterway is a joint responsibility of Iran and Iraq. Baghdad argues that the 1975 Treaty no longer exists; and Tehran states that, being a border agreement, it is valid for ever, and that such a document cannot be abrogated unilaterally.

1989

February

18   Iran's foreign minister, Velayati, reveals that Iraq is occupying 920 square miles of Iranian territory.

March

23   Responding to Baghdad's repeated calls for an immediate exchange of all prisoners of war, Velayati

urges Iraq to withdraw from all the occupied Iranian land forthwith.

28   Montazeri resigns as the successor-designate to Khomeini.

April

1   General elections to the Third National Assembly of Iraq are held.

June

3   Ayatollah Khomeini dies.

4   President Ali Khamanei is elected the Supreme Leader of Iran by the Assembly of Experts.

17   Arab Cooperation Council backs Iraq's claim to both banks of the Shatt al Arab and calls on the United Nations to clear the waterway of war debris.

July

28   Rafsanjani is elected president of Iran.

November

16   Iran's foreign minister proposes an immediate exchange of prisoners of war along with a simultaneous withdrawal of the two armies to the international border.

December

5   Iraq claims to have launched its first space rocket.

1990

January

11   The official Iranian and Iraqi news agencies announce that Tehran and Baghdad had welcomed the Soviet foreign minister's offer to host a meeting of the Iranian and Iraqi foreign ministers (under the UN aegis) to break the deadlock in the Gulf peace talks.

April

2   President Saddam Hussein declares that '[a] sophisticated binary chemical weapon' is available in Iraq.

APPENDIX II:

Iranian Armed Forces: 1980–88*

	1980	1988
FORCE RATIO		
Regular armed forces personnel/1000 inhabitants	6.3	13.2
Total Regular Armed Forces	246,000	644,800
GROUND FORCES		
(A) Regular Army		
Active	150,000	305,000
Reserves	400,000	350,000
(B) Revolutionary Guards Corps		
Active	Nil	250,000
Reserves	Nil	400,000
(C) Basij-e Mustazafin (para-military)		
Active	Nil	350,000
Reserves	Nil	2,650,000
In Service Equipment		
Battle Tanks	1740	1575
Armoured Fighting Vehicles	1075	1800
Major Artillery	1000	1750
AIR FORCES		
(A) Regular Air Force	70,000	35,000
(B) Revolutionary Guards Corps Air Units	Nil	4800
In Service Equipment		
Combat aircraft	445	90
Combat helicopters	500	341
Total helicopters	750	423
NAVAL FORCES		
(A) Regular Navy	26,000	20,000
(B) Revolutionary Guards Corps Naval Units	Nil	30,000
In Service Equipment		
Destroyers	3	3
Frigates	4	5
Mine warfare vessels	Nil	5
Missile craft	9	10

APPENDIX III:

Iraqi Armed Forces: 1980–88*

	1980	1988
FORCE RATIO		
Regular armed forces personnel/1000 inhabitants	18.9	63.3
Total Regular Armed Forces	242,250	1,000,000
GROUND FORCES		
(A) Regular Army		
Active	200,000	955,000
Reserves	250,000	Nil
(B) Popular Army (para-military)		
Active	250,000	250,000
Reserves	Nil	400,000
In Service Equipment		
Battle Tanks	2500	4500
Armoured Fighting Vehicles	2000	3200
Major Artillery	1000	2800
AIR FORCES		
Regular Air Force	38,000	40,000
In Service Equipment		
Combat aircraft	335	484
Combat helicopters	40	232**
Total helicopters	250	372**
NAVAL FORCES		
Regular Navy	4250	5000
In Service Equipment		
Frigates	1	1
Mine warfare vessels	8	8
Missile craft	12	8

* Adapted from various editions of *The Military Balance*, published by
The International Institute for Strategic Studies, London, and
Mednews: Middle East Defense News, published by Mednews, Paris.
The 1988 figures apply to the beginning of the year.
** In 1985 the helicopter fleet was transferred from the Iraqi air force
to the army.

APPENDIX IV:

The Algiers Accord 6 March 1975

During the convocation of the OPEC summit conference in the Algerian capital and upon the initiative of President Houari Boumedienne, the Shah of Iran and Saddam Hussein (Vice-Chairman of the Revolution Command Council) met twice and conducted lengthy talks on the relations between Iraq and Iran. These talks, attended by President Houari Boumedienne, were characterized by complete frankness and a sincere will from both parties to reach a final and permanent solution of all problems existing between their two countries in accordance with the principles of territorial integrity, border inviolability and non-interference in internal affairs.

The two High Contracting Parties have decided to:

First: Carry out a final delineation of their land boundaries in accordance with the Constantinople Protocol of 1913 and the Proceedings of the Border Delimitation Commission of 1914.

Second: Demarcate their river boundaries according to the thalweg line.

Third: Accordingly, the two parties shall restore security and mutual confidence along their joint borders. They shall also commit themselves to carry out a strict and effective observation of their joint borders so as to put a final end to all infiltrations of a subversive nature wherever they may come from.

Fourth: The two parties have also agreed to consider the aforesaid arrangements as inseparable elements of a comprehensive solution. Consequently, any infringement of one of its components shall naturally contradict the spirit of the Algiers Accord. The two parties shall remain in constant contact with President Houari Boumedienne who shall provide, when necessary, Algeria's brotherly assistance whenever needed in order to apply these resolutions.

The two parties have decided to restore the traditional ties of good neighbourliness and friendship, in particular by eliminating all negative factors in their relations and through constant exchange of views on issues of mutual interest and promotion of mutual co-operation.

The two parties officially declare that the region ought to be secure from any foreign interference.

The Foreign Ministers of Iraq and Iran shall meet in the presence of Algeria's Foreign Minister on 15 March 1975 in Tehran in order to make working arrangements for the Iraqi-Iranian joint commission which was set up to apply the resolutions taken by mutual agreement as specified above. And in accordance with the desire of the two parties, Algeria shall be invited to the meetings of the Iraqi-Iranian joint commission. The commission shall determine its agenda and working procedures and hold meetings if necessary. The meetings shall be alternately held in Baghdad and Tehran.

His Majesty the Shah of Iran accepted with pleasure the invitation extended to him by His Excellency President Ahmad Hassan Bakr to pay a state visit to Iraq. The date of the visit shall be fixed by mutual agreement.

On the other hand, Saddam Hussein agreed to visit Iran officially at a date to be fixed by the two parties.

H.M. the Shah of Iran and Saddam Hussein expressed their deep gratitude to President Houari Boumedienne, who, motivated by brotherly sentiments and a spirit of disinterestedness, worked for the establishment of a direct contact between the leaders of the two countries and consequently contributed to reviving a new era in Iraqi-Iranian relations with a view to achieving the higher interest of the future of the region in question.

APPENDIX V:

Treaty concerning the frontier and neighbourly relations between Iran and Iraq 13 June 1975

His Imperial Majesty the Shahinshah of Iran,

His Excellency the President of the Republic of Iraq,

Considering the sincere desire of the two Parties as expressed in the Algiers Agreement of 6 March 1975, to achieve a final and lasting solution to all the problems pending between the two countries,

Considering that the two Parties have carried out the definitive redemarcation of their land frontier on the basis of the Constantinople Protocol of 1913 and the minutes of the meetings of the Frontier Delimitation Commission of 1914 and have delimited their river frontier along the thalweg,

Considering their desire to restore security and mutual trust throughout the length of their common frontier,

Considering the ties of geographical proximity, history, religion, culture and civilization which bind the peoples of Iran and Iraq,

Desirous of strengthening their bonds of friendship and neighbourliness, expanding their economic and cultural relations and promoting exchange and human relations between their peoples on the basis of the principles of territorial integrity, the inviolability of frontiers and non-interference in internal affairs,

Resolved to work towards the introduction of a new era in friendly relations between Iran and Iraq based on full respect for the national independence and sovereign equality of States,

Convinced that they are helping thereby to implement the principles and achieve the purposes and objectives of the Charter of the United Nations,

Have decided to conclude this Treaty and have appointed as their plenipotentiaries:

His Imperial Majesty the Shahinshah of Iran:
His Excellency Abbas Ali Khalatbary, Minister for Foreign Affairs of Iran.

His Excellency the President of the Republic of Iraq:
His Excellency Saadoun Hamadi, Minister for Foreign Affairs of Iraq.

Who, having exchanged their full powers, found to be in good and due form, have agreed as follows:

Article 1

The High Contracting Parties confirm that the State land frontier between Iraq and Iran shall be that which has been redemarcated on the basis of and in accordance with the provisions of the Protocol concerning the redemarcation of the land frontier, and the annexes thereto, attached to this Treaty.

Article 2

The High Contracting Parties confirm that the State frontier in the Shatt al Arab shall be that which has been delimited on the basis of and in accordance with the provisions of the Protocol concerning the delimitation of the river frontier, and the annexes thereto, attached to this Treaty.

Article 3

The High Contracting Parties undertake to exercise strict and effective permanent control over the frontier in order to put an end to any infiltration of a subversive nature from any source, on the basis of and in accordance with the provisions of the Protocol concerning frontier security, and the annex thereto, attached to this Treaty.

Article 4

The High Contracting Parties confirm that the provisions of the three Protocols, and the annexes thereto, referred to in articles 1, 2, and 3 above and attached to this Treaty as an integral part thereof shall be final and permanent. They shall not be infringed under any circumstances and shall constitute the indivisible elements of an overall settlement. Accordingly, a breach of any of the components of this overall settlement shall clearly be incompatible with the spirit of the Algiers Agreement.

Article 5

In keeping with the inviolability of the frontiers of the two States and strict respect for their territorial integrity, the High Contracting Parties confirm that the course of their land and river frontiers shall be inviolable, permanent and final.

Article 6

1. In the event of a dispute regarding the interpretation or implementation of this Treaty, the three Protocols or the annexes thereto, any solution to such a dispute shall strictly respect the course of the Iraqi-Iranian frontier referred to in articles 1 and 2 above, and shall take into account the need to maintain security on the Iraqi-Iranian frontier in accordance with article 3 above.

2. Such disputes shall be resolved in the first instance by the High Contracting Parties, by means of direct bilateral negotiations to be held within two months after the date on which one of the Parties so requested.

3. If no agreement is reached, the High Contracting Parties shall have recourse, within a three-month period, to the good offices of a friendly third State.

4. Should one of the two Parties refuse to have recourse to good offices or should the good offices procedure fail, the dispute shall be settled by arbitration within a period of not more than one month after the date of such refusal or failure.

5. Should the High Contracting Parties disagree as to the arbitration procedure, one of the High Contracting Parties may have recourse, within 15 days after such disagreement was recorded, to a court of arbitration.

With a view to establish such a court of arbitration each of the High Contracting Parties shall, in respect of each dispute to be resolved, appoint one of its nationals as arbitrators and the two arbitrators shall choose an umpire. Should the High Contracting Parties fail to appoint their arbitrators within one month after the date on which one of the Parties received a request for arbitration from the other Party, or should the arbitrators fail to reach agreement on the choice of the umpire before that time-limit expires, the High Contracting Party which requested arbitration shall be entitled to request the President of the International Court of Justice to appoint the arbitrators or the umpire, in accordance with the procedures of the Permanent Court of Arbitration.

6. The decision of the court of arbitration shall be binding on and enforceable by the High Contracting Parties.

7. The High Contracting Parties shall each defray half the costs of arbitration.

Article 7

This Treaty, the three Protocols and the annexes thereto shall be registered in accordance with Article 102 of the Charter of the United Nations.

Article 8

This Treaty, the three Protocols and the annexes thereto shall be ratified by each of the High Contracting Parties in accordance with its domestic law.

This Treaty, the three Protocols and the annexes thereto shall enter into force on the date of the exchange of the instruments of ratification in Tehran.

IN WITNESS WHEREOF the Plenipotentiaries of the High Contracting Parties have signed this Treaty, the three Protocols and the annexes thereto.

Baghdad, 13 June 1975.

(Signed)   *(Signed)*

Abbas Ali Khalatbary   Saadoun Hamadi
Minister for Foreign Affairs of Iran   Minister for Foreign Affairs of Iraq

This Treaty, the three Protocols and the annexes thereto were signed in the presence of His Excellency Abdel-Aziz Bouteflika, Member of the Council of the Revolution and Minister for Foreign Affairs of Algeria

(Signed)

PROTOCOL CONCERNING THE DELIMITATION TO THE RIVER FRONTIER BETWEEN IRAN AND IRAQ

Pursuant to the decisions taken in the Algiers communiqué of 6 March 1975,
The two Contracting Parties have agreed as follows:

Article 1

The two Contracting Parties hereby declare and recognize that the State river frontier between Iran and Iraq in the Shatt al Arab has been delimited along the thalweg by the Mixed Iraqi-Iranian-Algerian Committee on the basis of the following:

1. The Tehran Protocol of 17 March 1975;

2. The record of the Meeting of Ministers for Foreign Affairs, signed at Baghdad on 20 April 1975, approving, *inter alia*, the record of the Committee to Delimit the River Frontier, signed on 16 April 1975 on board the Iraqi ship *El Thawra* in the Shatt al Arab;

3. Common hydrographic charts, which have been verified on the spot and corrected and on which the geographical co-ordinates of the 1975 frontier crossing points have been indicated; these charts have been signed by the hydrographic experts of the Mixed

Technical Commission and countersigned by the heads of the Iran, Iraq and Algerian delegations to the Committee. The said charts, listed hereinafter, are annexed to this Protocol and form an integral part thereof:

Chart No. 1: Entrance to the Shatt al Arab, No. 3842, published by the British Admiralty;

Chart No. 2: Inner Bar of Kabda Point, No. 3843, published by the British Admiralty;

Chart No. 3: Kabda Point to Abadan, No. 3844, published by the British Admiralty;

Chart No. 4: Abadan to Jazirat Ummat Tuwaylah, No. 3845, published by the British Admiralty.

Article 2

1. The frontier line in the Shatt al Arab shall follow the thalweg, i.e., the median line of the main navigable channel at the lowest navigable level, starting from the point at which the land frontier between Iran and Iraq enters the Shatt al Arab and continuing to the sea.

2. The frontier line, as defined in paragraph 1 above, shall vary with changes brought about by natural causes in the main navigable channel. The frontier line shall not be affected by other changes unless the two Contracting Parties conclude a special agreement to that effect.

3. The occurrence of any of the changes referred to in paragraph 2 above shall be attested jointly by the competent technical authorities of the two Contracting Parties.

4. Any change in the bed of the Shatt al Arab brought about by natural causes which would involve a change in the national character of the two States' respective territory or of landed property, constructions, or technical or other installations shall not change the course of the frontier line, which shall continue to follow the thalweg in accordance with the provisions of paragraph 1 above.

5. Unless an agreement is reached between the two Contracting Parties concerning the transfer of the frontier line to the new bed, the water shall be redirected at the joint expense of both Parties to the bed existing in 1975 – as marked on the four common charts listed in article 1, paragraph 3, above – should one of the Parties so request within two years after the date on which the occurrence of the change was attested by either of the two Parties. Until such time, both Parties shall retain their previous rights of navigation and of use over the water of the new bed.

Article 3

1. The river frontier between Iran and Iraq in the Shatt al Arab, as defined in article 2 above, is represented by the relevant line drawn on the common charts referred to in article 1, paragraph 3, above.

2. The two Contracting Parties have agreed to consider that the river frontier shall end at the straight line connecting the two banks of the Shatt al Arab, at its mouth, at the astronomical lowest low-water mark. This straight line has been indicated on the common hydrographic charts referred to in article 1, paragraph 3, above.

Article 4

The frontier line as defined in articles 1, 2 and 3 of this Protocol shall also divide vertically the airspace and the subsoil.

Article 5

With a view to eliminating any source of controversy, the two Contracting Parties shall establish a Mixed Iraqi-Iranian Commission to settle, within two months, any questions concerning the status of landed property, constructions, or technical or other installations, the national character of which may be affected by the delimitation of the Iranian-Iraqi river frontier, either through repurchase or compensation or any other suitable arrangement.

Article 6

Since the task of surveying the Shatt al Arab has been completed and the common hydrographic chart referred to in article 1, paragraph 3, above has been drawn up, the two Contracting Parties have agreed that a new survey of the Shatt al Arab shall be carried out jointly, once every 10 years, with effect from the date of signature of this Protocol. However, each of the two Parties shall have the right to request new surveys, to be carried out jointly, before the expiry of the 10-year period.

The two Contracting Parties shall each defray half the cost of such surveys.

Article 7

1. Merchant vessels, State vessels and warships of the two Contracting Parties shall enjoy freedom of navigation in the Shatt al Arab and in any part of the navigable channels in the territorial sea which lead to the mouth of the Shatt al Arab, irrespective of the line delimiting the territorial sea of each of the two countries.

2. Vessels of third countries used for purposes of trade shall enjoy freedom of navigation, on an equal and non-discriminatory basis, in the Shatt al Arab and in any part of the navigable channels in the territorial sea which lead to the mouth of the Shatt al Arab, irrespective of the line delimiting the territorial sea of each of the two countries.

3. Either of the two Contracting Parties may authorize frontier warships visiting its ports to enter the Shatt al Arab, provided such vessels do not belong to a country in a state of belligerency, armed conflict or war with either of the two Contracting Parties and provided the other Party is so notified no less than 72 hours in advance.

4. The two Contracting Parties shall in every case refrain from authorizing the entry to the Shatt al Arab of merchant vessels belonging to a country in a state of belligerency, armed conflict or war with either of the two Parties.

Article 8

1. Rules governing navigation in the Shatt al Arab shall be drawn up by a mixed Iranian-Iraqi Commission, in accordance with the principle of equal rights of navigation for both States.

2. The two Contracting Parties shall establish a Commission to draw up rules governing the prevention and control of pollution in the Shatt al Arab.

3. The two Contracting Parties undertake to conclude subsequent agreements on the questions referred to in paragraphs 1 and 2 of this article.

Article 9

The two Contracting Parties recognize that the Shatt al Arab is primarily an international waterway, and undertake to refrain from any operation that might hinder navigation in the Shatt al Arab or in any part of those navigable channels in the territorial sea of either of the two countries that lead to the mouth of the Shatt al Arab.

Baghdad, 13 June 1975.

(Signed)   *(Signed)*

Abbas Ali Khalatbary   Saadoun Hamadi
Minister for Foreign Affairs of Iran   Minister for Foreign Affairs of Iraq

Signed in the presence of His Excellency Abdel-Aziz Bouteflika, Member of the Council of the Revolution and Minister for Foreign Affairs of Algeria

(Signed)

APPENDIX VI:

United Nations Security Council Resolution 598
20 July 1987

The Security Council,

Reaffirming its resolution 582 (1986)

Deeply concerned that, despite its calls for a ceasefire, the conflict between Iran and Iraq continues unabated, with further heavy loss of human life and material destruction,

Deploring the initiation and continuation of the conflict,

Deploring also the bombing of purely civilian population centres, attacks on neutral shipping or civilian aircraft, the violation of international humanitarian law and other laws of armed conflict, and, in particular, the use of chemical weapons contrary to obligations under the 1925 Geneva Protocol,

Deeply concerned that further escalation and widening of the conflict may take place,

Determined to bring to an end all military actions between Iran and Iraq,

Convinced that a comprehensive, just, honourable and durable settlement should be achieved between Iran and Iraq,

Recalling the provisions of the Charter of the United Nations and in particular the obligation of all member states to settle their international disputes by peaceful means in such a manner that international peace and security and justice are not endangered,

Determining that there exists a breach of the peace as regards the conflict between Iran and Iraq,

Acting under Articles 39 and 40 of the Charter of the United Nations,

1. Demands that, as a first step toward a negotiated settlement, Iran and Iraq observe an immediate ceasefire, discontinue all military actions on land, at sea and in the air, and withdraw all forces to the internationally recognized boundaries without delay;

2. Requests the Secretary-General to despatch a team of United Nations observers to verify, confirm and supervise the ceasefire and withdrawal and further requests the Secretary-General to make the necessary arrangements in consultation with the parties and to submit a report thereon to the Security Council;

3. Urges that prisoners of war be released and repatriated without delay after the cessation of active hostilities in accordance with the Third Geneva Convention of 12 August 1949;

4. Calls upon Iran and Iraq to co-operate with the Secretary General in implementing this resolution and in mediation efforts to achieve a comprehensive, just and honourable settlement, acceptable to both sides, of all outstanding issues in accordance with the principles contained in the Charter of the United Nations;

5. Calls upon all other states to exercise the utmost restraint and to refrain from any act which may lead to further escalation and widening of the conflict and thus to facilitate the implementation of the present resolution;

6. Requests the Secretary-General to explore, in consultation with Iran and Iraq, the question of entrusting an impartial body with inquiring into responsibility for the conflict and to report to the Security Council as soon as possible;

7. Recognizes the magnitude of the damage inflicted during the conflict and the need for reconstruction efforts with appropriate international assistance once the conflict is ended and in this regard requests the Secretary-General to assign a team of experts to study the question of reconstruction and to report to the Security Council;

8. Further requests the Secretary-General to examine in consultation with Iran and Iraq and with other states of the region measures to enhance the security and stability of the region;

9. Requests the Secretary-General to keep the Security Council informed on the implementation of this resolution;

10. Decides to meet again as necessary to consider further steps to ensure compliance with this resolution.

SELECT BIBLIOGRAPHY

Abdulghani, Jasim M., *Iran and Iraq: The Years of Crisis*, Croom Helm, London, and The Johns Hopkins University Press, Baltimore, MD, 1984.

Algar, Hamid (trans.), *Constitution of the Islamic Republic of Iran*, Mizan Press, Berkeley, CA, 1980.

Arberry, Arthur J. (trans.), *The Koran Interpreted*, Oxford University Press, Oxford and New York, 1964.

Axelgard, Frederick W., *A New Iraq? The Gulf War and Implications for US Policy*, Praeger, New York and London, 1988.

Bakhash, Shaul, *Reign of the Ayatollahs: Iran and the Islamic Revolution*, I. B. Tauris, London, 1985.

Chubin, Shahram, and Tripp, Charles, *Iran and Iraq at War*, I. B. Tauris, London, 1988.

Cole, Juan R. I., and Keddie, Nikki R. (eds), *Shi'ism and Social Protest*, Yale University Press, New Haven, Conn., and London, 1986.

Committee Against Repression and for Democratic Rights in Iraq, *Saddam's Iraq: Revolution or Reaction?*, Zed Press, London, 1986.

Cordesman, Anthony H., *The Gulf and the Search for Strategic Stability: Saudi Arabia, the Military Balance in the Gulf, and Trends in the Arab–Israeli Military Balance*, Mansell, London, and Westview Press, Boulder, Colo., 1984.

Cordesman, Anthony H., *The Iran–Iraq War and Western Security 1984–87: Strategic Implications and Policy Options*, Jane's Publishing Company, London, 1987.

De Bock, Walter, and Deniau, Jean-Charles, *Des Armes pour l'Iran: L'Irangate Européen*, Gallimard, Paris, 1988.

Dishon, Daniel, Legum, Colin, and Shaked, Haim (eds), *Middle East Contemporary Survey: Volume V*,
1980–81, Holmes & Meier, New York and London, 1983.

Dishon, Daniel, Legum, Colin, and Shaked, Haim (eds), *Middle East Contemporary Survey: Volume VI, 1981–82*, Holmes & Meier, New York and London, 1984.

Dishon, Daniel, and Shaked, Haim (eds), *Middle East Contemporary Survey: Volume VIII, 1983–84*, Holmes & Meier, New York and London, 1986.

Farah, Elyas, *Evolution of Arab Revolutionary Ideology*, Arab Baath Socialist Party, Madrid, 1979.

Farouk-Sluglett, Marion, and Sluglett, Peter, *Iraq Since 1958: From Revolution to Dictatorship*, KPI Ltd, London, 1987.

Ghareeb, Edmund, *The Kurdish Question in Iraq*, Syracuse University Press, Syracuse, NY, 1981.

Graham, Robert, *Iran: The Illusion of Power*, Croom Helm, London, 1978.

Helms, Christine Moss, *Iraq: Eastern Flank of the Arab World*, The Brookings Institution, Washington, DC, 1984.

Hiro, Dilip, *Inside the Middle East*, Routledge & Kegan Paul, London, and McGraw-Hill, New York, 1982.

Hiro, Dilip, *Iran Under the Ayatollahs*, Routledge & Kegan Paul, London and New York, 1985.

Hiro, Dilip, *Islamic Fundamentalism*, Paladin Books, London, 1988.

Hussein, Saddam, *The Arab Heritage and Contemporary Life* (in Arabic), Dar al Hurriya li al Tibba, Baghdad, 1978.

Hussein, Saddam, *Iraqi Policies in Perspective*, Translation and Foreign Languages Publishing House, Baghdad, 1981.

Ismail, Tareq Y., *Iraq and Iran: Roots of Conflict*, Syracuse University Press, Syracuse, NY, 1982.

Karsh, Efram, *The Iran–Iraq War: A Military Analysis*, Adelphi Papers, The

International Institute for Strategic Studies, London, 1987.

Khadduri, Majid, *Socialist Iraq: A Study in Iraqi Politics since 1968*, the Middle East Institute, Washington, DC, 1978.

Khumayni, Ruh Allah, *Islam and Revolution: Writings and Declarations* [trans. Hamid Algar], Mizan Press, Berkeley, CA, 1981, and KPI Ltd, London, 1985.

King, Ralph, *The Iran-Iraq War: The Political Implications*, Adelphi Papers, The International Institute for Strategic Studies, London, 1987.

Laffin, John L., *War Manual I*, Brassey's Defence Publishers, London, 1986.

Marr, Phebe, *Modern History of Iraq*, Longman, London, 1985, and Westview Press, Boulder, Colo., 1985.

McDowall, David, *The Kurds*, Minority Rights Group, London, 1985.

McLachlan, Keith, and Joffé, George, *The Gulf War: A Survey of Political Issues and Economic Consequences*, The Economist Intelligence Unit, London, 1984.

Mofid, Kamran, *The Economic Consequences of the Gulf War*, Routledge, 1990.

Naff, Thomas [ed.], *Gulf Security and the Iran-Iraq War*, National Defense University Press, Washington, DC, 1985.

The National Security Archive, *The Chronology: The Documented Day-by-Day Account of the Secret Military Assistance to Iran and the Contras*, Warner Books, New York, 1987.

Nonneman, Gerd, *Iraq, the Gulf States and the War: A Changing Relationship 1980–86 and Beyond*, Ithaca Press, London and Atlantic Highlands, 1986.

O'Ballance, Edgar, *The Gulf War*, Brassey's Defence Publishers, London, 1988.

Rabinovich, Itamar, and Shaked, Haim [eds.], *Middle East Contemporary Survey: Volume IX, 1984–85*, Westview Press, Boulder, Colo., 1987.

Ramazani, R.K., *Revolutionary Iran: Challenge and Response in the Middle East*, The John Hopkins University Press,

Baltimore, MD, and London, 1986.

Seale, Patrick, *Asad: The Struggle for the Middle East*, I.B. Tauris, London, 1988.

Tahir-Kheli, Shirin, and Ayubi, Shaheen [eds.], *The Iran-Iraq War: New York Weapons, Old Conflicts*, Praeger, New York, 1983.

NEWS AGENCIES, NEWSPAPERS AND PERIODICALS

Arab News (Jiddah)
Arabia: The Islamic World Review (Slough)
Baghdad Observer (Baghdad)
BBC Summary of World Broadcasts (Reading)
Christian Science Monitor (Boston)
Current History (Philadelphia)
Daily Telegraph (London)
Al Dastur (London)
Economist (London)
Financial Times (London)
Foreign Affairs (New York)
Foreign Broadcast Information Service (Washington)
Foreign Report (London)
Guardian (London)
Al Hawadith (Beirut)
In These Times (Chicago)
Independent (London)
International Herald Tribune (Paris)
Iran Press Digest (Tehran)
Iran Times (London)
Iraqi News Agency (Baghdad)
Islamic Republic News Agency (Tehran)
Ittilaat (Tehran)
Jane's Defence Weekly (London)
Jumhourri-ye Islami (Tehran)
Al Jumhuriya (Baghdad)
Kayhan (Tehran)
Kayhan International (Tehran)
Keesing's Record of World Events (Harlow)
Khaleej Times (Dubai)
Le Monde (Paris)
Mednews: Middle East Defence News (Paris)
MERIP Middle East Report (Washington)
MERIP Reports (Washington)
The Middle East (London)
Middle East Economic Digest (London)

Middle East Insight (Washington)
Middle East International (London)
Middle East Journal (Washington)
Middle East Review (New Brunswick)
Middle Eastern Studies (London)
Nation (New York)
New York Times (New York)
Newsweek (New York)
Observer (London)
Orient (Hamburg)

Al Siyasa (Kuwait)
Sunday Times (London)
Survival (London)
Tass (Moscow)
Al Thawra (Baghdad)
Tehran Times (Tehran)
Time (New York)
The Times (London)
Wall Street Journal (New York)
Washington Post (Washington)

INDEX

For a name starting with Al, El, Ol or Ul, see its second part. A person's religious or secular title has been excluded.

Abadan, 10, 12, 17, 40, 41, 42, 43, 45, 48, 49, 52, 53, 54, 55, 146, 254
Abadan Island, 41, 52
Abdullah ibn Abdul Aziz (Saudi crown prince), 114
Abu Dhabi, 77, 116, 235
Abu Khasib, 180, 181, 182
Abu Musa Island, 14, 35, 77, 187
Abu Nidal, 147
Afghanistan, 37, 71, 73, 122, 162, 263
Aflaq, Michel, 18, 20, 24, 30–1, 93
Ahvaz, 38, 40, 41, 42, 43, 48, 49, 50, 52, 134, 162, 175, 222, 246
Alawi (Muslims), 18, 80
Albu Nasir tribe, 29
Alexandria, 223
Algeria, 16, 79, 128, 154, 157, 158
Algiers, 17
Algiers Accord (Iranian-Iraqi, 1975), 10, 17, 21, 25, 26, 28, 33, 38, 39
Ali ibn Abi Talib, 8, 21, 26, 34, 62
Amara, 95, 103, 137
Amiri, Hassan Ali, 65
Amsterdam, 82
Anglo-French-Israeli aggression (1956), 19
Anglo-Persian Oil Company, 10, 11
Aqaba, 79
Arab Baath Party, 18, 19
Arab Baath Socialist Party, see Baath Socialist Party
Arab-Israeli War (1967), 160
Arab-Israeli War (1973), 315
Arab League, 16, 27, 38, 69, 79, 91, 114, 115, 116, 153, 191, 233, 236
Arab Socialist Party, 19
Arabian Gulf, see Gulf
Arabian Sea, 15
Arabic language, 108
Arabism, 34, 66, 93, 258
Arabistan, 9, 12, 38, 75, 254; see also Khuzistan
Arabit, 186
Arabs, 10, 13; (Iran) 16, 35, 88; (Iraq) 3, 13
Arak, 33
Ararat Mountain, 9
Arbil, 16, 150
Ardebili, Kazem, 162
Ardeshir offshore oilfield, 187
Argov, Shlomo, 163
Arif, Abdul Rahman, 19, 26
Arif, Abdul Salam, 19, 23, 29
Armed Forces General Command Headquarters (Iran), 242
Armitage, Richard, 186

Arsuzi, Zaki, 18
Arvand, Rud, 8
Asghar-Owladi, Habibollah, 142
Ashura, 22, 114
Ashura offensives, 141
Assad, Hafiz, 5, 27, 57, 62, 80, 154, 155, 213, 216, 233, 234, 265
Assassination Attempts on the Life of President Saddam Hussein, 98
Assembly of Experts (Iran), 150–1, 242
Athens, 118, 161
Auja, 29
Austria, 1, 82, 127, 128
Azerbaijan, 46
Aziz, Tariq, 28, 35, 50, 63, 74, 82, 84, 100, 119, 123, 124, 132, 149, 160, 163, 245, 252
Azizi, Faroukh, 118

Baath Socialist Party and Baathists (Iraq), 12, 14, 16–21, 23, 24, 25, 26, 27, 29, 30, 34, 35, 52, 58, 62, 64–5, 66, 89, 90, 93, 94, 98, 109, 113, 148, 257, 258, 263, 264–5
Badr offensive, 136, 137
Baghdad, 22, 24, 28, 41, 58, 61, 87, 91, 135, 136, 182, 186, 190, 200, 248–9
Baghdad Pact, 11, 19
Baghdad-Tehran highway, 246
Bahmanshir River, 9, 53
Bahonar, Muhammad Javed, 69
Bahrain, 77, 78, 99, 127, 130, 155, 223
Bait al Muqqadas, 106; see also Jerusalem
Bait al Muqqadas offensive, 59, 60
Bait al Muqqadas-Two offensive, 199
Bait al Muqqadas-Three offensive, 200
Bait al Muqqadas-Five offensive, 202
Bakhtaran, 40, 262; see also Kermanshah
Bakhtiar, Shahpour, 36, 38, 62
Bakr, Ahmad Hassan, 20, 25, 26, 28–9, 30, 62, 63, 90, 93
Baluchis, 46
Bandar Abbas, 126, 189, 211, 220
Bandar Asaluyeh, 146
Bandar Khomeini, 91, 98, 102
Bandar Mashahr, 52
Baneh, 102
Bani-Sadr, Abol Hassan, 36, 43, 44, 46, 48, 49, 52, 69, 71, 118
Banias, 57
Bank of International Settlements, 109
Bar-Am, Avraham, 221
Bari, 231
Barikbin, Ahmad, 151
Barzan, 150
Barzani, Ahmad, 13
Barzani, Idris, 35, 59
Barzani, Mustafa, 13, 14, 16